# JOHN LYDGATE

JOHN LYDGATE

# JOHN LYDGATE

*A Study in the Culture of
the XVth Century*

\*

WALTER F. SCHIRMER

translated by

ANN E. KEEP

*University of California Press*

BERKELEY AND LOS ANGELES · 1961

University of California Press
Berkeley and Los Angeles
California

First published in German 1952
as John Lydgate: Ein Kulturbild aus dem 15.-Jahrhundert
by Max Neimeyer Verlag, Tübingen
This translation © 1961 Methuen & Co Ltd
Printed in Great Britain

# Contents

## PART I

# Contents

# Contents

## PART II

[ vii ]

# Contents

# Contents

[ ix ]

# Contents

*Letter to Gloucester* – Interruption and resumption – Historiographical approach – Books III to VII written as history – Interruption – Third stage: pragmatic historiography (Books VIII and IX) – Distribution of the work – *The Sodeine Fall of Princes in Oure Dayes* – Continuation of the theme in *Mirror for Magistrates.*

# Illustrations

# Illustrations

# Preface

The fifteenth century, overshadowed by the twin peaks of Chaucer and Shakespeare, has hitherto been insufficiently appreciated. In histories of literature this 'age of decline' is usually dismissed with a few remarks, mostly of a derogatory character. But this approach is an obstacle to proper historical understanding. Every age has its elements of growth and decay, and it is from this aspect, from the standpoint of development, that the fifteenth century must be judged – and also John Lydgate, its most representative poet. This monk, hitherto treated with derision instead of the respect that is his due, brought to a close the old literary era and paved the way for a new era to begin. His personality needs to be seen against the background of the age in which he lived. To glimpse him in his monastery cell at Bury St Edmunds we must needs peer through a lattice-work of historical dates, figures, and events. The picture of the period thus unfolded also makes it possible for us to appreciate Lydgate's literary vocation – a vocation of which he himself was unaware, and which was recognized only later. He considered himself a disciple of Chaucer; his writings were composed in dutiful response to the demands made upon him by his king, his abbot, and the era in which he lived. Yet in his apparently faithful adherence to old patterns there lay concealed the first tender shoots of a new literary epoch.

*Bonn, 1960*                                    W. F. SCHIRMER

PART I

PART I.

## Chapter I

### England at the time of Lydgate's Birth

*

In 1370, the year when Lydgate is thought to have been born,[1] the reigning monarch was still Edward III, in whose service Chaucer had grown to maturity, and whose court was one of the most splendid of the time. Its brilliance was heightened by the presence there of King John of France, awaiting payment of his ransom. Jean Froissart, who came to the English court in 1361 as secretary to the queen, Philippa of Hainault, describes in vivid colours and with the precision of an eye-witness the festivals, tournaments, and extravagant life led by the great lords. He regards Edward as the most glorious of kings and his consort Philippa as the most beautiful, devout, and munificent of queens. The treaty of Brétigny (or Calais), signed on 8th May 1360, so onerous to France, had ensured England's ascendancy; and comparison with the poverty of France made Edward's glory seem all the more resplendent. In return for the renunciation of his formal claim to the French throne he obtained complete sovereignty over Calais and Ponthieu and documentary title to Aquitania, i.e. Poitou, Guienne, Périgord, and Gascony, whilst as compensation for England's renunciation of the treaty with Flanders, which had now become redundant, the French renounced their Scottish alliance and agreed to fix John's ransom at three million gold crowns. Edward III's fiftieth birthday was celebrated in 1362 with unprecedented pomp, which seemed justified by the political and military successes he had won.

During Edward's reign art and literature, too, developed to full flower, externally through the patronage dispensed by the court and

---

[1] J. Parr, 'Astronomical Dating for some of Lydgate's Poems', in: *PMLA* 67 (1952), p. 256: 1371.

aristocracy, and internally through the growing spirit of independence, closely connected with the general strengthening of national consciousness. The University of Oxford became more national in character as a result of the measures taken by the king to prevent students from migrating to Paris; and in the same way English culture as a whole now lost something of its traditional cosmopolitan and clerical character. Englishmen gradually became less conscious of the common European heritage and more aware of their own national identity. This was apparent in architecture, with the development of the Perpendicular style, as well as in literature, with the poems of *Sir Gawain and the Green Knight*, *Pearl*, and of course with Chaucer. It was apparent even in the legal and ecclesiastical field: by the edicts of *De Provisionibus* and *Praemunire* of 1351 and 1353 the English Church obtained the maximum amount of independence from Rome that was in theory permissible. Churchmen sought to avoid appealing to Rome in cases which came within the competence of the king's courts, and accepting papal appointments to English bishoprics – aims which in practice, however, could not be fully attained, though compromise was possible in individual instances. The English clergy sided with the Crown, although they felt no animosity towards the Pope. Over the internal life of the English Church the papal Curia exercised no influence. All this would have been impossible without the growing material prosperity of the country, based mainly upon the wool trade, now becoming an English monopoly. The middle class, and particularly the City of London, were now coming to the fore. This trend was also shown by the fact that the London dialect used at court and in commerce was now becoming the generally accepted literary language.

These were the bright spots in a picture which also had its darker side. Langland's *Piers Plowman* is the vigorous expression of that other England, deliberately ignored in courtly literature, which was aflame with violent protest against abuses and deteriorating conditions. Even Froissart saw the dangers of the situation, and deplored the pride and cruelty of the English, and their hatred of foreigners. In 1369, when his patroness died, Parliament loudly applauded the resumption of the claim to the French Crown, and the Black Death ravaged the country for the third time, whereupon the adventure-loving historian took up service with a new master, Wenceslas of Brabant. In England the good old days were over. The French campaign proved unsuccessful. Crown Prince Edward, known as the

Black Prince, who had hitherto ruled over Aquitania with no small success, was mortally ill, and his military gifts failed him as the French, under their able commander Bertrand du Guesclin and their new king, Charles V,[1] avoiding an open battle, launched attack after attack and succeeded in splitting the English army. In 1374 the English possessions in south-western France were reduced to small strips of coast in the vicinity of Bayonne and Bordeaux. In England itself Edward III, who on the death of his wife had fallen completely under the influence of his mistress Alice Perrers, became a pawn in the intrigues carried on between rival groups of courtiers. In these conflicts his own sons took a prominent part: in the 'Good Parliament' of 1376 Edmund Mortimer (Earl of March), William of Wykeham, and Bishop Courtenay enforced certain reforms and brought about the banishment of Alice Perrers from the court; but these resolutions were reversed in a new parliament by the party of John of Gaunt, which relied upon the support of wealthy London financiers. It numbered Lords Latimer and Nevill among its partisans, and afforded protection to Wycliffe. The clash between John of Gaunt and Bishop Courtenay on 19th February 1377 in connexion with Wycliffe's summons to St Paul's Cathedral, in which the people took sides and the mob began to engage in looting, marked the beginning of an age torn by revolt and internal dissension.

This Edward did not live to experience. On Sunday 21st June 1377 he died in his palace at Sheen,[2] dominated by his mistress to the end. Even on his death-bed he spoke only of falconry and the chase. To his grandson Richard II he bequeathed a country on the verge of civil war, which moreover was embroiled in a struggle abroad that seemed to promise no chance of success. Richard, a child of ten, with golden locks and fine features, was crowned on 16th July. Since he was a minor, a Regency Council was established to rule on his behalf. It was in effect a coalition ministry, which counted among its members Courtenay, the Bishops of Salisbury and Carlisle, as well as the Earls of March and Stafford. The war with France, which had dragged on in desultory fashion, was resumed, and at home the conflict continued between the opposing doctrines of royal authority and parliamentary control. By and large this was a perpetuation of the regime of John of Gaunt. The war, however,

[1] King John was unable to raise the money for his ransom and returned voluntarily into captivity; he died in England in 1364.
[2] Cf. p. 25, n. 1.

[ 5 ]

came to a standstill with the death in 1380 of Bertrand du Guesclin and the French king, England's two most powerful adversaries. Like his English counterpart, the new ruler of France, Charles VI, was also a minor. In England there was mounting popular dissatisfaction with the Government and discontent at oppressive social conditions. This was the calamitous consequence of the Statutes of Labourers (1349 and 1351), promulgated after the first plague of 1348–9, whereby prices and wages were fixed at the level prevailing before the onset of the Black Death. But in the meantime social conditions had changed, especially owing to the scarcity of manpower, and the misery increased with renewed outbreaks of plague in 1362 and 1369. This was coupled with the great economic and social changes that brought about the collapse of the feudal system. As landed property passed from the aristocracy into the hands of the burgher class, to whom it served as capital investment, so the old economic system became untenable. Formerly there had existed something in the nature of a family bond between the noble landowners and their serfs; but the burgher bought the land and the serfs upon it with the object of exploiting them to the maximum. Thus the patriarchal relationship was broken between the farm-labourer and the employer who afforded him protection, and the natural consequence was that the labourer sought to leave the land if he had better opportunities of improving his position elsewhere. But since this was forbidden by his new master under the old feudal rule of *glebae adscripti*, the rural labourer inevitably came to feel himself a slave, deprived of all legal rights. Parliament, concerned to uphold the rights of the landed middle class, showed itself harsh and unrelenting, which inevitably produced a rebellious spirit among the villeins, who were also encouraged by the support they received from the lower clergy. During the reign of Edward III the intense national feeling had made the burden of taxes and dues bearable. In those days England had been the leading nation of Europe. But now that her armies had been unsuccessful and her foreign possessions lost, the discontent of the lower classes came openly to the fore. The semi-free peasants, too, who paid rent in lieu of personal services, sought to obtain a status equivalent to that of the freeholders and to secure all the rights assured to a *liber homo* by the Magna Carta.

The towns were also seething. In those already in possession of a charter and a municipal constitution, such as Winchester, Beverley, and Scarborough, there was an acute antagonism between *inferiores* and *potentiores*. The great majority of the non-privileged opposed the oligarchy of wealthy families who controlled municipal affairs, and in particular financial matters, accusing them of claiming rights but being unwilling to undertake responsibilities. In other towns that came within the domain of the Church, the bishops or abbots, such as Dunstable, and in market towns controlled by large monasteries, such as St Albans and Bury St Edmunds, the citizens were engaged in conflict with their ecclesiastical lords, demanding charters granting them the same municipal rights which towns on Crown land had gradually acquired. But the monasteries were administered on feudal lines (one Italian observer remarked that they resembled baronies rather than abbeys);[1] they were separated by a great gulf from the people and were just as unrelenting as Parliament. Finally, in London itself, in addition to the antagonism between *inferiores* and *potentiores*, there existed one between employer and employee. In every craft there were great entrepreneurs who did their best to prevent their apprentices from winning their independence. The apprentices banded together in bodies akin to trade unions, which struggled against the employers and the Statutes of Labourers, which was as disadvantageous to them as it was to the farm-labourers. Furthermore, a proletariat had already begun to form, consisting of unemployed apprentices, unskilled workers, and fugitive serfs from the countryside. The rigid social structure of the Middle Ages was no longer suited to the new conditions. The same was true of the ecclesiastical order. The Church, too, was faced with unrest, due not so much to the great schism that began in 1378, by which England was scarcely affected, but rather by Wycliffe and the Lollards. After the riotous scene at St Paul's in 1377 Courtenay appealed to the Curia, and in that year several Bulls were issued by Gregory XI condemning Wycliffe's teaching. Whilst Oxford afforded its eminent professor what protection it could, Courtenay summoned him once again to London. This led to another riotous outbreak, during which the citizens forced their way into Lambeth Palace. The breach between the higher clergy and Wycliffe's supporters became even greater when the so-called Lollards, or 'poor priests', began to popularize the teaching of their master in a cruder form and with an admixture of revolutionary ideas.

[1] *Relatione . . . d'Inghilterra*, ed. Sneyd, L., 1847 (Camden Society No. 37), p. 29: '. . . monasterij di San Benedetto, Certosini, o Cistercieni, i quali in vero sono più presto baronie, che luoghi di religiosi. . . .'

## Chapter 2

### Lydgate's Youth; the Monastery of Bury St Edmunds

\*

Far removed from this restless world, not far from the great Benedictine abbey of Bury St Edmunds, lay the quiet village of Lydgate,
near Newmarket. It was here in or about the year 1370 that John
Lydgate, the most important fifteenth-century English poet, was
born.[1] His family was probably of peasant stock, and his birth did not
predestine him for a distinguished career. But already as a child his
natural talents must have attracted attention in the monastery, for apparently in 1385, when fifteen years old, he entered it as a novice,
although by inclination he was better suited to a secular than to an
ecclesiastical career. The confessions set down by Lydgate as an old
man in his *Testament*[2] are of a general nature and relevant to almost
any childhood, but nevertheless these realistic sketches do possess
some autobiographical value. We see the lad retaining in his new
environment his rustic pugnacity and independent spirit, sitting in-
attentively in the monastery school, eager to play in the golden freedom outside. We see him stealing apples in the monastery garden, or
climbing the fence into the neighbouring vineyard when he ought to
be at Mass. During service he would occasionally steal away to play
marbles with his companions. The black habit of his Order was for
him no more than an outward article of clothing. These all-too-
human features, which the ageing monk deplores, seem to us rather

---

[1] F[all] o[f] P[rinces] IX, 3431: 'Born in a vyllage which callyd is Lydgate, // Be olde
tyme a famous castel toun; // In Danys tyme it was bete doun . . .' Ibid., VIII, 194: 'I
was born in Lidgate, // Wher Bachus licour doth ful scarsli fleete'. *Aesop Prol.*, 32:
'Haue me excusyd, I was born in Lydgate'.

[2] M[inor] P[oems], EETS, ES. 107 and O.S. 192, pp. 329 ff.

attractive, and provide a lifelike picture of a boy who was wide-awake and not given to reverie. These failings were treated with indulgence by the monastic authorities, and did not impair his noviatiate. On the other hand, we need not take so seriously as Lydgate does himself in his *Testament* the spiritual revelation he experienced shortly before his fifteenth birthday, when he saw painted on the monastery wall a crucifix with the superscription *vide*. Also later in life we find him delighting in 'vain secular history' and showing fondness for wine, which he deplores as sins of his childhood. On the whole it can be said that his secular tendencies helped to counterbalance his spiritual meditations. But medieval monasteries were cultural centres little affected by wars and other calamities, and a fitting abode for a pacific-minded man of Lydgate's temperament. Not that the great monasteries should be imagined as sanctuaries for those who sought to escape from worldly cares and lead an ascetic life. They participated in the life of the world at large in the first instance through the extensive hospitality which they all afforded, a particular feature of the great Benedictine monasteries and the houses of the Augustinian canons (prebendaries). They also took part in the political life of the country, frequently maintaining close links with the Crown. This was especially true of the highly-esteemed Benedictine abbeys of Bury St Edmunds and St Albans, described in detail, or at least frequently mentioned, by almost every chronicler between the eleventh and fifteenth centuries.

*

The monasteries' secular role was to some extent determined by their geographical situation. St Albans, Peterborough, York, and Durham lay upon the Great North Road, the only important highway between the dioceses of York and Canterbury, as well as between London, the seat of the central government, and the northern provinces. Canterbury was situated on the great road to the Channel used by all travellers to the Continent. At Gloucester, Tewkesbury, Worcester, and Shrewsbury there were bridges; Bristol was a port, and Winchester lay near a harbour of vital importance for the Continental trade. Eynsham was brought into contact with secular matters through its proximity to Oxford, whose scholars often enjoyed its hospitality.

St Edmunds was located in more peaceful surroundings. Where St Albans was the scene of important political negotiations, St

# John Lydgate

Edmunds was regarded rather as a place of rest and relaxation. King Henry VI was one of those who withdrew here to rest from affairs of state. The surrounding countryside was rich farmland. The counties north of London, from Suffolk westwards to Gloucestershire, at this time constituted the granary of England. To the north was the Great Fen, a belt of territory nearly forty miles wide and over fifty miles long stretching eastwards from Peterborough across Cambridgeshire to Brandon in Suffolk. These 300,000 acres of swampy land, mostly under water and covered in parts with reeds and rushes, provided the monastery with fish and waterfowl, whilst from the drier parts of the fen came equally valuable supplies of turf.[1]

The monastery where Lydgate lived all his life was situated in the old settlement of Beodricsworth, which occupied the site of the modern town of Bury. On a hill rising steeply from the grassy plain watered by the Lark, a small tributary of the Ouse, there stood the houses of the town. Its southern boundary was formed by the Linnet, a brook flowing into the Lark. On the plain, between the foot of the hill and the Lark, lay the monastery, today a ruin, but at that time an imposing group of buildings. The magnificent impression it evoked is described by John Leland in his inventory of English antiquities (1534):

'The sun doth not shine upon a town more beautifully situated . . . upon a monastery more famed for its endowments, size and splendour. One would think one were looking upon a whole town, so many gates are there, some of brass, so many towers, and a church unsurpassed by any other, adjoined by three more in the finest style, all situated within the precincts of the monastery. Through it winds a small stream, spanned by a bridge with twin arches.'[2]

---

[1] W. Denton, *England in the Fifteenth Century*, L., 1888, pp. 140, 144. Cf. *Chronica Jocelini de Brakelonda de rebus gestis Samsonis* . . . ed. J. G. Rokewode, L., 1840 (Camden Society); new ed. with trans. ed. H. E. Butler, L., 1949, pp. 150 ff.

[2] J. Leland, *Itinerary*, ed. Th. Hearne, 1744, IX, 50 ff. 'Quid ego hic pluribus collando curiam verbis? Unum hoc tantum addam, solem non videre urbem situ elegantiorem: (sic molli delicata pendet in clivo, et rivulus ad orientem defluit) aut coenobium illustrius, sive quis dotationem, seu amplitudinem, aut magnificentiam incomparabilem aequis rationibus expendat. Diceres plane coenobium urbem esse: tot portae, partim etiam aereae, tot turres, et templum quo nullum magnificentius, cui et alia tria egregio opere nitentia, uno et eodem coemeterio sita, subserviunt. Amniculus, de quo superius, mediis monasterii septis illabitur, duplici ponte arcuati operis pervius.'

1. A conjectural reconstruction of the Abbey of Bury St Edmunds

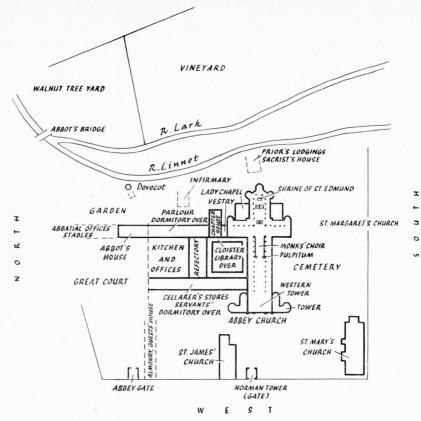

2. Plan of the Abbey of Bury St Edmunds

Both the monastery and the town were enclosed within rectangular walls, with large crosses at each of the four corners.[1] The most impressive aspect was that from the west; to Leland it suggested a wealthy walled town with many gates and towers. At the southern end of this West Front, almost in the south-western corner of the area surrounded by the wall, lay the church of St Mary's, a Norman building dating from the second quarter of the twelfth century. Its architects, Rodulph and Hervé, were also responsible for the church of St James' (approx. 1125), situated almost in the middle of the West Wall.

Flanked, as it were, by these two parish churches, rose the imposing abbey itself, over 500 feet in length and almost 250 feet in width. Entering the precincts of the monastery by way of the great churchyard gate in the ninety-foot-high Norman tower (partly still extant)[2] one was confronted at a distance of about 100 yards with the soaring West Front of the abbey, with its three towers, three doors, and four chapels. In Lydgate's day only the two octagonal side-towers were still standing. The great central tower, built under Abbot Samson, had collapsed as early as 1210 and had not been rebuilt.[3] But Lydgate was to witness the construction by John (de) Lavenham of the tower above the intersection of the nave and transepts. Visible for miles around, it brought the monastery great fame and renown. It is mentioned by William of Worcester as *campanile in medio ecclesiae navis*.[4] Today the church, begun under Abbot Baldwin and completed under Abbot Samson, is a mere ruin. But at the time it was a Norman edifice comparable in size to Durham Cathedral, although apparently with a Gothic campanile and other Gothic

---

[1] According to the description in: *Memorials of St Edmund's Abbey*, ed. Th. Arnold, 3 vols., L., 1890–6 (Rolls Series, 96); M. R. James, *The Abbey Church of St Edmund at Bury*, Cambridge, 1895 (Antiquarian Soc.); R. Yates, *Monastic Remains of Bury S. Edmunds*, I, 1805, II, 1843; S. Tymms, *Handbook of Bury St Edmunds*, 4th ed., 1872; J. Battely, *Antiquitates Si. Edmundi Burgi*, Oxford, 1745.

[2] The Norman tower, which according to Tymms was built by Abbot Baldwin in or about 1090, but according to other authorities by Abbot Anselm between 1121 and 1146, is generally described as the Great Gate.

[3] Since William of Worcester (see note below) only speaks of *campanile in medio ecclesiae navis*, it cannot be assumed that the West Tower was restored. Probably only the base was repaired and a belfry erected on top of it. Until the campanile was erected the Norman Tower served as a bell-tower. M. R. James, however, says: 'The central tower remained in ruins for more than a century. Finally John Lavenham, sacrist in the 14th century, rebuilt it and added a tall wooden spire' (p. 204).

[4] William of Worcester, who paced out the measurements above, is the author of a technical account dating from the year 1479 (Notebook in the library of Corpus Christi College, MS. CCX).

features, at least in the upper parts of the building, added during the extensive restoration work carried out after the pillage of 1327. The austerity of the architecture was counterbalanced by lavish ornamentation. The visitor needed to go no farther than the entrancegate in the Norman tower to find a sculpture of Our Lord in Glory; the bronze doors of the centre portal of the church were divided, on the Italian model, into panels with reliefs drawn from the New Testament. The interior was brightened by stained-glass windows, donated by Edward III, representing the lives of John the Baptist and Christ, by frescoes with verse inscriptions and by ornamental carvings. As one entered the church one found to one's left and right two chapels, and before one the great nave, supported by two rows of twelve pillars. Light poured in through the twelve brightly-coloured stained-glass windows of the south aisle and the adjoining south transept. In the south was located the cemetery, dating from the era of lay clergy (tenth century). From this angle the light could enter without hindrance, but in the north the cloister, a two-storeyed structure, blocked many of the apertures that had previously existed, so that the remaining windows, and the upper windows as well, had no coloured glass. But this deficiency was made good by the rich pictorial decoration of the north aisle, which also contained the tombs of several of the abbots. In the fourteenth century the roof of the nave, too, was enriched with paintings by the sacristan John Lavenham, whilst the painted roof above the choir dated from an earlier period. There were no fewer than fourteen altars in the church, not counting those in the choir and the chapel at the east end.

The visitor's attention was immediately caught by the stone screen dividing off the choir-stalls, where there were eighty seats for the monks. Surmounted by the great rood and figures of the Virgin and St John, it was the work of the sacristan Hugo (under Abbot Samson). Through the screen access was gained to the innermost part of the church, where the relics were preserved. The broad transept contained several altars dedicated to St John, St Nicholas, and St Giles; in the centre stood the choir altar, on both sides of which a staircase led down to the large vaulted crypt, with its twenty-four pillars. Entering the presbytery, and passing Abbot Baldwin's tomb, made of alabaster and embellished with a massive ornamental candlestick, one reached the imposing high altar. Upon it, or above it, was a carved crucifix executed by Hugo, who also worked the bronze doors. Behind the high altar, separated by painted doors, was the eastern part of the church, with the shrine of the saintly king and martyr Edmund. The shrine rested upon a Gothic stone base, with four candles perpetually lit placed at each corner; made of wood and in the shape of a church, it was lavishly decorated with silver and gold plate and jewels given by successive kings of England. Next to Edmund's sarcophagus there hung tapestries or paintings representing scenes from St Edmund's life. At the eastern end of the choir were three apsidal chapels, of which that in the centre was originally the Lady Chapel. In its place Abbot Simon de Luton built a new and more spacious chapel outside the church, adjoining the northern wall of the choir and the northern transept.

The northern transept of the church led to the other monastery buildings, all of which were situated to the north and east of the abbey itself. The first of these was the chapter-house, rebuilt and altered several times, and above all the cloister, reconstructed by Prior John Gosford after the sacking of 1327, which contained a statue of Abbot Anselm. Above it were the dormitory and library. The early fifteenth century was a great age for the collection of books and the foundation of libraries.[1] The foremost place was naturally taken by Oxford, with its university and monastic college libraries, but large collections were also held by Cistercian and Benedictine monasteries all over the country: there were some 2000 volumes in Bury, St Albans, and Canterbury, 1000 in Durham, 500 in Ramsey, and 350 in Meaux. Of the stocks of books in St Edmunds, which were chained to slanting desks, 322 manuscripts may still be identified today.[2] There is a *Registrum librorum Angliae* dating from the fourteenth century, which in the early fifteenth century was enlarged by John Boston, apparently the librarian of Bury St Edmunds, to include a total of 700 authors; he added a short biographical sketch of each writer and thus compiled the first dictionary of literature. This shows that Lydgate had at his disposal one of the finest libraries in the country. It may be assumed that many manuscripts were added during his lifetime, and perhaps by his instrumentality, for he had as his patron Humphrey, Duke of Gloucester, a humanist and the founder of the Bodleian Library, and also Henry VI, an ardent lover and collector of books, who founded Eton and King's College, Cambridge. Lydgate must have spent many hours working in the monastery library – unless, like many distinguished

[1] E. A. Savage, *Old English Libraries*, L., 1911 (The Antiquary's Books).
[2] After M. R. James; cf. Savage, pp. 58 ff., 63, 71.

monks, he was permitted to have a small writing-room, or *scriptoriolum*; it is perhaps a room such as this that we find represented in the picture showing Lydgate sitting at his desk.[1]

The large complex of buildings adjoining the great abbey church included, in addition to outhouses, the residence of the abbot himself. Much of this *camera*, as it was called, has been preserved. It faced on to the large courtyard, situated in the north-western corner of the precincts. Here, it may be assumed, the guest-house was also located. Access to this courtyard was gained through the Abbey Gate, a splendid Gothic building (still partly extant) and the principal entrance into the monastery. It contained a large room, in which from one of the windows facing east, visitors obtained a delightful view over the courtyard and the abbot's house, and beyond them the Lark and Linnet, winding their way between the beautiful gardens and the vineyard, and meeting under the three-arched Abbot's Bridge, to the fields and meadows of St Edmund's Hill and Eldo Grange. On the other bank of the Lark, on ground rising towards the east, was the monastery vineyard, once terraced and enclosed within a wall. The monastery school was situated outside the actual precincts, in the town of Bury; it was a solid stone building, which Samson, St Edmunds' greatest abbot, had in 1180 put at the disposal of Walter, the schoolmaster of the day, in gratitude for the tuition he had received. It was a free grammar school, where no fees were charged to the needy, and which, nominally at least, came within the jurisdiction of the abbot of St Edmunds.

*

In Lydgate's lifetime the monastery of St Edmunds, like that of St Albans, could already look back upon an honourable history of nearly 500 years, in which it had experienced times both good and bad.[2] It was founded in the reign of King Canute, in honour of King Edmund of East Anglia (*d.* 870), considered a saint and a martyr to the Danes, and was consecrated as a Benedictine abbey in 1032. Its first time of greatness was under Abbot Baldwin (1065–97),[3] who in

---

[1] In Pynson's edition of the *Testament* (reproduced in *EETS*, ES., 107).

[2] Exact account in *Memorials of St Edmund's Abbey*, ed. Th. Arnold, op. cit. There is no history of the monastery.

[3] Gasquet emphasizes that in the Benedictine houses the *abbas* was the absolute master. He was chosen by a vote (*per viam scrutinii*) or indirectly (*electio per compromissum*). The abbot appointed the prior and sub-prior, who were responsible for discipline within the monastery (*English Monastic Life*, L., 1904, p. 52).

accordance with a papal breve placed the monks directly under the authority of Rome.

Its second golden age occurred under Abbot Samson (1182–1210), an eminent personage whom Carlyle extolled in *Past and Present*. Samson, educated in Paris and the author of *De miraculis St. Edmundi*, was distinguished both as priest and secular administrator. He was a friend of King John and travelled to Rome on behalf of his monastery. The history of Samson and his times has been related by his chaplain, Jocelin de Brakelond, in his chronicle,[1] regarded by Carlyle, who translated it, as giving the most vivid picture of medieval life. The good relations that then prevailed between the monastery and the Crown continued after Samson's death; a guest-house was erected in which the king was fittingly entertained during his visits to the abbey.

Towards the end of the thirteenth century, however, harder times set in. It was difficult to remain neutral in the conflict between Crown and barons and at the same time uphold the monastery's privileges. This predicament led to differences with Henry III and Edward I. In 1296, after his victory over the Scots, Edward I held parliament in Bury St Edmunds, but in the following year confiscated the monastery's property owing to its failure to provide subsidies. Still more serious were the long-drawn-out conflicts with the citizens of Bury, who in 1327 burnt down the abbey and plundered it. We do not know which buildings were destroyed and which rebuilt, but in any case its golden age was now definitely over, and in the fourteenth century, under such weak-willed abbots as William de Bernham (1335–61), a moral decline began. During the reign of Richard II an ambitious monk by the name of Edmund Bromfield fraudulently obtained a papal provision, gained entrance to the monastery and temporarily drove out the abbot whom the monks had elected and who had been confirmed in office by the Crown.[2] These internal troubles (during the abbotship of John Tymworth, 1379–89), which Lydgate experienced, had hardly ceased when the political and social revolt of 1381 broke out. The political disturbances made themselves felt within the monastery walls, and the social unrest posed a threat to the monks' peaceful way of life. It might almost be thought that these events occasioned the note which

[1] Cf. p. 10, n. 1.
[2] A. H. Thompson, *The English Clergy . . . in the later Middle Ages*, Oxford, 1947, p. 167.

Lydgate strikes in his later works, one of the uncertainty of every-thing terrestrial and a yearning for celestial security, which, he holds, ought to be reflected in the political system on earth, even though this is necessarily imperfect. Rebellion stalked the land, and whilst the abbot had trouble in obtaining confirmation from the Pope, Wat Tyler's bands marched on Bury. Lydgate's life falls in a restless period of transition from the old feudal order to a new system, when the wealthy monasteries, which took tithes from the parishes and allowed the lower clergy almost to starve, did not know, or did not wish to know, how deeply they were hated by the parish priests as well as by their parishioners. The events of May and June 1381 must have been followed at St Edmunds with anger and trepidation: Essex and Kent in revolt, the Archbishop of Canterbury's palace sacked, London conquered, the Chancellor and Archbishop Simon Sudbury murdered, arson and the threat of wholesale civil war. In St Albans, which was situated on monastic land, the terrified abbot, Thomas de la More, was forced to give the townspeople the charter they had demanded for a century, but withdrew it on the following day when he received news that the young king Richard II had marched against the rebels and that Wat Tyler had been killed. On 13th June, the day when St Albans was threatened, John Wraw, a priest, with a great crowd of malcontents which included workers, townspeople, clergy, and even representatives of the country gentry, marched on Bury St Edmunds. As at St Albans, the monastery had for generations been at odds with the freedom-loving burghers. In the absence of the abbot the monastery seemed defenceless, and the townspeople joined with Wraw's men in sacking the houses of the monastery officials. Prior Cambridge, the abbot's deputy and leader of the intransigents, escaped, but was discovered and put to death; his head, together with that of Sir John Cavendish, the Chief Jus-tice, was exhibited in the market square. The panic-stricken monks, fearing a repetition of the sacking of 1327, now gave the townsmen a charter, and parted with their documents, silver plate, and other valuables. The atmosphere that prevailed during Wraw's one-week rule over Bury can be gauged from the story that one of the monks stood in the belfry looking eastwards and saw the rebels moving down the Rougham Road. But they withdrew, and the monastery escaped without suffering much damage. The rebels dispersed be-fore the advancing forces led by the militant Bishop of Norwich, Henry Despenser; Wraw was taken prisoner and hanged, and Bury was obliged to pay in compensation the extremely high sum of 2,000 marks (about £1,000). The last instalment was not paid until 1386. The revolt brought no change in the general situation; the feudal authorities soon regained their former power. To Lydgate, then a pupil in the monastery school, this will no doubt have seemed part of the natural order of things.

In suppressing the rebellion and restoring order the young king played an important part. In the eyes of the oppressed population he must have appeared as a man who had failed to keep his word; but this sentiment was soon forgotten in the upsurge of patriotic enthusiasm aroused by his wedding with Anne of Bohemia. Anne was the sister of King Wenceslas IV of Bohemia, who reigned as German Emperor from 1378 to 1400. Wenceslas had previously given support to Pope Urban, who was also recognized by England, and hopes were entertained – which in the event proved vain – that he would stir up the whole of Germany against the schismatic king, Charles VI, thereby placing England once again in a strong position *vis-à-vis* France. These hopes apart, the marriage of the young couple (both the king and his bride were only fifteen years old) in Westminster Abbey on 14th January 1382 was a splendid and moving spectacle. The young queen's womanly charm, good education, and high moral repute seemed to promise the country happier times. In 1383 the king and queen spent ten days as guests in the monastery of St Edmunds (a visit that cost the abbey 800 marks). If Lydgate was already there at that time (for the date 1385, traditionally given as the year in which he entered the monastery, is only conjectural), his childhood experience of this royal visit may well have laid the groundwork for his subsequent advocacy of the cause of the dynasty.

\*

The close relationship maintained with the Crown enhanced the monastery's sense of security, but should not be interpreted as reducing it to a position of subordination. The atmosphere that prevailed resembled that of a well-established *civitas*. The fact that the monastery walls also embraced the town of Bury, with nearly 4,000 inhabitants (at a time when London had 40,000), was a symbolic expression of the power exercised by the monastery over the town. It had a part in the election of the mayor, choosing whomever it pleased from the three aldermen put forward, and also had the right to declare the entire list of candidates invalid. It appointed the schoolmasters in

# John Lydgate

Bury and in certain other places. It also enjoyed independence from episcopal jurisdiction:[1] *monasterium sancti Edmundi de Bury, ordinis sancti Benedicti, ad Romanam ecclesiam nullo medio pertinentis.* The bishops did indeed seek to contravene the principle enshrined in this formula of the direct subordination to Rome of the great Benedictine abbeys, and to undermine the autocratic powers of the abbot, who ruled his monastery in patriarchal fashion, with his own staff of chamberlain, cellarer, almoner, and chaplain.[2] But their efforts did not have any marked success. In the middle of the fourteenth century the monastery stubbornly resisted the attempt by Bishop Bateman of Norwich to encroach upon its privileges. In the long jurisdictional struggle fought out between William Alnwick, Bishop of Norwich, and Abbot Curteys, in which the latter distinguished himself by his energy, the Crown sought to mediate in the monastery's favour, and the Duke of Bedford, then Regent of England, took the trouble to visit the monastery in person. There was scarcely one reigning monarch who failed to attend the festival of the monastery's patron saint, or at least to send his representative to the celebrations. In their correspondence with successive sovereigns the abbots adopted a self-confident, if deferential tone. When Henry VI stood in need of money for his wars, his letters to Abbot Curteys read like those of a supplicant. The monastery exercised considerable authority in the field of learning as well as in politics: in 1440, according to a letter written by the abbot of St Albans, Abbot Curteys was asked to send several scholars to the Council of Basle to uphold the institution of monasticism.[3] In 1446 Abbot Curteys was requested by the king, to celebrate Mass when the foundation stone was laid of King's College, Cambridge.[4] It was regarded as a great honour to become a lay

---

[1] Among the privileges of the abbot of Bury St Edmunds was the right to admit to lower orders members of his house and for this purpose to summon bishops to the monastery (e.g. Bishop Thomas Aladensis in 1401). The abbots went still farther: in 1410 and 1419 Abbot William of Exeter invited Archbishop John of Smyrna (John Leicester, who resided in Norwich from 1393 to 1423 as suffragan bishop) in a letter dimissory on the basis of Papal authority to consecrate several priests who were living within the 'liberties' of St Edmunds, but had no connexion with the abbey.

[2] Dugdale, *Monasticon*, III, 136: 'Sed S. Edmundi monasterium super firmam fundatum petram ut mons stetit immobilis faciesque ipsorum confusio cooperuit. Et quem admodum Berith et Asteroth a facie fugierunt beati Bartholomei Apostoli sic isti fugierunt impii nemini persequente. Deo tunc volente postea capti fuerunt et in foveam quam fecerant merito inciderunt.'

[3] *Memorials of St Edmunds*, III, 249 f., 188 ff., 242 ff., 246 f., 254 ff., 262 ff., 276 ff.

[4] 'Ye may doo þe service; as more plainly we have comaunded oure said cousin [Marquais of Suffolk] to sey unto you in oure behalve.' Ibid., III, 246 f.

member of the famous monastery, and under Abbot Curteys in particular we find many high-ranking officials and nobles as 'associates' of Bury St Edmunds.[1] The janitors and head cook of St Edmunds held office in hereditary tenure and possessed land in fief.[2] Bury was able to perform this important role because it was one of the wealthiest monastic houses in England. From landed property, leases, and in particular from the tithes of Suffolk parishes, the abbey had, in the thirteenth century, an annual income of almost £2,500 and could, without reducing its own domestic expenditure, devote more money to poor relief than any other abbey in England.

The eighty monks and twenty-one chaplains had at their disposal 111 servants, not including those living outside the monastery precincts. The servants received every day ninety-four loaves of bread and eighty-two gallons of beer. The monks' own fare consisted of the usual items, but on important feast-days there would be wine, sturgeon (a particular delicacy), bread of superior quality, and butter or cheese.[3] And there is abundant evidence to show that St Edmunds entertained its high-ranking ecclesiastical and lay visitors on a fitting scale.[4]

*

Documents dating from Lydgate's lifetime indicate the status which his monastery enjoyed; and notwithstanding the instance of childish insubordination mentioned above, as he grew older he will doubtless have felt a sensation of pride at being a member of this *civitas*. It is only tentatively that we can follow Lydgate's education and the reflection of the political events of the period in the life of the monastery where he resided. St Edmunds lacks the great historiographical tradition of St Albans, and the scanty and uninformative sources account for the absence until now of a history of this monastery. We do not know what discussions may have taken place among the monks about the 'crusade' that was launched in 1383 in

[1] E.g. the jurists John Brodwell and William Paston, the magistrate William Brewster, and the noblemen Richard Beauchamp, Earl of Warwick, and his wife Isabel and children Henry and Anna, Eleanor (wife of Duke Humphrey of Gloucester), William de la Pole, Earl of Suffolk, and his wife Alice (daughter of Thomas Chaucer). In 1434, after the visit of Henry VI, the Duke of Gloucester and all the leading courtiers were admitted. (*Victoria County History, Suffolk*, II, 71.)

[2] W. W. Capes, *The English Church in the Fourteenth and Fifteenth Centuries*, L., 1903, p. 291.

[3] *Victoria County History, Suffolk*, II, 67 ff.

[4] Cf. visits of Richard II (1383), Henry VI (1434), Archbishop Arundel (1400), etc.

support of the orthodox Flemings against their schismatic French overlords. They will scarcely have remained indifferent to it, for Bishop Despenser of Norwich, who had put down the revolt of 1381, is said to have been its leader, and Wycliffe, who condemned the fact that the enterprise was represented as a crusade on the grounds that this camouflaged its true nature, must have been regarded by the monks as their enemy. We do not know how they reacted to the authoritarian rule of Richard II, which followed the failure of this venture and the deposition of Despenser by the king. For even if the peaceful atmosphere may not have been disturbed by international developments (except perhaps by the widespread fear of a French invasion in 1386), the abbot and senior monks must have followed closely the king's unfortunate clash with Bishop Arundel in Parliament at Salisbury (5th May 1384), and the growing antagonism between Richard II and his uncle John of Gaunt. The fate of Michael de la Pole, the first Earl of Suffolk, will certainly have been discussed by those of the monks who took an interest in the fortunes of their country. De la Pole had been designated, with Arundel, tutor to the boy-king Richard II; as a friend of the sovereign and an old official from the days of Edward III, he was ill-disposed towards the ambitious barons, but in 1386 had to be dismissed from his office as Chancellor. The king's attempt to rule as autocrat had had as little success as the barons' attempts to establish an oligarchy. The conclusion of an armistice with France and Scotland had a calming effect. The country was in an exalted and joyful mood; the chroniclers, short of material, filled out their accounts with details about the weather, tournaments, and miracles, which shows that these were years of relative peace and contentment.

In these circumstances the monks could concentrate wholly upon the affairs of their monastery. One event of extreme importance was the election of a new abbot, necessitated by the death of John de Tymworth in 1389. His successor was William de Cratfield, who held office until 1415.[1] About his life we know little; but he had a

---

[1] List of the abbots of Bury St Edmunds:

| | | | |
|---|---|---|---|
| Uvius | 1020–44 | Thomas de Totington | 1302–12 |
| Leofstan | 1045–65 | Richard de Draughton | 1312–35 |
| *Baldwin* | 1065–97 | William de Bernham | 1335–61 |
| Robert I | 1100–2 | Henry de Hunstanton | 1361 |
| Robert II | 1107–12 | John de Brinkele | 1361–78 |
| Albold | 1114–19 | John de Tymworth | 1379–89 |

register[1] kept which gives a few details of Lydgate's ecclesiastical career.[2] According to this on 17th December 1389 Lydgate was admitted to minor orders for the office of sub-deacon; on 28th May 1393 he became deacon, and on 7th April 1397 was ordained priest by John Fordham, Bishop of Ely, in the chapel of the manor of Dounham.[3] There is less reliable information available about Lydgate's scholarly progress. As a novice he will doubtless have received instruction at the monastery school or at the school in Bury which

| Anselm | 1121–48 | William de Cratfield | 1390–1415 |
| Ording | 1148–56 | William de Exeter | 1415–29 |
| Hugo I | 1157–80 | *William Curteys* | 1429–46 |
| Samson | 1182–1211 | William Babyngton | 1446–53 |
| Hugo II | 1215–29 | John Boone | 1453–69 |
| Richard de Insula | 1229–34 | Robert de Ixworth | 1469–74 |
| Henry | 1235–48 | Richard de Hengham | 1475–79 |
| Edmund de Walpole | 1248–56 | Thomas Ratlisden | 1479–97 |
| Simon de Luton | 1257–79 | William Bunting | 1497–1514 |
| John de Northwold | 1279–1301 | John Reeve | 1515–39 |

One discrepancy must be noted. J. Battely (*Antiquitates Si. Edmundi Burgi*, Oxford, 1745) gives the following chronology of the abbots in charge during Lydgate's lifetime:

| Abbas | creatus | anno regni | rexit Eccl. annos | obiit |
|---|---|---|---|---|
| Joannes Tinmouth | 1384 | 7 Ric. II | 7 | 1390 |
| Guilielmius Cratefeild | 1390 | 13 Ric. II | 37 | 1427 |
| Gulielmus Exeter | 1427 | 5 Hen. VI | 2 | 1429 |
| Gulielmus Curtis | 1429 | 7 Hen. VI | 28 | 1457 |

According to Dugdale (L., 1846, III, 98), Cratfield was obliged to lay down his office in 1414 on account of illness; he died four years later (1418). Therefore Cratfield's rule lasted only from 1390 to 1414 or 1415. William of Exeter was elected on 13th July 1415 and died in January 1429.

[1] Registrum Cratfield, B. M. Cotton Tib. B IX (burnt) and Claud. A XII, unpublished, but reproduced in extracts in the Introduction to *Memorials of Bury St Edmunds*.

[2] On Lydgate's biography, cf. J. Schick's preface to his edition of the *Temple of Glas* and the prefaces to other works in *EETS*, esp. Steele's ed. of the *Secrees of Philisoffres*, *EETS*, ES., 66.

[3] A. Hortis, *Studi sulle Opere Latine di Gio. Boccaccio*, Trieste, 1879, p. 641, n. 2: 'Excerptum ex Registro Abbatiae S. te Ethldrade in Ely . . . qui liber vocatur Registrum . . . Episcopi Eliens. Frater Johannes Lidgate Monachus de Bury, ordinatus Presbiter per Johannem Fadham Episcopum Eliensum (John Fordham, who was Bishop of Ely from 1388 to 1425) in Capella magni Manerii de Dounham, die Sabat. 7° April. 1397.'

Th. Tanner, *Bibl. Britannico-Hibernica*, 1784, p. 489: 13th March 1388 [=1389] 'frater Joh. Lidgate monachus de Bury ordinatus ad omnes ordines in ecclesia de Hadham' [from: Registrum Rob. Braybrook, Bishop of London from 1381 to 1404]. The Registrum Cratfield shows that Lydgate received letters dimissory for the office of sub-deacon on 17th December 1389 (fol. 35b), deacon on 28th May 1393 (fol. 69b), and 'order of priesthood' on 4th April 1397 (fol. 85b). According to a MS. note in Tyrwhitt's copy of Wayland's *Fall of Princes* (B.M. 838 m. 17) Lydgate was ordained priest by John Fordham, Bishop of Ely, on Saturday, 7th April 1397.

came under the monastery's supervision.[1] He may have completed his education at the University of Oxford; this at least is the account given by Bale in his sixteenth-century biographical dictionary. We can imagine him residing in Gloucester Hall, for this was the college to which the Benedictines generally sent their young scholars.[2] In the fourteenth century Oxford could not rival the universities of Paris or Italy; nor have we any reason to assume that Lydgate possessed an exceptional thirst for knowledge. He acquired the usual instruction in theology, had a sound knowledge of Latin, and mastered French; it was by means of French translations that he became acquainted with works in Italian. We therefore need not suppose that as a young man he travelled abroad to further his education. If legends to this effect sprang up in later years,[3] this can be explained by his literary reputation, the beginnings of which can be traced to his years in Oxford.

For it was here, as is clear from a fifteenth-century manuscript note by John Shirley,[4] that he wrote his *Translation of Aesop* (*Isopes fabules*), which must be regarded as his first work.[5] The choice of a didactic animal fable seems well suited to Lydgate's general outlook; but Aesop's work was known in many versions the world over, and

[1] Papadopoli (Historia Gymnasii Patavini): 'A puero Monasticam D. Benedicti regulam professus est, primasque literas didicit in coenobio.'

[2] C. E. Tame, *English Religious Literature*, No. 2, L., 1871, Introduction: 'He was sent from the monastery of St Edmundsbury to Gloucester Hall, Oxford (MS. Ashmole, 59, II), it being the practice of the monastery to send all students for Oxford there; while those intended for Cambridge were sent to Gonville and Caius College. Gloucester Hall was supported by the contributions of the abbeys of St Edmundsbury, Glastonbury and 13 others.'

[3] Bale, who also speaks of Lydgate having studied at Cambridge, mentions his undertaking journeys abroad. Morley (*English Writers*) says that he studied in Oxford, Paris, and Padua. Schick (lxxxix) quotes a passage from MS. Harl. 2255 fol. 149 (= stanza 5 from *God is Myn Helpere*, M.P., p. 28):

> I haue been offte in dyvers londys
> And in many dyvers Regiouns,
> Haue eskapyd fro my foois hondys
> In Citees, Castellys, and in touns;
> Among folk of sundry naciouns
> Wente ay forth, and took noon hede:
> I askyd no manere of protecciouns;
> God was myn helpe ageyn al drede.

[4] Ashmole 59, fol. 246. On Shirley, cf. E. P. Hammond, *English Verse between Chaucer and Surrey*, L., 1927, pp. 191 f.

[5] Text in *M.P.*, pp. 566 ff.; ed. by P. Sauerstein, *Anglia*, IX (1886), 1–24; ed. by J. Zupitza, *Archiv*, 85, 1–28; cf. P. Sauerstein, *Über Lydgates Aesopübersetzung*, Diss., Halle, 1885.

there are traces of it in Langland, Barbour, and Chaucer. And there is little that is praiseworthy in these 959 lines; they lack the engaging quality, the vigour and rigid compression that characterize the treatment of Aesop 100 years later by Henryson, a Scottish disciple of Chaucer, who created a truly English poetic work on this theme. But Lydgate, who may have valued these fables, with their moral emphasis and assumptions, as illustrations suitable for inclusion in sermons, produced in these seven fables from Aesop[1] the first book of fables written in Middle English. His choice of the Chaucerian stanza testifies to his poetic ambition and his early fondness for the master whom all his life he was to hold in the highest esteem. His years at Oxford may be regarded as the beginning of his poetic career. Perhaps there is no reason to dismiss the statement by Bale and later biographers that he founded in the monastery a school of rhetoric where he taught sons of noblemen.[2] However that may be, already at this time Lydgate was thought of as a monastic poet, although it is a matter of conjecture which of his works he wrote prior to 1397.

Some of his pieces which are written in an unsophisticated style and serve practical or liturgical purposes may be ascribed to this period.[3] There is no evidence to support the view that Lydgate's religious poetry was written only in his old age. On the other hand, many of his secular works may also be dated to this early period.[4] Either through his school of rhetoric, or through frequent visits by men of rank to his monastery, Lydgate must have come into contact with noblemen who had literary interests, for, as we know, in Norfolk and Suffolk patronage on a provincial scale flourished with extreme vigour.[5] Most of Lydgate's works owe their origin to a commission.

---

[1] The Cock and the Jewel, The Wolf and the Lamb, The Dog and the Sheep, The Wolf and the Crane, The Mouse and the Frog, Two Suns, The Dog and his Shadow. Lydgate's source is the Latin version of the so-called *Romulus* (a prose rendering of the Latin verses of Phaedrus), which is close to the French version of Marie de France.

[2] Morley, quoting Bale, Pits, and others. (On his return from his studies and journeys abroad he opened a school for the sons of noblemen.) Warton and others believe this school to have been in the monastery of Bury St Edmunds; others hold that it was in London.

[3] E.g. *Misericordias domini cantabo*.            [4] *The Churl and the Bird*.

[5] S. Moore, 'Patrons of Letters in Norfolk and Suffolk c. 1450', in: *PMLA*, 27 (1912), pp. 188 ff.; 28 (1913), pp. 79 ff.

## Chapter 3

### *Henry IV*

\*

The year 1397, in which Lydgate was ordained, was also of importance in ecclesiastical and political history. William Courtenay, upon whom the title of Archbishop of Canterbury had been conferred after the murder of Sudbury in 1381, died in 1396. He was succeeded in the following year by Thomas Arundel, who held office until 1414, during the reign of three kings: Richard II, Henry IV, and Henry V. The archbishop had twice been a successful chancellor, and undoubtedly had a talent for politics; he manifested on several occasions his sympathetic and liberal attitude towards the poor and oppressed; but he was no scholar. Only once did Arundel pay a visit to St Edmunds, and that was in September 1400,[1] on completing a visitation of the dioceses of Norwich and Ely. He was received with highest honours and conducted into the church by the abbot; but the honours were accorded him solely in his dignity as archbishop, for St Edmunds was only subject to visitations ordered by the Benedictine provincial chapter.[2] In the monastery records there is no mention of Arundel, which shows that little direct contact existed between it and the archiepiscopal authority.

In the political sphere 1397 brought to an end the tragic life of Richard II. Three years earlier his consort, Anne of Bohemia, had died without bearing him an heir. It speaks in Richard's favour that he was devoted to this queen, who was a magnanimous protector of the poor and the Church, and who enjoyed a reputation unmatched by any other English queen in the Middle Ages. But he showed his

[1] *Memorials of Bury St Edmunds*, III, 153 ff.
[2] *Victoria County History, Suffolk*, II, 65, 71.

want of moderation by ordering the palace of Sheen,[1] where she had died, to be pulled down, in sorrow at his loss. Two years later, in January 1396, he forfeited popular support by marrying Isabella, daughter of King Charles VI of France. This was the prelude to his *coup d'état*: determined to avoid a repetition of the impasse of 1386, he had his enemies Richard, Earl of Arundel and Thomas, Duke of Gloucester (the youngest son of Edward III and Philippa), condemned to death and executed as traitors, and embarked upon twenty-two months of despotic rule which eventually led to his downfall. Richard was no coward, and scarcely ever has a tyrant shed so little blood as he. But the senseless injustices and petty arbitrary actions which infringed the liberties of his subjects aroused the feeling among them that so long as he was on the throne no one could be certain of his life or property. His friends had deserted him: his policy of peace with France estranged him from the nobility; his protection of the farm-labourers alienated the landowners, and the favour he showed the Lollards turned the clergy and monasteries (and probably also the peace-loving Lydgate) against him. The prevailing mood is revealed by the prose and verse pamphlets of the Langland era.[2] In the monastery of St Edmunds he will have found few supporters. When Richard, after returning from Ireland, left his army, he sealed his own fate. The way was now clear for his enemy, Henry of Lancaster, who was advancing against him. The 'Great London Chronicle' records laconically: 'Sentence of the deposicion of king Richard anno XXII°', and goes on to relate the events of the first year of the reign of the new king, Henry IV (1399–1413).

For the first time the chronicles contain a detailed description of the coronation celebrations with all their brilliant splendour. The coronation was performed in Westminster Abbey on Monday, 13th October, by Arundel, Archbishop of Canterbury. To the resounding chords of the *Te Deum* he anointed the king, who was kneeling upon a golden cloth before the high altar, in the presence of the lords spiritual and temporal, scarlet-robed dignitaries, and the aldermen

[1] The edifice dating from the reign of Edward III (in what is now Richmond Park) remained in ruins during the reign of Henry IV and was not restored until 1414, by Henry V. The chronicler Thomas Elmham calls Sheen 'a delightful mansion of curious and costly craftsmanship'. (Illustrated in J. Nichols, *The Progress and Public Procession of Queen Elizabeth*, 4 vols., L., 1788–1821, II, 412.) Henry V's building burned down in 1477 and was rebuilt by Henry VII as Richmond Court. Cf. J. H. Wylie, *The Reign of Henry V*, Cambridge, 1914–29, I, 212.

[2] *Political Poems and Songs (Edward III to Richard III)*, ed. Th. Wright, 2 vols., L., 1859–61 (Rolls Series).

# John Lydgate

of the City of London. On the preceding Saturday there took place the customary cavalcade from the Tower of London to Westminster through the densely thronged streets of the City, with fifty newly-created knights riding before their king. The coronation banquet and procession were held with the splendour and extravagance which on later occasions Lydgate was to describe in his verse. The festivities offered to the populace, ever eager for spectacle, followed the ancient custom already described in Walsingham's chronicle (when the City's welcome was extended to King Richard II in 1377). On this occasion, too, according to Froissart, there were erected in the wide street known as The Cheap seven conduits flowing with wine, and there were magnificent pageants in which, with music and pantomime, homage was paid to the king as he rode past, with an escort 5,000 strong. People jostled one another to catch a glimpse of their new sovereign, whose affability and generosity earned him general esteem; they rejoiced at the fact that this time the king was not a minor, but a man of mature years. Henry was now thirty-four, and his robust figure, handsome broad face, and pointed red beard inspired confidence. There was nothing stiff or haughty in his mobile and vigorous features. He was the very opposite of Richard. Restrained and tactful, an experienced soldier, widely travelled and well educated, he appeared to possess all the qualities necessary in a ruler. He had, it was true, none of Richard's charm or artistic sense, and only years would show that he lacked prudence and the capacity to perceive in time when crisis threatened.

Henry's position was far from easy. He did not need to attach undue importance to the few who remained loyal to Richard II and regarded his deposition as unlawful; and he was shrewd enough to reward his friends rather than to punish his adversaries. But the fact that he had only a victor's title to his crown, and that the rightful claimant was the eight-year-old Edmund Mortimer, Earl of March, obliged Henry continually to seek and maintain the consent of the majority of his subjects. Precisely because he could never face his Parliament in the same confident manner as a hereditary monarch, he was forced to set an example of constitutional government in the modern sense. To this extent 1399, if not exactly a turning-point in history, does at least mark a change which contemporaries keenly appreciated.

The change that now took place in ecclesiastical policy, however, to our eyes seems less progressive. The great princes of the Church had no scruples in withdrawing their support from Richard II, since he had shown himself in a poor light when endeavouring to suppress the dangerous attacks to which the Church had been exposed. Although Henry was the son of a man regarded as a patron of Wycliffe, and was himself not unsusceptible to the ideas of Church reform, he had recognized that Wycliffe's views, as advanced by the Lollards, represented a threat not only to the Church but also to the existence of the feudal order as such, of which the Church formed an important constituent part. Subsequently he gave Archbishop Arundel proof of his orthodoxy. The commons, too, who like the clergy and aristocracy saw their possessions endangered by the Lollards' denial of all property rights, had cause to be grateful for the protection promised to orthodox beliefs. Thus a law was passed according to which no one might teach or preach without permission of his bishop; it was the latter's duty to inspect and scrutinize books and pamphlets, his decision being enforced by the State. The king and lay peers stiffened the provisions of a bill tabled by the clergy whereby heresy was made punishable by death at the stake (*De haeretico comburendo*, 1401).

With the government in such firm hands, for monks as for the common people the 'restless times of Henry IV', as the chronicler Hall was later to call them, were none too alarming. The successive visits by foreign envoys were all marked by pageantry and public merry-making. In the winter of 1400–1 the king received Manuel Palaeologus, Emperor of Constantinople, who came in search of assistance against the Turks; he was followed by ambassadors from the German Emperor Rupert of the Palatinate (the successor of Wenceslas) to beg the hand of Henry's eldest daughter Blanche on the Elector Ludwig's behalf. In 1403 Joan of Navarre, King Henry's bride, was welcomed with all possible ceremony; after their wedding at Winchester the Lord Mayor and aldermen stood in wait for them outside London and accompanied them to Westminster for the coronation. Once again conduits flowing with wine were set up in the City, and pageants staged. The Burgundian ambassador, who arrived in 1410 to entreat aid against the Duke of Orleans, and the latter's envoy who came on a similar mission in the following year, were received with the same ceremonial. Such customs, though still upheld by the court, had now degenerated into mere outward show; relics of a bygone age of chivalry, they had been adapted to *bourgeois* taste. This was a phenomenon characteristic of both England and Burgundy in the fifteenth century.

In addition to these spectacles, inspired by the court and the burghers, there were great popular festivals in which the humble citizenry took part. A feature of these were the plays performed by guilds of artisans on Corpus Christi Day, with Biblical themes that had acquired a secular character. The London 'Great Chronicle' contains a reference to a play performed in 1408 which lasted for eight days. Among the authors of such allegorical secular plays, staged by the municipal authorities or by guilds of artisans, was the monk Lydgate (cf. Chapter 13).

Meanwhile, in the world of high politics trouble continued. Even before the mysterious, and probably violent, death of Richard II (14th February 1400) there took place a rebellion, the first of several, in which three earls and Lord Despenser himself were involved. The years that followed up to 1405 each had their fill of treachery, internal revolts, military expeditions to Wales, Scotland, and France, and conflicts between king and Parliament. Henry's personal strength, shrewdness, and statesmanlike qualities, as well as the fortunate turn of events, helped him to keep his throne, reach agreement with Parliament, and show firmness in his dealings with foreign countries. The Scottish threat was averted by the capture of the heir to the throne, James, whilst he was on his way to France. The commercial agreements, armistices, and treaties concluded in the years 1407 and 1408 with Flanders, Brittany, and the Hanse showed that the House of Lancaster had won general recognition in Europe.

The year 1408 at long last saw the inauguration of a more peaceful era: the 'London Chronicle' finds room to mention the severe frost, which caused the death of all the young blackbirds and thrushes. The capitulation of Aberystwyth to the Prince of Wales (later Henry V) pacified Wales and eliminated Owen Glendower; and with the death of Northumberland in the battle of Bramham Moor (19th February), the last battle on English soil for more than forty years, the revolts in the country came to an end. But now King Henry's health broke down. Repeatedly he was obliged to take to his bed, and the last five years of his reign (1409–13) were filled with the struggle between his relatives for high office and for supremacy in the Privy Council. On one side were ranged the Prince of Wales and his three uncles by marriage, the Beauforts; the other party was led by the venerable Archbishop Arundel, and for part of the time by the king's second son, Thomas.

Since Lydgate had frequent dealings with the members of the

former party, a brief survey of this struggle may not be out of place. Henry's eldest son, born in 1387 from his marriage with Mary de Bohun, called Henry of Monmouth after his place of birth, was 'chosyn and made Prince of Walys, Duke of Cornevaylle and Erle of Chestre, as Heyr Apparaunt to the kyng and to the crowne off England' at his accession by the king, who was concerned to legitimize the Lancastrian dynasty. He was a brilliant soldier, who had held Owen Glendower in check from 1403 to 1408 and finally brought about his defeat. During these years he spent the winter months at court, took his seat in Parliament, and showed his talent for diplomacy in the debates in the Privy Council. Henry of Monmouth became a well-known figure in London. He is said to have led a life of debauchery: 'he served Venus no less fervently than Mars,' wrote Thomas of Elmham in his panegyrical biography. But these rumours are in part based upon his hot-blooded temperament and overbearing manner, and in part deliberately exaggerated to stress the contrast with his later career. Characteristics more worthy of note are, in the first place, his ambition and love of action, which led him to seek the crown and engage in a struggle against Arundel, who exercised absolute power during the king's illness; secondly, a somewhat narrow-minded piety, which found expression in regular church attendance, fasting, and alms-giving. The orthodox beliefs held by his father on political grounds developed in his case into bigoted intolerance, prompted by an inner feeling of revulsion against the Reformers.

At first the young prince was a tool in the hands of his counsellors, the three Beaufort brothers, who were all older than he was but equally able and ambitious. The eldest of them, John, Earl of Somerset, died in 1410 at the early age of thirty-seven and thus remained a less colourful figure. The most important of the three was Henry, who already in 1404 became Chancellor and Bishop of Lincoln and Winchester. He was a blend of prelate and politician typical of the late Middle Ages – a pluralist, none too strict in his private moral life, imperious and quarrelsome, but as an administrator as capable as he was energetic. His interests in pastoral matters were minimal (he allowed his diocese to be administered by an agent); instead, he devoted himself fervently to politics, playing an influential and active role that was not always to the benefit of his country. His immense fortune, which he had acquired by means that sometimes smacked of dishonesty, he spent generously on patriotic causes.

The youngest of the three brothers, Thomas, who was made Duke of Exeter in 1416, though he later proved himself a good officer in the French campaigns of Henry V, was obstinate and violent. He had exerted pressure upon Henry IV to sentence to death and execute Archbishop Scrope, in defiance of the laws of the land. All the Beauforts were regarded as upstarts by members of the older aristocratic families. Sons of John of Gaunt by his marriage to Catherine Swynford, they were legitimized by Richard II in 1397 and later also recognized as legitimate by the Pope and by Parliament.

The conflict between the two parties was not concerned with differences over constitutional or foreign policy but was merely the result of personal antagonism. The king therefore did not intervene to put a stop to their quarrel. The last political event of his reign in which he participated personally, and which forms a prelude to the reign of his successor, was the war with France. Previously he had sought to avoid war by arranging a marriage between Richard II's widow (Isabella, daughter of Charles VI) and the Prince of Wales, a plan he had later abandoned,[1] but now reconsidered. In France civil war was raging. Charles of Orleans had taken up arms against the Duke of Burgundy, and the latter sent ambassadors to London to offer the hand of his daughter Anne to the Prince of Wales and to ask for military aid. Henry IV gave his consent, and also sent a small supply of arms, but simultaneously, in a most Machiavellian manner, carried on negotiations with the Orleanists, who offered him the whole of Aquitania as a bribe. This desire to interfere in the French troubles was based upon the calculation that France, torn by civil war, no longer presented a threat, and that in this situation England's concern for peace had become unnecessary, and that a war would be a lucrative proposition. This view was shared by the Prince of Wales' party, which suggested to the ailing king through Beaufort that he should abdicate. But Henry wanted to make war in person. Once more he summoned up the energy to undertake the strenuous journey to his royal country-seat at Eltham, where he attended the Christmas festivities (1412), and then went to London, where in February Parliament was due to assemble. On 20th March 1413 he died, aged forty-seven, clinging to the last to the idea of a crusade – a conception inherited from the age of medieval chivalry, which he handed on to his son.

[1] In 1400. But in 1401 the twelve-year-old Isabella was returned to France at the latter's request, and her dowry retained.

## Chapter 4

### Lydgate's Early Works; The Chaucer Tradition and Lydgate's first Epics

*

During the reign of Henry IV, or by monastic reckoning during the abbotship of William Cratfield, we have no documents on Lydgate apart from those quoted above (cf. p. 21). In spite of this it must be assumed that during this period the newly-ordained priest came to be known as a poet outside the precincts of his own monastery. The names of those who played a role in public or monastic life are to be found in documents, letters, and chronicles, but there is no mention in these of the poet Lydgate. Thus this important stage in his rise to fame can only be reconstructed tentatively, in particular since the dates of his works cannot be ascertained with any certainty. *The Complaint of the Black Knight*[1] and *The Flour of Curtesye*[2] are thought to have been written in the years 1400–2. These are courtly poems, remote from any contemporary allusion, which conjure up the good old days, executed with the life-affirming artistry of Chaucer and the French poets. That a monk of this period should have made his début with verse in this genre – for after his *Aesop* and a few lesser attempts attributed to him, the *Black Knight* is his first major work – necessitates a discussion of the literary situation of the time.

England, where for two and a half centuries French had been the sole colloquial and literary language, lagged far behind other European countries in developing a vernacular. None of the great

---

[1] *M.P.*, 382; ed. by E. Krausser, Heidelberg Diss., Halle, 1896 (reprint from *Anglia* XIX); cf. W. Skeat, *Chaucerian Pieces*, p. 245, and E. P. Hammond, *Chaucer Manual*, p. 413. Krausser gives the date as 1398–1412, Schick as 1402–3, and the *D.N.B.* as 1430.
[2] *M.P.*, 410; cf. Skeat, p. 266, and Hammond, p. 424.

medieval epics was first related in English. There was no English *Quest of the Holy Grail, Tristan, Parzifal, Divine Comedy*, or lyrical Troubadour poetry, and consequently there was no cultivated English literary language. When a truly great poet appeared in the person of Geoffrey Chaucer, it was his first task (as it had been Dante's task in Italy at the beginning of the fourteenth century) to create a literary language from one that had hitherto been broken up into a variety of dialects. And since he enjoyed the patronage of the English court, where he read his works, he had to conform to the taste prevalent in that milieu. As has already been mentioned, with Froissart quoted in support, the court of Edward III was entirely dominated by French taste, and Richard II continued this tradition in so far as he patronized English poetic works that followed French taste. Deeds of knightly valour and the worship of woman (*minne-dienst*), were, according to courtly etiquette, the prescriptive themes • in poetry. The desire to do justice to these themes, and in particular to learn a graceful mode of expression suited to the audiences at court, with more refined words adequate to convey deeply-felt emotions in a flowing and lilting metre, impelled Chaucer to translate the *Roman de la Rose*, and to compose artistic and artificial complaints – that is to say, complaints of courtly love and gallantry modelled upon the writers of the French allegorical school (Machault, Deschamps, Granson, Froissart). Chaucer's achievement in this respect was rightly recognized by the fifteenth century, and there is hardly a single poet in that era who refrains from paying homage to him. 'I may conclude with ye flower of Poets in our English tung, and the first that euer elumined our language with flowers of rethorick eloquence: I mean famous and worthy Chaucer . . .'[1] – these words of Lydgate's are repeated almost literally by three successive generations. Chaucer is the 'flour of rhetorique', the 'first finder of our faire langage', the 'noble Rhetor poete of bretaine'. The Scots, too, lauded the artistic mastery which produced a literary language equal in stature to Latin and French. His command of linguistic form in the style of the age earned him admiration: a non-real world of dreams and visions, birds of song, flower-strewn meadows, and fanciful architecture – all coupled with his elegant style, high-soaring thoughts, and strictly restrained expression of feeling. The modern

---

[1] *The Serpent of Division*. For the numerous eulogies in Lydgate's poetic works, cf. C. Spurgeon, *Five Hundred Years of Chaucer Criticism and Allusion*, 3 vols., Cambridge, 1925, I, 14 ff.

reader, who for the most part forms his judgement from the *Canterbury Tales*, usually fails to appreciate sufficiently to what extent Chaucer's significance is conditioned by the age in which he lived, just as he also overlooks his cavalier approach to the common man, so remote from the attitude of the *bourgeois*. The perspective afforded by distance does, however, enable us to appreciate one point: that the world portrayed in ornate courtly poetry was no longer suited to existing reality. As early as 1369 Chaucer had created, in his *Boke of the Duchesse*, a work of art of enduring validity by his skill in blending the world of convention and artificiality with his own personal experience of life and with true feeling (see, for example, the portrait of the Duchess Blanche). An illustration in MS. no. 61 in Corpus Christi College, Cambridge, shows Chaucer reading his works at the court of Richard II. His courtly style of poetry was the only accepted form. John Gower, Chaucer's contemporary and his equal in mastery of language, relates how on one occasion Richard, whilst sailing on the Thames (at that time the most fashionable thoroughfare in London, where the streets were so narrow and badly paved) called him over from his rowing-boat into his royal barge and urged him to write 'some newe thing'. This was later to become the great collection of tales known as *Confessio Amantis* (1390), which reveals the author not only as a moralist and gifted story-teller, but also as a courtier, bringing to life before us the outlook and taste of refined society – then still the class mainly concerned in promoting literature. We can see how even a man of middle-class origin such as Chaucer, who held office as page, valet, and scutifer at court, was anxious 'to stonden in his lady grace', how he accompanied his mistress to Mass, held her stirrup or rode beside her carriage, read or sang to her, or watched her by her needle-work or, if she was away from home, played with her pet dog or song-bird and chatted to her pages until she returned.

This sphere of life and the literature that gave expression to it necessarily appeared worthy of imitation in the eyes of *bourgeois* poets, and even of clerical ones. At the very time when Lydgate entered the arena of courtly poetry with his *Complaint of the Black Knight* a number of works similar in character were appearing. There were verse romances such as *Ipomedon*, *The Earl of Toulouse* and *The Sultan of Babylon*, which kept alive in popular form the tradition of wondrous miracles and chivalrous deeds; Sir Thomas Clanvowe, a well-known figure at Henry IV's court, wrote *The Cuckoo and the*

*Nightingale*, an elegant exposition of the ancient debate on love and wisdom; and Lydgate's contemporary, the poet Thomas (H)occleve (*circa* 1368–1450) translated Christine de Pisan's *Letter of Cupid*, a deep-felt defence of women against the attacks of Jean de Meung. Chaucer's death in 1400 naturally caused his courtly poetry to appear transfigured, as it were. Thus Lydgate's *Complaint of the Black Knight* is an act of homage to Chaucer, yet another perambulation through the gardens of the French allegorical school in which the poet had so often wandered. Both this work and *The Flour of Curtesye*,[1] like the majority of his poems, it seems, were written in response to a commission, for the Black Knight's followers implore a princess to receive them with favour, and the *Flour of Curtesye* is a Valentine such as poets were frequently called upon to compose. These are exercises in the best traditional style, so natural in tone that they were long attributed to Chaucer. It was Lydgate's ambition to strike precisely the right note. Thus *The Complaint of the Black Knight* resembles *The Book of the Duchess* in its subject-matter, and in style is reminiscent of the French school that originated with the *Roman de la Rose*. We find the love lament itself more tedious than its epic setting: there is less to hold our interest in the stiff allegories of Danger, Disdain, Malebouche, and Truth, the catalogue of true lovers, the invectives against the God of Love, and the plea to be granted a hearing, whereas Lydgate's descriptive talent enables him to effect a pleasing treatment of such old requisites as a May morning, birds, a river, and a bowery of flowers; and he concludes with an almost whimsical account of his writing down this tale one evening, pleading with the rising Venus on behalf of the lovelorn knight. The many touches reminiscent of Chaucer may lead us to interpret this in humorous fashion; but the poet himself is in great earnest, concerned to emulate his master's 'gaye style' (florid style). In this he succeeds, but unfortunately drives it to excess (the poem comprises 681 lines in ninety-seven Chaucerian stanzas). More felicitous in this respect is *The Flour of Curtesye*, a eulogy of the most perfect of women, modelled upon Chaucer's praise of Alcestis. In a mere 270 lines (likewise in Chaucerian stanzas, and terminated by a ballad in regular structure) an elegant, or at least pleasing, turn is given to the well-worn themes of the poet taking his morning promenade, abstract praise of his lady, allegories from the *Roman de la Rose*, and heroic women famous in history and mythology. Originality cannot be expected; for Lydgate

[1] M.P., 382, 410; cf. p. 31.

and the whole generation of poets that followed in Chaucer's wake the merit of their master's work lay in its style. It is from this proper but one-sided evaluation that all Lydgate's courtly love-poetry must be judged, irrespective of the date when it was written. To some works, such as *A Gentlewoman's Lament*,[1] an early date may be ascribed, as they are very pure and impersonal in form, modelled upon the complaints of the French masters, or Chaucer's *Anelida and Arcite*. Others, on the other hand, may be presumed to date from a later period: for example, the *Ballade of Her that hath all Virtues*,[2] written 'at þe request of a squyer þat serued in loves court', and the short *Complaint for Lack of Mercy*.[3] In this latter poem the style is characteristic of Lydgate in his maturity. The slightly satirical tone adopted in *The Servant of Cupid Forsaken*[4] suggests that Lydgate may occasionally have written a poem of this kind of his own free will; but most of them were commissioned – as was the vow of loyalty that occurs in one of the customary New Year poems, *A Lover's New Year's Gift*.[5] In all these works there predominate the two kinds of stanza which Lydgate preferred: the seven-line Chaucerian stanza rhymed ababbcc and the octave ballad stanza ababbcbc, usually with five-beat lines, rarely with four – metrical forms which demanded considerable artistry and mastery of language.

Throughout the fifteenth century the old themes continue to enjoy their former popularity: there were courts of love, testaments of love, books and letters of Cupid, houses and courts of wisdom and pleasure, temples of gold and glass, all gradually becoming rigid, mannered, and stilted. Here one has to ask oneself for which type of reader this literature was designed. Chaucer's select audience, with its taste sharpened on French literature, and its delight in allusions, wit, and irony had ceased to exist. The court of the sober-minded Henry IV no longer had the same brilliance as under the romantic Richard II, during whose unhappy reign many of the finest works of Middle English literature were composed. With the fading of semi-French culture the lay poet gave way to the cleric. Henry IV, who was inci-dentally fond of music, harboured good intentions of continuing the literary traditions of the court. In memory of his father, John of

---

[1] *M.P.*, 418 (fifty-six lines in seven octets with four-beat lines).

[2] *M.P.*, 379 (forty-nine lines in six Chaucerian stanzas and an envoy), written for 'Sir Othes of Holand'.

[3] *M.P.*, 381 (thirty-two lines in four octets).

[4] *M.P.*, 427 (seventy-two four-beat lines in nine octets).

[5] *M.P.*, 424 (seventy-one seven-beat lines in twenty-three tercets).

# John Lydgate

Gaunt, and his mother Blanche, whose praises Chaucer had sung, the king increased the pension granted to Chaucer by the Crown; he allowed Gower to dedicate to him his *Confessio Amantis*, and invited to his court the French poetess Christine de Pisan. But the restlessness of the age did not leave him the leisure to exercise patronage in systematic fashion. The burghers now also emerged as patrons of literature, and a radical transformation of the reading public was set in motion. One may well ask what relationship existed between the practical-minded urban commercial *bourgeois*, and the gentry that arose from them, and the courtly style which deliberately avoided all the burning issues of the day. An impression of life as it was lived at this time is provided by the correspondence of three generations of the Paston family,[1] with their constant monetary deals, lawsuits, and servant troubles. Whilst the poets were singing of eternal May and writing tales of chivalry in the traditional style, Lord Moleyns sent a band of armed men 1,000 strong to drive Margaret Paston from her manor house at Gresham, which was the object of a pending lawsuit, and demolish it entirely. Fifteen years later the Duke of Suffolk took similar unlawful action against the Pastons' house at Hellesdon. Whilst the poets continued to sing of love and pay chivalrous honours to the ladies of their choice, Agnes Paston whipped her twenty-year-old daughter until she consented to marry the wealthy fifty-year-old Scrope. One would hardly believe that people living in such conditions could appreciate the dream world portrayed in courtly poetry, were it not for astonishing evidence to this effect: Sir John Paston, a representative of the second generation of the family, who had been raised to the nobility, writes from London, whither his mother and brother had sent him to expedite proceedings concerning the family property, that he had injured his hand in a tournament: 'My hand was hurte at torney at Eltham upon Wednesday last. I would that you had been there and seen it, for it was the goodliest sight that was sene in Inglande this forty yeares of so fewe men.' And a list of books in the Paston library includes Lydgate's *Siege of Thebes, Seven Sages, La belle dame sans merci, The Temple of Glas, The Green Knight*, Ovid's *Ars Amandi*, and treatises on knighthood, war, and rules of chivalry. It may be supposed that the literary works suited to a world of knights and nobles were retained by the new *bourgeoisie* not only from a feeling for tradition, but also because they actually read them and held them in high esteem: the dream world

[1] *The Paston Letters*, ed. by J. Gairdner, 4 vols., 1901.

made the harsh reality more tolerable. During troubled times of war, pestilence, and social convulsion the yearning for a better life found expression in courtly literature and chivalrous romances, as it did also in the festivals, pageants, and tournaments that were performed by the burghers or for their entertainment. This makes it clear why it was possible for a poet and monk such as Lydgate to choose the theme of the *Complaint of the Black Knight*, and why its appeal was not limited to the public at court.

From the same period dates *The Churl and the Bird*,[1] a fable that may well be regarded as a parergon, and which carried on the tradition of Chaucer. It was natural that Lydgate should continue along the path he had trodden in his translation of Aesop, but this time he demonstrated his masterly qualities. The fable about the peasant and the bird, borrowed from the French version of *Disciplina Clericalis*, is related in the lively humorous tone adopted in the French *fabliaux* – didactic when ridiculing the slow-witted peasant who parts with his securely held possessions in exchange for something indefinite, full of suspense in the cleverly executed dialogue and perfect in the handling of the rhyme royal. This short work of 387 lines contains in the envoy a dedication 'vn-to my maistir' Chaucer, and is one of the most popular of Lydgate's minor works.

\*

His poetic talent drove him on to undertake tasks of greater magnitude. As soon as he found a patron, presumably some time between 1400 and 1403, he composed his first *oeuvre de longue haleine*, destined to remain one of his best-known works: the *Temple of Glas*.[2] Who commissioned it is not certain; Shirley says it was written '*à la request d'un amoreux*' to celebrate the union between a knight and his lady. It was probably designed as a festive poem for some wedding celebration. Since the motto of the lady eulogized in the poem is the same as that of the Pastons, *de mieulx en mieulx*, it is thought that

---

[1] *M.P.*, 468; Hammond, p. 102; cf. R. H. Bowers in *MLN* 49 (1934), pp. 90–4. Bowers publishes a manuscript mentioned neither by MacCracken nor by Hammond: Harley 2407, fol. 76r.–90v. (containing the illuminations of the garden, the peasant and the bird, and seven additional stanzas between stanzas 35 and 36 and another after stanza 40 (mainly dealing with the magic stone)). H. S. Bennett (*Chaucer and the 15th Century*) dates the fable to 1408.

[2] Edited by J. Schick, L., 1891 (*EETS*, ES. 60) with an authoritative monograph on Lydgate. Bennett dates it to 1410, after *Resoun and Sensuallyte* and *The Churl and the Bird*, which he dates to 1408; MacCracken gives the date as 1420 (*PMLA* 23 [1908], pp. 128 ff.).

William Paston commissioned it. In 1420 he married Agnes, the daughter of Sir Edmund Bury of Harlingbury Hall, Hertfordshire.[1] Chronologically this is improbable, but the occasion for which it was written may well have been a wedding feast similar to this given by some country squire. The lower gentry were eager to embellish with all manner of outward show marriages arranged on a highly commercial basis. The love allegory of the *Temple of Glas*, like Shakespeare's comedies for court circles in a later age, was designed to provide poetic adornment for an event of prosaic character. The work thus belongs to the same genre as *The Complaint of the Black Knight* and the *Flour of Curtesye*, and owing to its length (1403 lines) and ambitious scope may be regarded as the greatest of these courtly love-poems. The motifs are all familiar, and one is very often reminded of Chaucer's *House of Fame* and *Parliament of Fowls*, which likewise belong to the category of visions. The presentation, too, closely follows old models. In the customary introduction the musing poet is confronted with a dazzlingly bright temple upon a rugged cliff and obtains entrance to it through a hidden portal. The first part contains a catalogue of famous lovers of antiquity, represented pictorially, and a list of their love-laments, culminating in the lyrical complaint of a radiant beauty whose request Venus grants. The second part describes a knight, who stands apart from the crowd and delivers a monologue; it ends with his complaint and Venus counselling him to draw near to his beloved. The third part, which forms the climax, after a short narrative section depicts the knight's lyrical wooing and his lady's response, and the final words addressed to them both by the goddess. In the epilogue the poet awakes and decides to relate his vision in poetic form. The division of the theme into three epic cantos in heroic couplets, each ending with a long lyrical section in Chaucerian stanzas, shows Lydgate's talent for composition and a poetic promise comparable to that of Chaucer in *The Book of the Duchess* – although the form employed here is different; Lydgate is imitative in his choice of subject-matter and mode of expression and remote from life in his archaic book-knowledge and predilection for rhetoric.

[1] Cf. MacCracken, op. cit., pp. 128 ff., esp. p. 134; Moore, in ibid., 27, pp. 191 ff. MacCracken proves his thesis by the motto of the Paston family mentioned in l. 530 (of the B text group) and by the relations between the Pastons and the abbey of Bury St Edmunds: the judge William Paston (father of John Paston) was considered a patron of the monastery ('devotionem quam ergo Deum et nostrum habetis monasterium') and was a lay brother from 1429 onwards.

# Lydgate's first Epics

Lydgate's next major work, *Resoun and Sensuallyte*,[1] written in or about the year 1408, also has a worldly setting. But unlike the *Temple of Glas* it is not a mosaic of various reminiscences, but, like most of his works from this time onwards, is closely modelled upon a French prototype. Taking the allegorical love romance *Les Échecs Amoureux*, he expanded the first 5000 lines into 3500 short couplets. The poet finds himself checkmated in a game of chess by his beautiful partner, and anxiously turns to Amor, who instructs him in the arts of love: love and sensuality have been linked by Nature to preserve her work. But Pallas maintains that it would be unworthy of him to waste his life in the service of Venus. There follows a debate on reason and sensuality, that is to say, a discussion on chastity; the ways and means of remedying passionate love are indicated, and alternatives open to the lover once he has been cured, the *vita contemplativa* and the *vita activa*, dwelt upon in detail. Already in the original version the beginning of the tale was turned into an instruction in the art of living, and this is emphasized even more strongly in Lydgate's treatment, with the result that the work gives the impression of a moralistic allegory rather than an allegory of love. It is a fragment, evidently composed by the poet for his own delectation (for we do not know of its being commissioned), and discontinued after he had exhausted the material in which he was interested. It shows that Lydgate took no delight in story-telling, but liked to spread knowledge and learning. Of his old joy in narration and description nothing remains but the stereotyped picture of the advent of spring. All the other descriptive passages are crammed with popular philosophy in allegorical form: when Juno is mentioned, a full account is given of Jupiter's revolt against Saturn; Mercury occasions a genealogical digression on all the gods of Olympus; the judgement of Paris is treated *in extenso*; and the example of Phaeton is coupled with a catalogue of all those characters in antiquity who suffered misfortune through love. He is continually adducing examples from ancient mythology, with moral philosophical interpretation and sermonizing generally appended in the form of allegory. The work is thus less a romance than a treasure-chest of knowledge tricked out with elaborate description and rhetoric. Automatically one is reminded

[1] Edited by E. Sieper in *EETS*, ES. 84, 89, L., 1901–3, with comprehensive introduction. Cf. also Schick, in *Anglia Beibl.*, VIII, 134 ff. On the literature of chess, cf. A. Schmid, *Literatur des Schachspiels*, Vienna, 1847, and E. Sieper, *Les Échecs amoureux*, Weimar, 1898 (Literarhistor. Forschungen ed. Schick u. Waldberg, Heft 9; this has an exact summary of the contents and a comparison with Lydgate's work).

of Lydgate's contemporary John Whethamstede, abbot of the monastery of St Albans not far distant, who in his *Granarium* and *Pabularium* compiled a reference work to the treasures of antiquity which the Italian humanists had made familiar.[1] Lydgate provides an original counterpart to this in his combination of fable from the *Roman de la Rose* and allusions to chess with a dictionary in verse on mythology and the natural sciences. It is not unpleasant to read, and is characteristic of the transition from Middle Ages to Renaissance. We can visualize the author sitting at his desk, thinking that he is extracting the sum of learning from the books of antiquity, but unwittingly allowing the new eagerness for learning to enter into his text.

Lydgate's third major work of this period is his first one on a religious theme, a comprehensive *Life of Our Lady*, consisting of 6000 lines in Chaucerian stanzas (cf. Chapter 18). This poem, written between 1409 and 1411, often strikes us as lacking in taste and excessively lengthy. But it is one of his main works and is an early example of the new style in religious poetry that was to develop later. It was commissioned by Prince Hal, who subsequently reigned as Henry V.[2] This is the beginning of the close relationship eventually established between Lydgate and the Lancastrian dynasty. We have already noted that Lydgate and his fellow-monks were loyal supporters of Henry IV, in whom they saw an enemy of the Lollards. The king enjoyed popularity by reason of his deeds of chivalry at tournaments and his struggle against the infidels, and he also endeavoured to be a good churchman and a patron of the arts. It may be presumed that, on hearing of the existence of this monk with his poetic talents, he commissioned him through his son to write a *vita* of the Virgin, as a task befitting his abilities. From 1409 onwards Henry IV was ailing and avoided travelling; he had much on his hands, and may well have commanded the crown prince to represent him on a visit to the monastery. Prince Henry's patronage may at the same time have served as an act of grace towards the monastery, designed to strengthen the ties between it and the Crown.

---

[1] Cf. W. F. Schirmer, *Der englische Frühhumanismus*, Leipzig, 1931, pp. 92 ff.

[2] On Henry IV and V, cf. J. H. Wylie, *History of England under Henry IV*, 4 vols., L., 1884–98; *The Reign of Henry V*, 3 vols., Cambridge, 1914–29. On the queens of England, cf. A. Strickland, *Lives of the Queens of England*, Vols. II, III, L., 1877. Other works are: C. L. Kingsford, *Henry V*, 2nd ed., L., 1923; Sir W. Ramsay, *Lancaster and York*, Oxford, 1892; C. L. Kingsford, *English History in Contemporary Poetry, II: York and Lancaster*, 1914.

Possibly, however, the prince may have acted on his own initiative, for in later years he again sometimes commissioned Lydgate to write religious poems. His licentious days at the manor of Cheylesmore near Coventry were over, as was his soldiering in the Irish and Welsh campaigns. He too was in his own fashion a lover of the arts. Lydgate did not disappoint his princely patron. Whereas most legends were fairly short tales, in conformity with their prime purpose, Lydgate made his *Life of Our Lady* a voluminous epic. Only John Capgrave and Henry Bradshaw, of later poets, tried to follow his example, but met with less success.

When the *Life of Our Lady* was completed is not known – perhaps in 1411. In conformity with the usual practice, the author will have presented his work personally to his august patron. There is no authentic information whether a royal castle or the monastery of Bury was the scene where this solemn ceremony took place. In the illustrations that have been preserved[1] the author is represented kneeling, surrounded by ecclesiastical and secular dignitaries, who remain standing, and offering his book to the prince, shown seated upon a throne. This act symbolized the personal link between author and patron which, in addition to any links of intellectual sympathy that might exist, was founded upon a firm material basis: the author obtained protection and monetary reward from his patron, and in return enhanced the latter's fame and popularity. The prince who was later to reign as King Henry V will have accepted the dedication of Lydgate's work with gratitude, for despite his martial spirit and unimaginative earnestness he had leanings towards the arts; he had enjoyed a scholarly education, had his father's love of music, and was anxious to continue the literary traditions of the House of Lancaster. Thus after Lydgate handed over his *Life of Our Lady*, mention may have been made in conversation of the possibility of his writing a new work, one that seems to us more in keeping with Henry's inclinations than the life of a saint, and one that faced Lydgate with incomparably more exacting demands: a poetic treatment of the legend of Troy.

---

[1] As in MS. Cotton Aug. A IV (B.M.), Bodl. MS. Digby 232 (Bodleian, Oxford), Crawford-Rylands MS. (Manchester), Trin. Coll. MS. O.5.2. (Cambridge), Rawl. C. 446 (Bodleian, Oxford) – all of which contain the *Troy Book* (cf. p. 50, n. 8).

# Chapter 5

## Lydgate's Troy Book

*

During his brief but illustrious career Henry V, known for his triumphant victories, held ideas of feudal chivalry more appropriate to the high Middle Ages than to the *bourgeois* fifteenth century, an era of transition leading to the Renaissance. His outlook was, however, in keeping with the Indian summer atmosphere of medieval chivalry that prevailed at the court of the Duke of Burgundy.[1] The pointless wars of conquest in which he expended the strength of his country, the crusade which he regarded as the climax of his life's work, and the duel which he fought at the siege of Melun – all appear as strange anachronisms.

It is in the light of these views that his patronage of the *Troy Book*[2] must be seen. When the poet received his commission – from the precise astronomical data given in the prologue we even know the day and hour: it was on Monday, 31st October 1412 at 4 p.m.[3] – he may well have spent many a late autumn day in the monastery library meditating on his task. This well-known theme had been handled by several writers, particularly by Benoît de Sainte-Maure, in his *Roman de Troie* (1160), and by Guido delle Colonne, in a prose ver-

---

[1] Cf. O. Cartellieri, *Am Hof der Herzöge von Burgund*, Basle, 1926, and J. Huizinga, *The Waning of the Middle Ages*, London, 1924. On 10th January 1429 Duke Philip the Good founded the Order of the Golden Fleece for thirty-one knights of ancient noble families, with the object of reviving the old ideals of chivalry. Cf. Zoller, *Der Orden vom goldenen Vlies*, Altenburg, 1879; H. Kervyn de Lettenhove, *La toison d'or*, Brussels, 1907.

[2] Edited by H. Bergen, 4 vols., *EETS*, ES. 97, 103, 106, 126, L., 1906, 1908, 1910, 1935. Cf. W. Greif, *Die mittelalterlichen Bearbeitungen der Trojasage*, Marburg, 1886, and other works listed by Bergen. Guido's *Historia Troiana* is given in excerpts in Bergen, Vol. IV. The *Roman de Troie* of Benoît de Sainte-Maure has been edited by L. Constans, in 6 vols., Paris, 1904–8 (S.A.T.F.).

[3] 3rd November, according to Parr's calculation (*PMLA* 67 [1952], pp. 252 ff.).

3. Lydgate presenting his *Troy Book* to King Henry V

4a. Lydgate, in black, kneeling as he presents his *Troy Book* to King Henry V

4b. Lydgate at his desk

sion, *Historia Troiana* (1287). In addition to these French and Latin versions Prince Henry wished to have one in English; and Lydgate, though less moved by such sentiments of national pride, appreciated the significance of the undertaking. He chose to follow Guido[1] because he claimed to have given the true story, in contrast to the fables told by Homer, Virgil, and Ovid. For Lydgate was in agreement with his mighty patron that poets should relate 'nothing but the truth': they should narrate events as they had really happened, and thus keep alive the fame of the hero. Henry, who was fond of reading tales of this kind contained in ancient books, regarded the deeds of the heroes of Troy as examples of true chivalry and as an encouragement to men to avoid living in idleness. Lydgate had to do justice to this historiographic and pedagogic evaluation of the work. He therefore narrates most diligently, exhausting all the possibilities of his rhetoric, the entire set of Trojan tales, from the expedition of the Argonauts to the final fate of the Greek and Trojan heroes. In so doing he expands his Latin source, which he follows closely, to more than 30,000 lines, arranging them into heroic couplets, probably on the model of the *Canterbury Tales*. The customary asides in which he apologizes for his modest poetic talents[2] are all the more striking because he not only places himself on a lower level than Chaucer, but even the scholarly Guido. It was not until later, he says, that the Muse came to him – and it is characteristic that he should refer to Clio, the Muse of History. He confesses that he also lacks the art of rhetoric. His repeatedly expressed regrets at his rhetorical shortcomings reveal the scope of his poetic ambition and are all the more remarkable since to us his poetry seems excessively rhetorical. Of approximately 800 words borrowed from Romance languages – the 'aureate terms' introduced by Lydgate – over 200 are to be found in his *Troy Book*.

An analysis of one of the passages in which he expands on his source, such as the account of Achilles' body being thrown to the dogs,[3] gives a good idea of the place of rhetoric in Lydgate's method of narration. An accumulation of figures of speech, and particularly of anaphoras, which follow upon one another to the point of invocation, slow down the rhythm of the verse. The polysyllabic Romance words produce the sonorous musical effect to which he aspired. His verbose style is characterized by repetition of the same thought,

[1] The versions are compared by H. Koch, *John Lydgates Troy Book*, Diss., Berlin, 1935.
[2] E.g., II, 160.     [3] IV, 3204.

# John Lydgate

expressed with variations of language; by expletive phrases, indicative of carelessness (which, following Chaucer, he thought permissible in poetry); and by interpolation into his rhetorical tirades of explanatory historical comment and moral injunctions, which with other digressions repeatedly interrupt the flow of the narrative.

The great collection of tales connected with the siege of Troy was regarded by the author and his contemporaries not merely as a string of episodes but also as a historical work containing all the moral and political lessons which history was expected to teach. Into the leisurely unfolding narrative are woven erudition and worldly wisdom, exhortation, and didactic sermonizing, all of which combine to produce a richly embellished historical structure. Lydgate begins with Jason and the expedition of the Argonauts, tells the story of Hercules and the Golden Fleece, and, as a welcome supplement to this group of tales in which Mars occupies such a prominent place, adds the popular story of Medea's faithful love and the abduction to Greece of Hesione. The death of King Laomedon and the destruction of Old Troy bring the first book to a close. The second tells of Priam and the building of the new city. Hesione is to be fetched back, and when Antenor's endeavour fails, Paris is sent on a campaign of retribution. He returns in triumph with Helen; but the Greeks prepare for war and lead their army before Troy. Books III and IV relate in detail, and therefore somewhat monotonously, the battles fought between the two armies and the individual heroes. In these martial events the love element, which forms such an integral part of the epic proper, makes but a brief appearance, in the story of Troilus and Cressida and in Achilles' passion for Polyxena. In its place we have long speeches by the heroes, in which they discuss the issues of war and peace and the leadership of their armies. After the account of the surrender of the city Book V, the last, tells of the fate of the surviving Greek and Trojan warriors, in particular of Aeneas and Odysseus. An edifying conclusion is contained in the epilogue, which deduces from the tales the vanity of everything terrestrial and solicits divine blessing upon the patron of the work.

The subject-matter commonly treated in epics[1] was plentiful enough, and contained sufficient moments of suspense to produce an effect, even in the hands of Lydgate, who could not or would not compete with a born narrator like Gower. Throughout the Middle

---

[1] On Middle English epics on Troy, cf. J. E. Wells, *Manual of the Writings in Middle English*, New Haven, 1923, pp. 106 ff.

Ages there existed able story-tellers, and some of their talent was shared by the author of the *Troy Book*. One need only compare his account with Guido's dry *Historia*. Dull passages in his source he shortens or passes over entirely; the night spent by Jason in Medea's arms[1] he treats with a lighter touch; Hector's lying-in state[2] or the story of Pyrrhus[3] gain by being shortened, and by the addition of new material. Occasionally he divides up one of Guido's long chapters and sets off the incidents to advantage by adding an introduction of his own.[4] Sometimes, as in the case of Odysseus' adventures, Guido's dry enumeration of events is turned by Lydgate into an entertaining account.[5] His description is also more vivid when, as for example at the Calchas oracle, he keeps closely to the Latin text.[6] It has been suggested that Lydgate inserted technical details about military tactics, weapons, armour, and heraldry in order to please his patron, and this has been held against him. But in fact a description of this kind was of interest to everyone in those days, including the poet himself. The vigorous description of the battle of Tenedoun[7] does not suffer thereby; and the description of the armour of the Trojans[8] arrests our attention, as does also the duel between Pyrrhus and Penthiselea,[9] described in the style of the tournaments held in Lydgate's own day; both are of interest from the standpoint of cultural history.

The tribute paid to his talent for description is merited less by his portrayal of the characters, in which, as is only to be expected, he adheres to the traditional ideals (e.g., in the case of Helen),[10] but rather by his portrayal of the festival, in which he surpasses Guido (e.g. reception of Paris and Helen in Troy),[11] and the colourful account given of the eight-day festivities with their tournaments, feastings, and dances.[12] All this Lydgate had seen with his own eyes, as he has the pomp and splendour of armies drawn up in battle array, with the soldiers' weapons and the gold and silver crests of their helmets gleaming in the sun. He had heard the piercing trumpet-calls and the neighing of the horses,[13] whereas Guido has almost nothing to say about the first encounter between Greeks and Trojans. The imaginative scenes, too, gain in colour and vigour in Lydgate's version. The dry statement in the Latin text that the Trojan women watched their heroes leaving is elaborated by such details as, for example, that many of the women turned pale on hearing

---

[1] I, 2920.  [2] III, 5663.  [3] V, 2445.  [4] IV, 2401.  [5] V, 1781.
[6] II, 5941.  [7] II, 6341.  [8] III, 44.  [9] IV, 4295.
[10] II, 3642.  [11] II, 4097.  [12] II, 4179.  [13] III, 716.

the rustling of the banners as they were unfurled, or that others hid their faces and dared not look upon the armour gleaming in the sunlight, fearing for their husbands or loved ones.[1] Less commendable are the frequency and length of the speeches and counter-speeches of the individual heroes,[2] most of them extending to more than 100 lines. Lydgate's tedious prolixity interrupts and impedes the flow of his narrative. The same may be said of the laments for the dead, apart from those in which the fallen heroes are compared in catalogue-like fashion with figures frequently mourned in the past, thus making a claim to humanistic interest.[3] The lengthy but artistic account of the mourning of Paris,[4] in which lamentation and depiction of the mourners are combined with one of these catalogues, can be regarded as typical of this kind of description, whereas the lament for Agamemnon,[5] with the omission of passages dealing with the king's murder, serves as an example of the way in which Lydgate sometimes made his own interpolations into the narrative.

Of these interpolations those illustrative of nature have been singled out for praise.[6] There are a number of them in the *Troy Book*, inspired by and modelled upon Chaucer. Their freshness led to their being erroneously evaluated by modern criteria of observation and originality, whereas medieval artists sought to describe an ideal landscape and an ideal season. This accounts for the recurrent appearance of such artificial allegorical figures as Aurora, Titan, Phoebus, and Flora, for the designation of the seasons of the year in astronomical terms, adopted by Chaucer, and also for the constant recurrence of topics such as clear water, birds singing, morning stillness, green meadows, foliage casting shade, gaily-coloured flowers, etc. But Lydgate is genuinely attached to introductions and interpolations which are illustrative of nature, for he inserts them in places where Guido has nothing similar[7] or where he contents himself with a brief reference;[8] and he decks out his descriptions with such lively illustrative details that the modern reader gains the im-

---

[1] III, 516.

[2] Jason-Cethes, I, 1409; Priam, II, 1145; II, 1903; Hector, II, 2183; Agamemnon, II, 5239; IV, 153; IV, 3271; Hector-Achilles, II, 3785; Odysseus-Achilles, IV, 1701.

[3] Especially in the lament for Troilus, IV, 3003, and for Hector, III, 5422.

[4] IV, 3600.     [5] V, 1011.

[6] Cf. F. Reuss, *Das Naturgefühl bei Lydgate*, in *Archiv* 122, pp. 269–300; Moorman, *Interpretation of Nature in English Poetry*, 1905 (Quellen und Forschungen, Band 95); E. Ballerstedt, Über Chaucers Naturschilderungen, Diss., Göttingen, 1901.

[7] I, 1197; I, 623; I, 3431; III, 2745; III, 4449, etc.

[8] I, 3093; I, 3907; I, 1248; II, 3319; III, 1; IV, 3363; V, 586.

pression of something actually perceived at first hand. The lark soaring in jubilation, the glittering of the silver dew, the leaves of small white daisies, flowers red and blue—all these are vividly rendered, although they derive from the common stock of set idioms. The mention of cherries reddening and ripening in June, and ears of corn swelling, dew evaporating with the rising sun, and the first cutting of the hay evoke a picture of Lydgate wandering leisurely in the monastery garden and in the valleys of the Lark and Linnet. He had seen grapes damaged by autumnal frost hanging in the monastery vineyard; and he augmented the traditional nature pictures by drawing upon other images familiar to him, as to seafaring Englishmen generally: the calm sea, the sun setting behind the waves, and autumnal storms.

Other interpolations bear traces of Lydgate's own character. His romantic and chivalrous patron envisaged the *Troy Book* as a tale of military heroism and adventure that would inspire its readers to emulate such exploits themselves. The author did not share this conception of the work, and remarks that this tale of war, lust, and revenge merely pointed the moral of the transitoriness of life, fading as the flowers of summer.[1] For it was common practice to regard history as a mirror of the present and a guide to action; and Lydgate made use of every opportunity that presented itself, even at the cost of the narrative, to make the practical moral applications of his story clear to the reader. There are three themes in particular which are repeatedly treated in formal digressions: the theme of transitoriness, which Lydgate sees as a sermonizing monk, coupling it with general moral and religious teachings; the theme of war and discord, which as a pacific-minded poet he holds up for the edification of the rulers and the ruled; and the humanistic theme, which leads him as a scholar, widely read in the works which his library contains, to set down proudly and naïvely his knowledge of history and mythology.

All the digressions gain in significance and gravity as a result of Lydgate's conception of the art of poetry. Art consists solely in mastery of linguistic technique; for this reason the homage repeatedly paid to Chaucer is rendered to him only as an artist in words,[2] and in his asseverations of modesty he deplores his own lack of rhetoric.[3] The content of poetry must be truth, and the task

---

[1] V, 3546. On his favourite theme and image, cf. M.P., 780, 809.
[2] II, 4677; III, 550 and 4197; V, 3521.     [3] I, 4420; II, 160.

# John Lydgate

of the poet to criticize whatever is false. Accordingly the moralizing and sermonizing digressions are of various kinds: in addition to satire on the inconstancy of women[1] and praise of womanly virtue[2] there are shorter passages of worldly wisdom, such as an instruction on navigation by the stars,[3] the advice not to keep on blurting out one's own opinions,[4] to avoid envy and revenge,[5] and not to harbour suspicion of others unjustly.[6] The fact that this religious counsel is couched in verbose language is understandable in view of Lydgate's profession. Medea's indulgence in the magic arts compels him to point out, taking the events at the Crucifixion as his example, that only God can change the course of nature.[7] More interesting, since they reveal more of Lydgate's own personality, are the numerous digressions about Fortune.[8] This conception of fickle Fortune, enthroned upon the wheel of fortune, was popular in the Middle Ages, and in it Lydgate's religious and secular convictions coincided. His invective against the covetousness of the clergy[9] reflects the anger felt by the monks against the lay priests who had come to terms with the townspeople during the revolt of 1381 and who were later involved in feuds with the monastery. Personal experience may have prompted his sermon against love of gossip among ordinary folk.[10] The monastery had all manner of conflicts with the population of the surrounding countryside, and the remark that the common people are untrustworthy reveals the way in which the monastery identified itself with those in power.

Lydgate's attitude towards King Henry V, with whom he had become acquainted whilst he was still crown prince, showed for all its respect and humility the warmth, intimacy, and admonitory attitude of a father confessor. In conformity with his distinguished patron he emphasizes the values of a chivalrous life by extolling Hector and Troilus[11] and condemning Achilles for his lack of knightly virtues.[12] He censures Pyrrhus because he sacrificed Polyxena at his father's grave, for this was an unchivalrous act;[13] and the treacherous Antenor and Calchas stir him to irate outbursts.[14] King Henry, whose French conquests Lydgate welcomes, since he is convinced of the legality of Henry's claim to his inheritance,[15] ought to unite the two countries by employing the wisdom of true chivalry; then bloodshed

---

[1] E.g., I, 1840, 2100; III, 4265, 4820.  [2] E.g., III, 4361.
[3] I, 670.  [4] IV, 5451.  [5] II, 1067.  [6] I, 959.
[7] I, 1712.  [8] II, 1, 4245; III, 1976, 4077; V, 16, 1019.  [9] IV, 5833.
[10] IV, 4951; III, 5492.  [11] IV, 2752.  [12] IV, 2673, 2768.
[13] IV, 6849.  [14] IV, 5201, 5480, 6023.  [15] V, 3368.

will cease and the golden age return.[1] He calls on God to send the Prince of Peace home safely and to grant him a long reign.[2] Queen Catherine he urges to mediate between the two countries,[3] and ensure their prosperity, peace, and tranquillity.[4] Each of these hopes, expressed in the form of homage, is simultaneously both request and admonition.

We have already entered into a discussion of Lydgate's political digressions, which reveal his deeply ingrained love of peace. Although he must needs invoke the protection of Mars in this tale of war,[5] he places the Muses beside him; and in Book IV – at a time when the Crown Prince had become king and was engaged in his lengthy and sanguinary wars of conquest in France – there follows a whole chapter in which the author levels accusations against Mars:[6] murder and death are his delight; he is the source of anger and hatred, and to man signifies ruin, treachery, war, and captivity. When it is said of Troy: 'almost for nouȝt was þis strif be-gonne',[7] and the contrast repeatedly pointed between the insignificant causes of the war and its murderous course,[8] we can interpret this as a reference to the war with France, which was continually flaring up anew. It sounds like a warning addressed to Henry V when the irascible Priam is upbraided for failing to consider what will be the effect of his actions, and cautioned not to trust Fortune,[9] since military success is transient, and one may suddenly find oneself checkmated.[10] And he appears to have Catherine in mind when, in the plans for Achilles' wedding to Polyxena, his wife is hailed as the harbinger of peace.[11] Even in the envoy, which celebrates the radiant triumphant hero, it is pointed out that Henry holds both sword and sceptre in his hands – the sword with which to suppress obstreperous rebels, and the sceptre with which to rule over his poor subjects, who wish to live in peace and tranquillity.[12] These admonitions addressed to the sovereign are coupled with an earnest entreaty to the barons and great lords of the realm to preserve unity among themselves. For strife and discord are poison, the root of all trouble and disorder in every land.[13] It is a motto for the times, as well as a timeless one, when Lydgate says, in connexion with the quarrel between the Greek commanders: 'Lo what meschef lyth in variaunce // Amonge lordis, whan þei nat accorde'.[14]

[1] V, 3399.  [2] V, 3416, 3457.  [3] V, 3426.  [4] V, 3435; cf. pp. 133 f.
[5] I, 36.  [6] IV, 4440.  [7] II, 7855.  [8] *E.g.* II, 7851 ff.
[9] II, 1796.  [10] II, 1894.  [11] IV, 2614.  [12] Envoy 55; cf. p. 64 f.
[13] IV, 4513.  [14] III, 2342 f.

# John Lydgate

The view of the outside world which the Trojan tales invited was one fraught with anxiety. But to the scholar these tales also opened up the humanistic world, the peaceful atmosphere of the monastery library. This is shown by the third group of digressions, in which Lydgate vaunts his knowledge of the classics and, in particular, of mythology. As in *Resoun and Sensuallyte* we hear in the judgement of Paris further details about the attributes of the goddesses and their significance.[1] The Delphic oracle occasions a long digression on idolatry,[2] in which all the deities of antiquity are discussed; and in a second and more comprehensive mythological catalogue[3] Lydgate displays in an admirably concise manner a degree of learning which was remarkable for his time. It is only to be expected that one should find popular historical catalogues, in which, for example, an instructive and entertaining comparison is drawn between Helen's grief for Paris and the sorrows of women in the ancient world,[4] or between the lament for Troilus and famous laments of antiquity.[5] But it is surprising to find several descriptions of the ancient theatre and of the performance of tragedies.[6] The reformulation at this point of the poet's task, to relate the deeds of rulers, their chivalrous exploits, and their ultimate decline and death, through the intervention of Fortune,[7] foreshadowed Lydgate's main work, *The Fall of Princes*.

For eight years Lydgate worked on the *Troy Book*, completing it in the summer or early autumn of 1420. The four oldest manuscripts,[8] all written in a similar hand, and illuminated by the same English school of miniaturists, probably originated from the *scriptorium* of the monastery of St Edmunds, which endeavoured to provide a worthy setting for the great epic of its poet. Presumably one of these manuscripts was the copy dedicated and presented to the king.[9]

*

During the eight years which Lydgate spent working on the *Troy*

---

[1] II, 2488.    [2] II, 5480.    [3] IV, 6930.    [4] IV, 3655.
[5] IV, 3003.    [6] II, 860; III, 5422.    [7] II, 884.

[8] C = Cotton, Augustus A IV (B.M.); D2 = Digby 232 (Bodleian, Oxford); Rawl. 1 = Rawlinson C 446 (Bodleian, Oxford) – all dated 1420–35. B = Bristol MS. (City Ref. Lib.), Crawford-Rylands (Rylands Lib., Manchester) dated approx. 1470. Printed by Pynson in 1513 (B.M.).

[9] Following Tanner, D 2; it might just as easily have been C, B, or Rawl. 1. The illustrations are similar in all of them, but C is particularly luxurious in its format, with broad margins.

*Book*[1] much was happening in the history of the monastery and in the world at large. William Cratfield, who had been abbot since 1390, resigned in 1414 (or 1415) on grounds of ill health, and on 13th July 1415 William of Exeter was appointed his successor. During the fourteen years for which he held office an official register was kept,[2] from which we learn that the abbot, together with Richard Clifford, Bishop of London, and Cardinal Henry Beaufort (at that time still Bishop of Winchester, but who was later to play an important political role), were sent to represent England at the Council of Constance. William of Exeter is known to have been present at the conclave of 1417. Whether this prolonged contact with Continental princes of the Church and humanists was fruitful for him and his monastery from the cultural point of view we do not know; there are no letters similar to those written by Whethamstede to his monastery at St Albans which allow such inferences to be drawn. But the political role played by Abbot William certainly testifies to St Edmunds' increasing importance. It explains why Henry IV's brother, Thomas (de) Beaufort, then Duke of Dorset, came to Bury St Edmunds in person to settle the protracted dispute with the Bishop of Ely about the scope of the monastery's authority.[3] Although this object was not attained, Thomas Beaufort retained a lifelong attachment to Bury. In 1427 he was buried there (in the Lady Chapel), in accordance with the provisions of his will, in which he commanded that 1,000 masses should be read for the salvation of his soul and the souls of his parents.[4] A testamentary disposition such as this indicates the close financial and political ties that existed between the monastery and the Crown, and accounts for the fact that Lydgate, as a monastic and court poet, was increasingly called upon to lend support to political and dynastic interests. It was not until the critical times of Henry VI, however, that he was obliged to devote himself fully to this role, for which his pacific temperament made him little suited. So long as Henry V's triumphal march continued, there was no need for propaganda in poetic form; deeds spoke for themselves.

[1] Th. Tanner, *Bibliotheca Britannico-Hibernica*, ed. D. Wilkins, 1748, pp. 489 ff. According to the *Registrum* of William of Exeter ('in monasterio vixit A. 1415 ubi electioni Gul. Exestri adfuit') and Lydgate's own evidence in the *Troy Book* (V, 3469), he stayed at Bury in 1420.

[2] This registrum, mentioned by Tanner, is not mentioned in Arnold, *Mem. of St Edm.*, I, XI.

[3] *Mem. of St Edm.*, III, 201 ff. Arnold wrongly states Bedford, but cf. pp. 259-60 (text Beuford, *alias* Beaforde).

[4] Ibid., III, 259 f.

E

## Chapter 6

### Henry V

\*

King Henry V entered London in triumph on Friday, 7th April 1413, to the cheers of his people, who regarded him as their legitimate ruler. No one spared a thought for the Duke of March's lawful claim to the throne. It was not in vain that Henry IV[1] had fought for fourteen years against enemies at home and abroad to defend the throne he had usurped. The new king was of slender build and average height, with strong but graceful limbs and a handsome countenance; his cropped hair and heavy jaw gave him a resemblance to his father, although his thin lips and penetrating gaze suggested that he possessed greater power of decision. In the Tower, wearing a serious expression, he conferred knighthood upon fifty young men who then escorted him as he rode back along the traditional route, which was thronged by crowds: up Fish Street, across the Corn Market and Grace Church Street to Leadenhall, and then curving westwards through narrow, crooked streets and squares to St Paul's. This was the main thoroughfare in the City of London, which was then still a walled town.[2] From there the way led through Ludgate into Fleet Street, past St Clement's to the Strand, at this time a badly paved road, to the north of which still lay open fields; and then continued along what was later to become Pall Mall and the broad highway leading to the city of Westminster. Here the coronation took place on Sunday, 9th April. The king displayed an intense piety;

[1] Henry IV died on 20th March 1413. His body lay in state in Westminster, was taken to Canterbury, and there interred in the Trinity Chapel, next to the tomb of the Black Prince.

[2] Cf. map in R. Pauli, *Bilder aus Altengland*, 2nd ed., 1876. Cf. also the frontispiece to Stow's *Survey* (ed. C. L. Kingsford, L., 1908), which shows London in Elizabethan times and A. Ryther's map in *Chronicles of London*, ed. Kingsford, Oxford, 1905.

even at the banquet in the great hall over which he presided, attired in his coronation robes and surrounded by distinguished guests, with trumpets sounding fanfares and wine flowing in abundance, he would neither eat nor drink. During his nine-year reign the young ruler was to become the idol of his people. There is something attractive about his supposedly frivolous youth,[1] his delight in music, and soldierly courage. He was unaffected, but cold and lacking in imagination. Acceding to the throne at the age of twenty-five, he had forfeited his youth and assumed the functions of his royal office with unnatural self-control, as though he were a priest entering upon his ministry. He imbued his people with a spirit of patriotic enthusiasm, but did nothing for their welfare, since his mind was preoccupied with problems of foreign policy. He did not allow himself to be deflected from implementing his political designs by his bigoted religious outlook. Thrice daily he attended Mass, and, mindful of his father's dying words, *ecclesiam orna et honora*, he adhered strictly to orthodoxy in his religious beliefs. For his zeal in persecuting the heretics the clergy lauded him as a 'champion of the Church'.

Convinced of the justice of his claim to the French throne, he dreamed of conquering that country and then leading a reunited Christendom against the infidel Turk and, as he said on his deathbed, rebuilding the walls of Jerusalem after a final victorious crusade.[2] His contemporaries, on the other hand, thought more in terms of *Realpolitik*, and sought to develop English commerce and gain command of the seas. The *Lybelle of Englyshe Polycye* (approx. 1436–7), which may perhaps be attributed to Adam Moleyns,[3] commends Henry for his maritime successes, but regards his conquest of Normandy merely as a means of controlling the Channel. The objective this writer has in mind is the expansion of English trade. The author, unlike King Henry, discards the outworn outlook of the feudal era, and advocates a commercial policy that is incipiently capitalistic.

Yet the king's plans of conquest, in which romanticism and realism were curiously combined, had a compulsive power of attraction. When the poet (H)occleve offered him the dedication of his work

---

[1] On the legends about Henry's licentious youth, cf. Wylie, *Henry V*, I, 186 ff.

[2] Among the books borrowed from Caen there was a volume of chronicles of Jerusalem and a description of the first crusade by Gottfried von Bouillon (R. Pauli, *Geschichte von England*, V, 178).

[3] Clerk of the Council of Henry VI from 1436 to 1441, Bishop of Chichester in 1446; he died in 1450.

# John Lydgate

*Regement of Princes* (1411–12) the king gladly accepted, for it contained a poetic justification of his policy.[1] It is understandable that as a patron of the arts Henry was more interested in subject-matter than in form of presentation, and that he must have appreciated as history rather than as poetry both Chaucer's *Troilus* and the legend of Troy in general, which he commissioned Lydgate to treat.

When the king opened his first parliament at Westminster on 15th May he showed that he had a firm and purposeful policy. He set at liberty the pretender to the throne and allowed the Earl of March, now a grown man of twenty-two, to take his seat in the House of Lords. He had no cause to regret his magnanimity, for the earl remained loyal all his life. With equal determination Henry grappled with problems which his father had hesitated to tackle, such as the attitude to be taken towards the Lollards and the policy to be followed in regard to the French civil war.

When the Lollards, perhaps encouraged by the advent of a new ruler to the throne, became more audacious in their preaching, the king took the initiative and had their leader, Sir John Oldcastle (Lord Cobham), imprisoned and subsequently executed. A wholesale persecution of the Lollards ensued,[2] in which they were made to appear more dangerous than they actually were. After Lord Cobham's death supporters of Lollardry were to be found only among the lower clergy and townspeople. It thus completely lost its political character and became more and more of a sect. But the ruling class kept up the fiction that it was a political party, and poets had to depict their plans for revolution as a formidable threat. Such a description is to be found, for example, in the *Versus rhythmici in laudem Henrici Vi*.[3] In (H)occleve's Oldcastle ballad[4] the Lollards' secularizing tendencies were interpreted as communism. Ecclesiastical poets, on the other hand, sounded a moderate note in such matters, and in all Lydgate's voluminous works there are only a few lines of condemnation, and not a single satirical poem exclusively directed against Lollardry.

---

[1] (H)occleve sketches in *Regement of Princes*, pp. 191–6, the policy that should be adopted towards France: the war should be brought to a close by a marital union, and the rightful heir should then lead both kingdoms in a war against the infidels and convert them to the true faith.

[2] Decreed at the Parliament of Leicester in 1414.

[3] In *Memorials of Henry V*, ed. by Cole (Rolls Series), V, 151, and in Elmham, *Liber metricus de Henrico V*, ibid.

[4] *Anglia*, V, 36, stanza 57.

As far as foreign policy was concerned, the king's attitude was equally unrelenting. His father's most eminent counsellor, Archbishop Thomas Arundel, who advocated a peaceful settlement with France, was obliged to resign the chancellorship in favour of Henry Beaufort, and in the second parliament of the reign, held at Leicester, negotiations were entered into with the Burgundian envoy for a treaty of alliance. In the event the envoy's plea for the conclusion of an agreement was rejected, not because of the fact that the armistice with France was still in effect, but because Henry wanted to play the principal role and not act merely as a confederate of the Burgundians. In July 1414 he demanded 'the restitution of his ancient rights in France', that is to say, the renewal of the treaty of 1360 and recognition of the claim to the French Crown laid by Edward III. In order to avoid the use of force, France was summoned to give Princess Catherine to Henry in marriage, with the territory of the old kingdom of Anjou as her dowry. The French sent the English ambassador back without a reply;[1] war was in any case inevitable. On 16th June 1415 Henry V took leave of Joan, the queen-mother, and after a service at St Paul's set out in procession from the City, accompanied by the mayor, aldermen, and by representatives of the townspeople. During his journey, at Winchester on 30th June, a French legation tried to avert hostilities at the eleventh hour, but was confronted with demands known to be unacceptable. On the eve of the expedition's departure a plot was laid, but it misfired.[2] Henry could thus entrust his kingdom to the charge of the Duke of Bedford, who was assisted by Beaufort and a council of four prelates and five peers, in the knowledge that there would be no trouble at home. On Sunday, 11th August the fleet set sail from Southampton for France. It landed without opposition on the 13th, and Harfleur was taken. Despite this success the expedition did not at first fare well. But the king's military measures had the effect of inspiring his army with a great wave of patriotic and religious fervour. The good understanding reached with Flanders and the neutrality of the other maritime powers enabled him to cut France off by sea. This made the

---

[1] They took their stand on the Treaty of Arras of 4th September 1414, whereby the dauphin and the Burgundians undertook a pledge not to enter into any alliance with England. Despite this agreement Burgundy concluded a secret pact with England on 29th September, which led to a resumption of war between England and France.

[2] Richard, Earl of Cambridge, Sir Thomas Gray, and Henry, Lord Scrope wanted to make the Earl of March, Richard II's heir, king; but the latter informed the king, who had the conspirators executed.

risky venture of a sea-borne invasion possible. France was in a state of anarchy, ruled by a feeble-minded king and a dissolute dauphin, with no military leader or modern army which it could pit against the English. On Friday, 25th October 1415 came the decisive battle of Agincourt (now Azincourt), a magnificent victory, due as much to the English troops' enthusiasm for battle, which bordered on fanaticism, as to the skilful use of the long-bow, the national arm, and to good generalship.

Agincourt seemed to have inaugurated a revival of Edward III's glorious foreign policy, and when the victorious king entered London in triumph on 23rd November he was given a reception unrivalled since the days when the Black Prince had ridden into the City with the captives from Poitiers. He was met on the broad common of Blackheath, where today the Dover road runs, the spot where the Danish army had encamped in the days of Ethelred, and where Wat Tyler had gathered together his rebels. Here, where there was a broad vista over Surrey and Kent which included the royal palace at Eltham, and where Richard II had once gone to meet his second consort, Isabella,[1] there waited the Lord Mayor and aldermen, attired in scarlet trimmed with fur, mounted on horseback at the head of all the guilds and corporations. On London Bridge the royal coat-of-arms was put up, bearing the words 'grete lyons and Geauntes' (this being the description given in the 'Great London Chronicle'), and 'seynt George ryally armed' stood at the entrances to streets that were hung with draperies and where from roof-tops and windows the massed throngs chanted their hurrahs, clarions and trumpets sounded, and streams of wine poured forth from the conduits in Cornhill and Cheapside. At the fountain in Cornhill men garbed as prophets sang the psalm *Cantate Domino*; the cross in Cheapside was turned into a tower for the occasion, on the top of which a children's choir sang the *Te Deum*, with women standing below to greet the king with 'Noel! Noel! Welcome, Henry the fifte, kynge of England and of Fraunce!' In the midst of this dazzling splendour rode the victor, serious and taciturn, clad in a red cloak, escorted only by a few attendants. He had declined to have songs and poems composed in his honour, to show the world that he owed his victory to God alone. He wore neither helmet nor

---

[1] Blackheath became the customary spot for ceremonial occasions. It was here that Emperor Sigismund was welcomed in 1416, Catherine of Valois in 1421, Henry VI in 1432, and Margaret of Anjou in 1445.

armour, and at St Paul's knelt down in prayer. Then, attended by
sixteen bishops and abbots, he went in procession to Westminster.[1]
His train took five hours to pass. The victory of Agincourt, and the
subsequent festivities, have been described by contemporaries in
prose and verse.[2] Lydgate, as the *Troy Book* testifies, followed these
events with patriotic interest, but at the same time with the aloofness
of a monk to whom all worldly things seemed vain. Possibly he may
have been in London for the king's ceremonial entry, to which the
large monasteries sent their representatives. From his precise knowledge of the City it can be inferred that he was there several times, or
for lengthy periods; but definite evidence is lacking.

The king granted himself no rest. He heard Bedford's report
about the latest turn of events in the country – about the persecution
of the Lollards and the death of Owen Glendower; he consulted his
chancellor, Henry Beaufort, and proclaimed an amnesty to assuage
internal discontent. The ecclesiastical administration was in the
hands of Archbishop Henry Chichele (1414–43), who was as orthodox and intolerant as his predecessor Arundel (*d.* 1414), but showed
greater concern for education.[3]

Chichele was personally involved in the great event of 1416, which
is related in detail in the chronicles: the visit of the Emperor Sigismund. Sigismund had afforded protection to the Council of Constance, at which England was represented by Richard, Count of
Warwick. He now came to England to obtain support for the Council, which had hitherto failed in its attempts to persuade the Counter-
Pope Benedict XIII to abdicate. By overcoming the schism in the
western Church he sought to institute ecclesiastical reform by means
of an oecumenical council, and to mediate between England and
France so that both 'nations' should be able to act in concert at the
Council. An understanding had already been reached with Archbishop Chichele, and it was hoped to enlist the support of the king.
On 27th April Sigismund arrived in Calais, where he was received
with great ceremony, and then brought to London in a splendid

[1] Cf. Walsingham, *Annales* (Rolls Series), pp. 60–8; Pseudo-Elmham, *Vita Henrici Vi.*,
ed. T. Hearne, Oxford, 1727, p. 72; *Great London Chronicle*, entry under 23rd November;
*Brut*, p. 380; Wylie, II, 262 ff.; R. Withington, *English Pageants*, I, 132 ff.
[2] Cf., *inter alia*, Th. Wright, *Political Poems*; C. L. Kingsford, *Historical Literature in
the 15th Century; The First English Life of Henry V*, ed. by C. L. Kingsford, pp. 156 ff.;
Lydgate, *M.P.*, pp. xlvi f.
[3] Educated at Winchester College, he was influenced by the traditions of its founder,
William of Wykeham.

procession by way of Canterbury, Rochester, and Dartford. Between Deptford and Southwark Henry V himself rode out to meet him. On 4th May Parliament met in Sigismund's presence; by this time envoys from France had also arrived. Serious political negotiations alternated with lavish festivities and magnificent banquets. The German Emperor, who felt at ease at the English court, prolonged his visit in the hope of bringing about a mediated settlement between England and France. But Henry V, who was not anxious to conclude peace, except on the unacceptable terms of the previous year (restoration of the frontiers of 1360), skilfully exploited the follies of the Orleanists to win the German Emperor entirely to his side. On 15th August a secret treaty was concluded whereby Sigismund recognized the right of the King of England to the French Crown and promised him his aid. He returned to Calais on 24th August, his mission having failed and an anti-French alliance having been concluded. This turn of events had the consequence that at the Council of Constance the French 'nation' was driven into the opposing camp by the demand, presented jointly by the Germans and the English, that the election of a pope should be delayed until reform had been carried out. The upshot was that the Pope was elected but the old system continued, rendering Reformation inevitable. The schism was brought to an end with the election of Pope Martin V.

In the war between England and France, the following year saw Henry V's second invasion of Normandy. On 1st August he landed again at Harfleur. The moment was well chosen, for the Constable, Armagnac, was engaged against the Burgundians and had no troops to spare for the defence of Normandy. Henry treated the inhabitants indulgently, since he regarded them as his future subjects; they had only to swear allegiance to him as King of England. The general situation was governed by the fact that Isabeau of France proclaimed herself regent of the country, in opposition to her husband, and joined forces with the Burgundians. From now onwards France had two rulers.

# Chapter 7

## Lydgate and the Chaucer Family; The Siege of Thebes

*

The course of events in France disrupted the pattern of life on the idyllic country estate of Thomas Chaucer. This is clear from the *Balade at the Departyng of Thomas Chaucyer into France* (1417),[1] which reveals Lydgate's contact with the gentry, conveys an impression of his character, and shows his relationship with the family of the master whom he esteemed so highly. Unlike (H)occleve, whose famous portrait of Chaucer is the sole authentic one, Lydgate, it appears, was not personally acquainted with the poet to whom he so frequently paid admiring tribute.[2] In the *Troy Book* he rapturously exclaims that he has heard tell of Chaucer[3] – from the authoritative lips of his son Thomas. Thomas Chaucer[4] (approx. 1365–1434) was a wealthy country gentleman, who was for a time Sheriff of Oxfordshire and Berkshire, and in 1407 Speaker of the House of Commons, where he sat for Oxfordshire. He was a friend of Henry Beaufort, then

---

[1] *M.P.*, 657; *Notes and Queries*, 1872, I, 382; *EETS* (Thynne's *Animadversions*), App. VI; *Mod. Phil.*, I, 331.

[2] Lydgate mentions Chaucer more frequently than (H)occleve does (cf. C. K. Spurgeon, *Five Hundred Years of Chaucer Criticism*, pp. 107 ff., list of seventeen works with allusions and literary compliments). Schick takes the view that a personal acquaintanceship between the two men can be assumed if the 'master' whom Lydgate addresses in the envoy to *The Churl and the Bird* can be identified with Chaucer, although he points out that Lydgate also addressed other poets as 'master' (Edition of the *Temple of Glas EETS*, p. xvi, c, 77 f.).

[3] 'My maister Chaucer. . . Hym liste not pinche nor gruche at euery blot. . . . I have herde telle but seid alweie þe best.' (Cf. A. Brusendorff, *The Chaucer Tradition*, L., 1925, p. 30; Spurgeon, I, 25; Schick, p. ci).

[4] Cf. M. B. Ruud, *Thomas Chaucer*, Minneapolis, 1926 (Research Publications of the Univ. of Minnesota, Studies in Language and Literature, No. 9).

# John Lydgate

Chancellor and later Cardinal, and enjoyed the favour of the ruling dynasty. In 1402 he accompanied the king's daughter Blanche to Cologne, where she was married to the son of Rupert, the Count Palatine; in 1414 he was sent to Holland and Burgundy on secret as well as public missions; in the following year he conducted negotiations in France for the marriage of Henry V,[1] and was later a member of the Regency Council during the minority of Henry VI. But he did not make use of his opportunities for political purposes and withdrew to his country seat at Ewelme,[2] a sleepy little village a few miles south of Oxford, which looks much the same today as it did then. Here he lived hospitably with his wife Maude Burgersh and daughter Alice, making his home a centre of social and cultural activity. Among his guests were the humanists Humphrey of Gloucester and John Tiptoft, Count Thomas Montacute of Salisbury and William de la Pole, Count (later Duke) of Suffolk;[3] he was intimately connected with the Stonor family,[4] who lived not far away, and with William Moleyns,[5] who had an estate at Stoke Poges in Buckinghamshire and a house in Henley, only about ten miles from Ewelme. The poem to Thomas Chaucer eulogizes his virtues as a country gentleman, friend, and host. His friends, who had found at his house generous hospitality, cheerfulness, and the cosy atmosphere of a well-ordered home, mourn their host, now departed from them, and recall nostalgically their common delight in falconry and fox-hunting. Then Lydgate mentions by name Moleyns, now deprived of his companion, and concludes with a plea that Lucina (a humanistic circumlocution for the moon that controls the tides) should safeguard his friend whilst crossing the Channel, and with a prayer for his safe return.

This occasional poem of eleven Chaucerian stanzas brings out the personality of this country squire. It gives a lifelike portrait of

---

[1] H. A. Napier, *Historical Notices of the Parishes of Swyncombe and Ewelme in the County of Oxford*, Oxford, 1858.

[2] The manor at Ewelme ([N]ewelme), which on Thomas Chaucer's death in 1434 passed into the possession of William de la Pole, Marquis of Suffolk, as the husband of Thomas Chaucer's daughter Alice, is already mentioned in the *Domesday Book* (*Victoria County History*, Oxfordshire, I, 384 f., 389).

[3] Cf. S. Moore, *Patrons of Letters*, in: *PMLA* 27 (1912), pp. 188 ff.; 28 (1913), pp. 79 ff.

[4] *The Stonor Letters and Papers, 1220–1483*, ed. by C. L. Kingsford, Camden Soc., 3rd Series, Vols. 29–30, L., 1919. Thomas Stonor senior (*d.* 1431) married a relative of Thomas Chaucer's wife, and in 1431 Thomas Chaucer became the guardian of Thomas Stonor junior. The family remained friendly with Alice Chaucer.

[5] Not to be confused with the better-known Adam Moleyns, Bishop of Chichester, the author of the *Lybelle of Englyshe Polycye*. William Moleyns died in 1425, at the age of forty-eight.

Chaucer as a man who performs conscientiously the obligations of his high office, and who retires to his estates once his duty has been done. Lydgate makes no mention of the real cause of his dispatch to France, to take part in one of the several mutually insincere attempts to negotiate an armistice.[1] Lydgate felt at ease in the non-political atmosphere which prevailed at the manor of Ewelme, and many of his later commissioned works originate from the circle of friends who met there. Chaucer's daughter Alice, born in 1404, seems to have played an active part in this. Her second husband was Thomas Montacute, Earl of Salisbury, who in 1426 ordered the translation of Deguileville,[2] and it was as the wife of William de la Pole, Earl of Suffolk, her third husband, that she commissioned Lydgate's *Virtues of the Mass*.[3] Lydgate may also have made the acquaintance of his most famous patron, Humphrey of Gloucester, in the circle of friends associated with Thomas Chaucer.

Another poem which, according to a note on the MS., is related to Thomas Chaucer is *My Lady Dere*.[4] This is a eulogy offered by a lover taking leave of his lady. In sixteen elegant ballad stanzas with short lines the speaker affirms that he is happy only 'whenne I se my lady dere'. When she approaches the sun rises and makes me rejoice like the birds in May, and frolic like the deer in the forest. When I have to leave her, the sky clouds over and I clothe myself in black. May God reunite us soon again; but you, little poem, beseech her 'to be my souveraine lady dere'. The poem contains no reference whatever to real persons or their environment. But if we can trust the sub-title 'made at departyng of Thomas Chauciers on þe kynges ambassade into Fraunce', it indicates that there may still be other secular poems (courtly and perhaps also satirical ones) connected with the circle of friends that met at Chaucer's house.

After Thomas Chaucer's departure Lydgate's thoughts must often have been in France, for the master of Ewelme was for a time with the expeditionary army, and was presumably present at the entrance into Rouen, then the largest and wealthiest town in France, which fell on 19th January 1419 after a twelve-month siege. He did not return to England until October 1420.[5]

---

[1] On 1st October 1417. In addition to Chaucer, Richard, Earl of Warwick, was one of those who took part in these talks on the English side.

[2] See Chapter 16.    [3] See Chapter 19.    [4] *M.P.*, 420.

[5] Thomas Chaucer subsequently undertook missions to France in the autumn of 1424, together with John Tiptoft, to the Duke of Bedford, and in October 1431, to accompany Alionora Moleyns back 'from the waters of the Loire'.

# John Lydgate

With the fall of Rouen Henry V's position had so greatly improved that he could hope to win from the two rival parties in France, that of the dauphin and that of the queen, now in league with the Burgundians, everything that had hitherto been denied him: the frontiers of 1360 and the hand of Princess Catherine. By the peace of Troyes on 20th May 1420 Henry V, Charles VI, and Isabeau agreed to establish a personal union between the two Crowns. The French king signed a deed appointing Henry V his heir and providing that he should reign already during his own lifetime, 'because we are for the greater part of our time prevented by ill-health from giving to the affairs and governance of our realm the care that they deserve'. Henry V, 'heir to France', bound himself, as 'the most beloved son' of Charles VI and his consort, to marry Princess Catherine without a dowry – which meant nothing, since she actually brought with her the whole of France, the dauphin being disinherited because of his 'grave crimes'. It was further prescribed that the two thrones should pass to Henry's direct descendants. The Treaty of Troyes proved to be no more than a house of cards, not only because Henry V's successor lacked the power to put it into effect, but also because it took no account of the national realities of the age. The era of a Henry II or a Richard I was past. We do not know what were the views put forward in discussion by Thomas Chaucer's friends, of whom Lydgate was one. Whilst other poets wrote panegyric poems to Henry V, sang the praises of the battle of Agincourt,[1] or, like John Page in his poem *The Siege of Rouen* (1418–19), gave expression to the people's romantic and patriotic mood, Lydgate looked on affairs *sub specie aeternitatis*, in an epic seemingly valid for all time. This was his *Siege of Thebes*.[2]

\*

This work, written between 1420 and 1422,[3] was not the product of a commission. A eulogy of Chaucer, it was conceived as a continuation of the *Canterbury Tales* and written in its principal metre (in 2356 heroic couplets). For the modern reader it is pleasant to compare Lydgate's artistry with that of Chaucer, whom he esteemed so highly. He too begins with a prologue (ll. 1–176), in which we are

---

[1] Text in Th. Wright, *Political Poems and Songs*, 2 vols., 1859–61. The poem sometimes attributed to Lydgate is in fact not by him: cf. *M.P.*, xlv f.

[2] Edited by A. Erdmann and E. Ekwall, *EETS*, ES., 108, 125, L., 1911, 1930. For bibliography, cf. E. P. Hammond, *Chaucer Manual*, 1927, p. 456.

[3] Parr (*PMLA* 67 [1952], p. 256) calculates the date of writing as 1421.

5. Lydgate (*second from the left?*) and other pilgrims leaving Canterbury

6. Lydgate (*right*) and another Benedictine monk, perhaps his abbot,
kneeling in prayer before a prince seated on a throne

told that, upon recovering from an illness, he went on a pilgrimage, and at a tavern in Canterbury chanced to come across Chaucer's band of pilgrims. The innkeeper, a magnificently delineated character who gives the prologue a touch of lively humour, persuades Lydgate to join them. On the pilgrims' return journey the poet is the first to tell his tale. (This scene is represented in an illustrated manuscript,[1] which shows Lydgate riding a dapple grey horse.) This introduction, which is of greatest interest to the modern reader, is followed by the tragic tale which, like the *Troy Book*, is less an epic than a historical account, with passages of admonition and philosophical observation. The subject-matter, borrowed by the author from a French prose version of the *Thebais*,[2] is divided into three parts. The first (ll. 177–1046) relates the events leading up to the conflict. It begins with the legendary founding of Thebes, taking as its actual theme the fate of Oedipus and Jocasta. The second part (ll. 1047–2552) gives an account of the struggle for the succession to the throne between their two sons, Eteocles and Polynices; finally, the latter leaves Thebes for Argos, where he meets the knight Tydeus, who henceforward becomes the real hero of the story. The third part (ll. 2552–4716), which is as long as both the two preceding parts, deals with the theme mentioned in the title, the battle for Thebes. After a march dogged by privations the Greek army approaches; with it Polynices seeks to enforce the right of alternate rule which he had previously stipulated. Jocasta's attempt at mediation fails, and even Antigone and Ismene, who have won the love of the Greek heroes, do not succeed in persuading their brother to show indulgence. In the battle Tydeus is killed, and Polynices shares his fate. But the city falls only when the attack is entrusted to Theseus. An epilogue on the theme of war and peace brings the tale to its conclusion.

From an artistic point of view this work gains over the *Troy Book* by its brevity. Balance is achieved by division into parts of approximately equal length; descriptive sections and speeches alternate regularly, and the longer didactic parts are graded according to their content. The moral in the life of each character is pointed sententiously by means of proverbial expressions,[3] which constitute, so to speak, the backbone of the work. They also serve as breathing-

[1] Cf. illustration in MS. Roy. 18 D. II, f. 148.
[2] Cf. E. Koeppel, *Lydgates Story of Thebes: eine Quellenuntersuchung*, Munich, 1884.
[3] E.g., 591, 1014, 2700, 2876, 2945, 3415, 3666, 4126, 4458, and many others.

spaces which, interrupting the accounts of the lives of the several characters, with their many vicissitudes, emphasize the wisdom gained by all and incumbent upon all. Vivid realistic descriptions[1] help to make the narrative more lively. However, these questions of style, which in any case do not justify an all-too-favourable assessment of the work, seemed relatively unimportant to Lydgate, who was concerned rather with content.

From the *Troy Book* we know that he had no intention of writing a great romance, but an interpretation of life; and here again he is not philosophizing in an abstract way about virtue, vice, and the need for charity, but stating his position on the two burning issues of the day: the relations between a ruler and his people, and war and peace. Learned works[2] as well as fiction are drawn upon to bolster up the thesis which the whole *Siege of Thebes* is designed to demonstrate: that no durable achievement can be attained by means of falsehood, and that truth will always win the day.[3] The *Siege of Thebes* is even more outspokenly a 'mirror for princes' than the *Troy Book*, for the hero Tydeus is clearly conceived in the image of Henry V, and the allusion to the murder of Duke John of Burgundy[4] on 10th September 1419 serves Lydgate as a contemporary illustration of the veracity of his doctrines. Truth occupies first place among the virtues which ought to grace a ruler;[5] next in importance come kindness[6] and generosity.[7] Arrogance and disdain create hatred among a ruler's subjects, even though they may not dare to show their feelings openly.[8] He should not fritter away the people's wealth or bleed his subjects with taxation.[9] Tyranny is wrong,[10] and without the love of his people a ruler is powerless.[11]

Similarly, in the question of war and peace, there is an allusion to the Treaty of Troyes to point the significance of the siege of Thebes for the present day. Lines 3655-73, added by Lydgate, are directed to two different quarters. Just as in ancient Thebes, so also in contemporary England public opinion is divided: many are discontented at the long French war and wish for peace; but Henry V, and

---

[1] E.g., 902, 1302, 1257, 1443, 2330, 3581, 4479.

[2] Martianus Capella, Seneca and Boccaccio (*De casibus . . .* and *De claris mulieribus*).

[3] 2077, 2237, 1763.

[4] 3432; cf. also *Troy Book*, V, 3553. The murder of Duke John of Burgundy had the result that his successor, Philip the Good, now entered openly into an alliance with Henry V against the Dauphin.

[5] 1721, 1742, 1763, 1768, 1941, 2077, 2237.    [6] 244.    [7] 2682, 2701.

[8] 244, 258, 262.    [9] 2688.    [10] 2698.    [11] 283.

many nobles and commoners as well, belong to the party which
supports the war as a matter of honour, and Lydgate also gives expression to their sentiments.[1] Thus he acts as the mouthpiece of both
sides, but with a strong bias in favour of the peace party.[2] The young
men who urge war do not realize that it defeats both vanquished and
victor.[3] War, says Lydgate in his epilogue, destroys cities, devastates
countries, and impoverishes peoples; high- and low-born must suffer
from it, and one should beware of starting hostilities light-heartedly.[4]
In the *Troy Book*, written under patronage, Lydgate could not speak
so openly. In his *Siege of Thebes* he speaks his own mind, and can
dare do so since the Treaty of Troyes recently concluded promised to
inaugurate a new era. He incorporated in his work[5] the literal words
of the treaty, which had evidently made an impression upon him:
*ut concordia, pax et tranquillitas inter praedicta Franciae et Angliae regna
perpetuo futuris temporibus observentur.*[6]

[1] 4134 ff., also expanded by Lydgate.
[2] 4650, 4686; cf. the Jocasta scene, 3648, and 272, 1378, 3662.    [3] 4652, 4689.
[4] 4636, 4639, 4640, 4645, 4650.    [5] 4690 ff.    [6] Cf. Rymer's *Foedera*, IX, 901.

# Chapter 8

## Henry V's Last Years

*

The festivities that followed the peace of Troyes were, as the importance of the occasion demanded, on an unusually grandiose scale, even for an age accustomed to an excess of pompous ostentation. On 1st December 1420 Henry V rode into Paris escorted by the King of France on his right hand and Philip of Burgundy on his left. The jubilant welcome accorded him by the populace was soon superseded by a mood of disappointment.[1] The Parisians were not taken by the English king, who seemed to them stiff, haughty, and dictatorial. Until Christmas he remained in Paris, where his arbitrary manner of government and ruthless policy of dismissing Frenchmen from their posts deprived him of whatever popular affection he had once enjoyed. On 27th December Henry handed over command of his army to his brother Clarence and, accompanied by Catherine, journeyed via Rouen and Calais to England, whence he had been absent for three and a half years. From Dover the splendid cavalcade made its way to Canterbury, Westminster (8th February), and then to the royal palace at Eltham; the ceremonial entry into London did not take place until 14th February. As usual, the Lord Mayor, aldermen, and guilds waited on Blackheath, this time clad in white robes and wearing red hoods embroidered with the emblems of the craftsmen's corporations. As usual the streets were decorated, artistic pageants staged, and the fountains in Cheapside and Cornhill turned into conduits of wine. As usual the chronicles give a detailed account of the festivities, which lasted for several days and merged with the

[1] Wylie, *Henry V*, III, 224 ff. The French chronicler Chastellain is not unfavourably disposed towards Henry V; he calls him a Prince of Justice, and is even prepared to accept his unlikely claim to the French throne as an act of God.

celebrations of Catherine's coronation, which took place at Westminster on 24th February. On this occasion the royal banquet was particularly lavish; there were, for example, some 'soteltes', i.e. dishes made of malleable ingredients. The first dessert represented St Catherine disputing with pagan scholars, with a book in one hand and in the other a scroll with the inscription 'Madame la Roigne'. Next to it sat a pelican with its young, likewise bearing inscriptions in French. The next dessert, which must have given a lively impression of movement, represented a tiger pursuing a man, stopped in its tracks by a mirror. This man had robbed the tiger of a cub and ridden off, throwing down mirrors to protect himself. He says: *'par force saunz Droit Jay pris ce best'*, and the tiger replies: *'Gile the mirrour || ma fete distour'*.

The literal meaning of this is: Giles the mirror (which frightens the tiger by confronting it with its own wild-looking reflection) has made me turn round. It can also be interpreted symbolically: Giles, who in *Brut* is identified with St George, that is to say the King of England, has seized the French king's daughter and is now defending himself by his virtues.[1]

This foreshadows Lydgate's work in describing, and possibly even staging, royal receptions: the scrolls containing dialogue are related to his polemical poems in dialogue form, mummings and *tableaux vivants*, including the *dance macabre*.

In March and April 1421 the royal couple travelled north, to receive homage from the people in town and country and to visit the holy places of pilgrimage. But in York their journey had to be interrupted owing to the receipt of bad news. On 21st March Thomas, Duke of Clarence, had suffered an annihilating defeat at Baugé, in which he himself lost his life and his army was completely routed. In an effort to restore English supremacy, Henry hastened across to France. He took with him reinforcements, but these could be raised only by imposing forced loans upon the people, who began to manifest their discontent: the nation's readiness for sacrifice had been strained too severely and for too long. Parliament had refused to grant supplies. In the army, too, there was a spirit of disaffection. Disappointment at the failure of the peace of Troyes to justify expectations may have been responsible for the cruelty that distinguished Henry's French campaign. He met with stiff opposition:

[1] According to the 'Great Chronicle' and Fabyan; cf. F. J. Starke, *Populäre englische Chroniken des 15. Jh.*, Diss., Berlin, 1935 (Neue deutsche Forschungen), p. 65.

Meaux withstood a siege of seven months, and the dauphin retired beyond the Loire. It must have been in a mood of hopeful reconciliation that the hard-pressed king greeted Catherine, who, escorted by the Duke of Bedford, arrived from England on 25th May, fifteen days after the capitulation of Meaux. From Rouen she went to the Bois de Vincennes to visit her parents, the King and Queen of France. Here she met Henry, and they spent Whitsuntide together in Paris. The records do not state whether they were accompanied by their infant son, later King Henry VI, who had been born on 6th December 1421.[1] In any case Henry, who had been obliged to stay in France owing to the campaign, will have heard tell of him from Catherine's lips. The boy had been baptised by Archbishop Chichele, with his uncle John, Duke of Bedford, his great-uncle Henry Beaufort, and Jacqueline of Holland as godparents. The continuity of the new dynasty thus seemed assured.

In France, too, matters now seemed to have taken a more hopeful turn. Compiègne fell without a struggle, and the French nobility swore allegiance.

At this point Henry fell ill; feeling his end near, he drew up his political testament, commanding his heirs to pursue the phantom of a conquest of France. On 31st August 1422 he died in his camp at Bois de Vincennes, thirty-five years of age. His remains were brought home with unusual pomp.[2] First his body was embalmed, and then, on 14th September, taken from Vincennes to St Denis, where the monks and clergy held a burial service as though for a king of France. Afterwards the funeral train, led by the Duke of Bedford, went via Paris to Rouen, where a military and heraldic pageant was held. Here Thomas Beaufort, Duke of Exeter, took over and, accompanied by the widowed Catherine, escorted the bier to Dover via Abbéville and Calais. The coffin rested upon a carriage draped in black, over which was suspended a floating silk canopy. Upon a bed of gold and crimson cloth lay an effigy of the deceased, made of wax and leather, with the crown resting on its head, the sceptre in its right hand and the orb in its left. The carriage was drawn by six black horses, alternately bearing the blazons of England and France; in front and behind lamps were burning. The king's horse, led by the bridle, had painted on its collar the arms of King

---

[1] M. E. Christie, *Henry VI*, L., 1922, p. 3.
[2] For this, cf. the account in *Journal d'un bourgeois de Paris*, ed. by A. Mary, Paris, 1929, pp. 166 ff.

Arthur: three golden crowns on an azure shield.[1] In front of the cortège walked 500 knights in black armour, with their lances pointing downwards, and on either side were 250 soldiers with torches and banners. Behind rode the King of Scotland, the Dukes of Burgundy, Bedford, and Exeter, and other members of the upper aristocracy. At every halt the priests said requiem Masses. After two months the funeral procession finally reached its destination, and on 7th November Henry was laid to rest in Westminster Abbey, next to the tomb of Edward the Confessor, in the presence of Humphrey, Archbishop Chichele, fifteen bishops, and all the peers of the realm, who held lighted candles in their hands.

[1] Details from Chastellain, *Le miroir de nobles hommes de France*, I, 333. Otherwise the description here follows that of MacFerlane in the *Cambridge Medieval History*, with supplementary details from the main chronicles. Monstrelet (Book I, cap. 264) gives the following description: 'Near the car were the relations of the late king, uttering loud lamentations. On the collar of the first horse that drew the car were emblazoned the ancient arms of England, on that of the second the arms of France and England quartered, the same as he bore during his lifetime: on that of the third, the arms of France simply. On that of the fourth horse were painted the arms of the noble king Arthur whom no one could conquer: they were three crowns or, on a shield of azure.' (*Chronicles*, translated by T. Johnes, 1810.)

## Chapter 9

### Lydgate's Metre and Style

*

The funeral procession seemed to suggest the closing of an entire epoch: the Middle Ages. Its exaggerated forms found expression in the exuberant, in parts almost grotesque, splendour of Henry's funeral procession, as it did in the archaic chivalrous outlook of Henry himself, who sought to reign as a *rex christianissimus*. In life, as in the arts, the fifteenth century produced a peculiar ornate style which seems almost an anachronism. In architecture the buildings of fifteenth-century England have a superfluity of decorative ornamentation, so plentiful that it obscures the basic structural idea, producing an abstraction of form that does violence to nature. The minor arts, carved ivories, and book illustrations go even farther in this direction, their very essence often lying in the ornamental scroll-work. The same phenomenon is to be found in the music of John Dunstable, who had emulators in Burgundy and France as well as in England: the counterpart voices resemble an apparently disorderly interplay of melodic lines, so that the *cantus firmus*, the basis of the composition, is obscured by fluid polyphonous ornamentation (cf. the Lady Mass 'O Rosa Bella'). In poetry Lydgate's deliberately obscure and excessively ornate style tends to conceal his line of thought and the syntactical structure. When seen in due relation to its environment, the literary style of the fifteenth century ceases to appear strange and peculiar, but falls into place as organically suited to the pattern of the age.

As is evident from the eulogies of his 'master' Chaucer interpolated into many of his works, Lydgate himself believed that he was closely following his model, whereas in reality he was taking Chaucer's theories a stage farther. This is shown to some extent in his verse,

[ 70 ]

and to a much greater extent in the form of his language. In his versification[1] Lydgate never loses sight of Gower's and Chaucer's
achievement in making the stress of the verse coincide with that of
the word. He also seeks to adopt Chaucer's masterly skill in not employing a rhythmical formula rigidly. But in this striving for rhythmical variation he is only partly successful; his verses are indeed
smooth (not halting, as used to be maintained), but do not make for
such easy and natural reading as in the case of Chaucer. This applies
both to the four-beat line employed in *Resoun and Sensuallyte* and to
the five-beat line prevalent in all his remaining works. Chaucer varied
his basic iambic scheme by approximation to narrative prose, as a
consequence of which the verses read as though an experienced story-
teller were reciting them orally. Lydgate, who does not excel in
narrative, and whose verses, weighed down with 'aureate terms',
lose more and more of the quick flow of the metre they are modelled
upon, also gives the effect of artificiality in his verse variations, so
that his work is by no means easy to read. Lydgate's assurances that
his versification is faulty and that he mistakes long for short[2] are
customary rhetorical phrases springing from an assumed modesty
and mean the reverse of what they say. This is shown by Schick's
elucidation of the five different types of five-beat line:

A. The regular type, with five iambics, to which an extra syllable may occasionally be added at the end. There is a caesura
after the second foot: For thóuȝt, constréint, // and gréuous
héuinésse;

B. Lines with a trochaic caesura, built up like the preceding
ones, but with an extra syllable before the caesura: And máni a
stóri, // mo þén I rékin cán;

C. The type peculiar to Lydgate, in which the thesis is wanting
in the caesura, so that two accented syllables clash: For spéchelés
// nóþing máist þou spéde;

D. The acephalous, or 'headless' line, in which the first syllable has been cut off, leaving a monosyllabic first beat: Of musíke,
// ay díde his bísynés;

---

[1] The most valuable treatment of Lydgate's metrical usage is to be found in the
introductions to his works as edited in *EETS*, in particular those of Schick, Ekwall,
Sieper, and Locock. Cf. also A. H. Licklider, *Chapters on the metric of the Chaucerian
Tradition*, Baltimore, 1910, and E. P. Hammond, *English Verse between Chaucer and
Surrey*, pp. 83 f., and bibliography, pp. 98 f.

[2] E.g., *Troy Book*, V, 3483 f.

# John Lydgate

E. Lines with trisyllabic first measure: Thăt wăs féiþful fóund, // til hém depártid déþe (rare in the early period, but frequently used in *Fall of Princes*).

These five types by no means exhaust all the variants used by Lydgate, but they give a good idea of his peculiarly heavy, almost ponderous verse technique. It is artistic at the cost of naturalness. The combinations resulting from these five types also give the impression of artificiality, e.g.:

Combination of B and D: in which the first syllable is wanting, and there is an extra syllable before the caesura:

Wýth hir sústren // that ón Pernáso dwélle;

Combination of C and D: in which the first syllable and the thesis after the caesura are wanting:

Whér this kýng // róoming tó and fró.

These verses are arranged into the eight-line ballad stanza ababbcbc, modelled on Chaucer, for which he shows a predilection in his shorter poems, or the equally artistic Chaucerian stanza ababbcc. This is the main rhyme-scheme adopted by Lydgate in his major epic works. Only rarely, again following Chaucer, is the couplet used for narrative. Lydgate's treatment of these traditional forms of stanza is devoid of originality, but he manages them in such a way that the reader becomes conscious of his artistry. If, as in the case of heroic couplets, the artistically built framework of a stanza is wanting, the standard basic melody is dispensed with, and the metrical variations of the single line seem strange, to say the least, since in Lydgate's decasyllabic verse the margin between the metrical scheme and natural pronunciation is unusually great. This has led C. S. Lewis to call in question Middle English decasyllabic verse as such.[1] Already with Chaucer there are lines which, owing to the 'epic' caesura and the redundant syllable before and after it, as well as the omission of the first thesis, can hardly be read as decasyllabic. The line beginning with an arsis, the so-called 'line without anacrusis', was suited to octets, making for narrative tone and at the same time interrupting the monotony; such poetic licence or variation is incompatible with the metrical flow of decasyllables. Apparently, when adopting French decasyllabic verse, which, being unaccented, has no rhythm

[1] 'The Fifteenth-Century Heroic Line', in *Essays and Studies of the English Association*, Vol. 24 (1938), Oxford, 1939, pp. 28–42.

in the English sense of the word, Chaucer directed his attention partly to quantity and partly to accent; sometimes his ears were filled with the strange melody of 'heroic verse', and sometimes a more familiar native melody, closer to the narrative tone of the octosyllable. Thus we find, in addition to 'regular' decasyllables lines which ought rather to be read as two half-lines with two or three beats:

> *Whan Zéphirus éek*
> *with his swéte bréeth,*

Or:
> *Bút a góvernòur*
> *wýly and wíse.*

For Lydgate it is already normal to put more emphasis on accent than on the number of syllables and to show a predilection for the epic caesura. Verses such as:

> *Írows and wóod ànd maléncolík*

have a thoroughly undecasyllabic flow of metre, but are quite readable as half-lines of which each half has not less than two and not more than three beats.[1]

This interpretation of Lydgate's metrical style is appropriate chiefly to poetic works written in heroic couplets, not to those composed in short couplets, and still less to the works in the artistic Chaucerian and ballad stanza, which had the greatest appeal for him.

Turning now to Lydgate's use of language,[2] mention must first of all be made of his 'gilding', that is to say, refinement of language by introduction of so-called 'aureate terms', mostly polysyllabic and sonorous Romance words,[3] which were new or which he employed in an original way. Lydgate does exactly what Chaucer did before him, but goes further in piling words one on top of another. Not

---

[1] Lewis points to the 'native rhythm' to be found, for example, in Allingham's poem 'The Fairies' (*Oxford Book of English Poetry*, No. 769), in which the lines can be described either as two- or three-beat:

> *Up the airy mountain*
> *Down the rushy glen,*
> *We daren't go a-hunting*
> *For fear of little men.*

[2] Cf. the introductions and bibliographies mentioned on p. 71, n. 1, and also E. Tilgner, *Die Aureate Terms als Stilelement bei Lydgate*, Diss., Berlin, 1936 (Germanistische Studien, Heft 182), and the literature referred to here.

[3] Cf. G. Reismüller, *Romanische Lehnwörter bei Lydgate*, Leipzig, 1911 (Münchener Beiträge zur englischen Philologie, No. 48).

infrequently two such words appear in two successive lines: for example, in describing the colonnades erected in New Troy:

*Vowted a-boue like reclinatories* [*reclinatorium* = couch]
*þat called werne deambulatories* [*deambulatorium* = ambulatory]

In the invocations in Lydgate's religious poetry this is so frequent as to become a mannerism. In the 140 lines of the *Ballade at the Reverence of Our Lady Quene of Mercy* there are twenty-three first examples of this, and even two in one line: 'O glorious vyole, O vytre inviolat! Cristallin welle, of clennesse clere consignet, fructif olyve . . . itinerarie . . . bravie . . . diourn . . . denarie', etc.[1] These are the 'newe straunge termes' of a 'faire and dulcet langage'. By using such a florid poetic language Lydgate, in contrast to Chaucer, seeks to reproduce Latin words comprehensible to humanistic scholars, and words of marked sonority. Even where it is not a matter of new terms, he prefers the recondite polysyllabic and generally Romance word (merciable, redolent, benigne, curteyse) to the simple familiar expression. As a result of the example set by Lydgate, this 'poetic diction' came to predominate in fifteenth-century verse. Also in syntax[2] preference was given to the unusual or the archaic: almost invariably the object is placed before the verb, and the adjectives placed after the noun, as in French, for the sake of emphasis; adjectives are frequently used as substantives or as absolute adjectives, and continuous tenses employed.

Rhetorical flourishes are naturally the best means of attaining elevated poetic language. Almost throughout there is alliteration between noun and epitheton, and in many lines between almost every

---

[1] Many of these words have been accepted into the English language: e.g., abuse, adolescence, avaricious, capacity, commodious, confidence, credulity, deception, detestable, duplicity, equivalent, excel, fallible, fraudulent, gallery, immutable, incredible, musical, passionate, provoke, rural, solicitude, tedious, terrible, tolerance; others which have not been accepted have remained alien, e.g., amate (amiable), apayre (in pairs), barratour (quarrelsome), bealoncle (uncle), botraille (border), bravy (prize), celature (relief), citrinade (bright yellow), consignet (closed), corsifnes (corpulence), deambulatorie (ambulatory), deaurat (gilded), diourn denarie (daily wage), dislanderous (slanderous), diverticle (inn), ennew (dye), equipollent (equivalent), eurous (happy), facundious (eloquent), fardery (cosmetic), flaskisable (inconstant), fructyf (fertile), gardeviance (meat-holder), glawk (clear), hiems (winter), imputrible (unfading), lausioun (praise), muaunt (inconstant), obumbred (overshadowed), oppilate (blocked), pausacioun (pause for rest), polimite (brightly-coloured), reclinatory (couch), regitive (ruling), stoupaille (cork), tentorie (tent), weymentacion (complaint).

[2] A. Courmont, *Studies on Lydgate's Syntax in the Temple of Glas*, Paris, 1912 (Bibliothèque de la Faculté des Lettres, 28).

word: 'O *t*rusty *t*urtle *t*rewest of al *t*rewe'. Apart from the decorative effect, the chief purpose of the copious use of alliteration, this also gives added weight to the meaning – a practice which suited Lydgate, who, as has been said, always spoke with his forefinger raised in admonition. Of his rhetorical figures of speech, the use of the anaphora (particularly in invocatory religious style) is so excessive that it can be regarded as one of Lydgate's stylistic peculiarities. Repetition of expressions is characteristic of every style that aspires to solemnity of emphasis, but with Lydgate this becomes a fundamental feature of his style. It is not simply a matter of expressing the same idea by using two words (e.g., 'chaunte and synge'), or by combining them artistically, with the second word elaborating the first (e.g., 'with franc and with encense'); it is a matter of finding two or more expressions, not just for one word, but for a whole idea, e.g.: 'Thy mantel of miserycord on our mischef sprede // And er wo wake wrappe us under thy wede.' This already comes within the sphere of periphrasis and metaphor, and is suggestive of the style of the psalmist. Lydgate's metaphors and similes are striking and strange in their abstractness, even where concrete objects are compared. To call Maria a 'closid garden', a 'cristallin welle', a 'fructyf olive', etc., may be traced back to the exemplars of the Litany and the Song of Songs; and the periphrasis of the sun as Titan, of the pearl as 'margeryte', etc., are common to all medieval poetry. But it is a peculiarity of Lydgate's late style that metaphors are only to be understood by an intellectual effort, and at times only after careful analysis. In the prologue to the *Legend of St Austin* he expresses the simple idea that 'Augustine introduced Christianity to England' as follows:

> *This was doon by grace or we wer war*
> *Of tholygoost by the influence*
> *Whan foure steedys of Phebus goldene char*
> *List in this regioun holde residence;*
> *Who droff the char to conclude in sentence*
> *By goostly favour of the nyne speerys*
> *Til blissed Austin by goostly elloquence*
> *Was trewe Auriga of foure gospelleeris . . .*

i.e., just as Phaeton (who is, however, not mentioned) drove the horses of the sun (and without him Phoebus' chariot of the sun could not have filled wide expanses with light), so Augustine became the *auriga*, the charioteer of the four Evangelists, who brought the Word of God to England with the spiritual aid of the nine spheres, that is to say, of all the celestial powers.

Lydgate's late style culminates in an ornate decorative scroll-work of abstract ideas and a predilection for formulations that obscure the sense. Thus in the *Fabula duorum mercatorum* the situation that the two merchants have met and become friends is described as follows: Each one contemplates the appearance of his friend; meditation has deeply engraved upon him the other's form, stature, and countenance; their eyes have conveyed the message of their hearts; their minds were mingled in memory of each other, and drew nourishment from imagination.[1] This style echoes in miniature the singular composition of the tale, which (as we have seen from *Resoun and Sensuallyte* and the *Troy Book*) does not grow naturally, branching out in all directions like a tree; instead, the trunk, as it were, is cut short, branches are added here, there, and everywhere; and where they are broken off new shoots appear at unexpected places.[2] This is a new style, different from that of Chaucer, although descended from it.

It is wrong to apply modern criteria of judgement, and to consider Lydgate's obscure and involved diction as jarring, deplore his introduction of abstract terms, and maintain that he had no feeling for the poetic quality of words and did not use language in an imaginative, lively, and creatively artistic manner. It is not that Lydgate was incompetent, or that he was an aberration, or a singular phenomenon; we have here a new poetic style adapted to the taste of the fifteenth century, and Lydgate was its most characteristic exponent.

*Florida verborum venustas*[3] was also the ideal of the early humanists

---

[1] *Fabula duorum mercatorum*, ll. 50 ff.:

> Reuoluyth ech by contemplacioun
> Al of his freend the lyknesse and ymage:
> Thynkyng hath grave with deep impressioun
> Ech othris fourme, stature and visage;
> Her hertys eye did alwey her message
> And mynde medleth in the memorial
> And fet his foode in the ffantastical.

[2] Cf. W. F. Schirmer, 'Das Ende des Mittelalters in England' and 'Der Stil in Lydgates Dichtung'; both articles in *Kleine Schriften*, Tübingen, 1950.

[3] E. F. Jacob, 'Florida verborum venustas', in *Bulletin of the John Rylands Library*, 17 (1933), 264 ff. The phrase cited above appears in the Minutes of the Southern Convocation, 1417. Other phrases: *'ornata verborum series'* and, with reference to Chichele himself, *'in maturo et deliberato verborum eloquio satis floride declaravit'*.

who wrote in Latin. These are the words used by the author of Archbishop Chichele's *Registrum* to describe the florid style as taught by John de Norwich in his *Tractatus de modo inveniendi ornata verba*[1] and used by Abbot Whethamstede in his letters to the monks of St Albans.[2] These efforts to produce an artistic, exuberant, and refined Latin style are identical with Lydgate's efforts in vernacular poetry. Lydgate's position as a court poet and as a protégé of Duke Humphrey of Gloucester, who was highly esteemed as a patron, as well as his voluminous work, made him a model for others. For this reason the tradition that he also exerted an influence as a teacher, by founding a school of rhetoric at Bury St Edmunds, even though not in strict accordance with the facts, nevertheless points the way to a correct appreciation of his achievement.

[1] J. W. H. Atkins, *English Literary Criticism: The Medieval Phase*, Cambridge, 1943, p. 164.

[2] Cf. W. F. Schirmer, *Der englische Frühhumanismus*, pp. 88 ff.; R. Weiss, *English Humanism in the Fifteenth Century*, pp. 28 ff., and the unpublished thesis by Esther Hodge on Whethamstede mentioned by Weiss and Jacob.

PART II

PART II.

# Chapter 10

## Accession of Henry VI;
## Lydgate's first Political Works

*

At the death of Henry V his son and heir, later King Henry VI
(1422–61), was only nine months old, and his widow Catherine, the
Queen-Mother, was aged twenty-one. Since the new king's grandfather, Charles VI of France, died shortly afterwards (22nd October
1422), Henry VI also became King of France (known as Henri II),
in conformity with the terms of the Treaty of Troyes. The English
Parliament now resolved that Henry's uncle John, Duke of Bedford,
was to become Protector of England and chief adviser to the king;
and since John also became regent of France, in his absence Humphrey, Duke of Gloucester, was to rule as Protector of England,
assisted by a council.[1] Since Gloucester could only enact laws *de
assensu consilii*, supreme power *de facto*, though not formally, lay in
the hands of the Regency Council. Parliament itself, which had not
yet acquired the independence it won later, had to come to terms
with those in power at any given moment. Henceforth there were
three men in the forefront of the political scene: the two surviving
brothers of the deceased king, Bedford and Gloucester, and the
Bishop of Winchester,[2] whom Pope Martin V had raised to the rank
of cardinal. The tensions inherent in this triumvirate seem to have
attracted Lydgate's attention, and it is his anxiety for the future of his

[1] To this Council belonged the two Beauforts (Henry and Thomas), Archbishop
Chichele and three other prelates, the Earls of March, Warwick, and Westmorland,
Thomas Mowbray, Henry Percy (son of Hotspur), as well as three other barons and two
knights.
[2] R. Lodge, *Cardinal Beaufort*, Oxford, 1875; L. B. Radford, *Henry Beaufort*, L.,
1908.

country, now once again under baronial rule, that prompted his only prose work,[1] *The Serpent of Division*.[2]

The date when this work was written cannot be ascertained with certainty. On the basis of a note on one manuscript it has been ascribed to a very early date, approximately 1400,[3] but internal evidence suggests a considerably later dating: to the turbulent years after Henry V's death, when the peace of the realm was endangered. Lydgate states that he translated this minor work at the request of his highly-esteemed master,[4] identified by MacCracken as Humphrey, in his capacity as Lord Protector. Humphrey was a humanist who had already helped to stimulate English patriotic feeling by encouraging his secretary Tito Livio to write a life of Henry V in Latin; he is said to have commissioned Lydgate, by now a well-known poet, to write a life of Caesar in order to illustrate the dangers of civil war in the anxious days that followed Henry's sudden death. If this is so, *The Serpent of Division* may be ascribed to December 1422, a date substantiated by the final phrase of one MS.[5] Against this reasonable assumption it can be objected that Humphrey was not, like Bedford, a conscientious father of his country, who skilfully sought to forestall the dangers that threatened it under its infant sovereign. The work could therefore, it is argued, be attributed to some other noble patron, possibly even an opponent of Humphrey. But there is probably little truth in such conjectures, or in the view that the author was someone other than Lydgate. We may rather follow the editor in ascribing the work, on the basis of its content and style, to

[1] MacCracken's Lydgate Canon No. 12 (*M.P.*, xii) leaves open the possibility that Lydgate collaborated on *Brut*. For in the Harvard MS., AR 5, there is a copy of *Brut* (up to Caxton's Chap. 251, i.e. to the seizure of Owen Glendower, who married the widowed Catherine) with the conclusion (by Shirley): 'the whiche Cronycle was lamentabuly compylled at Paris by hem of ffraunce in theyre wolgare langage and nowe translated by Daun Johan lydgate the munk of Bury'. Cf. Robinson, in *Harvard Studies and Notes*, V.

[2] Ed. with introduction, notes and glossary by H. N. MacCracken, London and New Haven, 1911.

[3] According to Miss L. Toulmin Smith, a fifteenth-century copy among the Yelverton MSS. belonging to Lord Calthorpe shows that the tractate was written in December 1400 'by me, Daune John Lidgate'. Cf. her *Gorboduc*, introduction, p. xxi (cited by Robinson, in *Harvard Studies and Notes*, V, 183).

[4] 'At the request of his most worshipful master and sovereign' (in other MSS. the 'and sovereign' is wanting). On this and the following, cf. MacCracken's introduction to his edition of the work, pp. 1 ff.

[5] MacCracken's introduction, p. 4. For a contrary view, cf. E. P. Hammond, *English Verse between Chaucer and Surrey*, pp. 176 ff. On the dating, cf. MacCracken in *Mod. Lang. Rev.*, VII (1912) and VIII (1913), 103 ff.

him;[1] it is merely necessary to rectify his classification of it as a
humanistic *vita* of Caesar.

Its content is in any case noteworthy: an account of the rise and
fall of Caesar. The theme as such is no evidence of its being humanistic in spirit, since in general Caesar's fame lived on in the Middle
Ages as one of the nine *preux* or 'worthies', or else was debased to
serve allegorical purposes. But while most English historians make
only brief references to Caesar, Lydgate here gives the first comprehensive biography of him to appear in English. The 'olde bookes'
which he used as his source are not the works of the ancients, but
date from the Middle Ages: principally, a French version, which has
since been lost, of Lucan's *Pharsalia* and several chapters of the
*Speculum historiale* by Vincent of Beauvais.[2] Nevertheless Lucan's
pathos in describing the unhappy fate that befell the Roman people
makes itself felt in the works of all his imitators, and even where the
subject-matter is designed to serve only as a *memento mori* or *vanitas*
litany, it still reflects the warmth and colour of the original. Lydgate
was particularly susceptible to sombre pomp, and even though he
has no historical vision to compare with that of John of Salisbury in
his account of Caesar's life, *The Serpent of Division* is inspired by an
awareness of fate reminiscent of Lucan. Its purpose is, of course, to
illustrate by Caesar's life the horrors of civil war, which is not the
same point as Lydgate makes in his *Fall of Princes*, where Caesar's
fall is designed to show the fickleness of temporal fame.[3]

The thesis which he puts forward here is to be found throughout
Lydgate's work: so long as unity prevails, the kingdom will be
strong, but as soon as selfish ambition allows discord to creep in,
ruin will threaten. This theme is expressed right at the beginning so
clearly that one is tempted to regard the work as a final admonition
addressed to the English nobility immediately prior to the outbreak
of the Wars of the Roses. The Latin term *bellum civile* in the chapter
on the crossing of the Rubicon[4] serves as an explicit warning.

---

[1] F. Brie, in *English Studies*, 64 (1929), pp. 281 ff., pronounces himself against Lydgate's
authorship.

[2] Detailed discussion of the question of sources in the preface to MacCracken's edition
(see above). On Caesar's subsequent fame, cf. the literature given here and F. Gundolf,
*Caesar: Geschichte seines Ruhms*, Berlin, 1924.

[3] Cf. *F.o.P.*, Bk. VI, 2920 ff. It is impossible to say whether this epic preceded the
prose work or vice versa. There is a further parallel in *St Alban and St Amphabel*, I,
106 ff. (Caesar's conquest of Albion).

[4] Pp. 56, 20.

# John Lydgate

Imploringly he calls upon all ruling princes to learn the lesson from history that internal division brings in its train suffering, misery, and ultimately destruction;[1] it not only pits one man against another, but 'disseuerith and departith a man from God';[2] the envoy invokes Christ and the Scriptures as testimony.[3] The anxious warning of the threat presented to the country by internal discord takes up more room than the sermon calling for repentance and conversion which one expects from the pen of a monk. Only 'wilfulness and surquedaunce', or, as he says elsewhere, 'ambicious pride', are condemned;[4] in addition there is Fortune, which it is beyond man's power to influence, and the natural process of growth and decay, which succeed one another as inevitably as day and night. As in Books VI and VII of the *Fall of Princes* and in the great *Envoy to Rome*, the story is designed to make his noble and princely readers or listeners aware of this fact; as in his other works, his characters are for him not merely names drawn from mythology but real historical figures, and the miraculous signs and wonders, which he relates in detail,[5] convey the effect of conviction rather than sheer superstition. The speeches, particularly that by Destiny and the one by Caesar in the Rubicon scene, are likewise reminiscent of the *Fall of Princes* and of common humanistic usage.

This short prose tract, like Lydgate's long verse works, has been criticized as verbose and lacking in form and coherence. This is not wholly justified, for the thread of history is followed so clearly that MacCracken is able to distinguish thirteen points which he sets out systematically. First of all (1) an account is given of the Roman constitution, based upon the Senate and two counsellors, or 'dictators', an arrangement which in itself contains latent possibilities of conflict. Then we are told (2) of the campaigns of the two dictators Caesar and Crassus, and of Pompey, who on the death of Crassus (3) succeeds in persuading the Senate to recall Caesar. But Caesar carries out his conquests as planned and then (4) requests a triumphal procession. The subsequent digression explaining the nature of these triumphs is not inept, for the Senate's refusal (5), at Pompey's instigation, to allow him a triumph is in Lydgate's version the cause of the civil war. And since the work has been written in order to depict its horrors and to avert such a calamity by showing how insignificant the causes were, he pertinently adds the systematized explana-

---

[1] Pp. 58, 29 ff.  [2] Pp. 61, 12.  [3] P. 66.
[4] Pp. 56, 10; pp. 65, 28.  [5] Pp. 59 and 64. On *F.o.P.*, cf. Chapter 21.

[ 84 ]

tion (6) that there were three causes: firstly, a 'natural' one, corresponding to the changes of the seasons and the ebb and flow in nature and life generally; secondly, a 'common' cause, to be found in external conditions; and finally, an 'internal' cause, the 'wilfulness' and 'surquedaunce' of the individual. This interpolation interrupts the narrative, but does not divert the interest of the reader. After it, set off to advantage by being held back until this point, there follows (7) the Rubicon scene, which, despite Destiny's warning, brings about the fatal decision. An *exemplum* (8) of the horse's tail which cannot be pulled out all at once, but can be one hair at a time, stresses the dangers threatening the Roman Empire and its eventual collapse. The inevitable consequences are shown in two stages, the suspense being enhanced in each case by an introductory chapter (9 and 11) dealing with auguries and miracles; the first (10) is the civil war between Caesar and Pompey, culminating in the battle of Pharsalia, and the second (12) Caesar's fall. The work is rounded off by a concluding summary (13), and in many manuscripts also by a poetic envoy.

There is thus no need to emphasize the work's lack of form and to attribute this to the multiplicity of sources from which Lydgate obtained his material before translating it.[1]

MacCracken takes Lydgate to task for want of proportion in the work as a whole as well as in its individual parts. He argues that not only is the discussion of the causes of the war, and of the auguries and miracles before its outbreak, disproportionately long compared with the history itself, but that the sections, sentences, and single phrases are also lacking in proportion. These objections are valid if one regards, as the editor does, *The Serpent of Division* as a historical work. It is, however, not a chronicle, not a *vita* of Caesar, but a propagandist political tract, designed to show that discord has evil consequences for every community. This is the obvious truth which men continually forget, just as they do the fundamental religious and moral verities, which for this reason the Church again and again hammers into the minds of the faithful. Lydgate's task was thus analogous to that of a preacher: a generally accepted truth had once again to be brought home to a wider audience, and for this purpose he resorted to a sermon, a medium with which he, as a preacher at court, was only too familiar. Since he borrowed his *exempla* almost

---

[1] Pp. 2 f. of the edition mentioned: 'haphazard selection of such details as interested the writer from half a dozen works', 'singular want of proportion'.

# John Lydgate

exclusively from Caesar's life, the *Serpent* also provides a *vita* of Caesar; but from the point of view of structure it is not a chronicle, but a sermon, or rather a tract modelled upon a sermon. The passages containing purely historical narrative Lydgate disposes of in brief, 'compendiously'; the numerous episodes play the part of *exempla*; everything is in some respect a commentary on the theme. This brief work shows political propaganda developing out of what is in spirit and form a sermon.

Sermons were conventionally divided into five parts:[1] *thema, prothema, introductio, divisio,* and *discussio,* with the *thema* being repeated after each section. This repetition is clearly evident in the *Serpent.* Lydgate begins with a short sketch of Roman history from Romulus to the triumvirate of Pompey, Caesar, and Crassus, not for the sake of history, but in order to come quickly to the triumvirate, and thus be able to announce his theme:

> 'And thus all the while they weren of oon herte and of oon assente and voide of variaunce withinne hemselfe, the noblesse of rome flowred in prosperite; but als sone als fals covitise broughte inne pride and vayne ambicion, the contagious Serpent of Division eclipsed and appaled theire worthiness; concluding sothly as in sentence, that every kingdome bi division is conveied to his distruccion.'[2]

The next part is introduced by the sentence: 'Liche as this litill story compendiously shall divise.' Then follows 'briefly' the description of Caesar's dispatch to the north, his conquest of Britain, and the account given by King Cassivellaunus, because Lydgate needs a different authority for his *prothema* (designed to develop one aspect of the main theme). The formula that dissent has fatal consequences both in the kingdom and in the provinces, and a reference to Eusebius, introduce the story, told according to other sources, of Caesar's recall by Pompey and his refusal to submit, which provides the required repetition of the main theme. Now the *introductio* must follow, which had to attract attention and explain the purpose the author had in mind. The former aim is achieved by a vivid description of a triumphal procession (following the *Polychronicon*), the latter

---

[1] Cf. W. O. Ross, *Middle English Sermons, EETS,* OS., 209.

[2] MacCracken's ed., pp. 29, 25–50, 9. In a similar manner in Sermon No. 39 the story of the burning bush is told and from it the theme developed: 'So it may fully than be concluded as a trouthe þat . . .' (Ross, op. cit., p. 222).

by the connecting idea of Caesar being refused his triumph, which, according to Lucan, was the main reason for the civil war. This is the beginning of the *divisio*, in which we are reminded of the main theme. Now follows the main section, the *thema-divisio*, with the characteristic division into three parts. This had to be supported by some authority, and Lydgate therefore refers to Lucan, although he does not mention the three causes. It is thus probably the construction of the work, based upon that of a sermon, that explains why he gives three reasons for the war: 'necessarie' (proved by the example of nature), 'consuetudinarie' (proved by the wheel of Fortune), and 'voluntarie' (that is to say, based upon the false and misguided wills of those involved). Everything that follows serves the purpose of illustrating these three causes, particularly the last. In this *discussio* the *exemplum* plays a great part; it includes the warning given to Caesar by the old woman, the account of the swollen Rubicon (a warning by nature), the horse's tail story, and the numerous omens and warnings by the gods – each link in this chain of *exempla* being an 'evident tokyn of the sodeyne myschefe of deuysion', whilst the rendering of Caesar's triumphal procession, with the indication that he took over the government 'hooly undevided', illuminates the theme from a different angle (the power of 'unite'). All these historical images do not serve the purpose of giving a biography of Caesar, but of reinforcing Lydgate's argument, which is underlined once more in the final *exhortatio*: everyone ought to be mindful of the inconstancy of this earthly world, and those in power should realize, from the *exempla* given, the danger of dissension. Lydgate's *Serpent of Division* is thus no formless historical account, but a carefully built-up tract modelled upon a sermon.

As much care is devoted to the language as to construction. MacCracken is obliged to admit that the apparently shapeless long sentences are surprisingly effective when read aloud, that the meaning is clear throughout, and that the choice of words is most admirable, and even elegant, by comparison with other contemporary prose works. From this it ensues that Lydgate's prose follows the new type of sermon, directed less to the uneducated than to a discerning audience that knew how to appreciate diction. If one compares the prose of *The Serpent of Division* with similar passages in the sermons of the time,[1] Lydgate's frequent mythological allusions, for example, in the main part of the *thema-divisio* show a rhetoric that

[1] Cf., for example, Ross, in op. cit., p. 95.

can be called humanistic, and which surpasses the standard of rhetoric attained by ordinary priests. Thus Lydgate deserves some credit for the revival of English as opposed to Latin. He seeks to emulate, although only to a moderate extent, the efforts of the early humanists to develop English. He expands the colloquial language in particular by using words in pairs, a feature that is most striking when compared with contemporary sermons. This is most readily apparent in his specific mention of the three causes of the war, for which Lucan, as already shown, merely gave the initial stimulus. But since we are dealing with only a single prose work, and not a particularly extensive composition at that, Lydgate's significance as a prose writer is incomparably inferior to his importance and influence as a poet.[1]

The warning that Lydgate gave in this prose work was repeated more frankly in a poem. This was a prayer entitled *A Praise of Peace*,[2] which may be ascribed to the same period, but which marks the beginning of an era in the poet's life in which he concerned himself less with religious than with political matters. Lydgate had now become a poet whose services were sought by the Crown, nobility, and *bourgeoisie*. In the years that followed his links with the monastic world weakened, and the mundane but modest monk became, probably with reluctance, a respected figure in the public life of the country. This period, which for Lydgate was one of steady ascent, was simultaneously a time of preparation for the Wars of the Roses. In this poem (in twenty-four ballad stanzas), with a plentiful show of learning and allegory, Lydgate, distressed by forebodings of calamity, preaches the blessings of peace. The word *pax* comprises the initial letters of the peace-makers Prudentia, Auctoritas, and Christos (Χριστος). Misericordia, Equitas, and Caritas appear; and the seven daughters of the Holy Ghost, as well as Diogenes and Socrates, are invoked as lovers of peace. Then follows a survey of wars from the times of the Scriptures to the present day, ending in an imploring

---

[1] Lydgate is hardly mentioned in such studies of fifteenth-century English prose as R. W. Chambers, *The Continuity of English Prose*, EETS, 186; H. S. Bennett, in *Chaucer and the Fifteenth Century*, p. 177, and in *RES* 21 (1945), pp. 257 ff., and H. C. Wyld, 'Aspects of Style and Idiom in Fifteenth Century English', in *Essays and Studies* 26 (1940).

[2] *M.P.*, p. 785, also in Wright, *Political Poems and Songs*, II, 209 ('Prospect of Peace'). K. H. Vickers, in his *Humphrey Duke of Gloucester*, L., 1907, relates this poem to the events of 1443: 'he welcomed the attempts at peace in 1443' (p. 390). Cf. also, in regard to this poem, the story of the four daughters of God in his translation of Deguileville, chapter 16, p. 120 below.

prayer: the good knight Henry V died on his victorious campaign; may God now grant us peace between the parties, the peace for which Christ gave His life. This prayer expressed the mood of the English people, who were becoming more and more desirous of peace, and especially accorded with the sentiments of Catherine of Valois, Henry V's twenty-one-year-old widow, whom Lydgate had welcomed as a mediator and who now looked on the troubled future as an impotent spectator. From now on the ties between Lydgate, poet and pastor, and his royal patroness were to become closer.

## Chapter 11

### *Lydgate's Priorate at Hatfield*

\*

Lydgate's court connexions secured for him at this time a grant of land;[1] and it was apparently to this same quarter that he also owed his priorate at Hatfield, which inaugurated a new epoch in his life. This appointment was made in June 1423,[2] and took Lydgate into the vicinity of Windsor, thereby consolidating his links with the court and enhancing his role in secular affairs. Hatfield Regis,[3] or, as it is called nowadays, Hatfield Broadoak, in Essex, is situated more or less as far to the north-north-east of Windsor as Windsor is to the west of London. The priory[4] had been founded in the twelfth century by Aubrey de Vere as a 'cell' of the Abbey of St Melaine in Rennes. Under Robert de Vere (*d.* 1221), who called himself

---

[1] 21st February 1423. Cf. the documentation listed in Chapter 23. According to *Proceedings of the Privy Council*, ed. by H. Nicolas, III, 41: 'dimittantur, modo ad firmam dompno Johanni Lidgate et Johanni de Tofte monachi, Johanni Glastoñ et Willelmo Maltoñ Cappellanis ad nominacionem prefati Radulphi Rocheford. . . .'

[2] According to Tanner; cf. Schick, preface to ed. of *Temple of Glas*, p. 92. (Other data put the appointment as early as 1421.)

[3] On Hatfield Regis, cf. Dugdale (1846), IV, 432; *Victoria County History: Essex*, II, 107, and *History of the Priory at Hatfield Broad Oak*, ed. by G. Alan Lowndes (Trans. Essex Arch. Soc., II, New Series, Colchester, 1884), 117-52. On pp. 146 f. we read: 'John Lydgate was the next prior, named in a deed from John Clerk, Simon Doom, Richard Garden and Thom. Goos. This is the only deed in which Prior Lydgate is named and he only appears in the court rolls as being fined for a trespass by his cattle, for not repairing a fence, and not having a ditch secured . . . among the witnesses John Derham who succeeded him as prior. . . . The date of his [Lydgate's] appointment is uncertain and so the date of his resignation (before 1434 when Edw. Confield is mentioned in a deed as Prior).' Cf. also Dom. D. Knowles, *The Religious Houses of Medieval England*, L., 1940, and *D.N.B.*, under Vere, Earl of Oxford.

[4] On the map Anglia Monastica in Davis' *Medieval England* (Fig. 270) only the abbeys, not the priories, are given. There is no further information on Hatfield Broadoak to be obtained from the volume on Essex in the *Cambridge County Geography*.

*primus fundator* of Hatfield Priory, where he is buried, it seems to have become independent of St Melaine and to have entered into connexion with Bury St Edmunds. Permission to occupy these 'cells', of which there was a particularly large number in Essex, was granted by the abbot of the abbey in whose jurisdiction they came – in the case of Lydgate, William of Exeter, abbot from 1415 to 1429.

It is commonly assumed that Lydgate was prior of Hatfield Regis from 1423 to 1434, in which year (on 8th April) he obtained permission from Prior John to return to Bury St Edmunds *'propter frugem melioris vitae captandam.'*[1] This needs some correction. The available list of priors of Hatfield[2] unfortunately has a gap between 1395 (Prior William Gulle) and 1430 or 1432 (Prior John [Johannes] Derham). This fact alone raises doubts as to Lydgate's supposed eleven-year priorate.[3] Apparently Lydgate lived at Hatfield only between 1423 and 1426; subsequently he is known to have been in Paris, probably in the suite of the king or of certain senior officials, and to have remained there for several years – presumably until Henry's coronation in 1429. From 1429 to 1434 he was probably in London, Windsor, and Bury St Edmunds, and then (being only nominally resident at Hatfield, but in fact living at Bury) obtained through the *dimissio* mentioned above official sanction for his actual position. It

---

[1] Thus Tanner, and the MS. note in Tyrwhitt's copy of Wayland's *Fall of Princes*. The *dimissio* from the *registrum* of Will. Curteys (printed in A. Hortis, *Studi sulle opere latine del Boccaccio*, p. 641, n. 2) reads:

Dimissio Johannis Lydgate Monachi ab obedientia / Prioris de Hatfeld. Ex Registro Willi Curteys Abbatis / . . .

Johannes Prior Prioratus de Hatfeld Brodoke Ordinis Nigrorum Monachorum, Londonensis dioceseos, fratri Johanni Lydgate Commonacho et confratri nostro, salutem et sinceram in Domino caritatem; Licet in Prioratu nostro praedicto Habitu Regulari aliquandiu fueris conversatus, tamen cum, ut asseris propter frugem melioris vitae captandam, ex certis causis veris et legitimis conscientiam tuam in hac parte moventibus, ad Monasterium de Bury Sancti Edmundi, in quo dictum dudum ordinem legitime et expresse fueras professus, *regressum habere proponas*; NOS qui commissarum nobis animarum salutem ferventi desiderio peroptamus, ut ad dictum Monasterium vel alibi in loco ejusdem religionis congruo et honesto, sumptis pennis cum Maria contemplationis libere valeas convolare licentiam in Domino tibi concedimus specialem. (*My italics.*)

'In cuius rei testimonium praesentibus sigillum nostrum commune apposuimus. Dat. apud Hatfeld predict. VIII° die mensis Aprilis, Anno Domini Millesimo quadringentesimo tricesimo quarto.'

[2] In Dugdale, *Monasticon Anglicanum*, IV, 433.

[3] Schick also assumes, in his introduction to the *Temple of Glas*, p. 92, that Lydgate wrote his *Life of St Edmund* in Bury St Edmunds and that he saw Henry VI there in 1433.

may be assumed that this was granted in response to a petition by Lydgate, and that the wording employed by the abbot in his letter was that of Lydgate himself.

The office of prior of Hatfield, which Lydgate held for eleven years, from 1423 to 1434, must be regarded as a sinecure; the real Hatfield epoch, when Lydgate actually lived there, must be dated from 1423 to 1426. Which of Lydgate's works belong to this period cannot be ascertained with certainty. Perhaps one or two of his mummings can be ascribed to this era, and probably also some religious poems dedicated to his distinguished patroness, the Queen-Mother Catherine, to whom he must have been a kind of spiritual counsellor. As an occasional poem for St Valentine's Day he composed for her *A Valentine to Her that excelleth all*,[1] in twenty polished Chaucerian stanzas with the same rhyme 'c' recurring as a refrain. In conformity with the custom of choosing one's love on St Valentine's Day, the poet also makes his choice, listing the merits of women who have figured in poetry and in Biblical and secular history, ending each time with the words: 'But I love oon whiche excelliþe alle'. This refers to the Blessed Virgin. After giving an account of her life and that of other prominent saints, he concludes with an envoy of two stanzas addressed to Queen Catherine, whom he asks to endorse his choice. May the Virgin Mary protect the queen and her son Henry VI! The poem is essentially a panegyric to the 'noble pryncesse, braunche of flour-de-lys',' given an air of solemnity by the religious element.

To the same period, presumably written between 1423 and 1426,[2] either in Hatfield or later, during Lydgate's sojourn in Paris, belongs the edifying and patriotic story of *Guy of Warwick*.[3] This was an an-

[1] This is the title given by MacCracken, *M.P.*, 304 (ibid., p. xxx, 'to Her I Love Best of All'). O. Mahir, in his more accurate edition, *Einige religiöse Gedichte Lydgates*, Berlin, n.d. (1910, 1915), entitles it: 'A Poem on St. Valentine's Day'. Mahir dates it to the years 1422–9.

[2] Scholars have traditionally accepted an early date, 1423 or even 1420, but it seems advisable to place it in chronological proximity to *Pedigree* (see Chapter 15).

[3] There are two texts extant of Lydgate's poem, printed by Zupitza, *Wiener Akademieschrift*, 1873, pp. 623 ff., and by F. N. Robinson, in *Harvard Studies and Notes*, V (1896), 197 ff., as well as that in *M.P.*, p. 516. (Printed in part in Zupitza's textbook of Old and Middle English.) Robinson challenges Zupitza's dating (*circa* 1420) with the sentence: 'It was written at the request of Margaret Countess of Shrewsbury . . . so that it cannot have been earlier than 1442'. (In 1433 Margaret married John Lord Talbot and Furnival, who became Earl of Shrewsbury in 1442). This conclusion cannot be substantiated, since the note in the MS. about the patronage is not by Lydgate and naturally takes account of the subsequent higher rank of his patroness.

cestral tale commissioned by Margaret, Lady Talbot, and later Countess of Shrewsbury. In seventy-four ballad stanzas it relates the legend of the chivalrous pilgrim who by Divine Providence returns home in the hour of England's need, overcomes the Danish giant Colbrand, and then again leads the life of a pilgrim until he dies a blessed Christian death. But in Lydgate's version it loses all the charm possessed by the old epic poem of the same title. In this there was something captivating about the adventures of the knight who fought Saracen and Turk for the sake of his Felice; the battle descriptions were exciting, and the note of asceticism about the pilgrim who abandons his wife and worldly glory was at once unexpected and full of wonder. Lydgate's attitude was not that of the epic poet; he wanted historical truth and drew expressly upon one historical source, the Latin chronicle of Gerardus Cornubiensis.[1] In general he follows the chronicle accurately, making omissions only where the material is of purely local interest, and expanding it by verbose digressions and reiterations, mythological and Scriptural allusions, introducing images from nature and human emotions. His supplementary passages include a fairly long digression (stanzas 5–11), the prayer of King Aethelstan (stanzas 27–8) and the conclusion (stanzas 73–4). In contrast to the chronicle the digression, which contains the most rhetorical passage in the poem, precedes the description of the atrocities committed by the Danes, and makes the account that follows stand out in a didactic and moral light. God, he says, is more merciful in retribution than the tyrant; tyranny leads only to bloodshed. Similarly, Aethelstan's prayer is couched in Lydgate's invocatory style and the conclusion contains the usual *topos* of modesty.

*Guy of Warwick* is generally held up as a prime example of Lydgate's style at its worst. It can hardly be accounted a poetic work. But a comparison with its source reveals that Lydgate had his own conception of the theme, and recalls the ideas of his *Serpent of Division* and the *Pedigree* of Henry VI. *Guy of Warwick* may fairly be regarded as a piece of contemporary history: this view is borne out by the fact that it was taken over by the major sixteenth-century chroniclers (Fabyan and Grafton). With Lydgate the king is brought into prominence; his main concern is to preserve the institution of monarchy. This minor work must therefore be viewed against its historical background. This interpretation is also of importance from

[1] Printed in *Archiv* 146 (1923), pp. 49–52.

the biographical point of view. Lady Margaret Talbot, who commissioned Lydgate to write this work,[1] belonged to one of the most
notable aristocratic families. She was the eldest of the three daughters
of Richard de Beauchamp, fifth Earl of Warwick (1382–1439) from
his first marriage with Elizabeth, daughter of Thomas, Lord Berkeley. In 1433 she married John Talbot, first Earl of Shrewsbury
(1388–1453),[2] who had been sent to France in 1427 to lend support
to her father, had been appointed by Bedford 'governor' of Anjou
and Maine, but had then been taken prisoner in France, where he remained until 1433, when he was released under the provisions of an
agreement for the exchange of prisoners. We know little of Margaret
Talbot; she appears in the documents only as having escorted Queen
Margaret in 1445. She died on 14th June 1467. Her reason for granting Lydgate the commission may have been in order to show respect
towards her father. Of the latter it is known that he stressed his
descent from the legendary Guy of Warwick, and that a representative of the Sultan in the Holy Land (in 1408–10) is said to have related
to him the history of his ancestor, which had been set down in the
local tongue.[3] Doubtless Lady Margaret's choice fell upon Lydgate
because her father had been his employer and patron. Doubtless it is
also due to Beauchamp that his third wife Isabella, daughter of
Thomas, sixth Lord le Despenser, and his wife Constance commissioned Lydgate to translate from the French *The Fifteen Joyes of
Oure Lady*.[4]

[1] 'Here nowe begynneþ an abstracte oute of þe Croniclis in latyn made by Gyrarde
Cornubyence þe worþy croniculer of westsexse 7 translated in to Englisshe be lydegate
daun Johan at þe requeste of margarite Countas of Shrowesbury Ladye Talbot fournyual
and Lysle of the lyf of þt moste worthy knyght Guy of Warwike of whoos blood shee is
lyneally descendid.'

[2] On Margaret, cf. *Letters and Papers illustrative of the Wars of the English in France*, ed.
J. Stevenson, and *Chronique of Wavrin (Waurin)*, both in Rolls Series.

[3] Warton, *History of English Literature*, section III, 1.

[4] 'Translated out of Frenshe into Englishe by daun John the Monke of Bury at
instance of þe worshipfull Pryncesse Isabelle nowe Countasse of Warr lady Despenser.'

# Chapter 12

## Lydgate's Satires

*

A poet who was entrusted with tasks such as these, and who took Chaucer's style as his ideal, was naturally far removed from everyday or 'common' literature (though this was in effect a genre on a par with courtly poetry). But in those days satire enjoyed such popularity and was taken so much for granted (as is shown by the worldwide success of *The Ship of Fools*) that Lydgate also turned his hand to it, even though his gentle and modest manner put the pungency and wit of a true satirist beyond his reach. Thus he borrowed the Gallic artifice of describing something in a sense opposite to its proper meaning, called in rhetoric *per antiphrasim*; he translated, for example, the assertion by the '*plus grande Clerk du Parys*' that everything in the world was turning out for the best, and going forward – like a crab.[1] In a similar way he described how all classes lived model lives, honest and upright – as 'ryght as a rammes horne'.[2] More important than these *minutiae*, the effectiveness of which lies in the witty refrain, is the vivid description of the *Order of Fools*,[3] a commmonplace theme which Lydgate presumably introduced into English literature from French.[4] Possibly his sojourn in Paris provided the impulse for this, as it did for his *Dance Macabre* and other satirical poems. He invents an order of sixty-three fools, once founded by one Marcolf, under Bacchus and Venus. There is a long list of personified follies, who are each condemned in their respective refrains.

[1] *So as the Crabbe Goth Forward*, M.P., 464 (with the French original), in seven ballad stanzas.

[2] *Ryght as a Rammes Horne*, M.P., 461, in seven ballad stanzas.

[3] *The Order of Fools*, M.P., 449, in twenty-four ballad stanzas.

[4] Cf. the Anglo-Norman poem *Ci cummencent Les Trente-Sis Mestres Folies* (in the MS. Lydgate's poem bears the title *A Tale of Thre-score folys and Thre*).

# John Lydgate

Beginning with the chief fool, who scorns the laws and commandments of God and the Church, he scourges, in a gay medley, the
follies of extravagance, hypocrisy, clumsiness, vanity, covetousness, flattery, perfidy, gullibility, quarrelsomeness, licentiousness,
and laziness, finally invoking God's curse upon this foolish frater-
nity. From a brief summary this may give an impression of abstruse-
ness, but in the poem this does not jar; it has all the vividness and
realism of other works on this theme. *The Order of Fools* lacks the
vigour found in the poem *London Lickpenny*,[1] the authorship of
which was formerly ascribed to Lydgate; it is concerned with
generalities, suited to any place and time.

Less general in character are some stanzas describing the pillory-
ing of the deceitful miller and baker,[2] which may perhaps originate
from the poet's recollections of the damage that his monastery
suffered through such lamentable malpractices. In the magnificent
tale about the lazy farm-labourer Maymond[3] Lydgate, who was
better at fashioning ready material than contriving new, fell back
upon the Latin and French sources;[4] of these, however, he made
good use, adding local colour and Anglicizing the characters. Maymond becomes Jak Hare, the slovenly stable-lad, who lazily sleeps
well into the day, but is never absent from a drinking-bout; he
cheats his master in every conceivable way, especially by selling the
horses' forage, and using the money he thereby cunningly obtains
on beer or a game of dice. Then, returning home in a drunken state,
he disturbs his fellows by snoring and indecent behaviour. The
crudities, related in the true style of *The Ship of Fools*, are only to be
found in some additional stanzas, raising doubts as to whether the
author of this piece was Lydgate. For the same reason his authorship must be contested in the case of the wittiest and crudest satires
that have been ascribed to him, *Advice to an old gentleman who wished for
a young wife*[5] and the description of the corpulent beauty in *Hood of
Green*;[6] these must be attributed to an author who has remained anony-

---

[1] Annotated text and bibliography in E. P. Hammond, *English Verse between Chaucer
and Surrey*, pp. 237 ff.

[2] [Ballad] *Against Millers and Bakers. M.P.*, 448, in three ballad stanzas.

[3] *Jak Hare, M.P.*, 445, in seven ballad stanzas (with three additional stanzas).

[4] The story of Maymundus in the *Disciplina Clericalis* and the Norman poem *De
Maimound mal esquier*.

[5] Also known as *Prohemy of a Marriage*; printed in J. O. Halliwell, *Minor Poems of
Lydgate*, L., 1840 (Percy Soc.), p. 27.

[6] *A satirical description of his Lady* (alias: *Hood of Green*), in ibid., p. 199.

mous. In the same way the ballad *Warning to men to beware of deceitful women*,[1] in which an allusion has been detected to Lydgate's distinguished patron Humphrey,[2] can hardly be assigned to the Lydgate canon. In his hands such themes are toned down, as in his curtailed and colourless version of Map(es)' *Payne and Sorow of Evyll Maryage*,[3] or in the startling *Ballade on an Ale-seller*[4] in Canterbury, which probably dates from his early period. In the latter work he contrasts the ale-seller's inconstancy in love with the conduct of Griselda, Lucrece, and Penelope, and deplores it in the tone of a courtly complaint. The bold and gay tone adopted by wandering scholars was not Lydgate's *forte*. When he satirizes women's inconstancy *per antiphrasim*,[5] it turns out as a subtle and almost elegant trifle or as a small sermon, which would be cumbersome in style were it not for the swift-flowing short lines.[6] His more ponderous *Examples against Women*,[7] in which he sets out to stigmatize womanly infidelity, contains stanzas borrowed from the *Fall of Princes*, and has a solemn character hardly appropriate to its satirical purpose.

Lydgate was incapable of indignation; he was no zealot, and his tone is more akin to that of a fatherly counsellor. This is shown by one of his best occasional satirical poems, in which he directs his shafts against the horn-like hair-dress then popular among women in England as well as in France.[8] In this case the question of sources is of little importance,[9] for the praise given to comfortable domestic elegance, the learned catalogues and allusions, and the gentle tone, more mocking than spiteful, of this poem – all reveal the true Lydgate, true also in regard to the language and versification. He begins by sententiously recalling that all real beauty comes only

[1] Skeat's *Chaucer*, Vol. VII: Chaucerian Pieces, No. XIV. Cf. *M.P.*, p. xlix.

[2] K. H. Vickers, *Humphrey*, p. 335.

[3] *Payne and sorow of Evyll Maryage*, *M.P.*, 456. Twenty-two Chaucerian stanzas following W. Map's *De conjuge non ducenda* (in Th. Wright, *The Latin Poems attributed to W. Mapes*, L., 1841 (Camden Soc.), p. 77; French translation in ibid., p. 292).

[4] *Ballade on an Ale-seller*, *M.P.*, 429, in eleven Chaucerian stanzas, the final two fragmentary.

[5] *Ballade per Antiphrasim*, *M.P.*, 432, in four ballad stanzas, the final two fragmentary.

[6] *[Beware of] Doublenesse*, *M.P.*, 438, in thirteen ballad stanzas (in four-beat lines).

[7] *Examples Against Women*, *M.P.*, 442, in fifteen Chaucerian stanzas.

[8] *Horns Away*, *M.P.*, 662; E. P. Hammond, *English Verse . . .*, p. 110; Neilson and Webster, *The Chief British Poets of the Fourteenth and Fifteenth Centuries*, p. 222. In nine ballad stanzas. Cf. A. Abram, *Social Life in the Fifteenth Century*, L., 1909, pp. 150 f. (Parliamentary debates on and legislation against women's head-dresses and fashions.)

[9] A *Dit des cornètes* (in Jubinal, *Jongleurs et trouvères*, p. 87), similar to one by Jean de Meung.

from God and Nature, everything else being mere worthless frippery. Mother Nature in Alain's *De planctu naturae* had no horns, nor do the poets of antiquity speak thus of the famous women of their era, such as Helen, Penelope, Polyxena, and Lucrece. Horns belong to wild animals, not to gentle women. Noble ladies should take no offence at his words; they should set a good example by taking off their horns, for the greatest of virtues is modesty: this was shown by the Holy Virgin, who wore a simple head-cloth.

Different in style, and more important from the artistic point of view, is his *Bycorne and Chichevache*.[1] Its theme is again womankind, humorously satirized, but in form it has to be classified among the dramatic mummings or the pictorial poems drawn from the *Dance Macabre*. Bycorne (Bigorne) and Chichevache (Chi[n]chefache) are legendary monsters, which from the description given of them one may imagine as pictures; their meaning is elucidated by the text – spoken, as it were, by the poet.[2] The custom of accompanying tapestries or frescoes with verses was common, the best-known example being his *Dance Macabre*. On the other hand, in the *Dance Macabre*, as in the work before us, the dramatic element is so marked that it could be used for a proper performance with several speakers. As in the case of mummings, it was probably a pantomimic scene, elucidated by the accompanying text, which was read out aloud.[3] After an introduction, spoken by the author himself, he presents to us two monsters, each of which introduces itself to the audience with a fairly long speech, revealing its particular characteristics. Bycorne, who is female, is stout and fat, because she feeds on the vast number of henpecked husbands that exist. Of these, four representatives appear, who style themselves fodder for the hungry

---

[1] M.P., 433; Hammond, *English Verse* . . ., p. 113; Neilson and Webster, op. cit., p. 220; Dodsley's *Old English Plays*, L., 1780, vol. 12. Cf. R. J. Menner, 'Bycorne, husband of Chichevache,' in *Mod. Lang. Notes*, 44 (1929), pp. 455–7.

[2] 'ffirst þere shal stonde an ymage in poete wyse seying þees three balades.'

[3] This is shown by the words: 'than shal be portreyed two bestis . . . then shall ther be a womman devoured in the mowthe of Chichevache . . .', etc. Hammond (op. cit., p. 114) calls these remarks 'directions for representing the figures', which one can hardly construe as instructions for the painter (or weaver, for according to its sub-title the poem is 'þe deuise of a peynted or desteyned clothe for an halle, a parlour or a chaumbre'. These pictorial poems, as Hammond notes, have not yet been studied (she refers to Mâle's *L'art religieux* and the two works by Jubinal on tapestries, Paris, 1838 and 1840, and her own article 'Two Tapestry Poems by Lydgate', in *English Studies*, 43 (1910–11), pp. 10 ff.). In addition reference must be made to the *tableaux vivants* which are known to have been a feature of mystery plays and king's entries in France from the early fourteenth century onwards (cf. Chapter 13).

Bycorne. The second monster, Chichevache, who is male, is slender and starved, since he has to subsist on the scanty nourishment of obedient wives. Only a single spouse appears who on account of her obedience falls victim to Chichevache. At the conclusion, and as a sop to the women who have been satirized as domineering, there comes on an old man, who ruefully bemoans the loss of his faithful obedient wife, who has been taken from him by Chichevache. Like *Horns Away*, this is a mild satire, rendered humorous by the element of the grotesque. It is delightfully executed in nineteen Chaucerian stanzas. Where Lydgate obtained the stimulus for it has not been established. Critics have pointed to the envoy of Chaucer's *Clerke's Tale*, and to French models, which, however, cannot be identified with certainty. Since the tale of the two monsters was already known in Chaucer's day the motif was probably one that was widely familiar. This is also suggested by the fact that the person mentioned as having commissioned this work was a 'werþy citeseyn of London', which incidentally testifies to the response evoked by Lydgate's poetry in civic circles.

# Chapter 13

*

## Lydgate's Mummings

*

Pictorial poems such as *Bycorne and Chichevache* must be considered as falling within the range of 'mummings'.[1] These are short scenes in the form of dialogue or pantomimic presentations elucidated by a text in verse, which was read out before the audience. They are thus primitive forms of stage play, and are of importance for the later history of English drama. It is, however, not possible to analyse or classify them on the strength of our present knowledge, since masques,[2] pictorial poems, and 'king's entries'[3] overlap; and in addition to these there is the influence of the miracle plays and polemical poems in the English and French tradition, which cannot be left out of account. Lydgate's significance for the drama lies not least in the fact that he combined these different genres and influences into dramatic 'entertainments', intended for Christmas festivities in one of the royal palaces (Eltham, Windsor, or Hertford), or for festivities held by the municipalities or guilds, performed in banqueting halls or in the open air. They were written at different times, but form a single group from the stylistic point of view.

[1] My view finds support in the title added by Shirley: 'þe fourome of desguysinges contreved by Daun Johan Lidegate', 'þe maner of Straunge Desgysinges', 'þe gyse of a right'. This is the transcription of Hammond (p. 115) from MS. Trin. Coll. Cambr. R. 3.20. MacCracken (*M.P.*, 433) reads: 'þe couronne of disguysinges' and 'þe gyse of a mummynge'!

[2] R. Brotanek, *Die englischen Maskenspiele*, Vienna-Leipzig, 1902 (Wiener Beitr. z. engl. Phil., 15); A. Reyher, *Les masques anglais*, Paris, 1909; E. Welsford, *The Court Masque*, 1927.

[3] Authoritative modern study of the whole theme of pageantry: R. Withington, *English Pageantry, an Historical Outline*, 2 vols., Cambridge, Mass., 1918.

# Lydgate's Mummings

The *Mumming at Eltham*[1] may have been the first of these, for it can be linked with the Christmas festivities at Eltham Palace in 1424.[2]

The palace,[3] which today lies in ruins, resembled a fortress, with its ditches and battlements, inner courtyards and forty-six large rooms. It also boasted a banqueting hall in which, according to Froissart, Parliament occasionally met (1395), and which seemed expressly designed for theatrical performances. The palace was situated about two miles south-east of Greenwich, overlooking the park, with a view that extended as far as the steeple of St Paul's and the distant towers of Westminster Abbey. Once the favourite residence of Richard II and Anne of Bohemia, it was often visited by the three Henrys, especially at Christmastide.

Lydgate's *Mumming at Eltham* is not a theatrical performance in the modern sense of the word. The short text, comprising only twelve Chaucerian stanzas, may have been read aloud by Lydgate himself, for there is no mention of a herald or any similar person bringing in the 'balade' which elucidated the masque. The text, the first seven stanzas of which are addressed to the king, introduces the gods of antiquity that are to appear (Juno, Ceres, and Bacchus) and interprets the significance of their gifts, which are presented on their behalf by some merchants. They bring honourable peace, wealth, and joy, as the refrain has it. Mars may also have been represented, only to be driven away again, according to the verses, in view of the present union between England and France. Lydgate then turns to Queen Catherine, the young mother of the prince who is to become King Henry VI, whom the gods that appear want to relieve of her sorrows and anxieties, and whom they present with a further gift, the love and loyalty of her people. As their names are mentioned, the various figures step forward to render homage; and when they are once again in line the envoy, combining the refrains of the two parts, bids the royal couple farewell.

---

[1] *M.P.*, 672; in Brotanek, op. cit., pp. 9 ff. and 305 ff. Brotanek dates this mumming to Christmas 1427–8 without giving convincing evidence to support his statement. Kingsford says: 'Lydgate had devised mummings for the amusement of the little king in 1424 and 1428'.

[2] MS. note: 'Loo here begynnethe a balade made by daun John Lidegate at Eltham in Christmasse, for a momyng tofore þe Kyng and Cwene.'

[3] Eltham = eald-ham (old home). M. A. E. Green (=Wood), *Lives of the Princesses of England*, III, 335. Description with plan and illustration of the Great Hall in E. Hasted, *History of Kent*, 4 vols., Canterbury, 1778–99, I, 52. D. Lysons, *Magna Britannica*, 6 vols., L., 1806–22, IV, 398; *Archaeologica*, VI, 366–71.

# John Lydgate

Noteworthy in this is the expositor or commentator, who recalls the pictorial poems and *tableaux vivants* staged at the 'king's entries', and who plays a role similar to that of the 'narrator' who was then believed to have recited the comedies of Terence.[1] Lydgate has himself described in detail, in the *Troy Book*, the part played by the poet:[2]

> *Al þis was tolde and rad of þe poete.*
> *And whil þat he in þe pulpit stood,*
> *With dedly face al devoide of blood,*
> *Singinge his dites, with muses al to-rent,*
> *Amydde þe theatre schrowdid in a tent,*
> *þer cam out men gastful of her cheris,*
> *Disfigurid her facis with viseris,*
> *Pleying by signes in þe peples siȝt,*
> *þat þe poete songon hath on hiȝt;*

The text of the mumming is of no interest to the modern reader; the idea, suggestive of the Renaissance, of solemnly bringing on the gods of classical antiquity, Bacchus, Juno, and Ceres, to present gifts is of importance so far as this allegorical element, which Lydgate introduced (already in this pageant, which was presumably the first) hereafter remained characteristic of English pageants generally.[3] It is worthy of note that there is also a touch of apprehension: 'youre rebelles whiche beon now reklesse'. This seems to express the poet's sympathy for the anxieties of Catherine, the Queen-Mother, to whom he had offered consolation in his poem *That now is Hay sometyme was Grase*.[4]

Less solemn and more cheerful in tone is the *Mumming at Bishops-wood*.[5] Its date of composition remains uncertain. With its sixteen Chaucerian stanzas, it approximates in form to the mumming mentioned above. It is an entertainment – one might almost say an 'interlude' – at the banquet held by the circuit judges and high-ranking

---

[1] On the narrator, announcer, or conferencier (who probably also corresponds to the expositor in the Chester plays), cf. Creizenach, I, 5, and the plate in P. Lacroix, *Sciences et Lettres au Moyen Âge*, Paris, 1877, p. 534 (miniature from an early fifteenth-century manuscript of Terence, made for Charles VI). According to Creizenach, with whom Chambers (*Medieval Stage*, I, 397) concurs, this conception of the reciter arose through an erroneous reading of the abbreviation 'rec.', = recensor.

[2] *Troy Book*, II, 896 ff.

[3] Cf. Withington, *English Pageantry . . .*, I, 136.

[4] Cf. p. 200.

[5] M.P., 668, and in Sir H. Nicholas, *Chronicle of London*, 1827.

officials at Bishop's Wood on 1st May.[1] Bishop's Wood belonged to the Bishop of London and was situated far outside the City boundaries in what is now the borough of Stepney. The banquet had the character of a picnic: the guests disposed themselves on a meadow and were offered all manner of entertainment. One of these offerings was a scene of welcome of which Lydgate was the author. As the heading says, it was a 'balade', i.e., a poem written on a large sheet of paper, or a letter, presented by a page who steps out of the wood into the clearing. The page (or a narrator to whom he hands over the text) then reads out the dramatic scene: Flora, the Goddess of Flowers, who gives fresh life to all plants, animals, and men, wishing to delight the worthy personages here assembled, has sent her daughter Veere, the spring, to welcome them. The narrator then points to the Goddess of Spring, who now appears, adorned in a fantastical rich garment, and accompanies the text as it is recited with measured dance-steps and gestures. Freed from winter's grasp, the birds whirl in merry play and greet the day with song. The Goddess of Spring brings joy and plenty: to the princes victory, to the knights glory, to the people peace. Now the poet portrays the golden age that spring brings in its train: the winter of unrest will pass away, flowers of love will blossom forth, and truth and harmony will put forth buds. All social classes are living in concord, from the ruler down to the humble workman, each loyally performing his due. The Church, the Lord Mayor, the judges and officials will govern well, without oppressing the poor; justice will drive out all evil-doing. These are the tidings brought by Primavera, and a summer of joy is to follow. The envoy expresses the wish that the merry-making will pass off successfully, adding to the picture of Nature in spring a touch of humanistic fantasy: the Muses jubilating on Parnassus, whilst Calliope reads a poem and Orpheus sings a rondeau. Men and gods are united in jubilant celebrations.

This lively piece reveals most clearly the importance for English

---

[1] Stow, *Survey*, ed. Kingsford, I, 98 f.: 'I find also that in the month of may the Citizens of London of all estates . . . had their several mayings, and did fetch in Maypoles with divers warlike shows . . . and towards the evening they had Stage plays, and Bonfires in the streetes: of these Mayings we read in the reign of Henry VI that the Aldermen and Sheriffs of London being on May day at the Bishop of Londons Wood in the parish of Stebunheath [Stepney] and having there a worshipful dinner for themselves and other commers Lydgate the poet . . . sent to them by a Pursiuant [attendant on heralds] a ioiful commendation of that season containing 16 stances in metre Royal beginning: Mightie Flora, Goddes of fresh flowers.'

literature of these mummings which Lydgate introduced. The theme is new, and the author showed imagination and understanding in devising his fable. As can readily be seen, it combines two different genres: on one hand the pantomime-type pageants which Lydgate could see in London at the receptions of distinguished personages (such as St George represented by a *tableau vivant*, or the personified coat-of-arms wishing good fortune to the sovereign as he entered the City across London Bridge, or the scaffold tower in the Cheap from which maidens rendered homage with flowers and song); and on the other hand the pageant in a quite different sense – for the word is derived from *paginae* and relates to a scholastic drama. An example of this latter type is the *Pageant of Knowledge*[1] (287 lines in thirty-nine Chaucerian stanzas), a didactic work handed down in two versions, based upon an original by the poet Ausonius, author of *Mosella*.[2] In seven *paginae* there are successively enumerated, with a short explanation in each case, the individual social classes, the virtues or maxims of worldly wisdom, the seven liberal arts, the constellations and celestial spheres, the elements, the temperaments, the seasons and 'dysposicion' of the world, which is contrasted with the admirable constancy of the heavens. The whole pageant corresponded to the fifteenth century's inexhaustible desire for instruction: there is hardly another century that can boast of such a versatile, sober, and extensive didactic poetry. The material of instruction, which seems so dry to us, may have gained in vigour by the performance. Here the inventors of the *septem artes artificiales* appeared: Saturn and Ceres, who taught agriculture, Diana as mistress of the chase, Phoebus as inventor of the art of healing, and so on; four signs of the zodiac were brought to life; the temperaments could be represented, if not by separate figures, at least in mimicry by the narrator; and towards the end, when turning to the seasons of the year and the inconstant world, the work gains somewhat in richness.

These patterns were then developed and turned to good account in Lydgate's *Mumming at London*,[3] which was apparently played be-

[1] *M.P.*, 724, second version *M.P.*, 734. Printed in part, from a faulty manuscript, by Förster in *Archiv*, 104, 297 ff. (The second version in *M.P.*, 734 contains 144 lines in eighteen Chaucerian stanzas, and treats only the last part of the first version.)

[2] Cf. C. Brown and R. H. Robbins, *Index of Middle English Verse*, N.Y., 1943: No. 3183, and Bannatine MS., Hunterian Club, 1873, p. 123.

[3] *M.P.*, 682, and in Brotanek, op. cit., pp. 306 ff. *Ad* 'estates': the social divisions in the Middle Ages were not limited to three estates (clergy, nobility, and third estate), but every group, every profession, was regarded as an estate. On the dating of this mumming, cf. Withington, I, 106 f.

fore the 'greet estates of the land' in 1427. This allegorical masque, which served as an introduction to gay festivities with games and dances, must certainly have been well received. Since this mumming is closest to its model by Ausonius, it now seems the most archaic and long-winded (342 verses in short couplets). It is completely dominated by allegory, and is reminiscent of *Resoun and Sensuallyte* – also in its versification. The festivities at Eltham had been concerned with the significance of the gifts presented, but those who had brought them were conceived as real figures. Now, however, the figures themselves are allegorized; these are not the gods of ancient mythology that appear, but personified conceptions; they convey the 'morall plesaunt and notabell'. This time we have *tableaux vivants* (as we shall find them again in the Windsor mumming), elucidated by a commentator who has no part in the action. There are five scenes. First there appears Dame Fortune, whose characteristics are described in a long speech. Then come those capable of resisting her wiles: firstly Prudentia, with her three eyes, for the past, present, and future; secondly, Justice (Ryghtwysnesse), incorruptible and for that reason depicted without hands or eyes; thirdly, Fortitudo, or Magnyfycense, who inspired enthusiasm in heroes such as Henry V; finally Temperance (Attemperaunce), the description of whom turns into a formal sermon. The same tone also prevails in the humanistic catalogue of those whom Fortune has brought to ruin. The piece ends with the four being called upon to break into song.

Livelier in tone than this typical play adapted to *bourgeois* taste, and also different in form, is the *Mumming at Hertford*,[1] which was probably written in 1430.[2] This scene closely resembles the interludes, and like these shows the influence of the French *débats*. This progress from a narrator, interpreting allegorically the figures that appear, to a complaint by the 'rude uplandish people' to whom their wives

[1] *M.P.*, 675; ed. by Hammond in *Anglia*, 21 (1899), pp. 364 ff.; also in Neilson and Webster, op. cit., pp. 223 ff.

[2] Lydgate composed it 'at þe request of þe Countre Roullour Brys slayne at Loviers'. Since the donor of this commission cannot be identified, the piece cannot be dated with precision. Louviers in France was captured by Henry V in 1418, but this date is probably too early. On the other hand, the recapture of the town by the French in 1450 and its reconquest by the English, after a long siege, in the following year occurred too late for this to have been the occasion of its composition. Brys must therefore have been killed in one of the engagements that took place at Louviers during the intervening years, perhaps in 1430. As Withington arrives at the date 1430–1 independently of my reasoning (I, 107), this increases its probability.

give 'boisterous answer' justifies Chambers' view that Lydgate directed the development of the mumming into literary channels.[1]

The theme of the Hertford play is a description in the genre style of marital life among the lower orders, and is thus reminiscent of satirical plays such as *Bycorne and Chichevache*, and shares its humour. Six peasants complain about the tyranny to which they are subjected by their wives. The petition of the hard-pressed husbands is handed to the king and read out by his secretary or some such personage. There is the village elder Robin, whose wife Beatrix Bittersweete does not even keep a proper supper ready for him, and thrashes him when he complains. Ceceley Soure-chere, the wife of Colyn the cobbler, has a very sharp tongue and is given to drink – in short, everyone says his home is a veritable hell. The accused wives reply through a spokeswoman from their midst. She declares her readiness to represent their rights in a duel, for all the husbands' allegations, she says, are slanderous. After all (like Chaucer's Wife of Bath), they give their husbands the opportunity of exercising their patience and thereby securing entrance to the Kingdom of Heaven. Having heard plea and counter-plea, the king's representative gives an evasive ruling. Further investigation is still necessary, and the dominion of women is allowed to continue for another year. For the rest, the men are advised to beware of marriage. This lively play, reminiscent of a Renaissance farce, is surprisingly short for Lydgate (254 verses in heroic couplets), and reveals a talent for humour and satire to which he all too rarely gave expression.

It appears that Lydgate's mummings were written within the space of a few years (between 1424 and 1430), but no definite order can be assigned to them. His *Mumming at Windsor*[2] which in its outward form is closely connected with his Eltham mumming, may have been written during his stay in Paris, judging from internal evidence and the fact that it culminates in a pantomime or *tableau vivant*.[3] Shirley observed that it was a Christmas entertainment performed before the king at Windsor Castle, which from 1428 onwards was Henry VI's permanent winter residence; it can therefore be dated to Christmas 1429–30. In fourteen Chaucerian stanzas this short play tells of the conversion and coronation of King Clovis. Although Lydgate calls it a mumming, it is not a mumming proper but a prologue to a pantomimic representation of Clovis' conversion

[1] *Medieval Stage*, I, 396.    [2] *M.P.*, 691; Brotanek, op. cit., p. 317.
[3] See Chapter 17 (King Henry VI's Entry into London).

under the influence of St Clotilda. The saga of which he made use, to the effect that angels brought the French coat-of-arms (three golden lilies on a blue field) from heaven, contains an allusion to the proposed anointing of King Henry VI in Rheims. Lydgate was probably present at this ceremony, and the remark that Clotilda's piety saved France may be regarded as a counterpart to Joan of Arc, whose escorting of Charles VII to Rheims Lydgate had followed at close quarters, and whose activity he naturally regarded as inspired by a devilish counterpart of humility and piety. In the final stanza Lydgate pays homage to Catherine the Queen-Mother, whom he venerated so highly, and regarded as the embodiment of the right of the King of England to the French throne; here she is addressed as 'Royal Braunche, O Blood of Saint Lowys'. This Christmas play, of little literary merit, is the juridical thesis of the *Pedigree*[1] transposed into a warmer and more human sphere, given emphasis and solemnity by the Chaucerian stanzas and feminine rhymes.

Lydgate's two other mummings were commissioned by burghers and written for a civic audience. His *Mumming for the Mercers of London*,[2] in fifteen Chaucerian stanzas, was composed in the form of a letter – a form to which the author was most attached; it was performed by the silk merchants' guild on Epiphany Eve in honour of the Lord Mayor of London, William Estfeld.[3] The letter, in this case presented by Jupiter's messenger, is handed to a narrator, possibly the author himself, who reads it out aloud, pointing to the masked characters as they appear one after the other, and explaining their names and significance. Lydgate had little talent for invention; we find him employing the same artistic device in several mummings, as well as in other works such as *Bycorne and Chichevache*, which suggested to us tapestries and a commentator pointing with his stick, in the *Dance Macabre*, and again in the funeral procession in *The Fall of Princes*. Actually, in the case of this mumming performed before the worthy burghers, several commentators must certainly have been necessary, for the first thirty-four lines contain such an abundance of mythological names and classical and geographical allusions that his listeners' heads must have been spinning. Then they were told that the herald sent by Jupiter to London from Syria sees

---

[1] See pp. 118 f.  [2] *M.P.*, 695.
[3] Estfeld was twice Lord Mayor, in 1429 and 1437. 1429 is the more probable date for Lydgate's mumming, particularly since the latter contains no allusion to his being elected for the second time.

# John Lydgate

on his journey ships with French names that cannot be clearly understood and have to be interpreted allegorically. In London he appears before the Lord Mayor and announces the arrival of his companions, who had remained on board.

This is the poorest of his mummings; only the fantastical messenger, and perhaps also the skill of the narrator, can hold the spectators' attention. The zeal for learning among the *bourgeois* audience is severely taxed; Chaucer's entertaining cavalier approach seems more indulgent and less demanding. But this mass of knowledge was taken so seriously by the public of the period that Shirley made numerous comments on the margin of the manuscript.[1]

The last of the mummings was written for a performance by the goldsmiths' guild before the same Lord Mayor, Estfeld. In this *Mumming for the Goldsmiths of London*[2] (in fourteen Chaucerian stanzas) Fortune, in the capacity of a messenger, arrives on Candlemas Eve and hands a letter to the Lord Mayor, who is sitting at table after his meal. It contains the news that David and the twelve tribes of Israel have come to visit him and to present him with gifts. The performers bring with them the Ark of Covenant and announce that the town will be blessed with all good fortune so long as the reliquary and the presents it contains are safeguarded in the Mayor's house. The Levites are then called upon to sing a hymn of praise to God. Apparently Fortune recites her message herself. This play, with its procession of characters from the Old Testament, is unique in the literature of mummings and forms a counterpart to the one previously mentioned. Lydgate thus provided two mummings during Estfeld's mayoralty, one for Epiphany (6th January), when a mumming was always performed, and the other for the sacred Feast of Candlemas (2nd February). The themes correspond to the occasion on which they were performed, one being humanistic and the other theological.

[1] Marginalia to stanza 2: 'Mars is god of batayle. Venus is called þe goddesse of love. She is called Cytherea affter Cytheron, þe hill wher she is worshiped. Perseus is a knight which þat roode vpon an hors þat was called Pegase. þe nyen Muses dvelle bysyde Ellycon, þe welle . . .'

Marginalia to the catalogue of poets in stanza 5: 'Tulius a poete and a rethorisyen of Rome. Macrobye an olde philosofre. Ovyde and Virgilius weren olde poetes, þat oon of Rome, þat other of Naples afore þe tyme of Cryst. Frauncys Petrark was a poete of Florence. So were Bochas and Dante withinne þis hundreþe yeere; and þey were called laureate for þey were coroned with laurer in token þat þey excelled oþer in poetrye.'

[2] *M.P.*, 698; Brotanek, op. cit., p. 323.

## Chapter 14

### Lydgate's Didactic Poetry

\*

Even in the case of the mummings, where this is hardly to be expected, we have had cause to speak of didactic poetry; and this didactic tendency dominates the non-courtly literature written by and for the *bourgeois* public during Lydgate's lifetime. Apart from the literature of religious instruction and homilies (among which mention may be made of the paraphrase of the seven penitential psalms – a model of versification – by Thomas Brampton (approx. 1414) and, as a prose example, the excellent translation of Bonaventura's *Meditationes Vitae Christi* by Nicholas Love (approx. 1410)), there is also an abundance of didactic poetry in secular literature. We have John Walton's poetic rendering of Boethius' *Consolationes* (1410), which surpasses the prose version by Chaucer; we have the political tract *The Lybelle of Englyshe Polycye* (1436); there are many works giving historical and political information, and pieces of journalistic reporting such as *The Bataille of Agincourt, The Siege of Calais, The Ship of State,* and *The Rose of Rouen;* there are chronicles in prose, among which *Brut* takes pride of place, and, *inter alia,* pretentious didactic poems such as *The Court of Sapience* (1470?), formerly attributed to Lydgate. All these works may still be regarded as literature and evaluated accordingly.

But the new middle-class reading public of fifteenth-century England also needed didactic literature about ordinary human relationships. Such books of etiquette can no longer be regarded as literature, although they enjoyed high esteem in their time,[1] and were mostly written in verse, which seems inappropriate to us today. We

[1] The extent of their circulation is shown by the forty-three extant manuscripts of Lydgate's *Dietary* and twenty-two manuscripts of *Stans Puer.*

# John Lydgate

have books instructing parents how to bring up their children: *How the good wife taught her daughter*, *How the wise man taught his son*, and the famous *Babees Book*. We have the *Book of Courtesy* (approx. 1450), *The Master of Game* (1406), written by the Duke of York, and John Russell's *Book of Carving and Nurture* (ca. 1440), in which the author, who had been trained in Humphrey's service, sets forth the duties of the perfect butler, major-domo, valet, and carver. Finally, there is Peter Idley's *Instructions to his son* (ca. 1445), written in over 1000 Chaucerian stanzas, a formal epic of good manners and worldly wisdom.

If Lydgate emerged as the author of works such as these, this could only add to his reputation. First of all mention must be made of a little book on table manners, *Stans puer ad mensam*,[1] written in fourteen Chaucerian stanzas. It may be derived from a Latin original through the intermediacy of a French version.[2] The content follows the pattern of all these books on table etiquette, many of which are most informative as to the customs of the time.[3] Wylie[4] points out that the injunctions not to smack one's lips, lick one's plate, spread butter with one's thumb, or wipe one's mouth on the table-cloth were contrasted with the manners of trained domestic staff. At great feasts the servants would ride on horseback, much skill being required to keep their balance, with steaming bowls in both hands, whilst they forced their horses through the closely-packed throng. Lydgate's *Stans puer* is conceived on a less pretentious scale. He recommends his 'dere sone' not to pick his nose, play with his knife, or bespatter himself with gravy. Before a meal he is to wash his hands; he is not to drink too fast, must wipe his spoon clean, not leave anything behind in his bowl, and so on. More original than this, to our minds, is his short *Treatise for Lavenders*,[5] consisting of only three Chaucerian stanzas. This was written for Lady Sibille Boys of Holm Hale, of

---

[1] *M.P.*, 739; Hazlitt, *Early Popular Poetry of England*, 1866, III; *Babees Book*, ed. F. J. Furnivall, L., 1868 (*EETS*, OS. 36), which contains the original Latin versions. On the traditions of table manners, cf. A. Haufen, *Caspar Scheidt: Studien zur Geschichte der grobianischen Literatur*, Strasbourg, 1889 (Quellen und Forschungen, 32), in which pp. 14 ff. deal with books on etiquette in English and French.

[2] According to MS. Lansd. 699 and Ashm. 61 a translation from the Latin of Sulpitius Verulanus. Whether the poem *Stans puer . . .* attributed to Bishop Rob. Greathead (Grosseteste) has any close connexion with that by Lydgate remains to be investigated (Gröber's *Grundriss der roman. Phil.*, Bd. II, Abt. 1, Strasbourg, 1902, p. 384); English version attributed by Brandl to a disciple of Lydgate (*Grundriss der german. Phil.*, II, 690).

[3] E.g., *Babees Book*, p. 1.    [4] *Henry V*, I, pp. 6 f.

[5] *M.P.*, 723; Wright, *Rel. Ant.*, I, 26; Steele, in *Academy*, 1894, I, 395.

whom nothing is known except that she lived in Suffolk. Lydgate also dedicated to her a religious moralistic epistle.[1] The poet insists that her servants should take care with 'my lady's attire', since their wages are paid punctually. 'Wash everything until it is clean; two Latin verses will show you how to set about it: wine stains should be washed with milk, oil stains with lye of beans, ink stains with wine, and everything else with water.'

Two other works have more of the air of the monastery school-room about them, for they are paraphrased translations and annotations of Latin proverbs. *Duodecim abusiones*[2] begins with twelve 'absurd' Latin sentences which are set right in his translation e.g., *rex sine sapientia* – 'King, rule wisely'; the platitudinous nature of such sententious verses is overcome by the paternal admonitory tone:

> *People, obeye your kyng and the lawe;*
> *Age, be ruled by good religyon . . .*

*Four Things that Make a Man a Fool*[3] is a paraphrase, extant in three versions, each of one Chaucerian stanza, of the Latin phrase *quatuor infatuant: honor,*[4] *etas, femina, uinum,* with a fourth stanza demonstrating the vanity of 'worldly worship', and brought to a close by a fifth stanza, the *Balade de Bone Counseyle,* in which reference is made to Christ.

Less monastic in character is his *Nine Properties of Wine,*[5] which is more illustrative of Lydgate's cheerful secular outlook, and in particular of his fondness for wine (for he enjoyed the fruits of his monastery vineyard, and not, like Henry VI, merely the *vineae odorem delectabilem*).[6] This is likewise a paraphrase in rhyme royal of a Latin phrase, to the effect that wine clears the eyes, delights the heart, warms the stomach, heals wounds, and cleanses the gums. Further precepts for good health are contained in *A Dietary,*[7] one of the best-known contemporary collections of such rules. It consists of twenty-one ballad stanzas, of which the first three occasionally ap-

[1] See pp. 204 ff.
[2] *M.P.,* 707 (two Chaucerian stanzas); cf. E. R. Curtius, *Europäische Literatur und lateinisches Mittelalter,* Berne, 1948, pp. 501 ff.
[3] *M.P.,* 708.      [4] *honor* = advancement.
[5] *M.P.,* 724. The Latin original (six lines) in MS. Trin. Coll. Cambr. o.9.38, printed in Steele, *Secrees of Philisoffres, EETS,* ES. 66.
[6] R. Pauli, *Geschichte von England,* V, 281.
[7] *M.P.,* 703; *Babees Book,* p. 54; Halliwell, op. cit., p. 66; Neilson and Webster, op. cit., p. 221; cf. C. F. Bühler, 'Lydgate's Rules of Health', in *Med. Aevum,* III (Feb. 1934), 51–6. The 'Dietary' is in Brown's *Index,* 824.

# John Lydgate

pear separately under the title of *A Doctrine for Pestilence*. To keep healthy, the poet recommends one to be cheerful, avoid bad air, drink good wine, take walks in the garden, eat no fruit and only well-spiced white meat, and sleep long in the morning. These are the rules relating to feverish illnesses, which is what the word 'pestilence' means here. The general rules in this *Dietary* are not very different: to stay well, keep your head covered, exercise moderation, do not drink in the evening and do not eat too late. Make sure that the bread is good, do not work too hard, take walks in the garden, and abstain from taking a nap after luncheon. Put sage and rue in your drinks and guard against all intemperance: most illness comes from over-eating. If you have eaten too well, take care that you do not catch a fever. Moderation and a natural appetite are good guides which give relief when there is no doctor to be had. Then Lydgate turns from medicine to morality and recommends polite behaviour, love of truth, and piety. And towards the end he adds a second set of rules for good health: light the fire in the morning and evening to disperse 'black vapours', do not sleep after meals, do not drink at meals, and do not put too much salt into your food. One need not look for literary merit in this little work, but it does afford some insight into the life of the time. As a child of his era Lydgate had a fondness for didactic poetry of this kind. His last work, which he left uncompleted, was an adaptation of *Secreta Secretorum*, and belongs to this genre; and almost all his works have interpolations of purely didactic stanzas, or groups of stanzas.

## Chapter 15

### *The Regency during Henry VI's minority;*
### *Lydgate in Paris*

*

Lydgate's life takes its obscure course through the political history of the time, and we must now revert to this sphere for light on his further career.

After the death of Henry V the English political scene was dominated by the struggle for power between Henry Beaufort[1] and Humphrey of Gloucester.[2] Now forty-five years of age, and with an unusual amount of administrative and diplomatic experience behind him, Henry Beaufort knew more than anyone about the affairs of the realm, and would have been best suited for the office of regent. Parliament was also on his side, since the Duke of Gloucester, whom Henry had appointed regent in his will, did not possess Henry Beaufort's administrative talent or political sagacity. In an effort to comply with Henry's wish and at the same time to parry Humphrey's ambitions, it set up a Regency Council (6th November 1422) in which Beaufort had the decisive voice. Humphrey was permitted to act as Protector only during the Duke of Bedford's absence in France, with the result that he was unable to take the leading part in the affairs of the council. But from 1422 to 1425 there was little cause for concern. The Protector had enjoyed the artistic education of his father[3] and possessed an affable disposition that earned him his name of 'good Duke Humphrey'. But in later life he abused this respect by carrying on a feud against the faction led by Cardinal[4] Beaufort and

---

[1] 1377?–1447, uncle of Henry V (cf. p. 29).    [2] 1390–1447, brother of Henry V.
[3] K. H. Vickers, *Humphrey Duke of Gloucester*, L., 1907 (with extensive bibliography).
[4] Bishop of Lincoln in 1398, of Winchester in 1404, Cardinal from 1426.

# John Lydgate

subsequently by William de la Pole, Earl of Suffolk – both of them politicians of greater vision than himself.

Feeling cramped and restricted in England, Humphrey devoted himself to foreign affairs. In the autumn of 1422 he married Countess Jacqueline of Hainault and Holland, and in consequence laid claim to Hainault. In October 1424 he embarked upon an unsuccessful invasion which inevitably strained the Anglo-Burgundian alliance, the corner-stone of Bedford's foreign policy, and seemed to thwart all hope of lasting peace with France.

Lydgate was given the delicate task of composing a poem on the occasion of Humphrey's marriage. His attitude was probably akin to that of Archbishop Chichele, who favoured mediation. Both Chichele and Lydgate had close connexions with Humphrey: the former because he supported the idea of a national Church, whilst Beaufort backed the Pope; the latter because Humphrey was his patron. Thus his *Epithalamium for Gloucester*[1] (written in 1422–3, in twenty-seven Chaucerian stanzas) makes no mention of the political aspects of the marriage. At first sight it appears to be a clumsy eulogy of a poet anxious to please his patron, but on closer examination it becomes clear that in its content and structural harmony it is in fact a brilliant solution of a difficult task. The first part comprises an exaltation of love and matrimony, instituted by Jupiter, it is said, to promote peace. This thesis is authenticated by reference to mythology and ancient history. In the same way the marriage of Henry V and Catherine has put an end to the conflict between England and France, 'as I hope of hert and menyng truwe', and similarly Humphrey's marriage to Jacqueline should lead to peace and an expansion of territory (through the fateful dowry of Holland and Zeeland). At this point the second part begins, which contains a eulogy of the bride as an ideal of womanhood. A catalogue of women of antiquity constitutes the transition to the idealized description of Jacqueline; and in the third section comes the counterpart of this, a catalogue of men famous in antiquity, which serves to throw Humphrey into prominence. In conclusion a fourth part prophesies that as a result of the match good fortune will prevail in the land, as is shown by the perfect marriages of Mercury and Philology and others. The envoy contains the humble dedication to Jacqueline.

[1] M.P., 601; Hammond, in *Anglia*, 27, p. 385, and in *English Verse between Chaucer and Surrey*, p. 142 (with introduction, commentary and bibliography). Title in *M.P.*: *On Gloucester's Approaching Marriage*.

The marital bliss of which the poet sang was not to be of long duration. By 1428 Humphrey had already obtained a divorce and had married Eleanor Cobham, one of his first wife's ladies-in-waiting. The affair caused great commotion; and, interestingly enough, among the numerous protests there is also a poem by Lydgate, *Complaint for my Lady of Gloucester and Holand*,[1] in which, in a fabulous setting, he gives expression to his warm sympathy for the deserted Jacqueline and attributes Humphrey's conduct to witchcraft. In spite of this excuse, it seemed advisable for the poem to be circulated anonymously, with the result that Lydgate's authorship has occasionally been questioned. It is written in eighteen Chaucerian stanzas, but with four-beat lines, and is closer to modern taste and simpler than the pompous florid style that was most popular at the time.

The political blunder which Humphrey committed by venturing into marriage with Jacqueline was to some extent compensated by his release of King James I of Scotland (1423), the author of *Kingis Quair*.[2] James' return to Scotland put an end to the flow of Scottish recruits to support France in her struggle against the English. The common people now felt that times had become more peaceful: the 'Great London Chronicle' tranquilly records that on Sunday, 13th November the Queen-Mother, accompanied by the young Henry VI, travelled from Windsor to London, passing the night at Staines. On the following Wednesday 'the king with a glad chere sat in his mother's lappe and rode through the city of Westminster' – to Parliament, where the Speaker read an address of welcome.

With the passage of time the conflict between Beaufort and Gloucester[3] developed into an open breach. But at the Parliament of Leicester on 12th March 1426 Bedford brought about a reconciliation between the two men, which they sealed by shaking hands.[4] In 1426 the king spent Christmas at Eltham, where he was entertained

---

[1] *M.P.*, 608; Hammond, in *Anglia*, 27, p. 381.

[2] In this the king sings of his love for Henry Beaufort's niece, Lady Jane Beaufort.

[3] A duel between Humphrey and the Duke of Burgundy had been forbidden by Pope Martin V in a bull dated 24th April 1425. Cf. J. Stevenson, *Letters and Papers illustrative of the Wars of the English in France*, 2 vols. (Rolls Series), L., 1861, II, 412.

[4] *The Great Chronicle of London*, ed. by A. H. Thomas and J. D. Thornley, L., 1939: 'The same yeer John Duk of Bedford kom oute of ffraunce into England to see the governaunce off the Rewne and also for to putte in pees and reste certeyne debates and hevynesses hangyng bytwene the Duk of Gloucestre his brothyr and the Bishop of Winchester, chancellor of England, his oncle.'

by 'Jack Travail' and his troupe and the music of portable organs.[1]
At this time Lydgate must have already been in Paris.

\*

It was in or about 1426 (possibly in 1425, when Catherine the
Queen-Mother secretly married Owen Tudor) that the former monk
of Bury and nominal prior of Hatfield left for Paris. It has been suggested that Lydgate undertook this journey in the service of Lord
Richard of Warwick, Regent of France during Bedford's absence,[2]
just as in 1417 Thomas Elmham had accompanied King Henry V as
his 'official recorder'. As the example of Chaucer shows, it was not
unusual for a poet to be employed on a political mission. It is not
certain whether his journey was made at the behest of some body of
monks, or whether it was a secular mission, encouraged perhaps by
Catherine.[3] However this may be, Lydgate occupied a senior post on
Bedford's administrative staff as a kind of liaison officer. Journeys to
France were in those days no rarity. There was a constant movement
to and fro, less because of the dynastic union which the English
sought to bring about than because of French opposition to it. The
victorious Henry V had bequeathed a fateful legacy. The situation in
France was wretched in the extreme: the public highways were un-
safe owing to the danger of attack by brigands, and the whole country from Chartres to Hainault in the east and Abbéville in the north
had been devastated by the constant warfare. Cultivated land was to
be seen only where it was protected by a castle or fortified city, and
even in Paris the large number of dilapidated houses bore witness to
the widespread and increasing neglect.

Henry V himself had appointed to be his successor as Regent of
France John of Lancaster, Duke of Bedford (1389–1435), who was
almost the equal of the late king as soldier, administrator, and diplo-
matist. He accomplished the impossible: aware that English rule in
France was based on the alliance with Burgundy, he married in June
1423 Anne, sister of Duke Philip of Burgundy, whose likeness has
been handed down to posterity in the costly book of hours[4] which

[1] Rymer, *Foedera*, X, 387.

[2] Schick, in his edition of the *Temple of Glas*, p. xciii.

[3] Catherine was in close contact with her native land and had purchases such as wine,
silverware, and other household objects bought in Paris. *Letters and Papers*, ed. Stevenson, II, 265, 270, 275.

[4] The so-called Bedford Missal, or Bedford Book of Hours. B. M. Addit. MS., 18,
850.

she gave the king as a token of remembrance in 1430. In contrast to Henry, Bedford was popular with all Frenchmen of the Burgundian party; the French chronicle praises him highly, but his wise reforms could have only limited effect in a country that was athirst for freedom from foreign rule. He sought to maintain good relations with Burgundy (which had suffered as a result of Humphrey's escapade) as well as keeping the loyalty of the French.[1] After the Treaty of Troyes the administration of France was completely separated from that of England. Just as Bedford advocated the Regency Council in England, so also in France he adopted the *Grand Conseil*, the traditional organ of the French monarchy. This ensured the continued rule of the Burgundian government that had been installed in 1418. This pro-French government was the secret of his success and also the cause of his clash with Beaufort, which took place when the latter, accompanied by the young king, arrived in France in April 1430. There were two *conseils*, one in Paris and one in Rouen; for Henry V had taken Rouen at the point of the sword, and Normandy was therefore governed by a military administration. Paris had been won by the Treaty of Troyes and it was here that the *Grand Conseil*[2] was to ensure continuity of government, so that Henry VI should appear as the natural heir and successor to Charles VI. After the latter's death the Treaty of Troyes put an end, formally at least, to the special administration of Normandy, and Paris now became the capital of the Anglo-French state. Bedford had full confidence in his French counsellors, whom he also employed on diplomatic missions. He said that he had found his French subjects 'as loving and as kind as ever was people': they were to rank with the English soldiers as the king's 'true men and servants'.

In this administration, which had as its aim the pacification of the country, Lydgate was in his element. It may be assumed that his journey to Paris was welcomed, and perhaps even inspired, by Bedford, since the latter may well have met Lydgate on his visit to Bury St Edmunds in 1418, or at least must have heard of him later, since he subsequently became his patron.

When Lydgate came to Paris, Bedford was in England (from 5th

---

[1] B. J. H. Rowe, 'The Grand Conseil under the Duke of Bedford, 1422–1435', in *Oxford Essays in Medieval History presented to H. E. Salter*, Oxford, 1934, pp. 207 ff.

[2] Its members comprised thirteen Frenchmen (including Louis de Luxembourg, Bedford's uncle by marriage) and three Englishmen, and from time to time the commanders Warwick or Suffolk.

# John Lydgate

December 1425 to 5th April 1427). His deputy representative was Thomas de Montacute, or Montague, fourth Earl of Salisbury (1388–1428), a highly-esteemed public figure and capable officer. Already at the early age of twenty-six he had been sent by Henry V on a diplomatic mission to France, and had then held a command in the army, rising to the rank of lieutenant-general of Normandy. This Montacute, with whom Lydgate probably first became acquainted in Paris, was later one of the poet's most famous patrons. But before considering this point, we must mention another nobleman who shortly after Lydgate's arrival in Paris endeavoured to involve the pacific-minded and seclusion-loving monk into playing a political or propagandist role. This was Richard de Beauchamp, Count of Warwick (1382–1439), whose official title was 'lieutenant for the field in the absence of the regent Bedford'. Beauchamp had travelled widely in the Orient and in all countries of Europe and was a model of chivalry.[1] He may already have heard of Lydgate in 1414, since both he and Lydgate's abbot, William of Exeter, had been members of the English mission to the Council of Constance. It can be assumed that Lydgate met him at the home of Thomas Chaucer. Beauchamp had been sent with Chaucer to the armistice negotiations which had occasioned Lydgate's *Balade at the Departyng of Thomas Chaucyer into France*. Alternatively, Lydgate may possibly have met him in Windsor whilst he was prior of Hatfield. It was at the request of Beauchamp's daughter that Lydgate wrote the family history of Guy of Warwick. Thus they already stood to one another as patron to protégé; it was no stranger whom Beauchamp commissioned to write *The Title and Pedigree of Henry VI*.[2] This comparatively short work narrates in detail in a prologue (reiterated in the actual poem) how this genealogical tree, designed to prove Henry VI's claim to the French throne, had been compiled by a worthy French scholar by the name of Laurence Calot at the command of the regent, John of Bedford; and that he had translated it in Paris on 28th July 1427 at the command of the Earl of Warwick.[3] This is the accepted interpretation of Lydgate's verse, in which the exaggerations are deliberately designed to emphasize its propagandist character. Laurence

[1] 'His deeds of chivalry were collected by John Rous a generation later.' (MS. Cottonian Libr.). *D.N.B.*

[2] *M.P.*, 613, also in Th. Wright, *Political Poems*, II, 131.

[3] MacCracken (*M.P.*, 621) gives 1426, which cannot be correct, since Calot did not enter the king's service until 1427. Parr (*PMLA*, 67, p. 258) calculates the date as 28th July 1426.

Calot[1] was 'secretarius et notarius regis tam in regno suo Anglie quam in regno suo Francie', and his work was perhaps not just a learned treatise, but above all a real genealogical tree, magnificently drawn in detail, which was apparently added to Lydgate's poem as a pictorial supplement. By his unchivalrous murder of the Duke of Burgundy the dauphin is said to have forfeited all right to rule (one can feel Bedford's pro-Burgundian policy here!), and God has sent Henry V, a descendant of St Louis and a worthy ruler, in his stead; by the Treaty of Troyes and his marriage with Catherine, daughter of Charles VI, he has been declared the legitimate heir to the French throne. Because of the death in the same year of the kings of both England and France, Henry VI is entitled to the succession through his father's and his mother's line; may God grant him a long life (a prayer to which the detailed exposition of his horoscope is apparently designed to lend force). One gains the impression that Lydgate was short of subject-matter, and that he had some difficulty in composing these 329 verses (in heroic couplets). The praise given to the most clever and capable clerk Calot, with his 'rethoryk famous and eloquent', probably did not correspond to the facts. Lydgate's verse rendering was designed to popularize this proof of Henry's legitimate claim to the French throne.

Lydgate's years in Paris brought him into constant personal contact with English noblemen who professed some interest in the arts, as well as with French scholars and senior officials. This was one of his most productive periods, in which he completed several poetic commissions in addition to writing works on political themes. His translation of Deguileville and the *Dance Macabre* certainly belong to this period; so probably do several of his satires, which for the sake of convenience we have examined together, and some of his religious poems which in the absence of reliable dates for their composition may be discussed later.

[1] Cf. J. Otway-Ruthven, *The King's Secretary and the Signet Office in the 15th Century*, Cambridge, 1939, pp. 94 f. This shows that Calot was in the royal service from 1427 to 1444. His name occurs frequently in the documents of the English administration in France. In a petition for naturalization dated *circa* 1433 he states that he came to England at the king's command to serve as a secretary. He brought his wife and family with him. He was mainly concerned with diplomatic correspondence. In 1438 he returned to France; at this time the king wrote to the Duke of York, 'For as much as oure welbeloved secretarie, maister Laurence Calot, disposeth him at this tyme for to passe with yow into oure said duchie . . . we praye you that ye have him specially recommended'. He died in March 1444, and in the letter assuring his widow of a pension he is referred to as 'naguere en son vivant nostre secretaire'.

## Chapter 16

*Lydgate's Translations of Deguileville and the*
Dance Macabre

\*

Deguileville and his *Pèlerinage* are no longer remembered, but in their day, and for a century later, they were widely known and highly esteemed. The author, Guillaume de Deguileville (circa 1294–5 to a date later than 1358) was from 1316 onwards a Cistercian monk at the abbey of Chalis in Valois, near Senlis. It was here that in 1330–1 he wrote, as an account of a vision, the poem known as *Pèlerinage de la Vie Humaine*. The first version was taken from him before it had been completed and copies of it circulated. Indignant at this, some twenty-five years later he composed a second version, which he then sent to all those to whom the first version had been submitted. After this romance describing man's path through this earthly life Deguileville wrote the *Pèlerinage de l'Ame*, in which he narrated the passage of the soul from the Last Judgement through Purgatory to Salvation, and the *Pèlerinage de Jésus Christ*, a rendering of the exemplary life and death of Our Lord. This carefully thought out and organically built up trilogy, which was written without his being acquainted with Dante's *Divine Comedy*, has as its consistent theme the struggle between the forces of good and evil for the human soul; this is represented in the first part as a struggle between the virtues and the vices, in the second as an action at law brought by the devil before the celestial powers, and in the third as a great controversy between mercy and justice.[1] The commission to translate the *Pèlerinage*

---

[1] The three visionary romances have been edited by J. J. Stürzinger (Roxb. Club), L., 1893–7. They are described in outline in Gröber, *Grundriss . . .*, II, 1, pp. 749 f.; Abbé Joseph Delacotte, *Guillaume de Digulleville: Trois Romans-Poèmes du XIVe siècle*, Paris,

*de la Vie Humaine* was given to Lydgate by Thomas Montacute, Bedford's deputy and the second husband of Thomas Chaucer's only daughter and heiress Alice.[1] Thomas Montacute was not only an officer, but also a man of broad education; he was a friend of Christine de Pisan, a man who received a most appreciative mention in one of the French verse chronicles, and had a reputation as a poet.[2] '*Gracieus chevalier, aimant dictiez, et lui même gracieux dicteur*' are the words used by Christine de Pisan in her assessment of him.[3] The fact that Thomas commanded the translation may be attributed to his wife Alice. Lydgate must have received his commission in 1426, when the Count was in Paris. Judging from the luxurious dedication copy,[4] this patronage must have been a great honour for him. The frontispiece shows the pilgrim,[5] portrayed as an old man dressed in black, presenting the work to the young count, who is shown wearing armour; next to him is Lydgate, represented kneeling, as a Benedictine monk; the illustration is executed almost in the form of a portrait.

The book must have been completed before 3rd November 1428, for on this date Thomas de Montacute died from the effects of a wound he had received at the siege of Orleans. He was not the only English nobleman to appreciate Deguileville; there seems to have been a veritable cult of this somewhat obsolete writer. The Duke of Bedford, who like his brother was a great bibliophile,[6] apparently requested Lydgate to write a prose version of the *Pèlerinage de l'Ame*;[7]

---

1932. (Cf. also H. Traver, *The Four Daughters of God*. Bryn Mawr Monograph, VI, 1907.) The three epics are dated respectively 1330, 1355 (or alternatively 1335), and 1358.

[1] Alice Chaucer was only twelve years old when her supposed first husband, John Phelip, who was a friend of the king, died (1415), which leads H. A. Napier to the view that they were only engaged (*Historical notices*, op. cit.).

[2] The chronicle in verse has been edited by J. Webb in *Archaeologia* 20 (1824), pp. 1–442. Of his poems nothing remains.

[3] Ruud, *Thomas Chaucer*, op. cit., p. 87.

[4] Harl. MS. 4826, frontispiece (f. 1*); see Plate.

[5] He carries on his scrip a scallop as an emblem of his pilgrimage to Compostella.

[6] In 1425 he bought the library of the grandfather of Charles of Orleans, which contained more than 800 volumes, and took it either to England or to his castle in Rouen. On his death on 14th September 1435 the library was broken up. Cf. L. Delisle, *Recherches sur la librairie de Charles V*, Paris, 1907, pp. 138–41, cited by P. Champion, *Vie de Charles d'Orléans*, p. 225, and G. Doutrepont, *La littérature française à la cour des Ducs de Bourgogne*, Paris, 1909; on Bedford's activity as a bibliophile, cf. ibid., pp. 396–402.

[7] Brusendorff (*The Chaucer Tradition*, London, 1925, p. 228) has drawn attention to lost works by Lydgate and mentions a Shirley MS. which contained a prose translation of Deguileville and various minor poems by Lydgate.

# John Lydgate

and he may also perhaps have indirectly inspired the verse rendering of the *Pèlerinage de la Vie Humaine*. For not so long ago a Caxton print came to light containing an English prose version of the *Pylgrymage of the Sowle*, which has been ascribed to Lydgate.[1] This English version was patterned on a French version of Deguileville's poem by Jean de Gallopes, a priest from the diocese of Évreux, and also contains a dedication to the Duke of Bedford.[2] Thus almost simultaneously Bedford and Montacute both commissioned translations of Deguileville's two main works.

Shortly after Bedford's return to England, where he stayed from December 1425 to April 1427, he was presented with a bill, dated 7th August 1427, submitted by a certain Jean Thomas, a clerk, who is referred to later as a member of the *Capitulum Ecclesiae Cenomanniae*.[3] Thomas requests payment, and acknowledges receipt of the same, for the parchment he required for the Latin prose translation of Deguileville's *Pèlerinage de l'Ame*,[4] a translation which coincides in time with Lydgate's English verse rendering of the *Pèlerinage de la Vie Humaine* executed for Thomas Montacute. The two translators of Deguileville, both working for English patrons, may have been in contact with one another.[5]

[1] According to an offprint in the British Museum ('Reprinted from *Apollo*, Oct. 1931'): *John Lydgate's 'Pylgrymage of the Sowle': a newly discovered volume printed by Will. Caxton*, by W. L. Hare.

[2] 'Je vostre humble chapellain ay transpose de rime en prose le livre de icelui pelerinage de l'ame . . .', ibid. This 'Jehan Galopes', who is believed to have been a Welshman, also made a translation of the *Meditationes Vitae Christi* by Bonaventura, which he dedicated to Henry V (*circa* 1420).

Hare puts forward the following chronology, which, however, needs some corroboration and authentication:

| | |
|---|---|
| 1. Deguileville's *Vie Humaine* | 1330 |
| 2. Deguileville's *Pilgrimage de l'Ame* | 1335 |
| 3. Deguileville's *Jésus Christ* | 1358 |
| 4. Gallopes' translation of 2 | 1410 (?) |
| 5. Lydgate's translation of 4 | 1413 |
| 6. Lydgate's *Life of our Lady* | 1421 |
| 7. Gallopes' translation of Bonaventura | 1421 |
| 8. Lydgate's verse translation of 1 for Montacute | 1426 |
| 9. Gallopes' new dedication of 4 to Bedford | 1430 |

[3] J. Stevenson (ed.), *Letters and Papers*, op. cit., II, 691.

[4] 'Il est deu a moy, Jehan Thomas, clerk, demourant a Paris, pour ma peine et salaire davoir escript en parchemin, par lordonnance et commandement de monseigneur le regent le royaume de France, duc de Bedford, ung livre en Latin intitule Le Pelerinaige de Lame en prose; le quel contient XII cayers de parchemin, qui valent, au pris de XVI s. P. pour chacun cayer, XII l. T.' (Stevenson, *Letters and Papers*, op. cit., II, 415). Of Thomas and of the Latin prose version of the *Pèlerinage de l'âme* nothing is known.

[5] See below, p. 127.

[ 122 ]

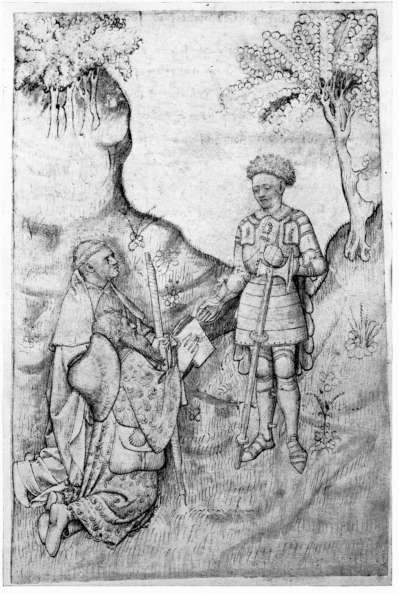

7. In the foreground, a pilgrim presenting *The Pilgrimage of the Life of Man* to Thomas Montacute, 4th Earl of Salisbury. On the extreme left, Lydgate in the habit of a monk

# Lydgate's Translations of Deguileville

Lydgate's *Pilgrimage of the Life of Man*[1] is based on Deguileville's second and more comprehensive version,[2] in which various additions enhance the interest, if not the artistic unity, of this allegory. A somewhat bald summary of the contents, excluding the additions, is as follows: a vision of the celestial Jerusalem prompts the author to undertake a pilgrimage thither. He finds Grace Dieu, who promises him her assistance and invites him to her house. Here he receives instruction in the dogmas and sacraments of the Church, and meets Moses, who provides the pilgrims with a sword and a key. He hears a polemical discourse between Nature and Grace Dieu on the transubstantiation of bread and wine, and encounters Penance and Charity. After didactic discourses between Aristotle and Sapience, Grace Dieu gives the pilgrim a Latin scroll containing the Creed and poems on God and the Virgin Mary. Then she equips him with armour which, however, proves too heavy for him, and after a lecture on body and soul Grace Dieu withdraws with a rebuke. The pilgrim is now confronted by Rude Entendement, from whom he is freed by Reason. He is joined by Youth, and at a cross-roads meets Labour and Idleness. On the advice of Moral Virtue he chooses the right path, but Youth leads him astray. He then meets Gluttony, Venus, and Sloth, who fascinate him by their conversation. After this he meets Pride and Envy and their attendants, has to defend himself against Wrath and Tribulation, and prays to the Virgin Mary (at which point a homily in prose by St Bernard is interpolated, which ends in a ballad on the Virgin Mary). The next danger comes from a meeting with Avarice and Heresy, whereupon the pilgrim holds discourse with Satan, who blocks his path, and finally tries to swim across the sea. In great distress he prays to the Virgin Mary (this is the *A B C* translated by Chaucer from Deguileville, which Lydgate here reverently inserts, in his master's rendering), and succeeds in saving his life by coming to some small islands, where he encounters Astronomy, Astrology, and Idolatry. He is harassed by the witch Conspiracy, and sees a revolving tower on which is the siren Worldly Pleasure. Finally, Grace Dieu sends a ship, on which are to be found the other monastic orders, as well as the castle of the Cistercians, inhabited by Obedience and Abstinence, Chastity and Poverty. He speaks to them and Prayer arrives, as a messenger from

[1] Ed. by F. J. Furnivall and K. B. Locock, *EETS*, ES. 77, 83, 92, London, 1899-1904.
[2] An English prose rendering (*circa* 1430) of the first version, which was of greater significance as a work of art, has been edited by W. A. Wright (Roxb. Club), 1869.

# John Lydgate

Heaven. The castle is stormed by Detraction, Treason, and Envy, who torment the pilgrim until the king gives orders for them to be seized. Then the author visits on his pilgrimage monasteries both good and bad, and receives instruction from Grace Dieu. Now Age and Sickness appear, as precursors of Death; Mercy consoles him; Prayer comes as a guide to Paradise, and Death causes him to breathe his last.

This adventurous pilgrimage, of which echoes are to be found in Bunyan, sets out to be a spiritual counterpart to the *Roman de la Rose*. It borrows not only Guillaume de Lorris' allegorical framework, but also Jean de Meung's encyclopaedic discussion of the most diverse subjects.[1] Consequently some sections, as for example those on Pride[2] and Avarice,[3] develop into substantial works in their own right. The book may in general be characterized as a didactic discourse combined with a romance, by which is meant that the reader's desire for knowledge and his imagination are both gratified in equal measure. Though there are many dull passages, the story is not uninteresting; the use of dialogue makes for dramatic suspense, and freshness is added by the author's evident delight in his narrative: for example, to illustrate cursing there is the tale of the monk who tears his stole on a cherry tree and curses it, with the result that he obtains no fruit the following year;[4] or, to portray flattery, the tale is told of the fox, the raven, and the cheese;[5] or again, to illustrate hypocrisy, there is the fable of the fox who feigns death,[6] and the simile that penance works on the human heart in the same way as a child hits an apple with his fist to make it soft.[7] The necessity of overcoming the body is compared with the oft-repeated efforts of an ant to climb up a heap of sand;[8] the movement of the spirit, in a sense contrary to that of the body, is likened to two concentric wheels turning in opposite directions,[9] and the light of the soul triumphing over the body is compared with the sun shining through the clouds, or the small lamp in a lantern.[10]

Most of these similes are taken from everyday life, and the shorter they are the more vivid is the effect of their frequently stark realism: for example, Venus, here equated with sensuality, wears a beautiful visor to conceal her ugliness;[11] Defamation devours raw meat like a

---

[1] Critical discussion with the *Roman de la Rose*, lines 13,198 ff., and esp. 13,255 ff.
[2] 13,985–14,603.       [3] 17,148–18,400.       [4] 2561.
[5] 14,247.       [6] 14,605.       [7] 4078.
[8] 10,099.       [9] 12,208.       [10] 9604.       [11] 11,365.

greedy dog;[1] Wrath has a steel saw in his mouth;[2] Envy is like a fish-net with a wide mouth and a narrow end;[3] Memory has eyes in his back;[4] Gluttony, full to excess, leaves behind it a slimy mark like a snail;[5] and the effect of the stars upon men's lives is no more than a prosaic indicator of divine power.[6] This vividness of description, which is far from all mysticism, can on occasion be repellent, as in the pilgrim's explanation of transubstantiation – how he has seen with his own eyes the conversion of the bread into 'rawh fflesshe' and the wine into red blood;[7] it can verge upon the grotesque, as in the description of the attendants of Venus,[8] or in the story that Avarice steals holy images from monasteries, retouches them, and then exhibits them in public alongside forged papal bulls, has bogus cripples and invalids kneel before them, who then have their bandages and plasters taken off and are discharged as healed.[9] If one also takes into account the persuasiveness of two- or three-fold repetition, one can readily see why this work was so popular. And since, as in the *Roman de la Rose*, almost all aspects of life are touched upon; since there is Aristotelian speculation as well as discussion of political and social questions; and since, despite some passages of criticism, the existing order is on the whole endorsed, it is understandable that Deguileville's *Pèlerinage* was also appreciated by the nobility and the ruling classes.

With regard to content and structure, there is little to distinguish Lydgate's translation from the French original; for, unlike his practice in the *Troy Book* and when treating other secular themes, he makes no major additions of his own, possibly out of respect for the subject-matter. He is satisfied with a prologue[10] in which, proceeding from the Fortune motif, he emphasizes the necessity of having a guide through life and, in conformity with his patron's wish, recommends to his readers the 'grete moralyte' of the *Pilgrimage*. His statement that regard should be paid to content rather than to form is probably seriously meant; but his customary apology that he is lacking in eloquence and artistic talent must, as always, be taken with a grain of salt. His work is embellished with over 150 new words with ample use of sonorous polysyllabic French words. They occupy a prominent place in the rhymes of this epic which, like the original, is written in short lines.

---

[1] 15,294.    [2] 15,556.    [3] 18,055.    [4] 8754.
[5] 12,852.    [6] 20,415.    [7] 3262.    [8] 13,420–14,220.
[9] 18,241    [10] In ninety-two heroic couplets.

The *Pilgrimage* is perhaps the first work in which Lydgate manifests a consistent style of his own. For where the principles he adopts here are later applied to the longer five-beat lines and also to the Chaucerian or ballad stanza, there results a more solemn flow of words; and where he treats another theme affording the poet greater freedom, there results an abstract circumlocutory style such as was characteristic of his later years. All this is of greater significance than the minor differences that emerge from a comparison of his translation with the original. Deguileville's work comprises 18,123 lines, whereas Lydgate's version has 24,832. His additions do not concern the subject-matter, and there is little expansion even in the parts which are emphasized most strongly: the description of the celestial Jerusalem,[1] the vivid description of Youth,[2] and the passage on the invigorating power of Nature.[3] Most of the expansion comes from amplifications, circumlocutions, expletives, repetitions of expressions or ideas, and similar characteristic rhetorical flourishes. In addition to these there are such learned and quaint etymologies as the derivation of Venus from venery,[4] and an admiring eulogy of Chaucer.[5]

\*

Lydgate may also have written other works during his years in Paris, such as his poem *Timor Mortis*,[6] a companion piece to his *Dance Macabre*, and others that may be classified as moralistic poems. *The Devowte Inuocacioun to St Denys*[7] ordered by Charles VII will have been written in Paris, and since the *Prayers to the Ten Saints*[8] generally begin with stanzas to St Denys and St George, these may also belong to this period. More important than these conjectures is the fact that Paris, which in the late Middle Ages still had much to offer, provided English literature and plastic art with the theme of the dance macabre[9] – a theme which, like that of Fortune in the fifteenth century, was of great significance as an expression of the mood of the age. In the colonnade which enclosed on three sides the cemetery of the Eglise des Innocents there was painted

[1] 323–53.   [2] 11,133–11,212   [3] 3434–523.
[4] 8150, marginal note: 'Venus dicitur a venandi'.   [5] 19,752 ff.
[6] See Chapter 20.   [7] See Chapter 19, section on Prayers.
[8] See Chapter 19, section on Prayers.
[9] The name (actually Macabrée) is said to be derived from the first painter of the dance macabre, and is connected with the Biblical Maccabaeus. It was popularized from 1485 onwards by the editions of Guyot Marchand.

in 1425 a dance macabre, the third of its kind in Europe,[1] and the celebrated precursor of a great number of similar paintings that were done later in France, England, and Germany.[2] Verses below these murals served to elucidate the theme; these versified texts soon became independent,[3] and even developed into dramatic plays. Either costumed figures of the king, soldiers, and death would appear, whilst the priest spoke cautionary or exhortatory lines, or else there would be regular dramatic performances with several speakers.[4]

Some French 'clerk', possibly Jean Thomas, drew Lydgate's attention to this dance macabre in the cemetery of the Eglise des Innocents, which had been painted a few years earlier[5] and was attracting great crowds; Lydgate translated the text and sent it to London. Some London burghers showed interest in it and, according to John Stow's testimony in his *Survey of London* (1598), at the suggestion of the town clerk, John Carpenter,[6] the dance macabre in English was written down to accompany murals, similar to those in Paris, which were painted in a cloister around Pardon Churchyard near St

[1] The first in 1312 (?) in Klingenthal, Little Basle, and the second in 1383 in Münden, Westphalia.

[2] In 1430 in St Paul's, London; in 1436 in the Sainte-Chapelle, Dijon; in 1440 in the Dominican cemetery, Great Basle; in 1440 in the Dominican Church, Strasbourg; in 1460 in the Hungerford Chapel, Salisbury; in 1463 in the Marienkirche, Lübeck, and many others.

[3] Cf. W. Seelmann, *Die Totentänze des Mittelalters*, Leipzig, 1893, and the bibliography in E. P. Hammond, *English Verse . . .*, op. cit., p. 130. Cf. further the bibliography by H. W. Eppelsheimer, *Handbuch der Weltliteratur*, 3rd ed., Frankfurt, 1960, pp. 181 f.; Y. M. Clark, *The Dance of Death in The Middle Ages and The Renaissance*, Glasgow, 1950; and H. Rosenfeld, *Der mittelalterliche Totentanz*, Münster, 1954.

[4] As, for example, before Philip the Good of Burgundy in Bruges in 1449. E. K. Chambers, *English Literature at the Close of the Middle Ages*, Oxford, 1945, pp. 52 f.: 'In a set of Latin verses, known as the *vado mori* poem, twelve representatives of all estates, from Pope to Pauper, speak appropriate couplets. That of the King runs:

*Vado mori, rex sum : quid honor, quid gloria regum?*
*Est via mors hominis regia. Vado mori.*

This may be the precursor of the lines known in France as the Danse Macabre, and in England as the Dance of Death. It has been conjectured that they may have owed their origin to a quasi-dramatic ceremony, in which a priest pronounced them from a pulpit, while appropriately clad figures, led by Death, passed to a tomb in the nave of the Church. But they are only known as attached to painted mural representations of such figures.'

[5] 'L'an mil quatre cents vingt-cinq fut faite la Dance macabré aux Innocents, et fut commencée environ le mois d'aoust, et achevée en caresme ensuivant.' *Journal d'un bourgeois de Paris*, ed. by A. Mary, 1929, p. 188.

[6] Carpenter, who was a friend of Reginald Pecock, held the post of Town Clerk of London from 1417 to 1438.

# John Lydgate

Paul's.[1] This must have been early in 1430, for it was in this year that young Carpenter was given permission to erect a 'chantry'.[2]

The verses provided an explanatory commentary to the paintings. It is striking how often Lydgate wrote works for such a purpose. His *Legend of St George* illustrates paintings in the guild hall of the London armourers; his satire *Bycorne and Chichevache* relates to pictorial representations; his *Pedigree* poem was probably written around a great genealogical tree; his lines on the *Kings of England* are texts written to accompany medallion portraits such as are found in old manuscripts; and even lengthy invocative poems[3] were written to go with paintings in churches.

Just as a song can only be properly appreciated if one considers the text together with the melody, so we ought also to examine Lydgate's verses together with the pictures they illustrated. This we unfortunately cannot do, since the paintings have not survived. Both the chapel and the cloister with its dance macabre paintings were pulled down in 1549 by Lord Protector Somerset, who used the stones from it to build his own palace. Thus we can only assess Lydgate's *Dance Macabre*[4] as a literary monument. His text, which can be dated to the years 1426–30,[5] reproduces the French original, as he says, 'not word by word, but following the substance'. His desire to retain the proverbial line with which each stanza terminates in the French text led him to take over much of the French rhyme-scheme; on the whole these eighty ballad stanzas keep closer than usual to the original, expanding it only slightly even in the longest version (700 lines). Each alternate stanza contains an exhortation by Death, with a rejoinder by the man or woman addressed in the stanza

[1] In addition to this, the first of the English dances of death, there were others in Salisbury Cathedral, Stratford-on-Avon, and elsewhere (Chambers, in *Oxford History of English Literature*, II, 2, p. 53).

[2] On 12th January 1430. The chantry is thought to have been erected in the Chapel of the Virgin Mary, over the ossuary on the north side of St Paul's. According to Dugdale (*History of St Paul's Cathedral*, 1658, p. 131) the dance macabre paintings were in the cloister around the Pardon Churchyard of the chapel mentioned.

[3] Cf. *The Image of Our Lady* (M.P., 290), which was an accompanying text to the painting of a saint given by Ralph Gelebronde.

[4] Standard edition by F. Warren and B. White, *EETS*, OS., 181, L., 1931, containing the two versions, which are distinguished from one another by the order in which the personages appear (represented by the Ellesmere and Lansdowne MSS.), and also the French original. The Selden MS., also with the French original, has been printed by E. P. Hammond, in *English Verse* . . ., op. cit., pp. 124, 426; Tottel's printing in H. Bergen's edition of the *Fall of Princes*, p. 1025 (*EETS*, ES., 123).

[5] Bennett dates it to 1424 (*Chaucer and the 15th Century*, Oxford, 1947).

that follows. Thus a number of men and women pass in a column before the reader's eyes: Pope and Emperor, king and cardinal, bishop, knight, lady, abbot and abbess, burgher and monk, lovers, usurer, jurist, and minstrel and child. One image after another is called to mind; we hear the illustrative text as though it were some words of warning spoken by a priest. It is indeed an illustrated sermon, given dramatic forcefulness by the arrangement of the stanzas in dialogue form. Detailed discussion of the artistic merits of Lydgate's work is made more difficult by his close adherence to his source and the traces that indicate that he contemplated revising it;[1] but this is in any case less important than to give a brief explanation of the power of attraction which the dance macabre theme had in Lydgate's day. By its very nature the theme of death is common to all humanity and valid for all ages; but in a century stricken by plague (1348–1450) its presence was felt in threatening proximity. Death is not represented as a comforter or as triumphant, but as a maliciously grinning skeleton. Such allegories and epics as *The Temple of Glas*, *The Black Knight*, *Troy Book*, and *The Siege of Thebes* still had about them an air of the medieval courtly world; but in the *Dance Macabre* theme a new world comes into view. Before the bony hand of Death all are equal, high and low; and with grotesque and mocking steps he dances away into the darkness, bearing with him those who in this world enjoyed honour and fame. This *bourgeois* satirical note finds expression chiefly in the text, whilst the pictures contrast the living and the dead,[2] making full use of the fantastical and ghostly element of the dance. The dance macabre was less well known in England than it was in France or Germany; Lydgate's main interest in the theme lay in the *Ubi Sunt* and Fortune motif, to which he was later to give expression in his magnificent historical work, *Fall of Princes*.

[1] The Selden MS. printed by Hammond (see p. 128, n. 4) of the original A group (from which the B group presumably derived) shows that Lydgate contemplated a revision with additional material, which, however, did not materialize. Some pages are lost, and the rest are bound together partly in the wrong order.

[2] The literary source is the French legend of the three dead men and the three live men (from the thirteenth century). Cf. Glixelli, *Les cinq poèmes des Trois Morts et Trois Vifs*, Paris, 1914, and Storck in *Zeitschrift für deutsche Philologie*, 42 (1910).

Chapter 17

## Henry VI's Coronation at Westminster and in Paris, and his Visit to Bury St Edmunds; Lydgate as 'Poet Laureate'

*

Lydgate had first-hand knowledge of the life of the mighty personages of the land. He probably also witnessed the coronation of the seven-year-old Henry VI at Westminster Abbey.[1] On 5th November 1429 the king rode through the streets of London, which were decorated with carpets and tapestries; with him rode his lords, clad in cloth of gold; behind him rode twenty-four newly-created knights, dressed entirely in blue, and before them the clergy, mounted and riding in rows of two. His escort was provided by the civic authorities in scarlet robes. Following the customary practice, stages were erected on which allegorical pantomimic shows were performed; of these mention is made in particular of the tower near London Bridge, packed with angels, and a small castle erected at Cheapside Cross, as well as the usual conduits flowing with wine, white and red. At Westminster Abbey on the morning of Sunday, 6th November, Cardinal Beaufort performed the coronation ceremony in the presence of all the bishops and several abbots fully robed. After he had been proclaimed by Archbishop Chichele, Henry made his way to the altar to be anointed and crowned with the great crown of St Edward. Two bishops stood by him 'helpyng hym to bere the crowne, for hyt was ovyr hevy for him, for he was of a tendyr age'.

[1] The description that follows is based on *Brut*, ed. by F. Brie, in *EETS*, 131, 136, pp. 450 f. and Gregory's *Chronicle* (Camden Soc.), L., 1876, pp. 164 ff.; cf. also M. E. Christie, *Henry VI*, L., 1922, pp. 51 f.

Catherine and her ladies-in-waiting were present at the ceremony and the subsequent banquet, when Cardinal Beaufort sat at the king's right hand. The task of giving literary adornment to the coronation festivities fell to Lydgate; indeed, it seems to have been he who was mainly responsible for the arrangements. The poem which he had written in Paris at the Earl of Warwick's command to prove Henry's hereditary claim to the English and French thrones[1] was circulated again, together with a *Roundel for the Coronation*.[2] In it he calls upon England and France to rejoice at the new scion sprung from the fleur-de-lys, in whom is joined the blood of St Edward and St Louis, and who has today been appointed by God to govern this realm. With his fanfares he seems to be trying to drown the menacing sound of the clash of arms drifting across from France. His magnificent *Coronation Ballad*,[3] by contrast, which was handed to the king, is more solemn in tone; it is spun out to form eighteen ballad stanzas, and resembles his *Prayer to the King, Queen, and People*,[4] which may also date from this period. In it the poet hails his most noble sovereign, who combines in his person the merits of the English and French saints and heroes, and to whom God has granted victory. But then his tone becomes admonitory: the king is exhorted to be firm in faith, to protect the Church, to live in concord with the great lords, and to show indulgence towards his subjects. The sonorous rolling verses suit his tone of admonition as well as they do the ostentatious eulogy; but they are followed by Scriptural and humanistic catalogues (listing Solomon, David, Samson, Joshua, Alexander, Caesar, and all the Roman emperors from Trajan to Constantine), which are tedious to us, although the ideas behind them accorded with the taste of the time. The mention of Sigismund, as a foe of the heretics, and of the present king's chivalrous father, Henry V, leads us back again from the central eulogistic part of the poem to moral exhortation. The life of Queen Catherine is held up before the young king as an ideal for him to aspire to, and in the envoy all these ethical injunctions are once again summarized: fear God and care for the Church, love peace and avoid war, show clemency and compassion towards the poor, and pay no heed to flatterers. All Lydgate's favourite ideas are woven into this eulogy; and they are

---

[1] *The Title and Pedigree of Henry VI*, cf. p. 181 f.
[2] M.P., 622; Wright, *Political Poems*, II, p. 314.
[3] *Ballade to King Henry VI his Coronation*, M.P., 624; Wright, op. cit., p. 141.
[4] M.P., 212.

emphasized in a decorative manner in the *Soteltes*[1] written for the coronation banquet. These 'subtleties' formed an artistic dessert served after each of the three courses; they are representations in miniature of the pageants staged in the streets. In both types of entertainment their allegorical and largely political significance requires elucidation. The poet has to provide on a tablet or scroll the interpretation of the significance of the small figures (in one stanza only in each case). At the festivities in Windsor in honour of the visit of the Emperor Sigismund (7th May 1416),[2] where we come across these 'soteltes' for the first time, they hardly needed any explanation: the scenes of St George girt in armour by the Virgin Mary and of St George fighting the dragon were eloquent enough as they stood, and only the scenes of the castle with St George and the king's daughter called for elucidation. At Henry V's wedding and Henry VI's coronation verses are required to explain the situation, and these are just as important as the pictorial representation itself. Those in power were anxious to present the young king as sovereign of both England and France. For this reason in the 'soteltes' the king is placed between two representatives of each nation – a device probably invented by the author. In the first 'sotelte' Henry VI appears between the royal saints, St Edward and St Louis, with the scroll above him, stating that Henry's robe shows the coats-of-arms of both kings combined. The ballad stanza beseeches God to grant that Henry may rule as wisely as his patron saints and equal them in chivalry and virtue. In the second 'sotelte' the king appears between Sigismund and Henry V, who are hailed as ideal sovereigns and enemies of heresy. The third 'sotelte' represents the Virgin Mary seated with the infant Jesus and holding a crown in her hand; beside her stand St George and St Denis, and before her kneels the young king, begging for mercy to enable him to rule justly over his two kingdoms. Both the pictorial representation and the verses repeat the ideas of the *Coronation Ballad*; both display more artificiality than art, in conformity with medieval taste.

At this time Lydgate received such an abundance of commissions and requests for poems that, with his diligence and constant readiness to oblige, he overstrained his modest talents and laid himself

---

[1] *The Soteltes at the Coronation Banquet of Henry VI*, M.P., p. 623, a version of which also appears in Fabyan's *Chronicle*; for the marriage festivities of Henry V, cf. above, p. 66 f.

[2] Gregory's *Chronicle*, op. cit., pp. 113 ff.

open to the reproach of later generations that he was a scribbler. Official commissions will have again been responsible for his ballad *On a New Year's Gift of an Eagle presented to King Henry VI*[1] and the prayer *Ab inimicis*.

The former, a ballad in ten Chaucerian stanzas, gives the impression of a poem dutifully composed by a poet laureate; it accompanied the New Year's gift of a signet ring or seal manual with an eagle carved on it, which the king was henceforth to make much use of.[2] According to a note by the scribe in the MS., it was handed over at Hertford Palace, where the king and his mother held a New Year's banquet, but there is no mention of the year (?1429). Like the majority of such poems, it is stiff and formal. The refrain, 'honnour and knighthoode, conquest and victorye', is pompous rather than genuine, and seems to have been written with one eye cast back to the reign of Henry V, for the queen-mother is referred to as though she were still the reigning Queen, and the second part of the poem, which is addressed to her, contains a refrain of its own: 'Helþe and welfare, ioye and prosparitee'. It consists of historical memoirs on the symbolic significance of the eagle, which is hailed as the king and queen of birds, and (once again looking back to Henry V and his marriage) an evocation of the peace that resulted from the alliance between England and France.

The other poem, *Ab inimicis*, or *A Prayer for King, Queen and People*,[3] generally ascribed to the coronation year 1429,[4] is more of a solemn prayer than a political document. It is a ballad in twelve Chaucerian stanzas, treating in circumlocutory fashion eight Latin petitions, which serve as the heading for each stanza; this is followed by an envoy of four stanzas, in which divine grace is invoked for Henry and his mother Catherine and the hope expressed that he

---

[1] *M.P.*, 649; Halliwell, op. cit., p. 213.

[2] Cf. the letter from Henry VI to Abbot Curteys of 17th September 1446 regarding the foundation of King's College Chapel, Cambridge: 'Yeven undir oure signet of thegle'. *Memorials of St Edmund's Abbey*, III, 247.

[3] This is the title given by MacCracken, *M.P.*, 212; O. Mahir prefers the title *Ab inimicis*; some MSS. have only one envoy stanza, and alter the dedication to Edward IV (Brown, *Index*, No. 2218).

[4] Sometimes dated 1427–8; it could have been written as early as 1425, before Catherine's marriage to Owen Tudor, because after this date Lydgate is usually content with formal phrases, whilst his tone here is more intimate. The poem says explicitly: 'And forgete nat, hys moder Kateryne, / When thou sittest in thy heuenly glorye ...'

John Lydgate

will soon be crowned king of England and France. A slightly varied refrain:

> *Kepe and preserue vnder thy myghty honde*
> *The kynge, the quene, the peple, and thy londe*

forms a link between the stanzas and the two parts of the prayer. It provides an impressive ending and enhances the effect of the gradual build-up towards the climax of the envoy, a direct invocation of God. There is nothing here of mysticism or of private devotions; in a prayer book Lydgate found some Latin verses from the *Pontificate* of Egbert:[1] '*Ab inimicis nostris defende nos Christe. Dolorem cordis nostri benignus vide. Afflictionem nostram respice clemens . . .*' – verses to which he took a fancy and which he placed before the individual stanzas as a fitting introduction to a general prayer for his king and country. The total effect is of a prayer for times of war, such as is incorporated into the Sunday service. One can quite well imagine it being said as part of a church service.

At the request of the Dean of Windsor, Lydgate also composed for the king a paraphrase of the 102nd psalm, *Benedic anima mea*,[2] generally dated to the years 1424–34. The poem comprises twenty-two eight-lined stanzas corresponding to the twenty-two verses of the psalm. In his paraphrases Lydgate is no longer content with a simple explanation. He overloads his verses with rhetorical embellishment, employing Scriptural texts like the jewelled hem of a priest's cassock.

His *Defence of Holy Church*,[3] which was presumably composed in 1431, was also addressed to a royal personage. With a great wealth of authoritative references and illustrations from the Scriptures he implores the 'most worthy Prince' to protect the Church against her enemies. This is the only theme which Lydgate champions. It is in fact not a religious poem at all, but belongs rather to Lydgate's political works.

*

[1] Archbishop of York, 732–66. His *Pontificate* is printed in *Publications of the Surtees Soc.*, vol. 27 (1853), p. 26.

[2] *M.P.*, 1; also in the more reliable edition of O. Mahir (op. cit.), who dates the poem to the years 1430–4.

[3] *M.P.*, 30, in twenty-one Chaucerian stanzas (fragmentary). Dating following Vickers, *Humphrey Duke of Gloucester*; cf. Bergen, *Fall of Princes*, vol. IV. The address fits neither the king nor Gloucester, although by its content the poem could apply to either.

[ 134 ]

In 1429, the year of the coronation, England's fortunes in France grew dimmer. On 7th May, led by Joan of Arc, the French relieved Orleans, which had been besieged since October 1428, and took captive the English commander William de la Pole, Earl of Suffolk; at Patay on 18th June they defeated and captured the English hero, John Talbot (the same man whose wife had commissioned Lydgate to write *Guy of Warwick*); then they marched through the midst of enemy-occupied territory to Rheims, where on 17th July Charles VII was anointed and crowned King of France. Preparations were even made for a march on Paris. Faced with the threat of catastrophe, Bedford turned to Cardinal Beaufort,[1] whose 'pilgrimage' consisted of sending a small army of crusaders which he had recruited at the Pope's request to Emperor Sigismund to fight the Hussites. Beaufort was willing to place 250 knights and 2500 marksmen at Bedford's disposal to save Paris from capture by the French, but the reinforcements sent to northern France had little effect. England had not only been driven from the Loire basin and a large part of the Champagne, but had also lost moral prestige. Bedford's seven-year rule had been discreet and conciliatory, and his shrewd policy of governing France through Frenchmen had made the Burgundian lay and ecclesiastical officials in Paris (always a stronghold of Burgundian influence) partisans of the English cause. The higher French clergy, too, and the University of Paris were loyal. But the general feeling was that Charles VII, who had now been crowned, would inevitably emerge victorious and that the English cause was lost. Philip of Burgundy was already in the process of coming to terms with England's enemies (armistice with Charles), and England sought to retain her alliance with Burgundy by ceding Champagne and Picardy. Joan of Arc's successes made it necessary for the English to transfer their headquarters from Paris to Rouen. Bedford now hoped that Henry's presence could offset the growing prestige of Charles VII in northern France. He wanted Henry to be solemnly crowned, if not in Rheims, then at least in Paris, with all ceremony,

---

[1] Henry Beaufort had renounced the post of chancellor in favour of Bedford (in order to make a concession to Humphrey), and Bedford had to allow him to take his Cardinal's hat, which Henry V had formerly refused to do. On the Day of the Annunciation of the Virgin (25th March) he was invested in St Mary's Church in Calais. Thus Henry Beaufort for the time being was removed from English politics, and since Henry's brother Thomas Beaufort, Duke of Exeter, also died in 1427 – he was buried in the Lady Chapel in Bury St Edmunds in accordance with his wish – the leadership of the constitutional party passed to other hands.

in accordance with French custom. Thus on St George's Day 1430 Henry VI crossed the Channel with a splendid suite. The hopes which Lydgate had expressed in his *Mumming at Windsor* and *Ab inimicis*, that Henry should be crowned king of France, were about to be fulfilled. However, Henry was obliged to delay for three months in Calais. During this time Joan of Arc was taken prisoner at Compiègne (23rd May 1430) and handed over by the Burgundians to the English. During the lengthy proceedings the king stayed in Rouen with his suite. It was here, in the market square on 29th May 1431, that the freedom-loving heroine was burnt at the stake. This was the only political mistake which Bedford committed, and the only blot on his reputation as a humane statesman.

About half a year later the ten-year-old king, accompanied by Bedford and Warwick and guarded by a large levy of troops, left for his coronation in Paris. His entry[1] into the capital on 2nd December was marked by great pomp and ceremony. Outside the city he was welcomed by the mayor, wearing a blue velvet robe, the chamberlain with his retinue clad in violet costumes and scarlet caps, and the president and members of Parliament, wearing red cloaks trimmed with fur. At the gate of St Denis the royal party were greeted by an enormous coat-of-arms with golden lilies on a blue field. The king was offered blood-red hearts from which white doves flew upwards, and a rain of flowers descended upon the procession. In the gateway the king was placed beneath a canopy embroidered with lilies and carried into the city on the shafts of lances by six men dressed in blue. Paris was decorated more gaily and more tastefully than was customary in London; in addition to conduits of wine and houses embellished with tapestries and draperies there were welcoming pageants and allegorical performances.

These pageants must be seen in conjunction with the mummings and similar pictorial representations which were provided by Lydgate with poetic accompaniment, as well as the pageants at king's entries in London. The cavalcade of the Goddess of Fame with her '*neuf preux*' and '*neuf preues*', which through a herald welcomed King Henry, has even been regarded as the direct prototype of the 'king's entry' into London (1432), and from this it has been assumed that

---

[1] Cf. the accounts in *The Chronicles of Enguerrand de Monstrelet*, tr. by Thomas Johnes, L., 1810, VII, 46 ff.; and *Journal d'un bourgeois de Paris*, pp. 248 ff.; also Withington, *English Pageantry*, I, 138 ff.

Lydgate was present when Henry entered Paris.[1] In any case the poet derived a lasting impression from such pageants, which were common in France at the time. *Tableaux vivants*, mostly with Scriptural themes, are known to have been performed at festivities and royal receptions in Paris as early as 1313.[2] In that year, when Philip the Fair gave a feast for Edward II of England and his consort Isabeau, the Passion was represented; in 1378 Charles V witnessed a rendering of the capture of Jerusalem. Froissart mentions pantomimes being performed at the entry of Isabeau of Bavaria, and the Bourgeois de Paris speaks of a '*moult bel mystère du Vieil Testament et du Nouvel, que les enffens de Paris firent, et fut fait sans parler*', performed at Bedford's entry on 8th September 1424.

The setting of these dramatic scenes was often based on sculptural works; in this way the Passion performed at the entry of Charles VI and Henry V of England into Paris took as its model the relief in the choir of Notre-Dame, which was rendered '*au vif*' upon a stage 100 feet long. For Henry VI's entry the themes of these *tableaux vivants* were much more diversified, but the emphasis was still on the pictorial element, and, in contrast to Lydgate's 'soteltes' and pageants, are intelligible without words. This applies to the forest erected in the street in front of the Church of the Innocents, through which, when the king arrived, a live stag was hunted, as well as to the performance of religious scenes, from the life of the Virgin Mary and the legendary tale of St Denis; it also applies to the political *tableau vivant* which portrayed Henry wearing both his crowns, flanked on one hand by the Duke of Burgundy and the Count of Nevers, who offered him the fleur-de-lys banner, and on the other by the Duke of Bedford and the Earls of Warwick and Salisbury, who bore the English coat-of-arms.

Like the Parisians, who thronged the streets and crowded at the windows in their eagerness to witness the spectacle, so also Isabeau, Charles VI's widow, surrounded by her ladies-in-waiting, looked on from the window of the Hotel Saint-Paul; and when the young king touched his hat to his grandmother as he rode past, she bowed her

---

[1] MacCracken in *Archiv.* 126, p. 99. For a contrary view, see Withington, I, 140. Brusendorff says that Lydgate took the figure of the goddess Fame from the *Roman de la Rose*, which shows that the allegory is of literary origin, as Withington suggests.

[2] On the following, cf. Gröber-Hofer, *Geschichte der mittelfranzösischen Literatur*, I, Berlin, 1933 (Grundriss der roman. Phil., N.F.), p. 166, and L. Petit de Juleville, *Les mystères*, Paris, 1880, I, 197 f.

head and turned away in tears.[1] The festive show was a mere façade. In Henry's suite there were scarcely any French or Burgundian noblemen to be seen. The civic and university authorities were obliged to attend the reception, but at the coronation at Notre-Dame on Sunday, 16th December, the officiating dignitaries were English, and instead of a French prelate it was Cardinal Beaufort who placed upon the king's head the crown (which, incidentally, had been brought from England). The ensuing banquet in the palace, in which the populace was to have participated, proved a disappointment, because the people crowded around too closely in their eagerness to secure a morsel, and because the meat had been cooked on the previous Thursday, which did not appeal to the French palate. The small size of the tournament seems to have provoked uninhibited criticism from the Parisians, although the Bourgeois excuses its brevity and economy by reason of the early onset of dusk and the winter cold.[2] The king returned to Rouen already on 26th December without having declared the amnesty that had been expected, and in February 1432, after having spent almost two years in France, he made his way to England.

*

If Lydgate, as we assume, was again in England from 1429 onwards, during the king's absence he will have stayed either at Hatfield or at Bury St Edmunds. The monastery experienced an important event in its history during 1429. Abbot William of Exeter died and was succeeded by William Curteys, a distinguished man whose abbotcy (1429–46) once again – and this not long before the outbreak of the Wars of the Roses – brought the power, wealth, and influence of his monastery to bear upon English domestic and foreign policy.[3] The energy with which Abbot Curteys took the administration of his monastery in hand is revealed by an order which he issued for more care to be taken in maintaining the library,[4] and by the restoration work which he undertook in the abbey. In 1430 the abbey was stricken by a major calamity; on 18th December of that year the

---

[1] *Journal d'un bourgeois*, p. 251.　　　　[2] Ibid., p. 253.

[3] There is no biography of Curteys.

[4] 'He issued an ordinance in which he declared books given out by the precentor to the brethren for the purposes of study had been lent, pledged, and even stolen by them. Some of them he had recovered and he hoped to recover more, but the process of recovery had been expensive and troublesome, both to himself and the people he found in possession of the books. He therefore sternly forbade the brethren to alienate books.' (E. A. Savage, *Old English Libraries*, 1911, pp. 61 f.)

south side of the great belfry, the so-called West Tower, collapsed, and in the following year the east side suffered the same fate. Curteys' *Registrum* assumes that the cause of this accident was either negligence on the part of the previous architect or vibration from the ringing of the bells (for there were nine bells in this tower). In the course of 1432 Curteys had the north and west sides of the campanile pulled down and obtained from Rome a free pardon for all who contributed towards the cost of reconstruction.[1] The new building, although it was not completed until a late date, must have been a noteworthy monument in the Perpendicular style.

During these years Lydgate slowly resumed his former way of life. He had a great task ahead of him: the translation of Boccaccio's *De casibus*,[2] commissioned by Humphrey of Gloucester. When Henry V, then Prince of Wales, had urged him to write the *Troy Book*, he had been faced with a task which only allowed him to make occasional comments – in the margin, so to speak – upon contemporary affairs. Now that he was armed with direct experience of events at home and abroad, he could turn a work concerned with the fate of great men into something more than pure entertainment. The historical theme offered him an opportunity to revive the once-flourishing tradition of monastic historiography, which was now cultivated only in a few Benedictine monasteries, such as St Albans, and had lost most of its former universality of outlook. This work was to occupy Lydgate over the next eight years, and was undoubtedly promoted to the best of his abilities by Abbot Curteys. For the monastery itself Lydgate may have composed at this time the *Kalendare*[3] and other religious poems. In his *A Defence of Holy Church*,[4] as we have seen, he invokes for the Church the protection of the secular power.

In 1432 Lydgate was charged with the responsibility for the official welcome given to the king on his return from France. If the coronation in Paris had been ineffective, then the reception in London had to be all the more pompous by contrast. The civic authorities entrusted the most distinguished poet of the day with the composition of a poem of welcome, *Pur le roy*. Apparently Lydgate was responsible not only for this poem, but also for devising and planning the tableaux and scenes described in these seventy-seven Chaucerian stanzas.[5] Lydgate seemed particularly well qualified for this task, for

---

[1] Such free pardons are mentioned as late as 1500.
[2] *Fall of Princes*, see Chapter 21.     [3] See pp. 174 f.     [4] See p. 134.
[5] Kingsford, *Chronicles of London*, Oxford, 1905, pp. xxv, 301.

monastic seclusion had not weakened his grasp of secular affairs. Three years prior to this event, at Henry's coronation at Westminster, his close connexions with the court had led him to write a 'ballade' entitled *Moost noble prynce of Cristin prynces alle*. During his sojourn in Paris the monk of Bury had been a court and political poet, and in his mummings had already revealed his talents as a 'master of the revels'. Such festivities, with their pageants and the descriptive or dramatic verses that accompanied them, are a feature of the contemporary scene. They are reported in detail in all the chronicles of the time,[1] and the description here is supplemented by the information contained in the new literary genre of 'king's entries'.

Lydgate had been present in person at many of these colourful pageants: at the reception of Henry V after the victory at Agincourt,[2] at the entry of Queen Catherine of Valois in 1421,[3] at the funeral procession that had brought Henry V's body back to London, and at the coronation of the young King Henry VI in 1429. On these occasions he had to stay in London, and will have resided at the beautiful town house known as 'Buries Markes' (now Bevis Marks)[4] in St Mary Axe, which belonged to the monastery.

In contrast to the reception in Paris, which was more dramatic and pictorial, in his London king's entry Lydgate lays emphasis upon allegory and makes supplementary use of the spoken word. One might regard this as a deliberate contrast; for the author of the reception in London is thought to have been an eye-witness of that in Paris. MacCracken concludes, on the basis of Carpenter's letter, that Lydgate stayed in France until Henry's coronation in Paris, and only returned with the king's suite; in my view this is an unwarranted assumption. For John Carpenter, the town clerk, who was a friend of Lydgate's and who had had the cloister painted with the dance macabre pictures, has also given in a letter an exact description of

---

[1] F. J. Starke, *Populäre englische Chroniken des 15. Jh.*, Berlin, 1935; C. L. Kingsford, *English Historical Literature in the 15th Century*, Oxford, 1913; R. Fabyan's *Chronicle*, ed. by H. Ellis, L., 1811; *The Great Chronicle of London*, ed. by A. H. Thomas and J. D. Thornley, L., 1939; *Chronicles of London*, ed. by C. L. Kingsford, Oxford, 1905; *Brut*, ed. by F. Brie, op. cit.

[2] Cf. *Gesta Henrici Quinti*, op. cit., pp. 60–7; *The First English Life of Henry V*, ed. by Kingsford, Oxford, 1911, pp. 156 ff.

[3] *Gesta Henrici Quinti*, pp. 297 ff.

[4] Bevis Marks, in Aldgate Ward: town residence of the abbots of Bury. It is described by Stow (*Survey of London*, ed. Kingsford, II, 73): 'One great house, large of rooms, fair courts and garden plots, sometime pertaining to the Bassets, since that to the abbots of Bury in Suffolk, and is called Buries Markes, corruptly Bevis Marks.'

Henry's entry into London,[1] and this letter is regarded by Mac-Cracken as the source for Lydgate's *Pur le Roy*. But allegory plays a major role in these verses and pageants at Henry's entry, and it is in the introduction of the allegorical element (in the mummings and king's entries) that Lydgate's great achievement lies. As a literary work it is little to our taste, but as a document of social history it can convey an impression of the life of the time.

*King Henry VI's [triumphal] Entry into London*[2] commences in the traditional way, with the season of the year being determined by the stars, and then passes on to the actual account: as joyfully as Jerusalem heard the news of King David's victory, so does London receive its king. The Lord Mayor and aldermen are mounted on horseback, clad in red ceremonial robes. The citizens have chosen white as a symbol of their sincere feelings toward their king (already here there is an element of allegory!). Genoese, Florentines, Venetians, and men from the Hanseatic towns, dressed in their native costumes, have all arrived for the ceremony. At Blackheath they wait for the king, and after an address of welcome (interpolated in prose) delivered by the mayor, John Welles, the procession sets out for London. At London Bridge is the first of the seven 'stations' that have been erected: a mighty giant, on whom there is an inscription announcing that he will protect the king against all his foreign foes. Next to the giant are antelopes bearing the coats-of-arms of England and France. At the second pageant, in the middle of the bridge, homage is paid to the king from a tower by three empresses adorned with golden crowns and precious gems: Nature, Grace (virtue), and Happiness (ffortune). Grace presents him with knowledge (sciens) and prudence (kunnyng), Nature with strength and beauty, Happiness with prosperity and riches. This, too, is indicated by large inscriptions, 'able to be redde with oute a spektakle'.[3] To their right the empresses have seven virgins in white garments decorated with symbols of the sun, who offer the king white doves as a gift from the Holy Ghost: strength, advice, prudence, fear, compassion, and

[1] Printed in Riley's *Munimenta Gildhallae*, III (Rolls Series), 457–64. MacCracken (*Archiv*, 126, pp. 75 ff.) sees in this letter not an official account (as Kingsford does), but a private letter to Lydgate. The parallels between the letter and Lydgate's poem, which MacCracken emphasizes, are not so striking when one considers that they relate to a description of what actually occurred. The identical wording is found only in the inscriptions on the individual pageants.

[2] *M.P.*, 630; *Chronicles of London*, ed. Kingsford, pp. 97 ff.; Halliwell, op. cit., pp. 1 ff.; H. Nicolas, *Chronicle of London*, 1827 (on this work, cf. Schleich, in *Archiv*, 96, p. 191).

[3] London Chronicle, Cotton Julius B II.

humility. To their left are seven more virgins in robes studded with stars. Greeting the king with words of welcome and a sung roundel, they present him with the crown of glory, the sceptre of purity and compassion, the sword of power and victory, the cloak of prudence, the shield of faith, the helmet of health, and the girdle of love and peace. The third scene is erected in Cornhill. It is a tabernacle of wisdom, in front of which stand the seven liberal arts, personified, in accordance with the humanistic practice of which Lydgate and his contemporaries were so fond, by figures drawn from antiquity: grammar by Priscian, logic by Aristotle, rhetoric by Cicero, music by Boethius, arithmetic by Pythagoras, geometry by Euclid, and astronomy by Albunisar. Not far from this *tableau vivant*, which is briefly explained to the king by the figure of wisdom, is the fourth pageant, erected at the conduit in Cornhill: seated upon a throne is a child dressed as a king, for whose education three women are appointed – Mercy, Truth, and Purity – and two judges with eight jurists. The significance of this scene is further emphasized by allusions to the Scriptures. In Cheapside, at the great well (there is a play on words here with the name of the mayor, John Welles), there is another pageant in honour of the mayor. This fifth scene represents an earthly paradise. Trees offer all manner of English and foreign fruit, and the conduit provides a choice of various kinds of wine, which are handed to the king by the virgins Mercy, Virtue, and Compassion. Lydgate does not fail to incorporate the fountain of wine, always a feature of these receptions, but adds a few humanistic names and the explanation that this is the wine of moderation, good conduct, and consolation. At this conduit Enoch and Elias pray for the king's salvation, their prayer being given in direct speech.

The procession now moves on to the sixth scene, at the cross in Cheapside: a castle built of green jasper and decorated with the coats-of-arms of England and France, Henry's 'pedigree' and the genealogical tree of Jesus, a symbolical representation of Henry VI's claim to both kingdoms, enhanced by its elevated religious connotation. Finally, the procession reaches the seventh scene, at the small conduit by the entrance to St Paul's churchyard, which represents the Holy Trinity. Angels carry a text announcing to everyone that they wish to protect the king from harm and to spread his fame. May he be blessed with joy and abundance, many years of good health, numerous progeny, the love of his people, and the goodwill of foreigners; may peace, tranquillity, and harmony prevail in both his realms. In front of St Paul's he is welcomed by the higher clergy, the archbishop and a number of bishops who are listed by name; then he is escorted by the Lord Mayor to Westminster, where, to the chiming of all the bells and the singing of the *Te Deum*, the abbot, surrounded by his monks, hands over St Edward's sceptre. This brings to a close the ceremony of the first day, Thursday, 21st February – or 14th February, according to other sources, a date which tallies better with Lydgate's work. On the following Saturday the Lord Mayor and aldermen present the king with £1,000 in gold as a gift from the City, together with an address (in prose). The work ends with a proud eulogy of London, the New Troy, city of all cities.

Owing to the large number of titles and names inserted, the metre is uneven.[1] The poem cannot be judged by modern criteria; it must be seen only in conjunction with the historical poetry of the day, such as the *Siege of Rouen*, and historical works of literary merit, and also against the background of the origins of the drama, in which Lydgate played a part with his mummings. His *Pur le roy* is a great step forward; the element of allegory becomes predominant,[2] and the words more important than the scene. After Lydgate's 'king's entries' these pageants develop from mere spectacle into a succession of addresses, a process which is completed at the wedding of Arthur and Catherine of Spain in 1501; the dumb figures here give place to actors who speak their roles, expressing their own volition and the meaning of the drama in a particular kind of verse. Another innovation in Lydgate's entry is the ornamental element drawn from antiquity in the figures of the seven liberal arts, which was to play a major part in the 'triumphs' of the Renaissance.

\*

The magnificent reception given to Henry in London had a deeper meaning in that the nation now transferred its interest from foreign conquests to security at home. In France the situation deteriorated further as the bonds between England and Burgundy became looser. In 1433, in the vain hope of cementing the alliance, Bedford had married (on the death of his first wife, sister of Duke Philip of

---

[1] Saintsbury cites stanza 67 as an example of his 'shambling metre' (*History of English Prosody*, L., 1923, I, 224).

[2] R. Withington, *English Pageants*, op. cit., I, xvii f., 80: 'What may be called the body of pageantry is the cars, but a procession of cars is only a corpse. The allegory or symbolism or history which the living characters bring, may be called the soul of pageantry.'

Burgundy) Jacqueline of Luxembourg, who was related to the house of Burgundy. True to the promise he had made to Henry V, Bedford still sought to hold on to France, but consented to remain in England until July 1434 as 'chief of the king's council'. Within the Regency Council a change had taken place from a conciliar to a curial system; the king was given a clerk of the council, whose function it was to maintain liaison between the central administration and the court; but under Adam Moleyns (1438) this office became identical with that of plenipotentiary secretary to the king, who often acted on his own under the minister in power. Thus the council became a purely consultative body, which met far removed from the court and maintained contact with the king only through his ministers. The king, for his part, consciously or unconsciously, became a willing tool of the minister in power, i.e., first of Beaufort and then of Suffolk. Henry VI's character is a controversial subject.[1] His interests were ecclesiastical and academic; matters of state interested him less than the canonization of Osmund and King Alfred, the prosperity of his foundations at Eton and Cambridge, and the promotion of grammar schools. Temperamentally he was well fitted, as his father and grandfather had never been, to establish the court as a centre of literature. Polydori Virgilio testifies to his 'liberal mind'. But he was a recluse who all his life loved monastic calm and seclusion. '*Vir simplex et rectus*' is the verdict of his chaplain and private secretary, John Blackman; he was a man who could endure with ease the longest church services, who disapproved of his nobles bringing their swords into church; pacific, chaste, charitable, averse to all luxury in clothing and angry only when there was an attack upon the authority of the Church or the Pope.[2] He was a man after Lydgate's own heart. He is said to have enjoyed his frequent stays in Bury St Edmunds '*propter aquarum ibidem adhaerentium dulces meatus . . . aerem salubrem et vineae odorem delectabilem*'.[3] There is probably some truth in the story that during his visit to Bury in 1433 the council suggested to the abbot that he should detain him there for a longer period – although this wish may have also sprung from concern for the king's health: that summer the plague raged so fiercely that the Parliament which

[1] F. A. Gasquet, *The Religious Life of Henry VI*, L., 1923.

[2] When opposition was expressed in Basle to the Papal bulls of Eugenius IV which in 1437 declared the Council of Basle terminated and transferred it to Ferrara, the king wrote imploring letters (*Correspondence of Thom. Beckynton*, Rolls Series).

[3] According to Curteys' *Registrum* (B.M. MS. Add. 7096 and 14,848), printed in *Archaeologia*, XV, 65 ff.

the king had opened in person on 12th May had to be adjourned, and after subsiding for a short time a second wave of the epidemic broke out during the winter.

On All Saints' Day 1433 Henry VI announced his intention of spending Christmas at St Edmunds.[1] At that time Abbot Curteys was at Elmeswell, where the monastery possessed some oak forests; he hastened back and ordered eighty stonemasons to enlarge and improve the abbot's house. He made arrangements with the mayor for a procession of 500 citizens, headed by the aldermen, to go to welcome the king. On Christmas Eve they waited for him on Newmarket Heath to escort him to Bury. The approach to the abbey was made from the south (the west side being dangerous on account of the possibility that stones might fall from the belfry, which had collapsed). When they entered the monastery precincts the great bronze doors of the abbey opened and some sixty to seventy monks came out, wearing costly surplices over their habit, preceded by men holding candles and bearing the crucifix. The monks stepped aside, and the abbot appeared in all his vestments, and next to him Bishop Alnwick of Norwich, who had come to welcome the king. Henry, then twelve years old, was dismounted by his tutor, Richard de Beauchamp, Earl of Warwick; he knelt down on a silk cloth, and the abbot sprinkled him with holy water and held out the crucifix for him to kiss. Then the procession moved into the church to the High Altar, singing the hymn *Ave rex gentis Anglorum* from the *Officium Sancti Edmundi*. The king prayed for a while at the shrine of St Edmund and subsequently made his way to the abbot's house.[2]

The king's stay lasted from Christmas Eve 1433 until St George's Day (23rd April) 1434. The presence of such an honoured guest meant that there was something in the nature of a royal court at Bury to disturb the monastery's tranquillity. At first the king stayed at the abbot's house, but after Epiphany moved to the house of the prior, not far from the east end of the church, in order to be closer to the vineyard overlooking the Lark and the open country beyond. Still farther to the east the courtiers hunted foxes and hares in the woods and meadows. Occasionally the king, too, participated in this

---

[1] Dudgale's *Monasticon*, III, 113 f., following Curteys' *Registrum*. The account is in *Memorials of St Edmunds*, again following the *Registrum*. Some additional details in F. A. Gasquet, *Greater Abbeys of England*, L., 1908, pp. 52 ff.

[2] For Lydgate's views on this visit by Henry VI, cf. *Life of St Edmund*, ed. Horstmann, *Altenglische Legenden*, 1881, lines 137 ff.

'mild kind of hunting'. On 23rd January the Court went to Elm(e)s-well, and passed the time until the festival of the Purification of the Virgin Mary in fishing and falconry. Lent was spent by Henry VI in the prior's house. He took part in all the ceremonies of Passion Week and Eastertide, acquainting himself with every part of the monastery. On Easter Tuesday, when the time fixed for his departure had come, Henry VI, the Countess of Warwick, the Duke of Glou-cester, and other members of his suite were admitted to share the religious privileges of the monks. This was a ceremony of the ut-most solemnity: the king prostrated himself before the shrine of St Edmund, followed by the Duke of Gloucester, the Earl of Warwick, and other members of his suite. Then they repaired to the chapter-house, where before the assembled monks the king publicly re-quested admission to their brotherhood, and from the abbot received the fraternal kiss. Finally, at a sign from his uncle Humphrey, the king gratefully took his leave; he shook hands with Curteys, and 'gleefully and gladly thanked him again and again'. He kept up his ties with St. Edmunds for the remainder of his days. Abbot Curteys requested Lydgate to write for the king a *vita* in verse of the founder of the monastery. The dedication copy (Harl. 2278) is a magnificent manuscript with illuminated letters, 120 carefully executed pictures, two portraits of King Henry and one of the poet himself kneeling before the shrine of St Edmund and presenting his work to the king (cf. Plate).

Ꝑ that whylom dyd his diligence
the book of Bochas in frenssh to translate
Out of latyn / he callyd was Laurence
this tyme twoofh remembryd / and the date
yeer Whan Kyng John thorugh his mortal ffate
Was prysonner brought to this Regioun
Whanne he first gan on this translacioun

In his prologe affermyng of resoun
Artificers havyng exercyses
may chaunge and tourne by good discrecioun
Shappys ffournyys / and newly hem devyse
make and vnmake in many sondry Wyse
As potterys which to that crafft entende
Breke and renewe ther vesselys to Amende

Thus men of crafft may of Dewe ryght
That been in Wyttyff / and have excercence
ffantasyen in ther inward sight
Devysys newe thorugh ther excellence
Expert maystrys han ther to lycence
ffro good to bettre for to chaunge a thyng
And semblably this auctorys in Wrytyng

8. Lydgate presenting King Henry VI with his *Lives of SS. Edmund and Fremund* in the Abbey Church at Bury, in the presence of Abbot William Curteys

PART III

PART III

## Chapter 18

### Lydgate's Saints' Legends

*

Lydgate's legends[1] play an important part in the history of this literary genre – if, indeed, legends can be regarded as literature, since
they developed out of Scriptural readings and sermons and have an
exclusively edifying and didactic purpose. The two collections of
legends compiled respectively in the south of England (Gloucester)
and the north of England (Durham) in the late thirteenth and towards the middle of the fourteenth century[2] are designed purely for
use in church. The compilers of these legends have little ambition to
create works of art; they desire only to relate the story of some holy
miracle. To fulfil this purpose they had no need of rhetoric, or of a
pompous introductory *invocatio*, of elevated epithets or learned explanations of the names referred to;[3] for them it was sufficient simply
to follow their sources. These legends, in which one may include
Barbour's collection, dating from the late fourteenth-century,[4] are
mostly written anonymously and have a non-literary character. This

---

[1] H. Quistorp, *Studien zu Lydgates Heiligenlegenden*, Diss. (unpublished), Bonn, 1951.

[2] Cf. the authoritative editions by C. Horstmann, *Altenglische Legenden*, Paderborn,
1875; *Sammlung altenglischer Legenden*, Heilbronn, 1878; *Altenglische Legenden, Neue Folge*,
Heilbronn, 1881. Also *Early South English Legendary*, L., 1887 (*EETS*, OS. 87); *The South
English Legendary*, 1956–60 (*EETS*, OS. 235, 236, 244); *Minor Poems of the Vernon MS.*, L.,
1892 (*EETS*, OS. 98). In Horstmann's introductions (esp. in the 1881 volume) is a
survey and outline history of legend-writing. Most recent study: Th. Wolpers, *Die
englische Heiligenlegende des Mittelalters*, Tübingen, 1961 (awaiting publication).

[3] These so-called *Etymologiae* or *Interpretationes nominum* (cf. Curtius, op. cit., pp. 488 f.)
play a greater part in Latin legend-writing (*Legenda Aurea*).

[4] They resemble one another in their objective narrative, simple diction, and unpretentious verse (short couplets), but not in their prologues (omitted, no doubt, in
ecclesiastical usage), which, like the occasional interpretations of names, foreshadow
Lydgate.

tradition of legend-writing continues to live on after Lydgate's death without his works having exercised any noticeable influence on it; just as the popular romances lived on after Chaucer as though his tales had never been written.

In addition to this popular form of legend, which was adopted by the Church from the last quarter of the thirteenth century onwards and which in Lydgate's day was still read out in place of the *lectio* at the festivals of the martyrs, there also developed a literary type of legend, catering for the tastes of a more cultured reading public; though no longer designed for use at divine service, it had not lost its religious content and thus did not seek to satisfy purely aesthetic demands. Among the several legends that paved the way for Lydgate a prominent place is occupied by Chaucer's *Seconde Nonnes Tale* and the miracle of the Virgin Mary in his *Prioresses Tale*.[1] These introduce the Chaucerian stanza in legend-writing and are the first legends in English to be written with a rhetorical flourish. They begin with invocations of God and the Virgin (in the case of the *Seconde Nonnes Tale* there is also a *propositio*), are embellished with explanations of the names referred to, and rendered impressive by interruptions on the part of the fictitious narrator, emotional epithets and ejaculations to show his interest in the story. These represent a new phase in the history of the verse legend which Lydgate took up and developed further. He is the most celebrated fifteenth-century practitioner in this genre.[2]

His legends begin and end with passages of epic scope. But where his later legends dedicated to St Edmund and St Alban have a heroic theme, his first, *The Life of Our Lady*,[3] depicts everyday life, for which a simple unpretentious narrative would have been more appropriate. In this work, commissioned by Henry V[4] and written between 1409 and 1411,[5] he shows his epic ambition by his elevated

---

[1] The Tales of the Man of Law and the Clerk could also be considered in this connection. They do not, it is true, tell of miracles, but only of withstanding trouble and distress. Like the legends, they are written in Chaucerian stanzas, which are reserved to these themes in the *Canterbury Tales*.

[2] G. H. Gerould, *Saints' Legends*, Boston–N.Y., 1916, p. 256.

[3] *The Life of Our Lady*. Part I, ed. by Ch. E. Tame in *Early Religious Literature*, L., n.d. [1871]. Part II is not contained in Tame's edition and must be read in the very old edition of 1531 (printed in London by Robert Redman: B.M., press-mark G 1122); cf. *Anglia*, XV, 291.

[4] Compilid . . . at the excitation and sterying of oure worshipful prynce Kyng Harry the Fifthe.'

[5] Dating according to Schick, in introduction to *The Temple of Glas*, p. cxii.

style, the wealth of sources consulted,[1] and the volume of the work. With its 6000 lines, it is the most complete life of the Virgin in English – more striking than Gower's attempt in French, which to our eyes seems more attractive.[2] Lydgate, it must be admitted, treats the theme in worthy manner, adopting an elevated tone of pious reverence. The popularity which his work attained is shown by the fact that forty manuscript copies have survived, as well as printed editions by Caxton and Redman. It is, however, not a *vita* and not an organic unity, despite its formal arrangement into four Books; it is rather a mosaic, a combination, swollen to epic proportions, of hymns, prayers, sermons, fragments of narrative, didactic digressions, and detailed descriptions – as is shown by the headings of its eighty-two chapters. Lydgate's conception of the legend is made plain by the fact that he adopts the thoroughly homiletic parts of the *Legenda Aurea* in his didactic digressions, with the object of enhancing the edifying effect.

A brief analysis may help to illustrate Lydgate's approach. The subject-matter, which in itself is not rich, is condensed to seven main points, which are not so much related as paraphrased: (1) the wedding of Joseph and Mary; (2) the Annunciation by Gabriel; (3) the argument between Joseph and Mary. This forms the content of the first two Books; the last two are more in the nature of a *vita* of Christ than of Mary, and contain the following main points: (1) the birth of Our Lord, which takes up almost one-third of the whole legend;[3] (2) the Circumcision; (3) the Three Kings; (4) the Presentation in the Temple.

As a prelude to the wedding of Joseph and Mary there is a prologue extolling the star of Jacob, and then three chapters in praise of Mary. The strange method adopted of restricting the whole narrative to a brief factual account, only a few lines long, can be explained by the large amount of space taken up by Lydgate's almost dithyrambic style. His aim is not to entertain but to extol, not to emphasize the human characteristics of the Mother of God but rather her supernatural majesty. His life of the Virgin, unlike any other legend, is an expression of his own personal piety; the prayers which he interpolates have no equivalent in the sources. His praise

---

[1] Mostly from the *Legenda Aurea*, from a Life of the Virgin Mary based upon the apocryphal Greek *Protevangelium* of James, from John of Salisbury's *Polychronicon*, and many other works.

[2] *Mirour de l'omme*, 27,480–29,945; in Gower's *Works*, ed. Macaulay, I, 305–34.

[3] 256 stanzas out of 832 (stanzas 375–631).

of the Mother of God, whom he invests with a halo, and his extolling of the Incarnation are among the finest pieces of poetry he
wrote in this field. Here we already find the invocatory style[1] which
he was to take to an extreme in his later religious lyrics.[2] With this
style the prayers are integrated naturally (for the first time in
Chapter 5: a modification of the Lord's Prayer).[3]

With the wedding of Joseph and Mary a little more narrative is introduced, only to be followed immediately by a hymn in praise of
chastity[4] and a lengthy dispute between Mercy, Peace, Righteous-
ness, and Truth on the redemption of man.[5] After an interval of
about sixty stanzas, Chapter 16 resumes the hagiographical narrative
with an account of the Annunciation by Gabriel, but it is then en-
cumbered by verses of praise. The reader who expects to find a *vita*
is taken aback, but must allow that these parts show Lydgate's
mastery of language at its best. He can treat this delicate subject with
great sensibility. He gives it charm and freshness by interpolating
images drawn from nature. These parallels with nature, which in
Lydgate's other legends often give an impression of conventional-
ity, illustrate in a gentle and lyrical manner the miracle of the Incarnation of the Word.[6] His somewhat ill-contrived introduction of

---

[1] Or 'apostrophic hymn style' (Tilgner).

[2] Cf., for instance, stanzas 50 ff. ('Sterre of the sea, and Goddys owne ancylle Quene of
this worlde, al weie of oon entent . . .', etc.) with the *Ballade at the Reverence of Our Lady*.

[3] Stanzas 64–76.  [4] Stanzas 118–27.

[5] This is the well-known allegory of the Four Daughters of God, which goes back to
St Bernard. This theme was made familiar to the English public by Nicholas Love in
his excellent English prose translation (1410) of the *Speculum Vitae Christi* (following
Bonaventura's *Meditationes Vitae Christi*). Cf. H. Traver, *The Four Daughters of God*,
op. cit. (p. 120 n. 1).

[6] The stanzas following the Annunciation of Gabriel may be considered the lyrical
climax of *The Life of Oure Lady*. (Since there is no modern edition available, I quote
chap. 19, stanzas 202, 205 ff.):

> 202 *And whan the aungel fro her departyd was*
> *And she allone in her tabernacle*
> *Rigt as the sune percith thourg the glas*
> *Thourg the cristal birell of spectacle*
> *Withouten harme, rigt so bi miracle*
> *In to her closet the faders sapience*
> *Entrid ys withouten violence*

> 205 *For alle the tresour of his sapience*
> *And alle the wisdome of hevene and erthe ther to*
> *And all the richnesse of spiritual science*
> *In her were shitte and closid eke also*

miraculous explanations for the Virgin Birth[1] seem to have appealed to the taste of his time. For this reason the entire main point (3) – the argument between Mary and Joseph, who is unable to comprehend the idea of *conceptio virginalis* – can be understood only when seen in the light of the age in which the work was written.[2] The part dealing with the life of the Virgin is brought to a close by a dignified prayer.[3]

The second half, dealing with the birth and youth of Christ, is at first a paraphrase of the Gospel story. After recounting Augustus' order and the birth at Bethlehem, he interpolates a prayer by Mary[4] and a retrospective glance at the Prophets, which he follows with the scene of the shepherds watching their flocks by night,[5] doing

> For she is the toure, withoute wordys mo
> And house of ivor in wiche Salomon
> Shitte alle his tresour in his possession

> 206  She was the castelle eke of the cristalle walle
> That never man mygt yit unclose
> In wiche the kyng that made and causeth alle
> His dwellyng chefe by grace gan dispose
> And liche as dewe dissendith on the roose
> With silver droppis, and of the leves faire
> The fresshe beaute ne may nogt appeire

> 207  Ne as the rayne in April or in May
> Causeth the vertue to renne oute of the roote
> The grete fairnesse ne appeire may
> On violettys and on herbis soote
> Rigt so this grace of alle oure grevous boote
> The grace of God amydde the lely white
> The beaute causeth to be of more delite

> 208  And as the cockle with hevenly dewe so clene
> Of kynde engendreth white peerlys rownde
> And hathe noo cherisshyng but the sune shene
> To his fostryng, as it is plainly founde.
> Rigt so this maide of grace moste abounde
> A peerle hathe closid with in her brestys white
> That from the dethe mygt alle oure raunson quyte

[1] Stanzas 221–60.  [2] Stanzas 293–368.
[3] Stanzas 345–50.  [4] Stanzas 410–15.
[5] Cf. the stanza:

> O mighty lorde we prayse and blesse the
> And worship eke with humble reuerence
> And glorifye thyne high mageste
> And thankinge gyue to thy magnyficence
> For thy glorie and thyne excellence
> O thou lord god o kynge celestiall
> O God thy father moste myghty founde at all.

justice to the theme of the Virgin by comparing her to a pomegranate,[1] eulogizing her[2] and paying homage to her in invocatory style.[3] Between these hymns to Mary are inserted accounts of miracles: the collapse of the temple in Rome and the drying-up of the wells, the attitude of the Roman Senate and the prophecy by Sibyl, the predictions by the prophets of Israel, and much else besides. After this long interruption the hagiography – of Jesus rather than of Mary – is continued with the Circumcision,[4] which is then interpreted symbolically and followed by digressions on the rewards awaiting those who believe in Him. A hymn to the Saviour[5] leads on to the Epiphany scene,[6] which, as the third main point in this section, is given emphasis not so much by the quality of the narrative as by rhetoric: one might almost say, by encrusting the simple Biblical garb with jewellery and precious stones. The structure becomes looser, with the hymns doing honour now to Jesus and now to Mary; the legendary framework is filled in by the arbitrary insertion of learned etymologies, which were a traditional feature.[7] After this frequent change of theme there again comes a scene from Mary's life; 'How Our Lady was purified',[8] but the Mother of God has now become an unapproachable majestic figure, and it is only in his hymns of praise that Lydgate approximates to the actual subject-matter of the Marian legend. The rest of the book is devoted to the Presentation of Christ in the Temple and a didactic elucidation of the significance of Candlemas. This gives a colourless ending to the legend, which has no claim to be judged as a narrative work but postulates a new elevated majestic style, in which the divine is placed at a distance from the everyday. The fluctuation between Mary and Christ as the subject of the story anticipates his later epic double legends.

That the stately religious poetry to which Lydgate aspired was feasible in a legend conceived on a smaller scale is shown by a comparison with his *Legend of St Margaret*,[9] based upon Latin and French sources,[10] and written between 1415 and 1426[11] at the request of Lady March.

[1] Stanzas 479–85.   [2] Stanzas 606–25.   [3] Stanzas 626–30.
[4] Stanzas 632–53.   [5] Stanzas 678–89.   [6] Stanzas 703–37 and 750–88.
[7] Cf. Curtius, op. cit., pp. 488 ff.   [8] Chap. 77, stanzas 789–802.
[9] *M.P.*, 173; C. Horstmann, *Altenglische Legenden*, N.F., Heilbronn, 1881, pp. 446 ff.
[10] Cf. lines 69 ff. Lydgate's version is scarcely distinguishable in this from the Margaret legend in the *Legenda Aurea*, which also served as a model for the concise compact form.
[11] The heading bears the date: A° VIII° h VI[i], i. e., 1429, which can, however, not be correct. The donor of the commission, Anne (1398/1403–1429/1432), daughter of Edmund, fifth Earl of Stafford, who fell at Shrewsbury in 1403, married in 1415

The dedication of this work gives us an insight into Lydgate's relationship with one of the most influential English aristocratic families of his time. It may be assumed that he was recommended to his patroness, Ann, Countess of Stafford, Buckingham, Hereford, and Northampton (1379–1438), by her daughter Anne, whom she outlived by many years. After the death of her first husband the Countess of Stafford married William Bourchier, a member of another family that extended patronage to Lydgate. Their son Henry, Viscount Bourchier (*d.* 1483), who was also a member of Bedford's suite in France, married Isabella, the younger sister of Richard, third Duke of York, a woman of literary inclinations. She enjoyed reading the legendary lives of saints by Lydgate and Osbern Bokenham; from the latter she commissioned a life of Mary Magdalene (1445). The family retained their literary interests in the next generation,[1] and it was for Lady Isabel Bourchier's son that Lydgate's friend Benedict Burgh, then rector of Sandon and vicar of Maldon, Essex, translated the distichs of Cato.

In form Lydgate's *Legend of St Margaret* is his most compact hagiographical work; as a work of art it is more valuable than the numerous other Margaret legends which have survived.[2] A reader who comes to it fresh from his epic legends and invocations to the saints may find the condensed treatment of this tale too unpretentious; but a comparison with other Margaret legends shows that this judgement is a relative one. The mere outward appearance of the work commands respect: its splendid seventy-seven Chaucerian stanzas form a striking contrast to the old versions in *septenarii* (and later in short couplets), and the division into prologue, legend, and envoy enhances its artistic effect. The prologue forms a connecting link between the asseveration of modesty and the likening of Margaret to a pearl shining forth like a treasure from an insignificant-looking casket. This is followed by the *invocatio* making Margaret his muse and the guardian of his patroness. In the principal part of the work

---

Edmund Mortimer, fifth Earl of March (the man who was the legitimate successor of Richard II but remained loyal to Henry V). Lydgate can thus only refer to Lady Anne as 'my lady Marche' after 1415. The *terminus ad quem* is 1426, for in this year Anne, who had been a widow since the previous year, married John Holland, Earl of Huntingdon (Wylie, *Henry V*, op. cit., I, 526 n.).

[1] S. Moore, *Patrons of Letters*, op. cit.; H. S. Bennett, *The Author and his Public in the Fourteenth and Fifteenth Centuries*, op. cit.

[2] E.g., Horstman, op. cit., pp. 225 ff., *circa* 1310; a later (and faulty) imitation of this version, pp. 236 ff., *circa* 1450; a much older text, early thirteenth century, pp. 489 ff.

the story of her youth is briefly summarized, and we move swiftly to the martyrdom itself. This is rendered impressive by the two great debates between Margaret and the Prefect and then, later, the Devil. These great disputations are separated by the Prefect's monologue, the trialogue between Margaret, the Prefect, and the People, and Margaret's prayer, spoken as a soliloquy. The envoy with its constant refrain is directed towards women readers who invoke the saint in time of need, and also to St Margaret herself, who is begged to intercede on her worshippers' behalf.[1] To the stateliness of structure corresponds a similar stateliness in the choice of subject-matter and manner of presentation. Everything unessential is omitted, such as the realistic details (e.g., description of the various kinds of torture) that were readily related in other versions. Everything human and commonplace is given elevation by the choice of words: Margaret is 'this holy virgyne, benygne and glad of chere'; her beauty is 'souereyne'; she is a lady descended 'fro grete noblesse'.

He gives an idealized portrait, in which Christian composure is blended with courtliness. There is an element of the grotesque in her fight with the dragon sent by the Devil, who devours Margaret and then bursts – but this fight could not be omitted, because it is an essential part of the legend, in art as well as in literature; instead, it is here elevated to a heroic plane. The maidenly heroine places her foot upon the head of the vanquished monster; the speeches that follow give the struggle a touch of grandeur.

These speeches, which to a large extent supplant the narrative, are characteristic. In the other versions there were also a number of direct speeches, but they are short, recalling the naïve expressions of emotion and monologues spoken by the figures in mystery plays to introduce themselves to the audience. Lydgate expands the speeches to one or more stanzas, introduces monologues, and reduces the number of speakers (for though he adds the figures of Christ, the Angel, and the Hangman, they do not speak). His legend thus evokes the same sensations in us as a French tragedy. The same striving after elevated style, the same heroic treatment of religious themes are also characteristic of his other short legends (which cannot be dated with precision).

[1] Prologue, stanzas 1–11; Legend, stanzas 12–74; Envoy, stanzas 75–7. Debates: Margareta and the Prefect, ll. 140–224; Margareta and the Devil, ll. 304–92. The Prefect's monologue, ll. 120–40; trialogue between Margareta, the Prefect and the People, ll. 239–66; Margareta's monologue prayer, ll. 461–87.

# Lydgate's Saints' Legends

In the case of his *Legend of St George*,[1] a stately and courtly note is already to hand in the subject-matter itelf. George is honoured as the guiding-star of chivalry, and his fight with the dragon, which forms the centre-piece of the story, presents him as a three-fold hero: as a chivalrous protector of women, a courageous fighter against monsters, and a devout champion of Christ. The other episode, his resistance to the heathen tyrant Dacian, forms a religious complement to his more secular fight with the dragon, and leads to the climax of his passion and death. The usual envoy is wanting; the prologue, which takes up three Chaucerian stanzas out of the total of thirty-five, merely heralds the theme, pointing the connexion with the foundation of the Order of the Garter. The legend is thus distinguished neither by its form nor by its content, but the verses flow smoothly, and the simple treatment of the action is vivid, particularly in the various phases of the fight with the dragon: the king's daughter going to her sacrifice in festive attire, the actual fight, the triumphal procession, and the final conversion and baptism of the people by the saintly knight. This is not accidental, for an introductory remark by the poet shows that he wrote this legend in honour of the armourers of London for their festival of St George. Adapting his tone to suit his patrons' taste, Lydgate makes it less elevated and extravagantly rhetorical as compared with the *Legenda Aurea*. The legend was designed to accompany pictures of St George's life that were painted on the walls of the armourers' banqueting-hall. From the initial stanza it can be concluded that the poem was recited by the poet himself when the frescoes were ceremonially unveiled. Certain passages, it seems, were selected to be inscribed on scrolls illustrating the pictures.[2] The advantages such a combination of word and picture presented for Lydgate's secular poetry are also valid in relation to his *Legend of St George*.

The *Legend of St Petronilla*[3] seems to be a small occasional piece which also follows the pattern of the *Legenda Aurea*. Its brevity (twenty ballad stanzas) is reminiscent of the *Legend of St Margaret*. As

---

[1] *M.P.*, 145; *English Studies*, 43, 10 ff. Lydgate's version follows, with many abbreviations, the *Legenda Aurea*. Dating (following Hammond): after 1426.

[2] Cf. Hammond in *English Studies*, 43, and G. H. Gerould in *PMLA*, 32 (1917), pp. 332 ff.

[3] *M.P.*, 154. Cf. MacCracken's canon (*EETS*, ES. 107), No. 126: 'Never before identified as Lydgate's, this piece is absolutely identical in style, rhyme and metre with other legends, even to the short 'oracio' at the end.' Other scholars attribute this legend to Lydgate's disciples.

was also the case here, every opportunity has been used to inflate the legendary account to resound to the saint's praise and to present her as an ideal of courtly womanhood. Apart from the artistic versification and polysyllabic rhymes the style of this little work has no particularly striking features. Only three episodes are related: Petronilla's patient submission when her father, St Peter,[1] momentarily cures the sick girl to edify a scoffing onlooker; her expectation of death in a prayer when she is being wooed by Flaccus; and finally the martyrdom of her companion and confessor on the orders of the infuriated Flaccus. The narrative comprises twelve stanzas and is set within a framework of a three-stanza prologue, introducing the *exemplum* of humility, faith, and patience in sickness, and an epilogue, likewise of three stanzas, in which the recurrent rhyme of 'pacience' exhorts the reader to exercise patience in time of sickness and pestilence. A four-line envoy assures the pilgrims on their way to visit her own holy relic at Bury that their prayers will be heeded.

The *Legend of St Petronilla* was thus evidently written for a divine service or ceremony on St Petronilla's Day – referred to in the legend as 31st May. Petronilla's skull was a relic preserved in Bury to cure feverish illness, and the leper hospital maintained by the monastery bore the name of this saint.[2] It may have been the plague epidemic of 1434 that prompted this composition; for Petronilla was the saint who gave protection against leprosy and plague; 'pestilence' is mentioned in line 158 of the poem; and Lydgate wrote several other religious works on this motif.

In this connexion mention must be made of the curiously colourless *How the Plage was Sesyd in Rome*,[3] a paraphrase of a miracle by St Sebastian in the *Legenda Aurea*, treated rather sentimentally and placed in a pretentious and affected framework. It is a poetic treatment of the mosaic of St Sebastian, a votive picture erected at the

[1] One interesting deviation from the source is that Lydgate makes Peter a more humane figure. It is not he who is responsible for Petronilla's illness, but 'Goodys prouidence'. Lydgate also made considerable abbreviations at the beginning.

[2] 'Hospital of St Petronilla or St Parnel for leprous persons near to the hospital of St John out of the South Gate, founded by one of the early abbots, ignored by Dugdale' (*Victoria County History, Suffolk*, II, 135 f.). 'Weever tells us in his *Funeral Monuments* that the skull of S. Petronilla was used to cure agues and that the bones of S. Botolph were carried about the fields, and prevented darnell and tares from growing' (M. R. James, *Abbey Church*, op. cit., p. 170). MacCracken writes: 'St Petronilla's Hospital is still to be seen at Bury St Edmunds (see a plate of it in Yates, *Bury St Edmunds*, Appx.).'

[3] *M.P.*, 159; source: a miracle in the appendix to the Sebastian legend.

time of the plague of 680 on an altar in the church of S. Pietro in Vincoli, Rome (not Pavia, as stated in the *Legenda Aurea* and by Lydgate). It is in fact only the nucleus of the legendary life of a saint or tale of miracles, but has the customary division into three parts: the prologue contrasts in an extravagantly rhetorical manner a catalogue of the famous physicians of antiquity with the superior divine art of healing; the principal part depicts the raging of the pestilence in Rome, Pavia, and other cities, and its sudden end when the altar to St Sebastian was erected; the conclusion reiterates the point that no man can do anything against the plague, but only God, who works miracles through His saints. The poem, which comprises only six Chaucerian stanzas and abounds in aureate terms, is of some interest in connexion with Lydgate's work as a writer of legends, but has no merit when seen in isolation.

By comparison his *Legend of Seynt Gyle*[1] (St Giles being a hermit who was highly regarded in England and Scotland) is indeed a work of art. Lydgate wrote it on the basis of a Latin text[2] in response to a short letter by an unnamed patron.[3] It differs from all earlier Middle English legends and all other legends by Lydgate: it is a hybrid work consisting of one epic and one hymnic apostrophic poem, composed in the difficult ballad stanza and condensed to the utmost.[4] In forty-six stanzas it tells the life of St Giles in the form of a direct address to the saint himself, in the second person singular; elsewhere this generally occurs only in the concluding prayer or in the invocation of the Muses in the prologue, but here it extends throughout the whole legend. For this reason the prologue (stanzas 1–5) and also the concluding prayer and envoy (stanzas 42–5, 46) seem to be less sharply differentiated from the main body of the legend. The work stands out by reason of the use of the affected diction common in prayers or invocations of saints, of rhymes that aspire to sonorous effect,[5] and the poet's success in overcoming the obstacle that the familiar second person singular lends itself to an intimate conversational tone rather than to the solemnity appropriate to a prayer. On the other hand, narrative composed in this invocatory style tends to

---

[1] *M.P.*, 161; C. Horstmann, *Altenglische Legenden*, N.F., Heilbronn, 1881, pp. 371 ff.
[2] Cf. lines 27 and 31. But Lydgate had a more detailed source than the *Legenda Aurea*: the Old French version by the Anglo-Norman Guillaume de Berneville (Soc. Anc. Text. Frç., 1881).
[3] This is probably a *topos* of modesty.
[4] 'For short metris do gladly gret plesaunce' (36), 'Prolyxite ffor to sette asyde' (38).
[5] E.g., the rhyme *-ioun* recurs in stanzas 20, 22, 23, 24, and 25.

become a dry summary of contents; the reader does not wish to have just a bald enumeration of 'thou hast done this, thou hast not done that', but wishes to hear how the events related took place; or where the poet does provide a narrative, one forgets his use of the second person singular, and finds its reappearance jarring.[1] The epic and lyrical elements do not harmonize, and the impression conveyed is of a work slighter than the motley tale by the Frenchman Berneville. Lydgate's aim is not to write in popular style; and the content, too, is directed to courtly and clerical readers. From Giles' life one episode only is singled out: the King of Burgundy, whilst out hunting, gives chase to the hind who brings Giles his food, and wounds him when he affords the animal protection; as penance he founds a monastery for him and appoints him abbot. Lydgate suppresses the idyllic features of the tale in order to emphasize the virtues of monasticism. This approach is underlined still more plainly by the account of the God-fearing attitude of King Charles and the bull given to Giles granting the monastery the right to exercise its religious functions freely and threatening its secular enemies with dire penalties. It is possible that Lydgate may have had actual events and persons in mind when he emphasized the monastery's independence vis-à-vis the secular power and portrayed St Giles as an ideal abbot. The readers for whom he wrote would easily identify such allusions, but here we must restrict ourselves to an assessment of the work as literature. This shows that there is much in the *Legend of Seynt Gyle* that foreshadows his later works on religious themes.

A further example of Lydgate's mannered style, somewhat different in nature, is the legend *St Austin at Compton*.[2] In this case the didactic purpose is all too evident, and is indeed already stated in the heading: 'Offre vp yowre Dymes', or 'Offer up your tithes'. Lydgate may have written this small piece in 1433 or somewhat later, at a time when the abbots were compelled to participate in the collection of tithes, at the request of Abbot Whethamstede[3] of St Albans or at the

---

[1] Despite its stylistically unsatisfactory intermediate position between an epic and a hymnic poem, this hybrid form lived on in the fifteenth century (e.g., in the Legend of St John).

[2] *M.P.*, 193; Halliwell, p. 135. Lydgate obtained his material not from the Legend of St Augustine in John of Tinmouth's *Sanctilogium* (fourteenth century), which was arranged alphabetically by Capgrave in the fifteenth century and later became known under the title of the *Nova Legenda Angliae*, but the Chronicle of Johannes Bromtonus, edited by the Bollandists as an appendix to the *Vita* of St Augustine in *Acta Sanctorum*, May, VI, 396.

[3] Cf. the dispute between the abbots and the two archbishops. The trial was held at Blackfriars in 1433. G. G. Coulton, *The Last Days of Medieval Monasticism*, C.U.P., 1950.

suggestion of his own Abbot Curteys. This remonstrance against Lollardry may be regarded as a justification of abbots and monasteries in general. The whole preface (nine stanzas) is an exposition in terms of church history of the obligation of the faithful to pay tithes. It is followed by a cautionary example in the form of the legend of St Augustine, apostle of England, who says Mass at Compton and becomes the instrument of a divine miracle. The former lord of the manor, who has been cursed by the former priest for refusing to pay his tithes, rises from the dead in ghostly form and, having shown remorse and done penance, is given absolution by the priest, whom St Augustine calls back to life. The conclusion is just a one-stanza envoy of the 'Go litil boke' type. Lydgate is concerned with the intrinsic miracle of the forgiveness of sins taking place in this resurrected *exemplum*-within-an-*exemplum*, not with the external aspects of the miracle and its narrative potentialities. The story is written in the didactic and edifying style of Lydgate's later period (in fifty-seven ballad stanzas), but is by no means so vividly told or so well constructed as were his legendary lives of the saints in the narrower sense of the term. He refers to himself as 'of wittis dul and old' (l. 407). In the prologue (the subject-matter of which is not particularly interesting for us, or, perhaps, for the poet either) he introduces such a wealth of unexpected and scholarly terminology that our attention naturally focuses much more readily on questions of style (cf. stanzas 5–7). At the beginning of the legend proper, when extolling England's apostle, this is intensified to the point where it becomes a rich symphony in which the sense is obscured (cf. stanzas 12–14). This style is ill-suited to the narrative, and deprives the account of the miracle of tension and suspense. As in Lydgate's later legends, the action is brought to a standstill and broken up by the long speeches, which serve a didactic purpose rather than a dramatic one. The final commendation of the contemplative life and the pious wish that the Church might not be troubled by heresy have a hollow ring about them, despite the stylistic effort expended, and the modern reader may concur in the description of the work in the envoy as a 'litil tretys' – though he will not regard this as a term of praise.

Dan Joos[1] is an account of a miracle which, like the Legend of St Austin, serves as an *exemplum*, but produces a totally different impression when judged as a work of art. This is one of Lydgate's most

---

[1] M.P., 311; Halliwell, op. cit., p. 62; also ed. by Horstmann, *Chaucer Society Originals and Analogues*, III.

appealing legends, not by reason of its subject-matter but rather the delightful manner of presentation, with hymns being introduced for decorative effect. The dry account given in the source[1] is elaborated, the theme of these twenty Chaucerian stanzas being praise of the Virgin and of this pious monk. The miracle, as told, concerned a monk who sang five psalms daily, the initial letters of which made up the name Maria; when he died, five roses bearing her name in golden letters grew out of his mouth. The characteristically hyperbolical description of this miracle is preceded by a four-stanza prologue, in which Maria is addressed as a Muse, and followed by an epilogue, also of four stanzas, in which spiritual love for Maria is contrasted with the sufferings and anxieties of earthly love. A miracle story such as this is more in keeping with Lydgate's gentle manner than the traditional popular tales of the holy martyrs. The legend's edifying function is fulfilled when the monk's sanctity is proved by a severe test; abstention from all pleasure and constant pious works are just as beneficial as trials of strength and the inhuman sufferings of the martyrs. To this extent the legend of brother Joscius (as he is called by Vincent) can be regarded as a model of the meditative and lyrical type of legend in Lydgate's work, which from an artistic point of view can be set beside the longer narrative type represented by the *Legend of St Margaret*. But throughout his life Lydgate aspired to the epic style, and in his later years he produced legends on an epic scale which are reminiscent of his *Life of Our Lady*, but less lyrical. There are two examples of this: the epic legends of St Edmund and of St Alban.

Lydgate's *vita* of St Edmund is an epic legend both by virtue of its elevated diction and its volume; it extends to three Books (3693 lines in Chaucerian stanzas). After relating the life of St Edmund, the martyred king of the East Angles and the patron of his monastery, he added (just as, in romances of chivalry, the son or grandson carries on the story of the hero) a *vita* of Edmund's nephew Fremund, King of Mercia, who avenges his uncle and also becomes a martyr himself. The sources[2] supplied a lucrative theme: a great hero, fighting for a

---

[1] The poet refers to Vincent de Beauvais' *Speculum historiale*.

[2] Lydgate's source was not the *Sanctilogium*, but the compilation in the Bodleian, MS. 240. (Cf. Horstmann, Appx. to his ed. of the *Nova Legenda Angliae*, Oxford, 1891, II, 575 ff.) In addition he used one of the sources of this compilation, the *Vita* of the Abbo of Fleury. The three additional miracles were later (MS. Ashmole 46) joined to the Legend of Fremund. The events of 1441 and 1444, which were almost contemporary with his compilation of this legend, may have been brought to his knowledge by oral

national cause, clashes tragically with the sons of Lothbrocus, and finally, like Beowulf, sacrifices himself for his people.[1] We know that Lydgate made no use of such narrative potentialities as this story provided, but that on the contrary he regarded a colossal turgid panegyric as more consonant with the dignity of an epic. He even added to these two *vitae* a third part giving an account of the miracles associated with St Edmund's remains and relics.

The overall arrangement of this double legend (which explains our title, *The Lives of SS. Edmund and Fremund*),[2] is clearly evident, even though the various parts are ordered in a somewhat confusing pattern.[3]

In a political speech the prologue identifies the three crowns worn by Edmund (that of his kingdom, of martyrdom, and of chastity) with the English, French, and heavenly crowns of Henry VI. This idea is repeated in a more familiar tone in a second prologue which introduces Book I. Lydgate states that he wrote the legend of Edmund, patron of Bury,[4] in his old age,[5] at the request of Abbot William[6] on the occasion of the king's visit to the monastery.[7] He then (as he does once more in the *Regi* envoy) acts as spokesman for all the monks of Bury, this last resting-place of the holy martyr Edmund: they regard it as their duty to pray that he may consolidate the happy bonds between the monastery and the reigning monarch; in return

---

tradition. For the Legend of Fremund, the Prologue cites the *Vita Burghardi* (printed in the Appendix to Horstmann, op. cit., II, 689 ff.), which Lydgate follows, though changing the order.

[1] I. P. McKeehan, *St Edmund of East Anglia: the Development of a Romantic Legend* (Univ. of Colorado Studies, XV), 1925.

[2] Horstmann, *Altenglische Legenden*, N.F., Heilbronn, 1881, p. 376.

[3] Prologue, lines 1–80; Book I, lines 81–1117 (of which lines 81–234 constitute a second prologue, lines 235–430 narrate, without a separate chapter heading, Edmund's childhood, and lines 858–1117, with a separate chapter heading, tell of his rule as King of the East Angles). Book II contains 1015 lines, which are in fact a continuation of the preceding text (which explains why the scribes who wrote the Ashmole MS. overlooked this division into a new Book). One chapter (lines 1–441, without a heading) tells of his Danish enemies, a second (lines 443–868, with a heading) of his martyrdom, and a third (lines 869–980, with a heading) of the miraculous finding of his head. Book III, which bears the heading 'Incipit vita Fremundi', contains, after the prologue (lines 1–182), the story of Fremund (lines 183–847), and then goes on to relate (which must really be a new Book) the miracles of St Edmund (lines 848–1456), and is terminated by a concluding envoy I (lines 1457–1520), an envoy II (lines 1521–55), and a *Regi* (lines 1556–62).

In MS. Ashm. 46 Edward IV appears throughout in place of Henry VI. Since Edward reigned from 1461 to 1483, but Lydgate died in or about 1450, the variants of this MS. cannot be his.

[4] I, 228.     [5] III, 80.     [6] I, 187 ff.     [7] I, 137 ff.

they hope and expect that he will become the guardian and defender of the Church, and in particular the church of St Edmund, and constitute the embodiment of an ideal Christian ruler. The customary declaration of modesty which follows is appropriately linked to a prayer addressed to the patron saint himself.[1] It is only now, after the first 300 lines, that the story proper commences, or rather that we are given a series of scenes from Edmund's life and passion. The most memorable passages in this are solemn or festive scenes, such as Offa's appointing Edmund his heir at his death, Edmund's coronation, or such curiosities as the description and allegorical interpretation of his imaginary coat-of-arms, the first mention of this in legends of Edmund's life. Occasionally his favourite ideas appear, e.g., that a noble mind is the result of noble descent,[2] that war is wicked,[3] and that a ruler must hold in his hands both the sceptre of peace and the sword of justice[4] (the latter being stressed more strongly than before owing to the troubled state in which England now found itself), and that the royal power must yield before the virtue of humility and the omnipotence of God.[5] Proverbial phrases[6] and similes drawn from nature[7] are integrated into this epic; and there are only a few humanistic flourishes[8] in which he displays his knowledge of antiquity. Of his sermonizing there remains in fact only the admonition to preserve the peace, which he endeavours to combine with a heroic treatment, in that the martyr is represented as an ideal knight.[9] He seems to forgo all personal remonstrance in order to attain a style in the grand manner. This does not make it attractive reading for our taste; the long speeches in which the martyr reveals his sentiments cannot replace for us the suspense provided by genuine narrative, and for the modern reader tales of miracles have lost their original quality of heroism and grandeur. What has been said here about the tale of St Edmund applies with even greater force to the *Vita Sancti Fremundi*, which follows a similar structural pattern: first the prologue, containing a commendation of holy miracles, followed by a catalogue of martyrs (as learned and pompous as the prayer to St Edmund, with its gems, astral spheres and celestial hierarchy), and then a declaration of modesty in the humanistic manner.[10] Only after 200 verses does the actual story commence, and then Lydgate fails to perceive, or deliberately bypasses, its epic

---

[1] I, 200–34.  [2] I, 347 ff.  [3] II, 419 ff., 433 ff.  [4] I, 848, 870 ff.
[5] E.g., I, 256, 379.  [6] I, 396.  [7] E.g., I, 312.  [8] E.g. I, 558 ff., 832 ff.
[9] II, 640, 646 ff., cf. also passages referred to in n. 3.  [10] III, 78 ff.

charm. Owing to the frequent interpolation of miracles this *vita* is further removed from the poet's epic ideal than his life of St Edmund, and approximates more closely to the tone usual in saints' legends. This is particularly the case in his description of the miracles of St Edmund,[1] which begin in the middle of Book III and really constitute a separate book. After an account, taken from actual history, of Ethelred's oppression at the hands of the conqueror Sveyn and the comforting miracle of the tyrant's sudden death,[2] there follow lesser miracles verging more and more upon the anecdotic and which at the end are simply listed in summary fashion.[3] They have been selected from the great compilation of St Edmund without regard for chronological order, for the sake of their paraenetic and edifying purpose. The irrational way in which they have been added shows that Lydgate did not know the art of composition in our sense of the word. We should have expected these miracles to follow directly upon the Edmund legend. Apparently they are for Lydgate not only a climax after a gradual build-up of tempo, but also a fortissimo followed by a concluding prayer couched in the magnificent invocatory style of his later period. For all the dexterity apparent in their recurrent rhymes, these eight ballad stanzas[4] recall his *Prayer for the King, Queen, and People*: the work is a profession of loyalty to his king, 'thenheritour off Ingelond and France', from which there radiates a warm humanity. The epic closes with an envoy[5] in five Chaucerian stanzas, embellished with humanistic and mythological allusions, and a final stanza containing a dedication to the king.[6]

This final stanza and the envoy are not to be found in a later MS., *The Miracles of St Edmund*,[7] containing additional miracles attributed to this saint, but in which the dedication is altered in favour of Edward IV.[8] These fifty-eight ballad stanzas, probably written in 1444 as an addendum to the *Legend of St Edmund*, do not have a heroic tone and differ from the main body of the legend also in their metre. They are three tales of children who met an accidental death but were restored to life as a result of prayers to St Edmund. Horstmann's suggestion that this represents a first draft is less likely than the conjecture that it is an independent work. Its realistic details and

[1] III, 848–1456.     [2] III, 848–1106.     [3] III, 1314–1456.
[4] III, 1457–1520.     [5] III, 1521–1555.     [6] Called *Regi*: III, 1556–62.
[7] Printed by Horstmann, *Altenglische Legenden*, N.F., Heilbronn, 1881, pp. 440 ff.
[8] See p. 163, n. 3.

# John Lydgate

allusions to actual celebrations of miraculous events in the monastery give it an individual touch. In their tone these moving tales are reminiscent of Chaucer's *Prioresses Tale*. The mention made of Abbot William Curteys[1] and the emphasis laid on the Abbey's privileges[2] give us an impression of life within the monastery.

Much that has been said here about *The Lives of SS. Edmund and Fremund* also applies to the parallel work *The Lyfe of Seint Albon and the Lyfe of Saint Amphabel*,[3] written in 1439, i.e., six years later. The abbot of St Albans, Whethamstede,[4] was an ambitious man who aspired to the role of patron of the arts. He wished to have a work written about the patron saint of his monastery similar to that composed by Lydgate for Bury St Edmunds. In compliance with his patron's wish,[5] the poet wrote a companion piece, arranged on the same plan, containing a life of St Alban together with the *vita* of Amphibalus, who converted him to Christianity. It has three books and contains 4724 verses in Chaucerian stanzas, with some interpolations in ballad stanzas. The patron's satisfaction at the finished product is shown by the princely scale of the remuneration which the author received (100 shillings in the currency of the time) and by the fact that his magnificent MS. was placed before St Alban's altar in the abbey. To the modern reader this work seems an ungainly monster, even more shapeless than all Lydgate's other legends. But this only shows that our ideas of structural technique have no equivalent in medieval aesthetics. Lydgate must have regarded this legend as his best, since it surpassed his others in rhetorical embellishment. To the literary historian it represents the final stage in the process, which we can trace from its earliest beginnings, whereby Lydgate's artistic as-

---

[1] l. 354.  [2] E.g., ll. 384 f. and concluding stanza.

[3] Ed. by C. Horstmann, in *Festschrift zum 50-jährigen Bestehen der Königstädtischen Realschule zu Berlin*, Berlin, 1882.

[4] On John Bostock, known as Whethamstede, cf. W. F. Schirmer, *Der englische Frühhumanismus*, Leipzig, 1931, pp. 82 ff., 143 ff.; R. Weiss, *Humanism in England during the 15th Century*, Oxford, 1941, pp. 30 ff., and the unpublished thesis of H. Hodge, *The Abbey of St Albans under John Whethamstede* (cf. Weiss, p. 30).

[5] Cf. the note at the end of the MS. Trin. Coll.: 'Here endith . . . which glorious Lyves were Translatyde oute of Frenssh and Latyn by Dan John Lydgate monk of Bury, at Request and prayer of Masteir John Whethamstede, the yere 1439, of his Abesye XIX.' Lydgate himself says that he wrote the poem in honour of St Alban 'at the request and biddyng of my father the abbot of that place' (I, 881), and flatters Whethamstede by saying that according to the etymology of his name ('of his name the Ethymologie is sayd of an home or stede of whete') he was a great collector and compiler of books, and had compiled a volume of biographies of ancient poets and philosophers with sayings drawn from their works (I, 890, 897 f.).

pirations consistently grew. To do him justice, it must be recognized that the epic sweep of the Alban legend finds its justification in the material, which dates back to the myth-shrouded days of the origins of English Christianity: Edmund was 'kyng, martir, and virgine', Alban was the 'prothomartyr of Brutes Albion'. Lydgate sets out to create a national Christian epic in the grand manner, and characteristically gives the work enormous volume by fitting the various pieces together like a mosaic. The legend is preceded by an account of the hero's chivalrous youth; Book III tells the story of his life, and also of the martyrdom of the subsidiary hero; the conclusion is provided by his *inventio* and *translatio* (which perform the function of the miracles in the *vita* of St Edmund). As in the latter work, the theme is provided with an extravagant apparatus of prologues, introductory and concluding prayers, digressions, and episodes. Lydgate went about his work carefully, as is shown by his choice of source material. In his endeavours to make Alban appear as a model of chivalry he was assisted by the *Tractatus de Nobilitate, Vita et Martyrio Albani et Amphibali*, in which the lives of the two saints were already combined to form a single entity. But his main source for the legend itself was the *Interpretatio Willelmi*, written by a monk of St Albans at the end of the twelfth century; for this account, with its rhetoric and pathos and many long speeches, corresponded more closely to his own purpose than Bede's matter-of-fact version.[1]

Book I,[2] which is relatively concise, commences with the usual flourish of modesty, in which the author states that he cannot rank with the masters of antiquity; characteristically enough, he mentions the great epic poets Homer, Virgil, and Lucan. After invoking the aid of Clio and the Almighty he moves on to his historical account, which reaches far back into time. In the days of Diocletian King Severus, in accordance with ancient custom, sends a party of English youths to Rome to obtain the accolade of knighthood. The Pope seeks to convert them, and succeeds in the case of Amphibalus, the son of a Welsh prince. The ceremony in which the knighthood is conferred upon him and the ensuing tournament, in which the noble 'Albon' from Verulamium receives the victor's prize, and is then kept in Rome by the Emperor for seven years, is described in detail in Lydgate's usual style, so that it takes up more space than the tale

---

[1] In the *Historia ecclesiastica*. Lydgate took the accounts of the saint's *inventio* and *translatio* from this work and from Matthew Paris.
[2] It has 931 verses, as against 2003 verses in Book II and 1800 in Book III.

itself. Symbolical and moralistic interpretations are inserted, as well
as speeches, all of which have a retarding effect upon the narrative.[1]
As is apparently Lydgate's intent, we have the impression of reading,
not a legend, but an epic. The narrative itself also has an epic quality: in Britain disturbances break out, which are put down by a sena-
tor with the aid of three legions; but he is subsequently defeated by
the Duke of Cornwall, elected King of Britain. Alban is sent to
England with a delegation to represent Diocletian at his coronation.
In his absence Rome resolves upon the persecution of the Christians
and Amphibalus flees to Verulamium. This brings to an end Book I,
which is rounded off by some *verba auctoris*. The aureate terms,[2] the
long-winded sentence structure, and the Latin constructions emulating those in the source[3] render the story more obscure than one
would think from this summary.

Book II, containing Alban's conversion and martyrdom, also begins in an epic manner with the classical nature pictures introducing
the various sections, which the modern reader often finds more attractive than the story itself.[4] Alban, who governs in the capacity of
'Steward of Britayne', is converted to Christianity by Amphibalus.
When the latter is denounced by a pagan he exchanges clothes with
his friend. He is then sentenced to death by the army sent by Diocletian to England to persecute the Christians. After enduring martyrdom with fortitude, he is transfigured and performs miracles. The
subject-matter is not so rich as that in Book I. Lydgate seeks to attain
epic fulness by preaching a moral lesson. The didactic discourse on
the nature of Christianity pronounced by Amphibalus when effecting
his conversion of Alban[5] extends almost to a quarter of the total
length of Book II. Despite all the effort at rhetoric it exhausts the
reader, whose interest is aroused only when he comes to Alban's
passion.[6] This forms the climax from the point of view of language.
In grandiose invocatory style Lydgate pays tribute to Christ as Hero.
Christ is the 'mighty champion, the famous stronge Achilles', who
triumphs over death and Satan. When the narrative is resumed the

[1] E.g., the speech of the English leader before Diocletian, I, 589 ff.

[2] E.g., I, 225, I, 256 f., I, 500, etc.

[3] Which are especially apparent when compared with later additions (in the copy in
the B.M.) by a Benedictine monk of St Albans, who avoids Lydgate's pretentious
Latinizing style (cf. Horstmann's note).

[4] Cf. Prologue (II, 1–64), the prelude to the conversion (II, 219 ff.) and especially the
two stanzas introducing the martyrdom (II, 856 ff.).

[5] II, 1–643; esp. the passage 'This is our belefe' (II, 204–358).

[6] II, 571–89, esp. 583 ff.

scene in which Alban and Amphibalus exchange clothes occasions a digression on other famous pairs of friends (David and Jonathan, Orestes and Pylades, Achilles and Patroclus, etc.), in an effort to replace the lack of lyrical eloquence by arousing scholarly interest in the subject-matter. The protracted speeches in Alban's trial make the reader inclined to sympathize with the hero, whose 'desyre . . . was only this, shorte processe to make'. Unlike his master Chaucer, Lydgate cannot create dramatic suspense by dialogue; nor has he Gower's talent for story-telling to help him make the ensuing accounts of miracles grip our attention. Though the modern reader is bound to criticize it on such grounds, Book II is nevertheless the most important part of the work. Its object was both to laud Alban as a saint and ideal chivalrous prince, and also to proclaim the triumph of Christianity in the Passion of Our Lord. This is why it begins with a panegyric of Alban, has in its centre Alban's dream (interpreting Christ's Passion), and concludes with a song of jubilation addressed to the pillar of light, the angelic host, and to Alban as a *vir egregius*.

In the third and final book, in which we are told that as a result of Alban's miracles the people of Wales were converted to Amphibalus' teaching, the poet in Lydgate gives place to the pastor and teacher. Occasionally we are impressed by one of his great rhetorical gestures, as for instance when he mentions God or Christ,[1] but on the whole the account given of the persecution of the Christians in Lichfield and elsewhere is colourless; so, too, is the story of the 999 conversions brought about in Verulamium, the massacre of the newly-converted Christians, and the vision of the 'martyrs of Verolamy towne' ascending to Heaven. For Lydgate these were sublime themes, on which he lavishly expended his eloquence. The conclusion of the book is of particular interest, in that it is largely a historical account.[2] When the heresies of Pelagius were spreading in England, St Germanus and St Lupus came from France and, after praying at St Alban's grave, suppressed the heretics. But time and again new outbreaks occurred, until Offa erected the abbey and Benedictine monastery of St Albans over the grave of the saint. This historical account, with its many dates and names, is a product of the historiographical ambition which Lydgate began to develop with his *Fall of Princes*,

---

[1] E.g., III, 639 ff., III, 646 ff.

[2] The chronology is as follows: death of Alban in 293, *inventio* by Germanus in 449, *translatio* in 793.

but it displays little of his former verve and is overshadowed by the concluding prayer, which contains several lines in which God is besought to show favour to King Henry VI and 'his riall quene Anna'.[1]

\*

To conclude, one may divide Lydgate's legends into four types. First of all there is the *narrative legend*, which can probably be assigned to his early period; it follows the traditional form fairly closely, but differs from it in its more elaborate structure, and introduces something fresh and original in the attempt at elevation and heroic tone. Of the three legends which belong to this category only that of *St Margaret* may properly be considered a legend; in the case of *St George* the sacred element of his passion is overshadowed by his chivalrous and secular triumph in his fight with the dragon, whilst the legend of *St Petronilla* is above all a eulogy of patience of the Griseldis type, with a holy miracle added.

It thus constitutes a bridge leading to the second type, the *miracle legend*, in which the miracles are described in a lyrical manner. The most outstanding example in this category is that of *Dan Joos*, whereas *How the Plage was Sesyd in Rome*, which also belongs to it, must be assessed merely as a brief sketch for an account of this type. One gains the impression that legends such as these were more in accordance with Lydgate's own temperament than descriptions of martyrdom.

This fact may also explain the existence of the third type of legend, the *experimental legend*. As far as its content is concerned, the legend of *St Giles* is purely and simply the tale of a miracle, longer and more diversified than *Dan Joos*, but differing in form from the legends of the second category. It is a not very felicitous attempt to avoid a simple tale and to enhance the lyrical strain found in *Dan Joos* by an approximation to the invocatory style used in prayers. The other legend which belongs to this category, that of *St Austin at Compton*, is in content also the tale of a miracle and by no means a story of martyrdom. In this the mannered style is carried to an extreme; the

---

[1] The prayer to St Alban has fifteen stanzas (III, 1696–1800) with the refrain: 'O prothomartyr of Brutes Albion!' The lines addressed to the king are: III, 1777 ff.

'Anna' refers to Anna of Armagnac, daughter of John IV, Duke of Armagnac, who was offered in marriage to Henry VI. The marriage plans may be dated to the years 1441–3; thus either the composition of the work was delayed until then, or else the supplicatory lines must have been added later.

shorter narrative form is abandoned in favour of erudition and breadth of treatment.

It is true that the number of lines is less than in the legend of *St Margaret*, but intrinsically it constitutes a transition to the fourth and last type of legend, the one that is most characteristic of Lydgate: the *epic legend*. To this category belong, as an early example, his *Life of Our Lady* and the two double *vitae* of his later period: *The Lives of SS. Edmund and Fremund* and *The Lyfe of Seint Albon and the Lyfe of Saint Amphabel*.

The striving after epic grandeur, after the heroic, after solemn pathos, which was alien to Chaucer and his generation, marks Lydgate's poetry out as the fulfilment of the fifteenth-century ideal. It was responsible for the enormous volume of, for example, his *Troy Book*, for the style of his translation of Deguileville, and for the theme of his *Fall of Princes*. In the case of religious poetry, where his theme was laid down in advance, the new style showed itself chiefly in the use of heavy turgid language. In hagiography, where secular and religious features were combined, his striving after the grandiose led to the creation of new forms of literary legend. Lydgate's achievements were only designed to appeal to a small circle, and found but few emulators. The legends written for the people and for church use, for example, show no trace of his influence. But those who aspired to the calling of poet, such as Bokenham,[1] Capgrave,[2] and Bradshaw[3] (to mention only the most important fifteenth-century hagiographers) did follow his example.

[1] Osbern Bokenham (1392?–1447) was a monk in the Augustinian monastery of Stoke Clare in the south-western corner of Suffolk. In 1443–6 he wrote *Legends of Hooly Women* (*EETS*, OS., 206), in which he refers to himself as a disciple of Lydgate. He followed him in his use of rhetorical prologues and glorification of the saints, but surpassed him in the use of complicated verse structure. In his hands (unlike Lydgate's) the actual legend remained a simple paraphrase. Unlike Lydgate again, the upright Augustinian father, proud of his native dialect, adopts a gentle and often humorous tone.

[2] John Capgrave (1393–1464) was a scholar who became Provincial of the Augustinian friars in England in 1456. Using a Latin source, he wrote a *Legend of St Catherine* (8372 lines in Chaucerian stanzas, edited by C. Horstmann, *EETS*, OS. 100 (1893); cf. Dibelius in *Anglia*, 23–4 (1900–1)) and *Vitae* of St Augustine and St Gilbert (*EETS*, OS. 140). Capgrave shares Lydgate's tendency to epic scale, and his *Legend of St Catherine* combines, in the manner of Lydgate's double legends, the fourteenth-century *Conversio* of Catherine with the familiar material of the *Vita* and the *Passio*. As a conscientious historian he is fond of making his own critical comments, which Lydgate avoids. Like Lydgate, he had King Henry VI and Humphrey as his patrons.

[3] Henry Bradshaw (*d.* 1513), a Benedictine monk of Chester, wrote a Life of St Werburge (*EETS*, OS., 88).

# John Lydgate

Bradshaw achieved great success with his readers[1] in his endeavour to venerate the saints as members of the *ecclesia triumphans* who had emerged victorious from life's struggle and were endowed with all honour and power. To obtain this aim he blended the style of courtly poetry with that of clerical poets who wrote in Latin. He resembles Lydgate not only in this but also in his predilection for compilations from several sources, in his historiographic ambition, and in his rhetoric and pathos.

Bokenham took over principally the symbolism which Lydgate, following Chaucer's example, had introduced into the English legend from the old ecclesiastical and medieval Latin literature. He was less successful in reproducing the edifying note struck in his sermons, in which he portrayed a Deity at the same time saving and healing and also punishing and avenging.

In the case of Capgrave the rhetorical rendering of emotion which Lydgate borrowed from Chaucer degenerated to a point where it became intolerable.

Bokenham and Bradshaw also exaggerated Chaucer's blending of the religious with the chivalrous to such an extent that their women saints resemble sisters to Chaucer's Blanche and their men saints knights of Christ.[2] With Bokenham the heroization, in which Lydgate goes beyond his Latin models, becomes stereotyped.[3]

But none of Lydgate's emulators ventured to follow him in his endeavour to introduce the humanistic world of antiquity into the religious sphere, to sing the praises of Christ as Orpheus, Hercules, and Achilles, to make the Romans and Trojans progenitors of the Saints, or to invoke the Muses in a religious legend.[4]

Thus in this sphere Lydgate remains the fifteenth century's greatest innovator.

[1] In the meantime Lydgate's ornate diction had become popular among the public. Bradshaw wrote: 'for no clerke in-dede. But for marchaunt men, hauyng litell lernyng' (St Werburge, ll. 2015 f.).

[2] On the other hand there are connexions with patristic literature: as befits a *miles Christi*, Alban appears as a knight of God in full armour (II, 884 ff.), which Bokenham takes over as 'Christes owene knight'.

[3] Bokenham exaggerates Lydgate's royal epithets to such a pitch that he portrays Magdalene as 'gloryous apostolesse' and Agatha as 'crownyd as a quene'.

[4] This applies to the legend-writing of the fifteenth century. For the topics cf. Curtius, *Europäische Literatur und lateinisches Mittelalter*, pp. 240, 249.

## Chapter 19

*Lydgate's Religious Verse*

\*

The difficulties that confront the modern reader in understanding and evaluating Lydgate's religious poetry are increased by two factors: one of a general nature, affecting medieval religious poetry as whole, and the other applying specifically to Lydgate's work. We shall look in vain for expressions of personal piety in the religious lyrics of the Middle Ages. (Even the devotional poetry of the thirteenth-century Franciscan friars does not contain direct intercourse between the individual and God.) To a large extent the deliberate avoidance of the expression of individual emotions inevitably gave religious art in general, poetry included, the – to our eyes alien – character of 'applied art', in that the poets, who in most cases were monks or officiating clergy, endeavoured to put their verses to practical use in divine service, and regarded this as the real purpose of their art.[1] Such well-established genres as penitential poems, prayers, and paraphrases are all almost completely bound up with the liturgy; in addition to these there are commentaries on the mass, calendars and other poetic works that often touch upon the mnemotechnic, which in their day had their justification in the religious purpose they were designed to fulfil.

The second difficulty is that Lydgate's sense of style seems alien to us. For he did not carry on the traditions of Latin and early Middle English religious lyrics (a tradition which still has some appeal for us today), but exaggerated the bombast and affectation present in fourteenth-century verse, so that to us his verse appears rigidified, and too mannered for genuine religious poetry. The style

[1] F. A. Patterson, *The Middle English Penitential Lyric*, N.Y., 1911 (Columbia Studies in English, Series 3, Vol. 4).

[ 173 ]

of such poetry needs to be evaluated by criteria which we are un-
accustomed to apply.

Since we have hardly any firmly-established chronological data to
go by, we cannot approach his religious poetry from a biographical
angle,[1] but must classify it according to categories. In doing so we
shall begin with his poetry applied to practical ecclesiastical purposes
and proceed to those that are freer and more valuable as works of
art.

*

The most obvious example of the former type are his sermons in
rhyme, of which the tone, style, and length all indicate that they were
designed to be read out from the pulpit. The importance attached at
that time to sermons can be seen from the *Artes praedicandi*; this, it
may be assumed, was studied with particular thoroughness by clerics
who belonged to a monastic order.[2] The only text we have that can
be ascribed to Lydgate with any degree of certainty, entitled by its
author *Merita Missae*,[3] gives us no opportunity to examine the various styles of sermon[4] or their traditional structure,[5] for it is a simple
instruction for laymen,[6] in which Lydgate cannot refrain from including illustrations drawn from history: Godfrey of Bouillon, Charle-
magne, and King Arthur.

In the tradition of the so-called calendar verses we possess a work
generally attributed to Lydgate, entitled *A Kalendare*,[7] containing all

[1] The attempt made here to ascribe the more simply written poems to his early years
and the more pretentious ones to his later life must be regarded as an experiment. The
traditional view that Lydgate's religious poetry belongs to his later years is only partly
correct. The basis of this assumption is a passage in his *Testament* in which the poet
says that when he saw a crucifix he came to the conclusion that all his earlier poems
were 'veyne fablys', and that he would in future devote himself to more worthy matters;
this, however, must be regarded as a *topos*, since the vision is said to have occurred
before he was fifteen years old. He will probably have written religious verse throughout
his career, although it is quite possible that he may have written more of it in his later
years.

[2] Cf. G. R. Owst, *Preaching in Medieval England*, Cambridge, 1926. For a popular
description of the service books with which medieval clerics were familiar, cf. C.
Wordsworth and H. Littlehales, *Old Service Books of the English Church*, L., 1904.

[3] Approx. 100 couplets, printed in *The Lay Folk's Mass Book*, ed. by C. Simmons
(*EETS*, OS., 71, pp. 148 f.); cf. Owst, op. cit., pp. 52, 277. MacCracken challenges
Lydgate's authorship in *M.P.*, xlvi, n. 1.

[4] Old simple manner (*expositio secundum ordinem textus*), formal manner (with historical
and allegorical interpretation), and popular manner (with anecdotal matter).

[5] Cf. p. 86.

[6] 'To the lewde that can not rede / But the pater noster and the Crede. . . .'

[7] *M.P.*, 363; ed. by Horstmann, in *Archiv*, 80, pp. 115-35. In fifty-one Chaucerian
stanzas with a concluding ballad stanza.

the festivals of the Church year arranged month by month, with the dates in the margin accompanied by verses to elaborate their significance. Lydgate may have written these himself or have expanded on some earlier work; in either case this will have been a thankless task, which as a monastic poet he could not evade. Indeed, he performed it with some skill, even though he lacked the talent for compression. For us this list of saints is interesting in that it shows which festivals were observed in a great monastery such as Bury St Edmunds; seen historically, it is the first attempt of its kind in English poetry after the Norman Conquest. One may imagine this practical calendar with its readily-absorbed information lying open in the sacristy or monastery library, and the monks consulting it as they passed to refresh their memories about the festivals of the coming week.

Also designed to serve purely practical needs, but more ephemeral, is his description, or 'ordenaunce', of the London *Procession of Corpus Christi*,[1] the great annual festival at which the holy sacraments were escorted through the streets by members of the furriers' guild, carrying hundreds of wax torches.[2] Lydgate did not describe the externals of the Corpus Christi procession but gave an explanation in verse of the meaning of the festival. He was probably commissioned to write it by the authorities of his monastery. In these stanzas, which are apparently only a fragment,[3] he treats his theme with a wealth of learned exegesis, proceeding from the antecedents of Holy Communion in the Old Testament, then going on to the New Testament, and concluding his account (which is reminiscent of his legends) with an exhortation to receive the sacrament in worthy manner. The arrangement of his images was predetermined by the order followed in the actual procession,[4] which apparently consisted of a succession of pageants bearing enactments of dramatic scenes, as in the mystery plays.

The fourth of these pieces written for the monastery is a commentary on the Mass. This is a set of three didactic poems – a triptych, one might say – in which the main part, *The Virtues of the Mass*,[5]

---

[1] *M.P.*, 35; Halliwell, op. cit., p. 95. In twenty-eight ballad stanzas. (*M.P.*, xxiv: 'Procession at Corpus Christi'.)

[2] Stow, *Survey of London*, ed. Kingsford, II, 230 f.

[3] Cf. the concluding remark: 'Shirley kouþe fynde no more of þis Copye'. It can in any case only be a matter of a few missing stanzas.

[4] Sub-title: 'Here foloweþe an ordenaunce of a precessyoun of þe feste of corpus cristi made in london'.

[5] *M.P.*, 87; ed. by Huth in *Fugitive Tracts*, I, under the title *The Interpretation and Virtues of the Mass* (*M.P.*, XX, *Vertues of the Masse*).

# John Lydgate

is flanked by two shorter poems: the introductory 'Exortacion to Prestys when they shall sey theyr Masse'[1] and the final 'On Kissing at Verbum caro factum est'.[2] The poem has a total of 94 ballad stanzas, of which eighty-three comprise the main part, seven the exhortation to priests, and four the conclusion. From the point of view of its size and the technical skill employed it may be considered a notable opus, although it is unremarkable when judged as a work of art. The introductory exhortation to the clergy to prepare themselves for communion in a fitting manner by prayer and to conduct themselves in dignified fashion when receiving the host is turned by Lydgate into a grandiose declamation with a special envoy[3] – too sonorous, perhaps, for the thin content. The same applies to the concluding brief explanation why in church one kneels to kiss stone or earth, wood or iron. But here the style is more appropriate, for he is explaining the symbolic meaning of earth (= the humanity of Christ), iron (= the spear and nails), and wood (= the Cross), which taken together remind the kneeling worshipper of Christ's Passion. Both poems are, as it were, side-altars to the High Altar – companion pieces to the main part of the poem, which is a self-contained whole, with its own prologue and envoy. This commentary on the Mass was written at the request of the pious Countess of Suffolk[4] and was designed for domestic use. The main part interprets the meaning of the gradual prayer *Judica me Deus* by paraphrasing the 42nd psalm, the verses of which, in Latin, are placed before the individual stanzas. After a detailed explanation of the priests' vestments there follows an elucidation of the various parts of the office and the related hymns and prayers. Mention is also made of the Creed, the triple Sanctus, and the prayer for the quick and the dead. Then Lydgate inserts a prayer of his own, which to some extent is a prelude to the paraphrase of the Lord's Prayer which ensues. The *Agnus Dei* leads the poet to consider his favourite Song of Songs, and then, after a few brief digressions on the blessing, again to draw a comparison between the *Ite missa est* and God leading the children of Israel through the Red Sea. This really brings the poem to a close; but, as is so often the case when he is dealing with solemn

[1] In the manuscripts sometimes placed before *Virtues of the Mass* and sometimes afterwards; *M.P.*, 84.

[2] *M.P.*, 116; in Halliwell, op. cit., p. 60, under the title *A Call to Devotion*.

[3] Stanza 7 (not in all MSS.).

[4] 'interpretatio missae ad rogatum dominae Countesse de Suthefolchia' [Alice Chaucer].

subjects, Lydgate does not know where to stop, and adds a digression, or rather two digressions, giving St Bernard's and St Augustine's explanations of the beatifying effects of the Mass. Only at this point do we have the envoy, the 'Go lytyll tretyse . . .'.

Two other paraphrases of the Lord's Prayer by Lydgate are his *Pater noster qui es in celis*,[1] which probably dates from his early period, and an exposition of the seven demands of the Pater noster. The former is a simple and pious verse rendering of the Lord's Prayer, composed in short lines of four beats, which was an unusual form for Lydgate. Its practical purpose (for use in church services) is evidenced by its designation as 'Oracio dominica'. On the other hand, his didactic and garrulous *Exposition of the Pater noster*[2] must be ascribed to his later period, probably to the year 1445. 'I doubt', the poet begins by saying, 'whether I ought to dare venture upon such a task at my advanced age and with my failing memory.' The long-winded preliminary observations, the digressions, and the outpourings of learning detract from the solemn effect aspired to and give the impression of familiarity. We cannot imagine ourselves listening to a prayer spoken before a congregation, as we can with some of his other pieces of a similar nature; instead, we are listening to a lecture on practical theology delivered by an old man to a novice.

Likewise coming within the category of 'applied art' (even though it cannot be shown that they were used in church) are Lydgate's poems of supplication, most of which were composed in pursuance of some request. This group comprises several poems on the plague, probably written during the severe epidemic of 1434,[3] as well as the verse legend *How the Plage was Sesyd in Rome*.[4] The latter, as we have seen, was originally inscribed over a votive picture in the church of S. Pietro in Vincoli. It was now made to serve as a means of warding

---

[1] *M.P.*, 18, seven ballad stanzas. Heading in text: *The Pater Noster Translated*.

[2] *M.P.*, 60; in O. Mahir, pp. 1 ff., under the title *Pater Noster*. Forty-two ballad stanzas: prefatory observation, lines 1–96; explanation of the seven requests of the Pater noster, lines 96–288; epilogue, lines 289–336.

[3] 'Parliament was adjourned several times on account of pestilence in London' (*Rolls of Parl.*, IV, 420 (1433), V, 67 (1444), V, 143 (1449)); and sometimes even the Justices postponed their business (*Proceedings of the Privy Council*, IV, 282 (1434), cited by Abram, p. 165). Cf. *Brut* (1434): 'A grete pestilence in London, bothe of men, women and children; and namely of worthy men, as aldermen . . . and also thurgh England þe peple deyed sore' (p. 407); cf. further Ch. Creighton, *A History of Epidemics in Britain*, Cambridge, 1891; *Pestblätter des 15. Jh.*, ed. P. Heitz, with introductions by W. L. Schreiber; Hecker, *Epidemics of the Middle Ages*, 1843. If it was not the plague epidemic of 1433–4 that occasioned Lydgate's poems, then it must have been that of 1438–9.

[4] *M.P.*, 159; cf. Chapter 18.

[ 177 ]

off the plague in London by the addition of a final stanza, written in a style differing from that of the rest of the poem. His *Stella celi extirpauit* may have undergone similar retouching. Of this we have two versions; if our hypothesis is correct, then the version in seven ballad stanzas connected by a refrain[1] must have been the earliest. The other version is by contrast less colourful; it comprises only four stanzas[2] and ends with a stanza borrowed from a prayer to the Virgin Mary[3] which does not belong here at all; it may have been written when the plague flared up again in the following year. In any case the shorter version, with its concluding plea for long life, wealth, and heavenly bliss, is pitched in a lower key than the earlier version, which is more vivid and rises to a magnificent invocation in the final stanzas. The prayer is to be found in the *Horae*, among those addressed to the Virgin.[4] The last of Lydgate's poems dealing with the plague, *De Sancta Maria contra pestilenciam*,[5] is less an invocation to avert the plague than a solemn declamation, in rolling cadences, honouring the Mother of God.

A further group consists of the *Quindecim signa judicii* poems,[6] Lydgate's contribution to these is, however, devoid of any artistic merit. Under the title of *The Fifftene Toknys aforn the Doom*[7] he treats the St Jerome theme in an extremely unimaginative manner, taking one day after another and discussing each one separately.

Other pieces of a similar nature are Lydgate's paraphrases of psalms and hymns for monastic purposes, which he was probably commissioned to write by his monastery; but in these he was able to display his qualities as an artist in words. In *Misericordias Domini in eternum cantabo*[8] the title and refrain are borrowed from the 88th (89th) psalm; it was apparently written at a relatively early date, and forms a counterpart to the secular hymns of martial glory, such as David's song of victory over Goliath. In his religious poetry Lydgate did not adhere to the habit, familiar to us from his secular

---

[1] C. Brown, *Religious Lyrics of the 15th Century*, Oxford, 1939, pp. 208 ff. (seven stanzas).

[2] *M.P.*, 295.         [3] *Prayer to Mary*, *M.P.*, 296.

[4] E. Hoskins, *Horae Beatae Mariae Virginis* . . ., pp. 165–6 (cited by C. Brown, op. cit., p. 335).

[5] C. Brown, op. cit., p. 206; eleven Chaucerian stanzas. In the colophon the person who commissioned it is identified as Canon William Cotson.

[6] Examples and parallels in Brown's *Index*, Nos. 408, 776, 1823, 2920, 2921, 3349, 3367, 3368, *48.

[7] *M.P.*, 117. Also in Th. Wright, *Chester Plays* (Shakespeare Society Series, 1847, II, 222); cf. Köppel in *Anglia*, Anzeiger, 24, 55. Eleven ballad stanzas.

[8] *M.P.*, 71, in twenty-four ballad stanzas.

poetry, of bringing in a wealth of names drawn from mythology and the Scriptures, from ancient history and literature. *Deus in nomine tuo saluum me fac*[1] is an early counterpart to his later *De profundis*. It is a paraphrase of the 53rd psalm, which in some parts is rendered faithfully; one verse of the psalm precedes each of the nine ballad stanzas. The slightly varying refrain comes from the absolution after public confession, so that one may presume this to have been used in the liturgy as a penitential hymn. In its dignity and intimate tone it is radically different from his *De profundis*,[2] a garrulous paraphrase that is alien to modern taste; written at the request of Abbot William Curteys, it was a rendering of the 129th psalm (used in the requiem mass for the dead).[3] As is shown by the last stanza, it is designed to be used in divine service, perhaps even to be suspended on the wall as a motto. It resembles the style of his later period, as exemplified by the last of the Pater noster paraphrases which we have discussed. A personal introduction tells how the poet came to write the work; then follows a digressive discussion, probably based upon theological commentaries, of the history of this psalm and its applicability; and then comes the main part, the paraphrase itself, in which each stanza is headed by a verse from the psalm; finally, the whole work is rounded off by a pertinent conclusion and a personal epilogue. The style of this hymn, probably written between 1445 and 1448, is smooth and sonorous, but nevertheless distorted to the point of mannerism.

The potentialities of Lydgate's style at its best are evident in his paraphrase of Ambrosius' hymn *Te Deum Laudamus*,[4] which was similarly composed for use in the service. We have here a sonorous translation and variation of the hymn sung daily after the celebration of Mass, in thirteen ballad stanzas (and a refrain), with a strong infusion of Latin lines.[5] There are, however, two points that mark this paraphrase out from others of its kind: it does not adhere strictly to the order of ideas in the Latin hymn; and it develops almost into a hymn of praise to the Son of God, who is hailed as the heroic conqueror of death. Of similar significance, and presumably dating from

---

[1] *M.P.*, 10; also in F. A. Patterson, *The Middle English Penitential Lyric*, p. 72.

[2] *M.P.*, 77, in twenty-one ballad stanzas.

[3] The psalm occurs in the missal, in the *Missa pro Defunctis*.

[4] *M.P.*, 21; cf. W. O. Wehrle, *The Macaronic Hymn Tradition in Medieval English Literature*, Washington, 1933, pp. 124 f.

[5] Latin passages are also incorporated which are not contained in the *Te Deum* as sung today.

N

the same period, is the paraphrase of the well-known passion hymn *Vexilla regis prodeunt*,[1] ascribed to Venantius Fortunatus. Here, too, the basis is an older Latin version which differs from that familiar nowadays; from it several verses have been incorporated into the English text, whilst others serve as mottoes or headings for each of its nine ballad stanzas. Thus this poem, only part of which is translated and paraphrased, is addressed to readers acquainted with Latin. It renders well the hymnic character, the lapidary manner of expression, and the solemn tone of the original. By contrast, the grandeur of the Latin original is lost in Lydgate's rendering of the Christmas hymn *Letabundus*[2] by Bernard of Clairvaux, which he expands to thirty-nine ballad stanzas. This was presumably composed as a New Year hymn for the pupils of the monastery school. It is rendered unwieldy by the arbitrary interpolation of Latin tags, tedious by the profusion of Biblical knowledge, and rigid by the bombastic splendour of the language. For the first Latin verse, 'Laetabundus exultat fidelis chorus', he uses a circumlocution of no less than forty-eight lines. The content, which is highly didactic in tone, also gives the impression of immobility and stagnation. This long-winded lecturing manner produces an effect that is scarcely poetic; the stanzas follow one another in jerks, as incoherently as the invocations of his later period, and are held together only by their common relation to the God whom they extol.

*

In this type of composition Lydgate had little opportunity to realize the epic ambition which, as we know, he showed in his secular poetry. Only two of his religious poems are epic in scope: his *A Seying of the Nightingale* and his *Testament*. The former[3] is a fragment, as is clear from a note in the manuscript: 'Of this Balade Dan John Lydgate made nomore'. Further conclusions as to its dating[4] must

---

[1] *M.P.*, 25 (in Brown's *Index*, No. 2833: 'ascribed to Lydgate'). For other adaptations of this hymn, cf. Brown, Nos. 3403, 3404, 3405.

[2] *M.P.*, 49. The original is in H. A. Daniel, *Thesaurus Hymnologicus*, II, 61. Cf. W. O. Wehrle, op. cit., p. 22, where he prints a version which elucidates some of the distorted and incomprehensible Latin words that appear in MacCracken's edition.

[3] *Lydgate's Minor Poems: the two Nightingale Poems*, ed. O. Glauning, *EETS*, ES., 80, London, 1900. Also in MacCracken's ed., *M.P.*, 221. Fifty-four Chaucerian stanzas.

[4] 'As this statement was no doubt copied by Stow from his Shirley original, we may fairly compare it with the like entry in the Lydgate and Burgh's Secree of Secrees (? 1446 – Schick), after the poet's decease, and conclude that the cause of the break-off

remain in the realm of conjecture. The poem is not so shapeless and careless in structure as is commonly maintained;[1] it is rather that Lydgate's manner of composition is utterly different from that of his Latin model. This model is the famous poem *Philomela* by the greatest thirteenth-century English composer of religious lyrics, John Peckham, who in this work gave expression to the soul's yearning for its celestial abode.[2] Peckham's Passion poem is concise in its use of words and precise in its composition: the song of the nightingale, lasting from morning until its death in the evening, represents the mystic experience of a single day, in which the hours correspond to the stages of redemption. This construction was retained in the translation of *Philomela* made by one important English poet,[3] which was formerly attributed to Lydgate, but does not apply to the paraphrase we are discussing here, which follows a course of its own. Lydgate's work commences in the epic manner with an astronomic determination of the season and a description of spring (transposed to the evening). The only one of all the jubilant birds to remain awake is the nightingale, whose song the eavesdropping poet compares to vespers (complyne). This forms the transition to the main part, the actual Passion poem, which treats the traditional subject-matter in five sections.[4] In the first we are told how a heavenly messenger appeared before the poet in a dream and explained to him the religious meaning of the nightingale's song; this is then developed more fully and in a more didactic manner in the second section, a meditation on the Crucifixion. The third part, introduced by a veneration of the name of Jesus, reproduces in traditional form Christ's words on the Cross. There is more originality in the next sections: a meditation on Jesus' death and His last cry to God. The style is here more elevated than in the rest of the poem, and this is continued in the final section, from which there are probably only a

---

in the Nightingale poem was Lydgate's death. This is borne out by the character of the metre, as the many examples of type D [the acephalous or headless line] tend to prove a late date.' (Note by Furnivall in Glauning's ed., p. xxxviii.)

[1] MacCracken, *M.P.*, p. xxxiv.

[2] C. Vötter, *Die Nachtigall des hlg. Bonaventura*, Munich, 1612; M. Diepenbrock, *Geistlicher Blumenstrauss*, Sulzbach, 1862 (with Latin text); Anon., *Des hlg. Bonaventura Philomela oder Nachtigallenlied*, Lingen, 1883.

[3] Printed in Glauning's ed.; cf. MacCracken, *M.P.*, p. xxxiii.

[4] Divided as follows: introduction, stanzas 1–6; main part: Passion: I, interpretation of the nightingale's song, stanzas 7–16; II, *memento Jesu*, stanzas 17–21; III, Christ's words on the Cross, stanzas 22–33; IV, *meditatio*, stanzas 34–42; V, raising of the Cross, stanzas 43–8; conclusion, stanzas 49–54.

few stanzas missing. The descriptions of nature in the introduction are here translated to the religious plane, and the Song of Songs is also drawn upon for words and images to exalt the theme of profane love. The poem thus does have order and shape, whilst at the same time, in the verses describing the nightingale, it strikes a personal note. Nevertheless, it cannot be considered an important work of art: its epic volume results from loose aggregation of its several parts, not from inner motivation.

The same criticism may also be levelled against the *Testament of Lydgate*,[1] a work of his later period.[2] It is a conglomeration of five different parts, distinguished from one another by changes of metre; it has a total of 118 ballad and Chaucerian stanzas.[3] Its autobiographical references give this work a particular appeal for the modern reader, whilst at the same time these references are incorporated into the cult of Jesus, the resulting duality leading to some charming and effective contrasts. It surpasses by far the *Seying of the Nightingale*, and thus merits more detailed analysis on our part. The prologue, a panegyric of Jesus, begins with a great invocation, which gains by contrast with the next scene depicting the humble monk inside his cell. The contrast is heightened by the fact that Jesus is no longer conceived as the Man of Sorrows in the Franciscan tradition, but as the Hero King before whom even the mightiest of men, as the refrain constantly repeats, must bow down in all humility.[4] The solemn content is matched by the rich texture of choice language. The popular device of a vision, the meaning of which is indicated by means of an anagram, leads up to the final climax, after which, to point the contrast, the action is again transferred back to the poet himself, by broaching the theme of his confession, which he makes under the protective hand of Jesus (*testamentum in nomine Jesu*). At the bedside of the ageing and ailing poet there appears, in the guise of a lady shrouded in black, 'remembraunce of myspent tyme', as he puts it. She is followed by her sister Meditation, who presents him with an awful reckoning. This gives the poet cause to muse upon the year with

---

[1] *M.P.*, 329; Halliwell, op. cit., p. 232.

[2] Dated 1448–9.

[3] Prologue, stanzas 1–30, ballad stanzas; *Testamentum*, stanzas 31–56, Chaucerian stanzas; Jesus, stanzas 57–79, ballad stanzas; Jesus (confession), stanzas 80–100, Chaucerian stanzas; Jesus Vide, stanzas 101–18, ballad stanzas. The parts composed in ballad stanzas have a refrain, i.e., 'c' rhymes throughout.

[4] From the Epistle to the Philippians, II, 10: 'ut in nomine Jesu omne flectatur coelestium, terrestrium et infernorum.'

its ephemeral seasons that has sped past so rapidly, and upon human life, which has passed by with similar rapidity. The second part thus contains a retrospective view of the poet's youth in the form of a description of spring; this is incorporated by drawing a parallel with man's own springtime in his childhood – both themes leading to that of inconstancy. The modern reader will scarcely wish to dwell upon the content, and will not be unduly troubled by the fact that in the hands of the ageing poet the rigid scheme of the composition here breaks down; he will instead be fascinated by the autobiographical allusions and the appealing images of spring[1] contained in this description of Lydgate's own youth – even though, in accordance with medieval custom, this was couched in general terms.

The third part, which bears the heading 'Jesus' and 'Oratio praevia humiliter confitentis', is a prayer preliminary to confession, belonging to the group of penitential lyrics;[2] its theme refers back to the first part of the work. He entreats Jesus, victorious and triumphant on the Mount of Calvary, mercifully to hear his confession. The refrain, 'Graunt or I deye shryfte, hosel, repentaunce', gives his plea a note of urgency that makes it reminiscent of the Litany. A Latin prayer[3] compiled from the psalms leads into the concluding supplication for mercy. It is only in the fourth part, likewise entitled 'Jesus', which really follows on from the second part, that we come to the actual confession.[4] Although this confession is kept in such general terms that it could apply almost to anyone, the realistic

---

[1] Almost every verse of the Introduction to the *Canterbury Tales* has an analogy here, in an affected version.

[2] The *Meditation* attributed to Lydgate by MacCracken (*M.P.*, 43) is to be classified with the penitential hymns according to its theme, but differs from them radically in its treatment. It represents an attempt unique in Lydgate's works to find an effective form for the theme of confession. From the standpoint of its metre, too, the hymn follows a distinctive pattern: it has 180 lines in heroic couplets. It begins with a nature picture of spring and an account of intensifying sensual lust, followed as a contrast by a speech by the soul on the putrefaction of the body. The poet then moves on to discuss the judgement between the blessed and the damned, and ends with a sermon which as it were is addressed to himself: better thyself, lest God be angry with thee. C. Brown (*MLN*, May 1925, XL, 282 ff.) denies that this poem, based upon a Latin work of the thirteenth century, *De humana miseria tractatus*, is by Lydgate, and sees in it a work which Chaucer said he wrote, but which has not yet been identified, *Of the Wreched Engendring of Mankinde*. Dr. Bergen agrees with this view.

[3] Its five lines are each paraphrased in one stanza. The passages are from Psalm xxxiv. 3; Psalm xxx. 17; Psalm xlv. 1 (freely adapted); Jeremiah xvi. 19.

[4] The third part follows on from the first. This is also the case with the metre: Parts I and III are in ballad stanzas, Parts II and IV in Chaucerian stanzas. Cf. p. 182 n. 3.

scenes of monastic life permit inferences to be drawn with regard to
Lydgate's own youth. For a novice to shirk early morning Mass
may have been a sin that was committed in many monasteries; but
for him to run into the neighbouring vineyard and pick grapes can
only apply to the monastery of Bury St Edmunds. His references to
games of marbles and to his independent rustic spirit revolting
against the monastery rules are also based upon his own recollections,
whereas the remaining confessions of sensual lust, excessive eating
and drinking, and other infringements of the Benedictine rules
correspond to the traditional patterns. Again, his conversion at the
age of fifteen on seeing a crucifix bearing the inscription *Vide* is
less significant for Lydgate's biography than it is for the theme of
his *Testament*: it introduces the fifth part, headed 'Vide', which
represents Jesus' Passion for the sake of mankind and is in essentials
a paraphrase of the Biblical version. Innumerable paraphrases of this
kind exist, and since this one is devoid of any distinctive personal
note it makes the final section of Lydgate's *Testament* disappointing
from the standpoint of content and aesthetically colourless. Thus in
its entirety this work is no epic, but a blend of prayer, self-incrimi-
nation, and exhortation, strewn with descriptions of nature and
parallels between nature and human life. These structural defects
apart, the *Testament* is nevertheless one of Lydgate's most interesting
poetic works from the biographical point of view; and it is also
significant in literary history, since it is one of the most outstanding
examples of veneration of Jesus in literature.

To this cult of Jesus also belong Lydgate's Passion poems. These
are a blend of two established genres, the *planctus Mariae* and the
words of admonition spoken by the Redeemer from the Cross. The
fusion may be considered a not entirely felicitous one, since both the
lament at the Cross and the Saviour offering up His sacrifice drag the
divine down to the human plane, where it can only survive if it is
represented in a moving manner. In popular religious poetry of the
fifteenth century the visible and scenic tended to be emphasized;
motherhood was painted in idyllic colours, and thus a portrait was
produced of the Virgin Mary that made her thoroughly human.
But Lydgate could not and would not continue this tradition, whereby Christ's torments were represented as suffering capable of moving
ordinary mortals. A meek and mild man, he was more sensible of
*consolatio* than *compassio*; and since it did not lie within his power to
express mystical ardour, his manner of treatment inevitably made his

theme appear trite. Being aware of this, he sought to compensate for it by increased elevation of style; but though this may have been appropriate to Maria portrayed as Queen of Heaven or to Christ cast in heroic mould, it was not suited to a humanized depiction of Christ.

The earliest of these poems is perhaps *The Dolorous Pyte of Crystes Passioun*.[1] This was designed to serve as text to a picture of the Crucifixion, and was written – presumably at the request of his abbot – in praise of an indulgence which could be purchased at the monastery.[2] In the Middle Ages such circumstances of composition do not necessarily preclude the theme from being treated in an artistic manner, and these seven ballad stanzas, with their recurrent refrain containing the words 'dolorous pite', were indeed worked upon with care. Lydgate exerted every effort to give stanzas 3 and 6 a heroic character and to elevate the style in stanza 6, but the result is nevertheless unsatisfactory from an aesthetic point of view. This also applies to his *Prayer upon the Cross*,[3] a treatment of the same theme that is even more skilfully executed.[4]

Lydgate is not at his best in short poems; his talent for rhetoric needs space. For this reason his *Cristes Passioun*,[5] a lengthier poem in which he can give rein to his eloquence, is more characteristic of his work: the traditional content is here drowned in the aureate style. The best of his poems in the *planctus* genre is *The Fifteen Ooes of Christ*.[6] This is a Passion or penitential poem that recalls his *Fifteen Joys of Mary* and similar rosary poems; the lament motif is here expanded into a great hymn to Jesus by the addition of a *meditatio* and repeated invocations. It is a long poem (in forty-two ballad stanzas),

[1] *M.P.*, 250.
[2] On the picture, cf. stanza 1 ('my bloody woundis, set here in picture'); on the indulgence, cf. the last stanza.
[3] *M.P.*, 252; also printed by Furnivall, *Political, Religious and Love poems*, EETS, OS., 15, and by B. Behr in *Archiv*, 106, 63. By the addition of a 'burden' Lydgate's poem was turned into a carol in the sixteenth century (R. L. Greene, *Early English Carols*, Oxford, 1935, p. 187), and set to music for four parts by Sheryngham.
[4] Its five ballad stanzas are linked by a refrain and recurrent rhymes, so that there are only three rhymes in the whole 40 lines. Careful arrangement enables the envoy (stanza 4) and the author's prayer, entitled *oratio* (stanza 5), to follow on after the actual poem, which takes up the first three stanzas.
[5] *M.P.*, 216, fifteen ballad stanzas. For a Scottish version of part of this poem, possibly by Dunbar, cf. Brown's *Index*, No. 2497, and *PMLA*, 46, p. 220 f.
[6] *M.P.*, 238. 'A Scotch version different from this is in Arundel 285, and another metrical version in Rawl. poet 32. A prose translation is in Harley 172, with an interesting prologue' (MacCracken).

which claims to be a translation from the Latin. Since Lydgate's paraphrases are freely adapted from the original, and since the structure of this piece is not rigid, this claim may refer to some Latin lines. The poem begins in the form of a prayer: 'O blyssed lord my lord, O Cryst Iesu'; after the third stanza it turns into an enumeration of the main stages of the Passion, with the occasional interpolation of a stanza entitled 'Oracio'. When the scene on the Cross is reached it becomes a lament, in which hymnic and invocatory stanzas (or parts of stanzas) alternate ever more rapidly with narrative stanzas relating the events of the Passion. This conveys the impression of the poet's meditation on the Cross being disturbed by successive spasms of pain. The epithets used in referring to Jesus are carefully chosen and heaped up: Mighty Jesus, Lion of Judah, King of kings, Unconquerable Knight of the Spirit. Even in the *planctus* proper, of which we have only one example (*Quis dabit meo capiti fontem lacrimarum*),[1] the heroic tone is still maintained: Maria's laments relate to herself, and not to Jesus, who is hailed as Samson, the hero Eleazar, and Hercules.

Among the mystical poems concerned with the person of Jesus a special place is occupied by *Christe qui lux es et dies*,[2] a fairly close paraphrase of a Latin hymn.[3] The central core, stanzas 2–4, is a nocturnal prayer which forms a self-contained whole;[4] it is preceded by one stanza of prologue and followed by two of epilogue (a supplication for protection against enemies and a eulogy of the Trinity). The curious form is of interest: each stanza has a line from the Latin hymn as a heading, which is reiterated in English translation as the first line of the stanza, and occurs again in Latin as the last line of the stanza. This form, not known elsewhere in macaronic poetry, can hardly have been devised by Lydgate himself; it must be related to the traditional hymnody, with which this piece is closely connected. According to its form, therefore, this poem ought to be

---

[1] *M.P.*, 324; ed. by Holthausen in *Festschrift zum Geburtstag des deutschen Kaisers*, 1908. For the title, cf. Jeremiah ix. 1–19. Ballad stanzas linked by a refrain.

[2] *M.P.*, 235, seven ballad stanzas in short lines with a Latin *cauda*; cf. Wehrle, op. cit., p. 138. Brown's *Index*, Nos. 614–19 (a version in couplets, *PMLA*, 54, p. 387; a version in quatrains in MS. Harley, 685; three versions by Ryman, *Archiv*, 89, p. 196, 325–6).

[3] Sub-title: 'Translacion of þe ympne: Criste qui lux es et dies . . . in wyse of balade'. This hymn is not contained in the modern breviary (which in its present form goes back to the seventeenth century), nor in the Benedictine breviary, but may have been included in an earlier one.

[4] Cf. *To Mary the Star of Jacob*, *M.P.*, 282.

classified with his Marian lyrics, in close proximity to the speech by
the child Jesus to His Mother.[1]

*

Lydgate's prayers do not hold any special position among his
religious lyrics. Devised for use in divine service, they were embellished with the splendour and magnificence of a priest's vestments.
*The eight Verses of St Bernard*[2] form an appropriate starting-point.
This is a prayer, extant in two versions, used by King Henry V at
Mass in his chapel between the elevation and consecration of the
host. We are consequently confronted with an early work, which
must be placed beside his epic *Life of Our Lady*. In support of this
view one may point to the short lines, which Lydgate avoided in his
later works, and the simple manner of expression. It remains uncertain whether from the almost identical wording of one stanza we
may conclude that at the same time he wrote his *Prayer in Old Age*.[3]
In this the short lines of the *Verses of St Bernard* are recast into five-
beat lines by the addition of adjectives. The polysyllabic rhyming
words of the additional stanzas seem to suggest that it was composed
at a later date.

The prayer *To St Robert of Bury*[4] displays originality. This is a
saint's legend in miniature, framed by an invocatory introduction
and an epilogue stanza. To our minds this little poem is far removed
from being a prayer, but yet it is evident from its last line that it was
designed to be said in prayer at services in St Robert's Chapel, or
to be incorporated into the service held in honour of this saint.

There is also an original flavour about the *Prayers to ten Saints*.[5] A
wealth of material is here compressed into twelve ballad stanzas, the
refrain being so placed that two ballads are formed out of it. Of
these the first, which has an envoy, extols five male saints: St Denis,
St George, St Christopher, St Blasius, and St Giles, and the second
praises five heroic women saints: St Catherine, St Margaret, St
Martha, St Christine, and St Barbara. This arrangement distinguishes
this work from conventional litany poems,[6] as also does its heroic

---

[1] *The Childe Jesus to Mary the Rose*, M.P., 235.

[2] *M.P.*, 206, 209, in nine and eleven ballad stanzas respectively, in short lines.

[3] *M.P.*, 20, in four ballad stanzas. The first stanza is identical with the ninth in the
*Verses of St Bernard*.

[4] *M.P.*, 138, in five ballad stanzas.   [5] *M.P.*, 120.

[6] Cf. Patterson, op. cit., No. 4, from line 67 onwards (also in *EETS*, 98, p. 19), and
No. 14, stanzas 1, 3 (also in Wright, *Songs and Carols*, Percy Soc., 23 [1847], p. 76).

conception. Since St Denis and St George are the first characters to appear, it seems that Lydgate may have written this work whilst he was in Paris.

In addition to this poem, in which ten saints are honoured collectively, he penned several more isolated invocatory stanzas which for some reason or other were not brought together to form a composite work. Among these are the *Prayer to St Thomas*,[1] a brief invocation probably intended to be included in the church service. This is an occasional piece, which cannot be compared with his long *Prayer to St Thomas of Canterbury*, to be discussed presently.[2] There are also the final prayer to St Giles[3] borrowed from the legend of this title, the three inter-connected ballad stanzas *To St Katherine, St Margaret, and St Mary Magdalene*,[4] the *Prayere to Seynt Michaell*,[5] designed for use in divine service on the feast-day of this saint, and the *Prayeer to Gaubriell*[6] which resembles it. The longer *Prayer to St Leonard*[7] can claim to be considered a self-contained whole, for it is more elaborately constructed: an invocatory stanza is followed by three stanzas addressed to this saint as patron of the exiled, the poor, the sick, and the trouble-stricken, and it ends with a summary in the final stanza and envoy. The style recalls the *Prayers to Ten Saints*, but it was composed at an early date (1422), for the wealthy hospital of St Leonard at York.[8] An early date may also be assigned to his three ballad stanzas *To St Ursula and the Eleven Thousand Virgins*,[9] an invocation in the form of a short supplication for use in church.

Lydgate wrote a number of such prayers reminiscent of the litany (consider, for example, his frequent use of the refrain 'and help them in ther neede'),[10] of which the three ballad stanzas *To St Ositha*[11] are a perfect example. In these he develops his invocatory style, which reaches its zenith in his hymns of praise, a kind of prayer at which he excelled. This applies for instance, to his *Prayer to St Edmund*, the

---

[1] *M.P.*, 139, in two ballad stanzas.      [2] *M.P.*, 140; cf. p. 190.
[3] *M.P.*, 171, in four ballad stanzas.      [4] *M.P.*, 134.
[5] *M.P.*, 133.                               [6] *M.P.*, 133.
[7] *M.P.*, 135; Halliwell, op. cit., p. 205. Five ballad stanzas and a six-line envoy.
[8] MacCracken: 'Norwich?'; Halliwell: 'made at [?] York.'
[9] *M.P.*, 144; Halliwell, op. cit., p. 178.
[10] The same refrain occurs in *To St Ositha, St Edmund* (*M.P.*, 124), and *St Thomas* (*M.P.*, 140).
[11] *M.P.*, 137. St Osyth (Osgyþa), *circa* 680, was the daughter of Frithuweald, King of Surrey, and Wilburgh (the daughter of King Penda), and was the wife of Sigehere, King of East Anglia. There was a St Osyth's monastery at Walbrook, and a St Osyth's priory 4½ miles west of Clacton-on-Sea (sixteenth century).

*Fifteen Ooes of Christ,* and to some of his Marian ballads. Lydgate achieved a mastery of technique already during his years in Paris. Evidence of this is provided by his *Devowte Invocacioun to Sainte Denys,*[1] a splendid prayer written for Charles VII of France,[2] probably in or about the year 1426, when Lydgate was in France, and presumably based on a French original. It is a veritable *tour de force,* for not only the refrain but all the rhymes recur throughout all the nine ballad stanzas, so that the sixty-six lines contain no more than three rhymes.[3] This gives the work a Romanic imprint, enhanced by the great rhetorical invocations of the divinely appointed patron saint of France in the introduction and conclusion.

The same majestic style is found in his *Prayer to St Edmund,*[4] the patron of his monastery, which he probably wrote on his return there from Paris. Some epithets used are the same as those in the prayers to St Denis. Lydgate presents St Edmund as a warrior king and a knight in shining armour, a role for which he was indeed fitted. With its sonorous verses and vivid imagery it surpasses the more abstract prayer to St Denis, and is eminently suited for services in the monastery on grand occasions, when it would be recited amidst great ceremony. Actually, the same could be said of two further prayers to St Edmund which were embedded in the great legendary *Lives of SS. Edmund and Fremund,* written in 1433. The first one[5] implores the monastery's patron saint to render the poet assistance in composing the legend that follows; the second one,[6] in which the rhyme remains constant in all the stanzas,[7] is reminiscent of the invocation of St Denis. Its theme is magnificently summarized in the refrain: 'Pray for thenherytour off Ingelond and France!'. As in his early prayer for Henry VI, *Ab inimicis,*[8] Lydgate manifested the verve which he always showed in his verses for this sovereign. There

---

[1] *M.P.,* 127.

[2] 'made by Lydegate to Sainte Denys at þe request of Charlles þe Frensshe Kynge to let it beo translated oute of Frenshe in-to Englisshe.'

[3] Eighteen rhymes on 'ffraunce', thirty-six on 'felicitee', and eighteen on the refrain word 'preyer'. The sixty-six lines extant are merely a torso; the poem should properly have seventy-two lines.

[4] *M.P.,* 124. Alternative titles: *A Glorious Prayer to St Edmund* and *An hooly preyer.* Twelve ballad stanzas linked by a refrain.

[5] Lines 200–34 (Book I) (cf. Horstmann, *Altenglische Legenden,* N.F., Heilbronn, 1881, p. 380). Five Chaucerian stanzas.

[6] Lines 1457–1520, eight ballad stanzas.

[7] Three rhymes in sixty-four lines (sixteen on -esse, thirty-two on -e, sixteen on -ance).

[8] *M.P.,* 212; O. Mahir, No. 49.

# John Lydgate

can be no doubt that this prayer to St Edmund is at the same time a eulogy of the king, as was also his *Prayer for King, Queen, and People.* It constitutes a climax in his religious poetry; and modern taste finds its patriotic-cum-religious rhetoric more appealing than the hymns of praise to Jesus and the Virgin Mary, which seem to us strained and stilted.

Lydgate was at once both a court and a monastic poet; and the farther he departed from this blend of patriotism and religion that was so suited to his rhetorical talent the more evident – and from our point of view the more artificial – his style became. This is shown for example, by his second *Prayer to St Thomas of Canterbury,*[1] which was probably written at the request of the monastery situated there.[2] It contains the litany-like refrain of his first *Prayer to St Edmund*[3] and the same heroic note, with its associations of ostentatious show; but since Lydgate felt less close affinity with St Thomas than he did with his King, Henry VI, or the royal patron of his monastery (whom he always seemed involuntarily to identify with Henry), the impression produced by his *Prayer to St Thomas* is in some way less effective. For this reason it has generally been attributed not to Lydgate himself but to one of his disciples.[4] The same is true of his two poems addressed to St Anne: of these the short *Praise of St Anne,*[5] comprising a mere two Chaucerian stanzas, deserves to be mentioned only because it served as a forerunner or preamble to his great *Invocation to Seynte Anne,*[6] a prayer commissioned by Countess Anne of Stafford. It certainly does not lack majestic splendour, but as there is less occasion to adopt a heroic tone in the case of a woman saint, his magnificent verbal display gives an all too artificial impression (e.g., in stanza 8), and to the modern mind sometimes verges upon the ridiculous. Only the final lines, in which Lydgate goes on to speak of Christ, make the heroic tone again apposite, and here he once more strikes the stately and dignified note that is proper to a hymn of praise.

*

[1] *M.P.*, 140, in fifteen ballad stanzas.
[2] Cf. stanza 13 (in which he entreats Thomas to pray for his church, town and monastery) and the envoy (stanza 15).
[3] 'And pray for alle þat calle the in ther neede'; in the *Prayer to St Edmund* (*M.P.*, 124) this sometimes occurs in this form and sometimes with variations.
[4] MacCracken writes: 'Never before ascribed to Lydgate, this prayer . . . bears every mark of his style, metre and rhyme' (Canon, No. 129).
[5] *M.P.*, 130.          [6] *M.P.*, 130, in eleven Chaucerian stanzas.

Marian hymns are the most prolific branch of medieval religious poetry,[1] and they are correspondingly numerous among Lydgate's works. Here we find in close proximity the traditional (i.e., popular) element and the new (i.e., pompous) style. We may consider first, as forerunners of his actual Marian hymns and paraphrases, two short pieces, evidently written at an early date: *The Image of Our Lady*[2] and the hymn *The Child Jesus to Mary, the Rose*. The former resembles the poem *How the Plage was Sesyd at Rome* in that it was also composed to order, as the accompanying text to a painting in one of the Roman churches, that of S. Maria del Popolo.[3] It would be of some interest from a biographical point of view if we knew more about the two men who donated the painting, Rauf Gelebronde and John Thornton.[4] It was written with technical skill, but is of no particular significance as a work of literature. The second of these pieces, *The Child Jesus to Mary, the Rose*,[5] is a hymn that still has a certain appeal for us today. Its three Chaucerian stanzas, linked by a refrain, recall the flowing rhythm of many Marian hymns. This apparent unpretentiousness and naturalness obscures the subtlety contained in the unchildlike theological discourse delivered by the infant Jesus to His Mother. Lydgate seeks to raise the content to an exalted spiritual plane to forestall the tendency for this type of hymn to sink to the level of a popular idyll. He adopts the same practice in his *Magnificat*,[6] a hymn addressed to God the Father, which forms part of his *Life of Our Lady*.

We may begin our examination of Lydgate's Marian poetry proper by considering the number of paraphrases which he made of well-known hymns (or at least, hymns that were well-known at the time), most of them treating the theme of the Joys of the Virgin. One of these is the [*Translacyoune of*] *Gaude Virgo mater Christi*,[7] a feeble work

---

[1] Th. Wolpers, *Geschichte der englischen Marienlyrik im Mittelalter*, Diss., Bonn, 1949. Cf. *Anglia*, 69 (1950), pp. 3–88.

[2] M.P., 290, in five ballad stanzas.

[3] The modern church of S. Maria del Popolo was built between 1470 and 1490 on the site of the chapel, erected in 1099 to free the district from the demons of Nero's grave, which was situated here.

[4] A 'gentylman Rauf Gelebronde' donated it at the insistence ('at the coste and contemplacion') of the Archdeacon, John Thornton (*praebendarius* of London in 1423).

[5] M.P., 235.

[6] Printed and edited by Tame, *Life of our Lady*, in op. cit.; Bannatyne MS., Hunterian Club, 1896, II, 64–7; Ritchie, in Scottish Text Soc., N.S., 22, pp. 60–3. Seven ballad stanzas.

[7] M.P., 288.

# John Lydgate

consisting of five Chaucerian stanzas framed by a prologue and envoy. Each stanza has a Latin heading giving one *gaudium*, which then forms the subject-matter of the stanza that follows. Lydgate dispenses with the invocations customary in other versions of this hymn, and attempts a narrative, which produces a rather unimaginative rigid impression. He wrote it, we are told, 'by night as he lay in his bedde at London'. His *Ave Maria!* (also known as *Salutacio angelica translata*)[1] likewise belongs to the *Gaude* tradition. This contains not five but seven joys,[2] in nine ballad stanzas, of which the concluding lines, in Latin, repeat with variations certain words in the concluding line of the preceding verse. The Latin *caudae* are incorporated in a meaningful manner, their short lines lending an element of melodiousness to the ballad stanzas. Nevertheless Lydgate's languid brocaded style can hardly be considered suitable to be sung. Each stanza opens with 'Hayle! glorious lady', or some similar invocation. Another work which may be noted here is the fragment, twelve ballad stanzas in all, that begins with the words 'Heyll blessid Marie'.[3] Yet another paraphrase, the hymn *Ave regina celorum*,[4] contains only a sprinkling of Latin phrases. Its style, as well as an allusion it contains to the plague of 1448,[5] indicate that it was written during his later period. This adaptation of the antiphons to Mary still to be found in the modern breviary is less a hymn than a prayer of glorification for use during the fast between Candlemas and Easter. Many of the invocations and epithets applied to Mary seem to us too far-fetched, and even tasteless; however, at the time (and also later, in the lyrics of the seventeenth-century Jesuits and the verse of Crashaw which was based on these lyrics) this *argutezza* was regarded as a worthy offering to the Virgin. A hymn of praise similar to these, but which gives a more melodious impression, is *Regina celi letare*.[6] Into this a Latin Easter hymn[7] has been worked in such a manner that a verse of the Latin

---

[1] M.P., 280; cf. Wehrle, op. cit., p. 139.

[2] The figure varies. Cf. p. 193, n. 6.

[3] Included in the canon by MacCracken as *Verses to the Virgin*, but not printed in M.P. (Brown, *Index*, *34).

[4] M.P., 291, in six ballad stanzas with a Latin refrain, which serves as a title.

[5] Wehrle, op. cit., p. 136: 'These lines were probably suggested by the thought of the Black Death which in 1348 [i.e., 1448] spread its ravages far and wide.'

[6] M.P., 293.

[7] The well-known antiphony *Regina caeli laetare*, which from 1742 onwards has taken the place of the *Angelus domini* as a prayer at Eastertide when the angelus bell is rung. In the breviary it is appointed for Eastertide, in place of the *Ave regina caelorum*, the prayer said before Easter. Cf. *Horae Eboracenses* (Publ. Surtees Soc., 132, Durham, 1920).

hymn constitutes the concluding lines of each of the five English ballad stanzas.[1] In general it displays the same sophisticated erudition as his *Ave regina*.[2]

Two of his other Marian hymns belong rather to the category of prayers: firstly, *To Mary, the Star of Jacob*,[3] a nocturnal prayer also in the *Gaude* tradition, written to order (like *Christe qui lux es*); and secondly, *Prayer to Mary, in whose Help is Affiaunce*,[4] which again makes only moderate use of invocations. Some of the benefits which Mary is asked to confer (long life and riches, as well as eternal bliss) may seem of somewhat dubious moral validity, but did not seem inappropriate to the faithful of those days.[5] In general this piece, like the preceding one, may be classified as a small parergon. There follow six other lengthy works: two variants summarizing the *quindecim gaudia* and four Marian ballads, which reveal Lydgate's later style in all its splendour and mannerism. The motif of the Joys of Mary originates in Latin hymnody; in the thirteenth century it was presented in a gentle lyrical mood, and in the fourteenth century in a more forceful manner which was the preliminary stage in the emergence of a litany-like prayer of salutation. The number of joys, originally seven, was later expanded to fifteen, a figure which in England became traditional.[6] The joys did not always remain the same: e.g., the more popular *de epiphania* replaced the *ascensio*, and the *de nativitate* was superseded by the 'experience of tranquillity'. Lydgate, however, sought to give elevation to his theme, not to present an idyll. In his hands the morning dew, for instance, turned to glittering gold and silver. Instead of the popular features that were now generally becoming more and more pronounced he deliberately preferred to

---

[1] Cf. the old macaronic poem in Wehrle, pp. 103 f.

[2] In a second version the first line, in Latin, recurs as a refrain and the other three lines form the headings of each stanza (as in the *Gaude virgo*). Many Marian poems and religious poems generally which display Lydgate's stylistic characteristics are probably not by him but by one of his disciples. Cf. MacCracken, *Lydgatiana*, in *Archiv*, 131, pp. 48 ff.

[3] *M.P.*, 282, in seven Chaucerian stanzas.

[4] *M.P.*, 296, three ballad stanzas in litany style.

[5] The same entreaties occur in *Stella celi extirpauit* (II, stanza 4) (*M.P.*, 296).

[6] The figure fifteen comes from the psalter (150 psalms); otherwise the Church speaks of the seven joys and seven sorrows of Mary, although these figures vary (today there are fourteen stations of the Cross, whereas in former times there were seven, and still are only this number in some old churches). The modern 'joyful rosary' has only five mysteries, but in former times the figure was not fixed at five, since the rosary had not then been stabilized in its modern form. Such rosary hymns are not official pronouncements of the Church, but the private work of local priests.

strike an exalted spiritual note. This can also be seen from the fact
that his hymns now increased in length. In *The Fifteen Joys and Sorrows of Mary*,[1] which attains almost epic proportions, he makes sparing use of the aureate style. It has an engaging introduction, with
autobiographical touches, reminiscent of the *Boke of Duchesse*; with
the following content: 'recently early one morning, meditating on
the inconstancy of life, I read a book about Fortune which had as its
frontispiece Mary in a Pietà; in it were listed the fifteen joys and
fifteen sorrows, and a man was shown kneeling and saying a Pater
noster and ten Aves at the end "of ech ballade" (i.e., after each of the
joys and sorrows).' And so it was that he came to compose the hymn
that followed, beginning with the *primum gaudium*. After each joy of
Mary, most of which are one stanza long, there are the words:
'Pater noster and 10 Aves'. The *gaudia* are therefore in fact invocations, like those in the litany, and the whole work can be described as
a rosary poem. The verses on the *gaudia* come to an end at stanza 21;
he then writes: 'tremblyng in euery membre my penne quakyng,' and
this is followed by the rather wearying enumeration of the *dolores*. The
same theme is treated in the pompous style of his later years in his
*Fyfftene Ioyes of Oure Lady*,[2] which were apparently translated from
the French for Princess Isabella, Countess of Warr, Lady Despenser.[3]
The construction is rigid, the joys alone being related; as in the
preceding poem, they are, as it were, spoken by the precentor, with
the congregation responding with 'Ave Maria'. The heaped-up
invocations serve the purpose of overwhelming the reader's senses
in a manner similar to that employed by metaphysical writers like
Crashaw.

This was also the purpose of the next of his ballads to be considered, which are perfect examples of his invocatory style. A forerunner of these was the four-stanza *Prayer to the Blessed Virgin* included in his translation of Deguileville.[4] In his Marian hymn

---

[1] *M.P.*, 268, forty-five Chaucerian stanzas (of which four belong to the prologue and
three to the envoy). For the theme, cf. the unpublished poem *Sorrows of the Blessed Virgin*,
in forty-five Chaucerian stanzas, listed in Brown's *Index*, No. 4089.

[2] *M.P.*, 260, in twenty-eight Chaucerian stanzas.

[3] Probably Isabel, daughter of Constance le Despenser (sister of the Duke of York
and widow of Lord le Despenser). In 1411, when only eleven years old, Isabel married
Richard Beauchamp, Lord of Abergavenny, and after his death in 1422 married his
cousin and namesake Richard Beauchamp, fifth Earl of Warwick.

[4] 'O blyssed mayde fflour off alle goodnesse' (Brown's *Index*, No. 2395). *EETS*, ES.,
83, pp. 454 f.

*Gloriosa dicta sunt de te*,[1] composed for the Bishop of Exeter,[2] Lydgate expands the seven verses of the psalm to 232 lines and employs an excess of stylistic artifices, but nevertheless reveals himself as, one might say, the poet laureate of the Church. Mary, radiating royal majesty, is equated with Jerusalem, the celestial Jerusalem of the Apocalypse, built of precious stones: jasper as the symbol of virginity, sapphire as the symbol of truth, and chalcedony as the symbol of purity. *To Mary the Quene of Hevene*[3] is also noteworthy as a work of art as well as from the standpoint of literary history – not so much on account of its theme, which follows the *gaudia* tradition, but on account of its lavish orchestration. Entire stanzas consist of invocations, creating a tension which then ebbs away in the refrain. The epithets used are ingenious and startling. Some stanzas, such as the fourth, are veritably enigmatic with their erudite allusions; but for all their unusualness they still maintain the form of a rosary or litany. *Ave Jesse virgula*,[4] a paraphrase of a Marian hymn that has since been lost, is an intermediate form between a litany hymn and a hymn in its own right. As in all his Marian lyrics, Lydgate adds nothing original to the content[5] and seeks to compensate for this by using far-fetched epithets in regard to Mary: for instance, he makes borrowings from a lapidary, gives a threefold interpretation of her name as an anagram, draws on the Song of Songs, and inserts Latin phrases. All this counted at the time for elevated style, although to our ears it sounds artificial and overdone, and impairs the hymn's value as literature. It is a veritable arsenal of aureate style, though more shapeless than his *Ballade at the Reverence of Our Lady, Qwene of Mercy*.[6]

---

[1] *M.P.*, 315 (alternative title: *Balade of Oure Ladye*), in twenty-nine ballad stanzas, following Psalm lxxxviii. 3, which is in the Mass appointed for the feast of the Immaculate Conception in the *Missale Romanum*.

[2] Probably Edmund Stafford, who was Chancellor from 1396 to 1399 and again from 1401 to 1403, was consecrated Bishop of Exeter on 20th June 1395 and died on 3rd September 1419. The other bishops of Exeter during the time in question were: Thomas Brantingham, consecrated 12th May 1370, died 23rd December 1394; John Catterick, transferred from Coventry 20th November 1419, died 28th December 1419; Edmund Lacy, transferred from Hereford 3rd July 1420, died 18th September 1455.

[3] *M.P.*, 284, in ten and a half ballad stanzas, of which three and a half form the envoy, each one linked to the next by a refrain.

[4] *M.P.*, 299, in nineteen ballad stanzas.

[5] The designation of Maria as an offspring of Jesse recurs time and again in poetry and art at this time. For examples of this in poetry, cf. the sequences of the school of Adam of St Victor; for examples in art, cf. in particular sculptures and church windows.

[6] *M.P.*, 254; ed. by Skeat, in *Chaucerian Pieces* (Chaucer, VII), 275 ff. Detailed analysis in W. F. Schirmer, *Der Stil in Lydgates religiöser Dichtung*, in *Kleine Schriften*, Tübingen, 1950, pp. 40ff.

O

# John Lydgate

This invocation of Mary, which extends to twenty Chaucerian stanzas, is one of the many versions of a hymn that Lydgate could read in Deguileville's original as well as in Chaucer's adaptation (*A B C*). In content it keeps close to its models: the first three introductory stanzas, in which ballads on spiritual love are compared to advantage with those on worldly love, are followed by invocations of the Virgin under the most varied appellations and using the most varied images, which follow one another like the gleaming beads of a rosary. The prototype of this was in the Bible (the Psalms and the Song of Songs) and in the Latin hymnody; but Lydgate accentuates the invocations to such an extent that they obscure the clarity of his sentence structure like the decoration on a cathedral in the Perpendicular style. He distorts entirely the basic pattern of the litany: *invocatio* (O Maria), subject (Thou), verb (aidest), and object (sinners); with Lydgate the *invocatio* takes up the greater part of the stanza, often as much as six lines, and the actual sentence drags on briefly at the end, in the seventh line; occasionally it is quite stunted, and the entire stanza consists of invocations.[1] The abstract treatment, based upon secular lyrics, produces a fatal effect. This graceful abstract style lent itself to the description of emotions and moods, such as were treated in secular ballads, but not to religious lyrics. Lydgate fused his secular with his Biblical model. He achieved neither vividness nor proper atmosphere, but an impression of something enigmatic, of something that had to be meditated on and puzzled out afterwards. Thus his endeavour to attain an elevated poetic diction that would express his search for the sublime, by accentuating the eloquence inherited from Chaucer, produced a style that could be read only with difficulty. He succeeded in increasing the possibilities that existed to express and formulate ideas, but in doing so substituted for faithfulness of representation conceptual formulae which often obscured the sense, together with a sonorous verbosity. Both his aims and his achievements are related to the *dolce stil nuovo* that had made its appearance a century earlier and to the poetry of the *Pléiade* a century later.

The evolution of the new style was the result of changes in religious attitudes. The naïve pious fervour of the Franciscans corre-

---

[1] Proper sentences (and thus a narrative account) occur only in stanzas 1–3 and in part of stanza 14. In stanzas 7 and 8 the sentence is compressed into two lines, in stanzas 4, 11, 13, 17, and 18 to one line, and in stanza 6 to half a line. In stanzas 5, 9, 10, 12, 15, 16, 19, and 20 the invocations take up the entire stanza.

sponded to an unpretentious natural style, which may still be found
in secularized form in many fifteenth-century carols. This feeling of
religious intimacy bridged the gulf between man and God and presented the Deity in more human form. Lydgate, in contrast, sought to
restore the sacred character of the religious lyric. He therefore had to
avoid the exaggerated courtly tone, in which (already in the thirteenth century) even the traditional liturgical forms of addressing
Mary, *domina* and *virgo* ('leafdi' and 'maiden'), had been qualified by
adjectives that were undeniably courtly. He distanced himself also
from Chaucer's *A B C*, although here the courtly element is combined with the elevated imagery found in the hymnody of the early
Middle Ages and of Dante. Lydgate does not, like Chaucer, make use
of his faculty of persuasion; under the influence of Latin hymnody
he seeks to bring about a reinvigoration of the invocatory style. He
is not concerned, as Deguileville had been, to supply an exact description of Mary's authority; his purpose is to sing the praises of
her dignity, abounding virtue, and sublime majesty. Zealous emulation of the Latin authors makes his style ornate with invocations until
it is as heavy and stiff as rich brocade. But this has its *raison d'être*
as the expression of a new attitude towards religion. We no longer
sit with the Holy Family at a common table; we are far below them.
Christ is no longer 'sweet' or 'dear', but 'mighty' and 'heavenly'.
Mary is no longer the consoling lover or the mother playing with her
child; nor is she the courtly lady, Chaucer's 'lady brighte'. Instead
she is the queen of heaven, the image radiating mercy, enshrined in
mystical ornamentation. Hence his revelling in her brightness and
splendour (where courtly lyrics would have emphasized her beauty);
hence his abstraction, his representation of the spiritual or moral
essence of images which he no longer visualizes in the flesh. In
his efforts to attain 'grettest solemnyte' Lydgate went beyond the
Latin hymnists both in his ideas and in his language. He brings the
Middle Ages to a close and opens the way to the new era of the
Renaissance. The graceful elegant courtly style gives way to a style
characterized by majesty, heroic dignity, and solemn grandeur.

## Chapter 20

### Lydgate's Moralistic Didactic Verse

\*

In contrast to his religious poetry, Lydgate's didactic or moralistic verse, devoted purely to secular themes, is written in a less pretentious style. A work that occupies an intermediate position between these two genres is *The Pyte to the Wretched Synner*,[1] a text accompanying an image of the Virgin, which combines a resemblance to the Marian lament with a call to penitence. The subject-matter of such poems, which were well suited to a monk, consisted of variations on the theme of the inadequacy and transitoriness of human existence. Thus, for example, he demonstrates the absurdity of human things in all their contradictoriness: a mighty king – and a poor country; almsgiving – and forced levies; chivalrous and cowardly conduct, which, he says, 'may wele ryme but it accordith nought'. With this refrain the eleven ballad stanzas of *Rhyme without Accord*[2] seek to show up satirically the faults of the various social classes, which are set off in the final stanza by a plea for divine succour. This is the popular theme of the *Order of Fools*,[3] which Lydgate had already adapted in a lengthier satire, and which he now took up again in the two versions of *They that no While Endure*,[4] employing a refrain that also occurs in the *Fall of Princes*.[5]

Lydgate was fond of gnomic poetry such as this; and his *Tyed with*

[1] M.P., 297, in five ballad stanzas (entitled: *On the Image of Pity*).

[2] M.P., 792; Halliwell, op. cit., p. 55 (*On the Inconsistency of Men's Actions*).

[3] Cf. Chapter 12.

[4] M.P., 818 and 820; seven and eight Chaucerian stanzas respectively.

[5] F.o.P., I, 12, and III, 10. Lydgate often took moralistic passages out of his version of this great historical work, and gave them an independence which they did not merit aesthetically: e.g., his *Death's Warning* (M.P., 655), in seven Chaucerian stanzas, intended as a *memento mori*, to which he added a new introductory stanza.

*a Lyne*[1] is composed in the same manner. MacCracken classified these pieces under the characteristic collective title: 'little homilies with proverbial refrain'. In most of them the whole content is stated in the refrain or in the first line, so that modern editors have taken these lines as appropriate titles. A more detailed discussion here of these minor works would be superfluous. One of them is *See myche, say lytell, and lerne to soffar in tyme*,[2] which in one MS. bears the heading '*proverbium*'. Many of these poems contain attractive wording and lively comparisons, as, for example, does the *Song of Vertu*,[3] but such details are drowned in the monotonous flow of aphoristic sayings. *Every Thing to his Semblable*,[4] an enumeration of all the craftsmen, classes, and professions with their corresponding occupations, develops into a catalogue that is not without interest for the cultural historian; but Lydgate lacks the delight in narration necessary in order to give a real picture of medieval life. *Say the Best, and Never Repent*[5] begins well with a narrative opening that puts the reader at his ease, but this is soon lost from view, and the pretentious 'ballade' which precedes it, with its moral maxims extending to five Chaucerian stanzas, does all that is required to kill the theme by sheer exhaustion.

In addition to these short popular moralistic pieces one may distinguish a more learned group, seeking to produce their effect by a prolix enumeration of model personages from the Scriptures, history, and mythology. For example, *Consulo quisquis eris*,[6] which likewise treats the theme of the imperfection of human nature and the transitoriness of all things temporal, acquires a special note by its touch of erudition, although it is no more ingenious than his short moral pieces or small sermons. It consists of two parts divided from one another by *verba translatoris* (stanza 8). The first part, probably the translation of a medieval Latin poem, puts forward the maxim 'when in Rome, do as the Romans do', which in the second part is superseded by more fitting precepts. These maxims are often far-

[1] M.P., 832; Halliwell, op. cit., p. 74 (*On the Instability of Human Affairs*), in twelve Chaucerian stanzas.

[2] M.P., 800, in five Chaucerian stanzas

[3] M.P., 835; Halliwell, op. cit., p. 216 (*The Triumph of Vertu*), in thirteen ballad stanzas.

[4] M.P., 801, in twenty-five ballad stanzas.

[5] M.P., 795; the ballad in five Chaucerian stanzas, and the text in sixteen more ballad stanzas (short lines).

[6] M.P., 750; Halliwell, op. cit., p. 173 (*The Concords of Company*); Furnivall, in *Political, Religious and Love Poems*; in fifteen ballad stanzas.

# John Lydgate

fetched; to *The Cok Hath Lowe Shoon*[1] (twenty-two ballad stanzas) one feels inclined to apply Lydgate's own words that although it rhymes, 'it accordith nought'. Nevertheless this sermon has passages that are entertaining even today, and brings to life for us this zealous, kind-hearted monk with his multifarious interests. Occasionally, to heighten the effect, he groups the parts of the poem in a dexterous manner; for instance, in *A Ditty upon Haste*[2] the first part, which is sententious and popular, is followed by one that abounds with erudite examples from antiquity and quotations from classical authors, while its concluding stanzas build up to a climax that one ought to turn from wickedness to a virtuous life, to Christ and His Passion. In the case of one of these poems, *That now is Hay some-tyme was Grase*,[3] a note by the scribe Shirley enables us to determine the circumstances leading to its composition. Lydgate wrote this ballad 'at þe commaundement of þe Quene Kateryne as in here sportes she wallkyd by the medowes that were late moven in the monthe of Iulij'. We can visualize the monk, who has risen to the rank of court poet, accompanying the royal widow on a walk, in his capacity as her ecclesiastical adviser, and consoling her by referring to the mown grass that has been put out to dry for hay-making; everything temporal is transitory; grass turns to hay and roses fade; in winter the nightingale's summer warbling will be stilled, and old age will disfigure all the beauty that now blossoms so sweetly. And he then goes on to say what Villon was later to celebrate in song, in *Où sont les neiges d'antan*: the famous women of the past, the heroes of antiquity, the knights upon whom Fortune once smiled – all have been 'layd full base' by Death. Everything on earth perishes; only in the celestial Jerusalem is there grass that is ever fresh and never turns to hay. The young Catherine, tragically afflicted by her sudden change of fortune, may have uttered the request that these comforting words should be written down, and thus that afternoon in July 1424,[4] spent perhaps in the park at Baynard's Castle in Surrey, forms an imaginary back-cloth to a poem of which the basic notion was drawn from Psalm 89 (90), vv. 5–6 and Is. 40, vv. 6 et seq.

[1] M.P., 813; Halliwell, op. cit., p. 150 (*Advise to Tittle-Tattlers*); Th. Wright, *Political Poems and Songs*, L., 1861, II, 215 (*On the truce of 1444*).

[2] M.P., 759, in twenty ballad stanzas.    [3] M.P., 809, in seventeen ballad stanzas.

[4] The dating is conjectural. It was only after Henry V's death that Lydgate had the opportunity to enter into a closer relationship with Catherine. In 1424 she obtained Baynard's Castle as her residence; the affair with Owen Tudor took place in the following year, and in 1426 Lydgate left for Paris.

Lydgate's eloquence on this theme of the transitoriness of this earthly world is inexhaustible. Occasionally he adapts it to the narrow framework of human relationships, telling us that we ought not to let ourselves be troubled by evil gossip – *A Wicked Tunge wille Sey Amys*;[1] occasionally he adapts it to the wider framework of the world at large, as in *The World is Variable*,[2] a poem neatly ensconced between an introductory description of the season and an envoy, 'Goo, litil bille'. It would be wrong to infer that the tone of gentle complaint that occurs in these short sermons represents Lydgate's own personal attitude; yet his references to ancient Rome, the golden age, and the chivalrous ideals formerly upheld by knights and poets call to mind his *Fall of Princes*. The similarity between the ideas expressed here and the conservative political views of Henry V and his successors suggests that this poem was composed some time between 1430 and 1440.

Cast in the same mould of indulgent exhortation is the short sermon *A Freond at Neode*.[3] The romance-like opening is calculated to attract the listener's attention: it describes how the poet, wandering early one morning in the grove, hears a lark in song. Its song, of the mutability of fortune and the friend in need, introduces the didactic element. The *exempla* drawn from the classics and the Scriptures, with authorities cited, are lightly disguised in narrative form, and reach their climax in the customary final pious invocation of Christ. This the scribe (Shirley?) commends as 'polletyke', i.e., a cleverly constructed ballad. To a still greater extent this might be said of *Look in Thy Merour, and Deeme Noon othir Wight*.[4] Here the same theme is set within a framework of an introduction indicating the season and a 'go litel bille' envoy, and interest in the long expositions is sustained by a wealth of erudite material, frequently of an unusual kind. The imperfection of all creatures is illustrated less by reference to mythology and the classics than by a discussion of the qualities of the animals, following the pattern of the bestiaries. The way in which some gem of moral wisdom or some maxim is embedded in the assorted mass of abstruse knowledge has a certain fascination of its own, particularly since Lydgate introduces much

---

[1] *M.P.*, 839; in Chaucer, ed. Skeat, VII, 285, as *Ballade of Good Counsel*, in nineteen Chaucerian stanzas.
[2] *M.P.*, 844, in fourteen ballad stanzas.
[3] *M.P.*, 755, in seventeen ballad stanzas.
[4] *M.P.*, 765; Halliwell, p. 156; in twenty-seven ballad stanzas.

that is novel (e.g., that the swan wears mourning on its beak and legs). If in the moralistic and sententious poems of the type of *Tyed with a Lyne* it was the monk in Lydgate that was speaking, here he appears as a child of the inquisitive fifteenth century.

To modern taste these poems gain in attractiveness the closer they approximate to Villon's theme of *Ubi sunt*. . . .[1] For this reason we are justified in giving prominence to *As a Mydsomer Rose*.[2] This deals with the various talents which man possesses, and demonstrates that appearances are deceptive. The description of the constant changes taking place in the world of nature leads on to a discussion of the mutability of Fortune in human history. The continuous theme of the transitoriness of this earthly life, repeated in the refrain of each stanza, acquires particular impressiveness by being combined with the *Ubi sunt* theme (introducing the catalogue of names). The crowning climax is reached with the martyrs, whose sufferings can be compared, not to the rose that blossoms but one summer, but to the five roses representing the five wounds of Christ, 'Off whos five woundys prent in your hert a roose'.

The most vigorous of these moralistic poems is *A Thoroughfare of Woe*.[3] It is generally dated 'after the death of Henry V' because it mourns his passing; but it should really be ascribed to a later date, to the 1430s, for it also mourns the death in the battle of Orleans on 3rd November 1428 of Thomas Montacute (the second husband of Alice Chaucer), who had commissioned Lydgate's translation of Deguileville. It is a precursor of the *Fall of Princes*. Chaucer's verses from the *Knyghtes Tale*,[4] to the effect that this world is but a 'thurghfare ful of wo' and that we are pilgrims on our way through it are supported by *exempla* taken from the Bible and the history of the world (in which English history is allotted a good deal of space, with a review of the events of the recent past). The usual religious ending is shifted here further towards the middle of the poem, and so the poet is able to conclude with the 'mirror for magistrates' theme and the eulogy of his 'maister Chaucier, chief poete of Bretayne'. It is less the composition that deserves to be singled out than the verve with

---

[1] Cf. C. H. Becker, *Ubi sunt qui ante nos in mundo fuere*, in *Aufsätze für Ernst Kuhn zum 70. Geburtstag*, 1916, and E. P. Hammond, *English Verse* . . ., pp. 169 ff.

[2] M.P., 780; Halliwell, p. 22 (*On the Mutability of Human Affairs*), and also in Thom. Gray's *Works* (see Appx. 1); in fifteen ballad stanzas.

[3] M.P., 822; Halliwell, p. 122 (*Wretchedness of Worldly Affairs*), in twenty-four ballad stanzas.

[4] A 2847-8.

which the poem begins and the rhetorical effect it produces. The preaching on the theme of transitoriness is enhanced by being cloaked in the Fortune motif. In the mourning for Henry V, for the Dukes of Clarence and Exeter, and for Montacute this theme acquires a forcefulness that is not to be found in the other poems in this group. Less colourful are the two poems *Song of Just Mesure*[1] and *Mesure is Tresour*,[2] both of which refer to the proverb 'Measure is treasure' and deal with order in the universe and moderation in everyday life.

*Amor vincit omnia mentiris quod pecunia*,[3] in which an envoy from the *Fall of Princes*[4] is adopted as a refrain, is a meditative complaint: 'Love is sette bakke, gold goth byfore, and mede'. With its wealth of allusions drawn from antiquity, this poem is clearly designed for an audience that has benefited from a humanistic education. The keynote of the transitoriness of this world, common to all these moralizing pieces, leads to a sermon on the theme: with God there exists a love that is superior to the love of a Delilah, riches that surpass those of Croesus, and beauty that exceeds that of Absalom. The theme of the venality of this earthly world is treated with great vividness and at a very mundane level in *London Lickpenny*, but this work is no longer ascribed to Lydgate. The poet prefers to supply a sermon and meditation for the benefit of those brought up in the humanistic tradition.

Of these laments on the theme of transitoriness his *Timor mortis conturbat me*[5] is thought to be his best. This genre, which had its origin in the office for the dead,[6] rapidly became popular. There developed a particular type with a fixed theme and metre: three rhyming lines and an unchanging refrain, *'Timor mortis conturbat me'*. This contains a forceful monkish sermon about the vanity of this world and the horrors of death, ending with a plea to God for salvation. Lydgate's poem, one of the earliest examples of this genre, stands somewhat apart, since it retains the ballad stanza, in which the point is made gently instead of being driven home, and since he does not develop the theme of the horrors of death. Thus the shattering

---

[1] *M.P.*, 772; Halliwell, p. 80 (*On Moderation*), in thirteen ballad stanzas.
[2] *M.P.*, 776; Halliwell, p. 208; in nineteen ballad stanzas.
[3] *M.P.*, 744, in seventeen ballad stanzas.
[4] *F.o.P.*, III, 4, *Envoy*, also often as a separate poem.
[5] *M.P.*, 828, in sixteen ballad stanzas (short lines).
[6] Further details and early examples in F. A. Patterson, *The Middle English Penitential Lyric*, op. cit. A fourteenth-century macaronic poem is in Wehrle, op. cit., pp. 89 f.

effect which the *memento mori* prayer is designed to produce fades out
in the final stanza, which has an air of pedantry about it despite the
ornate style. Owing to the numerous *exempla* the *timor mortis* theme
becomes an *Ubi sunt* poem, similar to the *Mydsomer Rose*; in the
stanza of the 'ladyes that were so fressh of face' the accumulation of
names, 'Ester, Judith, and eek Candace // Alceste, Dido and fayr
Eleyne', has a poetic quality that appeals to us as well; it may have
inspired Dunbar to write his moving *Lament for the Makaris*.

It is striking how easily Lydgate moves from a religious theme to
general moralizing. The poem *Benedictus Deus in donis suis*,[1] the title
of which is presumably taken from a passage in one of the psalms,
and which MacCracken has classified among his religious poems, is
actually a secular moralistic poem. So great is the profusion of words
that the catalogue of names lacks the urgency appropriate to the
*Ubi sunt* theme. In the case of *God is myn Helpere*[2] we can have doubts
as to its classification, for it begins as a prayer of thanksgiving, but
from stanza 6 onwards changes to the theme of fickle Fortune, and
then expatiates on the inconstancy of temporal things, health, the
weather and seasons, returning only at the end to praise of God as
the infallible succour.

The *Epistle to Sibille*,[3] a paraphrase of one of the Proverbs of
Solomon, is from the point of view of its content also a secular didactic piece; in the words of the scribe, its theme is the 'þeschewing
of ydelnesse'.[4] Each verse of the original is paraphrased in half a
stanza to one stanza, regardless of its applicability to English conditions. It comes as no surprise to find that the verse on the transitoriness of all things mundane, '*fallax gratia et vana est pulchritudo*'
(stanza 17), is the most successful. After stanza 18 the theme is exhausted; there follow the *verba factoris* recommending women to
lead a life of active piety, and then the envoy, 'Go lytel pistel, and
recommande me // Vnto my ladye which cleped is Cybille.' This
poem is of interest for the reference it contains to the person to
whom it was addressed, or who commissioned it. This was the same

---

[1] *M.P.*, 7, in nine ballad stanzas.

[2] *M.P.*, 27, in thirteen ballad stanzas (short lines). Line 89 of this poem is identical
with the introductory line of the ballad *Who seith the best shal neuer repent*, where it also
serves as a title (*M.P.*, 795).

[3] *M.P.*, 14, in twenty Chaucerian stanzas. Proverbs of Solomon: 31, 10 ff.

[4] The Proverbs of Solomon prompted Lydgate to change to a moralistic theme, for
their purpose lies in the realm of practical ethics. Cf. E. Sellin, *Einleitung in das AT*, 5th
ed., 1930, p. 136.

## Lydgate's Moralistic Didactic Verse

Lady Sibille Boys of Holm Hale[1] to whom he dedicated his *Treatise for Lavenders;* she apparently belonged to the circle of Lydgate's patrons.

All these pieces are not so much works of art as the routine products of a monastic poet.

[1] MacCracken: 'Lady Sibille [Boys] of Holm Hale?'. Further details are wanting.

# Chapter 21

## *Lydgate's* Fall of Princes

\*

The theme of the transitoriness of this earthly life was not only Lydgate's favourite topic but also that of the age in which he lived. The theme of melancholy, so aptly suited to the spirit of the times, had already been treated with vigour and sombre dignity in his *Dance Macabre*. He now returned to it in his *Fall of Princes*,[1] his most comprehensive work (36,365 lines). So overpowering was the impression it created that it became the epic of this war-torn century. We may perhaps find it uninspiringly monotonous on account of its prolixity and padding, and may reproach Lydgate for his lack of imagination and insight into character. But the sonorous solemnity of the verse,[2] which at times has the measured pace of a funeral march, makes this his greatest work. It has the pomp and ostentation of a procession of mourners, with the wheel of Fortune as background and an imploring speech to the living to keep the peace and maintain their personal

---

[1] *Fall of Princes*, ed. by H. Bergen, *EETS*, ES., 121–4, 4 vols., L., 1923–7. (Vol. IV contains a detailed study of the manuscripts and printed editions, excerpts from Laurent and Boccaccio, and a glossary). E. P. Hammond, *English Verse* . . ., gives excerpts with an introduction and notes, pp. 150 ff., 438 ff. Cf. also: A. Hortis, *Studi sulle Opere Latine di Boccaccio*, Trieste, 1879; E. Köppel, *Laurent de Premierfait und Lydgates Bearbeitungen von Boccaccios De Casibus: Beitrag zur Literaturgeschichte des 15 Jh.*, Munich, 1885 (Habilitationsschrift); F. Brie, 'Mittelalter und Antike bei Lydgate', in *Englische Studien*, 64 (1929), pp. 261 ff.; W. F. Schirmer, 'Lydgates Fall of Princes', in *Anglia*, 69 (1950), pp. 301–34; E. P. Hammond, 'Poet and Patron in the *Fall of Princes*: Lydgate and Humphrey of Gloucester', in *Anglia*, 38 (1914), pp. 121–36; W. Perzl, *Arthurlegende in Fall of Princes*, Diss., Munich, 1911; F. Werner, *Ein Sammelkapitel aus Lydgates Fall of Princes* (Münchner Archiv der Phil. des M.A. und d. Renaiss. ed. F. Wilhelm, Heft 5), Munich, 1915 (on Chapter 8 of Book I).

[2] *F.o.P.* is written in Chaucerian stanzas with occasional interpolations of ballad stanzas (in the envoys to Arsinoë, Antiochus, the Scipios, etc.: IV, 3445; V, 1590, 1846; VII, 246; IX, 2017, 3239, 3541, 3589.

integrity in this time of war and threatened civil strife. It is the first work in English to reproduce the heroic ideal of antiquity and to represent the heroes of classical legend and history in a dignified manner, without reinterpreting them in the light of Christian and chivalrous principles.[1]

Lydgate's achievement was made possible by the model on which it was based, Giovanni di Boccaccio's *De casibus virorum illustrium*. This Latin prose work, written between 1355 and 1360, relates in the chronological sequence usual at the time the blows dealt by Fortune to the great men – and women[2] – of legend and history. It is not simply one of the compilations of 'tragedies'[3] so popular in the Middle Ages, but a theatrical spectacle staged with consummate artistry. A long line of unfortunates, beginning with Adam and Eve and ending with King John of France (taken prisoner at Poitiers in 1356), passes lamenting before the author, who sits in his study and writes down the story of each of them. This succession of tragedies is enlivened by the disputations that take place between the author and his characters, who appear to him in a vision (e.g., between Boccaccio and Brunhild, Boccaccio and Petrarch, Fortune and Poverty), by digressions with comments by the author (e.g., the chapters summarizing pride, disobedience and womanly cunning), whilst relief is also afforded by chapters in which groups of persons appear (e.g., Pauci flentes, Conventus dolentium, Infelices quidem). This makes for variety and rhythm in a theme that would otherwise be monotonous. The numerous ironical remarks about the wickedness

---

[1] Brie (op. cit.) seeks to show that the *F.o.P.* was of signal importance for the new humanistic conception of antiquity, and emphasizes this thesis unduly. Nevertheless the passages which he cites to show appreciation of and enthusiasm for heroic subjects are indeed remarkable (cf. Mucius Scaevola, II, 918; Leonidas, III, 2297; Alcibiades, III, 3284; Epaminondas, III, 4635; Regulus, V, 421). Admiration for the freedom-loving heroes Cato (III, 1226) and Juba (VI, 2727), and for the last Scipio (V, 2787) even leads to suicide, otherwise severely condemned, being spoken of with approval. In describing Alexander (IV, 1198) and in some other remarks love of fame and posthumous glory are mentioned without reproach as being un-Christian. Yet, in opposition to Brie's thesis I should like to add that Lydgate's advocacy of the heroes of antiquity (such as Epaminondas or Regulus) can be explained by his patriotism, and that his mild matter-of-fact manner allows him to set down much of which he did not necessarily approve. We shall come back to some of these points in the text.

[2] The Latin *vir* here has the meaning 'human being'.

[3] The medieval conception of tragedy is defined by Lydgate in *F.o.P.*, V, 3118:

> *This may be weel callid a tragedie*
> *Be discripcioun takyng auctorite;*
> *For tragedie, as poetes spesephie,*
> *Gynneth with ioie, eendith with aduersite.*

and stupidity of those whom Fortune has entrusted with power over their fellow-men were, so to speak, flashes of lightning heralding a new stormy era. With nicely-calculated impartiality Boccaccio designed his work to appeal to various social milieux: firstly, his equal regard for Biblical and profane history and his rich portrait-gallery of figures from antiquity were addressed to humanists and scholars; secondly, his moralistic didactic thesis, in which he set out to show that all the buffetings of fate result from egoism, pride, and ambition and serve to teach princes wisdom and moderation, is often reminiscent of the examples given by medieval preachers, and appealed to the mass of *bourgeois* readers, as well as to those who retained an old-fashioned outlook; thirdly, his malicious remarks and the letter of dedication to his middle-class friend Mainardo dei Cavalcanti[1] galvanized those who were in a revolutionary frame of mind; lastly, the eminent, too, were attracted by the work, not by its teaching on everyday moral and political issues, but because it dealt with people like themselves. Thus we find Charles d'Orléans – also a fallen prince – calling for a manuscript to be sent him so that he might read it whilst he was a captive in English hands.

Translations of Boccaccio's work into vernacular languages soon followed. The most famous of these was the French prose version *Des cas des Nobles Hommes et Femmes*, written between 1405 and 1409[2] by Laurent de Premierfait,[3] a clerk of the diocese of Troyes. Laurent belonged to the group of littérateurs at the court of Philip the Bold of Burgundy, of which the most famous member was Christine de Pisan. His translations of Boccaccio[4] were commissioned by the Duc de Berry (1340–1416), who, like Humphrey, enjoyed a reputation as a bibliophile and patron of the arts but was at the same time a false and scheming egoist. (It was a strange stroke of irony that made these two noblemen the patrons of Boccaccio's mirror for princes.) Laurent's wide knowledge of history encouraged him to add to his source a profusion of historical, biographical, and geographical data. These comments on all the persons and places mentioned doubled the

---

[1] 1363. It was this version of *De casibus*, and not the expanded one of 1374, which Premierfait utilized: cf. note 2.

[2] This is the second, expanded translation, which Lydgate utilized; the first one, which was more literal, was written in 1400.

[3] His surname was derived from the name of a village near Arcis-sur-Aube. On Laurent, cf. the dissertation by H. Hauvette, *De Laurentio de Primofato*, Paris, 1903.

[4] As well as *De casibus*, Laurent translated the *Decamerone* (1411–14); he also translated the classics, *inter alia* Cicero for the Duke of Bourbon.

volume of the work. Although these additions to the subject-matter were for the most part taken from ancient authors, from the humanistic point of view the book represented a step back from Boccaccio. Reading *De casibus* would give an unsophisticated man courage in adversity; but Laurent made of this a veritable historical encyclopaedia, embracing everyone from Adam to the personalities of the mid-fourteenth century. The most regrettable changes were those which reduced its value as a work of art: the process of amplification resulted in the loss of *De casibus'* dramatic conciseness and the rhythm of its condensed and detailed chapters. As no new ideas were added to compensate for this extra breadth, the work is tedious for us to read today. But at the time when it was written this did not impair its popularity, and the most famous French painter of the day, Jean Fouquet, was called upon to illuminate the precious MS. copy which later passed into the possession of the Duc de Berry's descendants.[1]

Whether Lydgate had already examined this book, which was well known in France, when he was in Paris, or whether his attention was drawn to it by Duke Humphrey, we do not know. In any case Humphrey commissioned him to translate the work whilst he was Lieutenant and Warden of England during Henry VI's absence in France (April 1430 to January 1432), possibly in May 1431.[2] The task took the poet, now no longer a young man, almost eight years to complete. He treated the subject-matter in verses, which does not seem inappropriate, but unfortunately took as his source not Boccaccio but Laurent, which explains its disproportionate size and certain other shortcomings. On the other hand, Lydgate's translation has something original about it: it differs in the angle of approach. Boccaccio regarded his princes with hostility and bitter scorn. Although he gives it as his intention to teach those in power wisdom and moderation by means of the *exempla* he narrates, he nevertheless seems convinced that they have forfeited all sense of decency by their arrogance, extravagance, and vindictiveness, and that their bad example has a corrupting effect upon the people. One can thus detect a strong democratic and revolutionary note in his mirror for princes. But Laurent and Lydgate both genuinely sought to write so that princes might benefit from their teaching. They took the old-

---

[1] Written by Pierre Faure in 1458. Now Munich MS. Cim. V.a 4.

[2] The reference to Humphrey's zeal against the heretics (Prol., 400 ff.) refers to the suppression of the Lollards in Oxford, Salisbury, and London in the spring of 1431. An execution took place in Oxford in May 1431 probably in the presence of Humphrey.

established view that a prince's subjects existed for his sake, not the reverse. Laurent was obsequious; he flattered those who rewarded him, and his lack of character makes all his invective against tyranny and vice appear as a harmless theoretical exercise. Lydgate was different: he wrote as a priest in an admonitory tone, but without Boccaccio's crudities – he cut out his satire on the clergy and added more fervour to his lukewarm condemnation of the heretics. But he also wrote as a man of the world, as a courtier and aristocrat who held the people in contempt. Nevertheless he tells princes his opinions and calls on them to rule their subjects benevolently, justly, and unselfishly, since they hold their power from God. As is only to be expected, he does not censure his patron, but he does praise the domestic virtues.

Lydgate also shows originality in the artistic structure of the work. For he added envoys summarizing all the more important tragedies, thereby attaining a rhythmic effect similar to that achieved by Boccaccio. Honest as he was, Lydgate credits his patron Humphrey with having inspired this rhythm.[1] If this is indeed so, then one must pay tribute to Humphrey as a man of considerable aesthetic discernment; but it must be pointed out that the prologues and ballads which Lydgate interpolated, as well as the extensive cuts he made (usually with skill) in his French source, testify to the same effort to obtain rhythm.

The work is divided into nine books varying in length from nine to twenty-seven chapters. It begins with a prologue of 469 verses in which Lydgate indicates his source and, like Laurent, points out the advantages which an amplified translation has to offer. A narrative, in his view (and this is of significance both for an understanding of contemporary taste and for an evaluation of Lydgate's work), ought to have epic breadth – it should not be, as he puts it, 'constreynyd vndir woordes fewe' (93). It is in this way that he says he will treat the tragedies that Fortune has brought about. He sets off his usual flourish of modesty by giving a detailed discussion of the work of Chaucer. This appreciation, probably written with his patron's approval, allows him to emphasize the position formerly held by poets at their princes' courts; it closes with a eulogy of Humphrey in exaggerated terms which is, however, understandable in view of Lydgate's genuine sympathies for him as a book-lover and an enemy of the Lollards.

[1] Prologue to Book II (verse 146).

Then begins the long succession of great men lamenting their fate, starting with Adam and Nimrod, passing on to the Greek legends (the milieu on which he had relied for his earlier tales of Thebes and Troy), and concluding with the story of Samson and Delilah and Canace's letter. Several of these tales still show some of the old medieval delight in narrative, e.g., those of Meleager, Thyestes, Hercules, and Canace's letter[1] (the last-named being mainly based upon the account by that excellent narrator Gower). But by and large it is rather his turns of phrase, expressed as concisely as proverbs,[2] that appeal to the reader, as well as his envoys, which could often stand as separate poems in their own right. The tales themselves are employed in the traditional manner as pegs on which to hang a mass of encyclopaedic humanistic learning and pronouncements on the issues of the day.

Already in Laurent we find a large number of additions. Despite this the reader who casts a critical eye over the work can observe time and again how Lydgate endeavours to add yet more material, drawn from new sources, in an effort to obtain exhaustiveness. We can see that, inspired perhaps by Humphrey, he has studied Ovid's *Metamorphoses*; this is particularly evident in the tales of Medea, Minos, Scylla, the Minotaur, Hercules, Narcissus, and Pyrrhus.[3] For the story of Jocasta[4] and the subsequent events, which are only briefly summarized in Boccaccio and Laurent, he fell back upon his own *Siege of Thebes*, working some points out with greater precision. In the tales of Troy,[5] on the other hand, he is content to point proudly to the fact that he has dealt with these matters in his *Troy Book* and to refer the reader to it for further information. From another famous work by Boccaccio, *De genealogiis deorum*, he took occasional points of detail;[6] whilst for his Biblical stories he relied chiefly upon the Vulgate.[7] A 'mirror for princes' offered the opportunity not only for parading humanistic scholarship but also for cautionary sermons and a lightly disguised discussion of contemporary political topics. Many of these admonitions were a recurrent feature in such works, but others represented Lydgate's own ideas about the times in which he lived. For instance, the envoy to the tale of Oedipus declares that

[1] 4845, 3844, 5038, 6882 (in each case Book I).
[2] As in the account of Hercules and the résumé of the tales of Troy: I, 5104, 6042.
[3] 2171, 2411, 2483, 2658, 5216, 5552, 6735 (in each case Book I).
[4] I, 3158.      [5] I, 5937.
[6] E.g., in the stories of Orpheus, Ixion, Hercules, and Pyrrhus.
[7] As with Deborah, 2930, Gideon, 3048, and Samson, 6336.

# John Lydgate

internal strife endangers the existence of a kingdom.[1] This is admittedly a truism, on a par with other precepts such as that peace and justice are essential, or that princes ought to love their subjects; nevertheless, in view of the conditions prevailing in England, such general observations did have a specific meaning. This was made still more clear in the envoy to Atreus and Thyestes, where strife between relatives is stigmatized as unnatural and displeasing to God.[2] Humphrey may perhaps have seen in this a blow directed against his uncle Beaufort, just as he may also have interpreted his own efforts to curry popular favour as compliance with Lydgate's injunction to show love for one's subjects.[3] In condemning the war started without due cause (in the Marpessa envoy)[4] he broached a more delicate theme. But rulers were used to reading the 'mirror for princes' in a 'platonic' sense.

Lydgate proceeded in the same way in his treatment of Book II. But here, it might be said, he unexpectedly found himself confronted with a new task. We hear of Saul, Rehoboam, Lucrece, Virginia, Dido, Cyrus, the early history of Rome and its chequered fortunes – i.e., we have Biblical and ancient history, and less mythology than in Book I. But whereas he could read up the history of distant pagan deities and heroes in humanistic works (which also supplied curious details for him to include in his account), he was now called upon to consider people who lived nearer his own time. This meant that he had to compose their biographies himself and incorporate them into his overall historical pattern. The question of human responsibility and guilt arose in the mind of the reader and made the figure of Fortune problematical. His words of general admonition and exhortation acquired a topical political significance, and his whole position as a detached ecclesiastical observer was called in question.

In the prologue we are told that it is not Fortune[5] that brings about the fall of princes but 'vicious lyuyng',[6] and that Fortune

---

[1] 'kyngdomys deuyded may no while endure' (I, 3822).
[2] 'in kynredis to fynde frowardnesse' (I, 4223).     [3] I, 4502.     [4] I, 5888.
[5] On the important role played throughout medieval literature (and especially in the fifteenth century) by Dame Fortune, cf. A. Doren, *Fortuna im Mittelalter und in der Renaissance*, in *Vorträge der Bibliothek Warburg*, 1922–3; H. R. Patch, *The Goddess Fortune in Medieval Literature*, Camb., Mass., 1923; ibid., 'Chaucer and Lady Fortune', in *MLR* XXII (1927), pp. 377 f.; K. Hammerle, 'Das Fortunamotiv von Chaucer bis Bacon', in *Anglia*, 65 (1941), pp. 87 ff. E. Lommatzsch summarizes the literature on this question in the *Zeitschrift für rom. Philologie*, 1944. Cf. also K. J. Höltgen, 'König Arthur und Fortuna', in *Anglia*, 75 (1957), p. 35.
[6] II, 46.

exercises no influence over virtuous princes. This shows the intellectual dilemma in which Lydgate found himself. It was expressed still more clearly in the detailed dispute between Fortune and Cheerful Poverty in Book III:[1] on one hand the entire world is portrayed as a fatalistic drama of the fickleness of Fortune and the transitoriness of earthly glory; on the other hand history is seen as a manifestation in this world of divine justice. Lydgate fails to extricate himself from the toils of this contradiction. He condemns wicked Fortune as false, fickle, double-dealing, and deceitful,[2] but then goes on to say that it is not Fortune that is blind, but the tyrants themselves.[3] The preacher in Lydgate was loath to accept without qualification Boccaccio's shoulder-shrugging view that tyrants deserved their fate; he tones down his assertion that '*et ainsi dame Fortune se ioie des roys et aussi de tous aultres nobles hommes*' by adding the ethical point that Fortune humbles the mighty if they overstep their authority.[4] In the great scene in Book VI[5] in which the goddess Fortune appears to the author this contradiction becomes the pivot of an argument: the poet condemns her as the source of all evil, whilst Fortune excuses her fickleness as an inherent characteristic, with which one can as little argue as with the changing of the seasons. Lydgate is anxious to show the hand of God at work in human history, but persists in retaining the figure of Fortune, which has really become superfluous.

In Book I the discussion of contemporary topics, which forms an indispensable part of the text, was concerned with general moral principles, but in Book II we have the beginnings of a formal theory of politics (though not an original one). As a churchman Lydgate demands that wise princes should not interfere in ecclesiastical matters and should honour the holy Church.[6] The clergy hold for him the same position in the state as the soul has in the human body. This was an opinion shared by the high-ranking nobles and prelates with whom Lydgate as a courtier had close links; and the House of Lancaster was especially concerned to maintain a good understanding with the Church. His discussion of monarchy is noteworthy. Lydgate's age has been called by historians the era of 'the Lancastrian experiment' or 'premature constitutional government',[7] since

---

[1] III, 204–707.  [2] III, 3007–8.  [3] IV, 967.

[4] 'Aboue ther offis that wrongli list presume' (V, 2292).  [5] VI, 1–518.

[6] This is the lesson of the story of Uzziah (II, 2766–7) and the Belshazzar envoy (II, 3550); cf. also II, 2767.

[7] Adams, *Constitutional History of England*, L., 1928, p. 216 (ch. IX); cf. also Hatscheks p. 169.

# John Lydgate

Parliament showed a growing tendency to restrict the prerogatives of the sovereign.[1] This mixed form of government, with its quasi-modern air, was justified from the standpoint of constitutional theory by the jurist and courtier Fortescue. In contrast to Fortescue, Lydgate provides a defence of absolutist rule which seems to foreshadow the Stuart era. Unlike Laurent,[2] he makes no mention of popular election but only of hereditary right. The ruler is not responsible to the people, as Boccaccio had argued in his dedication, nor to God and the people, as is Laurent's intermediate view,[3] but to God alone. The love of the people for their sovereign ought to be fostered for his own sake, since it is to him that they owe obedience.[4] Love and obedience are the forces making for a firmly-established order.[5] It is clear from this that Lydgate's static outlook on politics does not make him a forerunner of the theorists of absolutism in Tudor and Stuart times, but rather indicates that he derived his ideas from St Augustine: *pax* (Lydgate's ideal),[6] *ordo* (based on the estates of the realm),[7] and *justitia* (the rights and obligations between the ruler and his subjects).[8] This medieval conception as advanced by Lydgate underwent some important modifications as a result of the events of his own day. When he speaks of the sovereign's power, he makes the point that royal blood and exalted descent are of little value without God's grace.[9] The story of Cyrus teaches that one should submit if God is pleased to raise someone of humble birth to wealth and power[10] – a sentence designed to bolster the claims to legitimacy of Henry IV and the Lancastrian dynasty, but one which could as easily be turned to good account by ambitious nobles. Such statements, and others of a similar nature, make Book II something of a political tract; and indeed the chapter headed by the editor 'On good government'[11] is based in part on John of Salisbury's *Polycraticus*.[12]

His subject-matter and the sources he utilized encouraged Lydgate to venture into the thought-world of the humanists. Alone the

---

[1] Parliamentary control over public revenues, parity of the Commons in legislation, Parliamentary control of the general policy of the government.

[2] *EETS*, ES., 124, p. 189.     [3] Ibid., p. 172.

[4] III, 3988; II, 547, 1460.     [5] II, 535, 538.

[6] Rejection of wars of aggression (II, 3960 and elsewhere).

[7] On the divinely-sanctioned social order of estates, cf. II, 869; I, 4229, and elsewhere.

[8] The rights of the people are in fact merely freedom from oppression (II, 909).

[9] Astyages wrongly thought that 'noblesse cam be discent off blood / And nat be grace, nor as the heuene stood' (II, 3037, 3081).

[10] 'Wher God list forthre a lyne / Outher to richesse or dominiciouns' (II, 3342–3).

[11] II, 806–917.     [12] Prologue and Books V–VI.

sentence that it is the scholar poets who preserve the glory of princes for posterity[1] is thoroughly humanist in tone. So, too, is the envoy to Rome,[2] in which he displays for the first time his stately sombre diction (its melancholic beauty was later to find consummate expression in Villon's *Ballade des dames du temps jadis*). In the tale of Mucius Scaevola[3] he praises the ancients' heroism and steadfastness, without any Christian bias; and in the eloquent eulogy of Lucrece which he translated, at Humphrey's suggestion, from the latter's copy of Coluccio Salutati's *Declamation*,[4] he even speaks favourably of her suicide,[5] although elsewhere such action earns his censure. But after his panegyric to Dido[6] he does consider it necessary to insert a satirical envoy to widows[7] in which he cautions them against following Dido's example. It would be a pity, he says, for the 'noble matrones' – may God preserve them in their weakness – to do so; rather should they take themselves lovers and keep them on a tight rein. In the tale of Gyges, which is almost entirely Lydgate's own work, we have another example of his satirical humour, in singular contrast to the dignified and almost solemn tone adopted in the rest of the work.[8]

After Book II was completed in or about the year 1433, an interruption ensued whilst Lydgate turned his attention to the *Legend of SS. Edmund and Fremund*. The interruption may also have had a deeper motivation in the problems arising out of the nature of his material. For this Humphrey, who not only commissioned this work but also supervised its progress, was not free from blame. Time and again he gave Lydgate books from his library: Ovid's *Metamorphoses*, Josephus' *De antiquitatibus judaicis*, and Coluccio Salutati's *Declamation of Lucretia*. Lydgate groaned under the weight of the advice given him by his patron and revenged himself by sending him his *Letter to Gloucester*,[9] a begging-letter '*in tempore translacionis libri Bochasii pro opportunitate pecunie*', in which, adopting Chaucer's felicitous manner, he describes the sorry state of his purse. He compares himself to a ship stranded by the ebbing tide; the only

[1] 'Or wheroff komth ther laude in reportyng / Sauff that clerkis han wreten ther histories' (II, 815).
[2] II, 4460. [3] II, 918.
[4] Cf. E. P. Hammond, 'Lydgate and Coluccio Salutati', in *Mod. Phil.*, 25 (1927–8), pp. 49–57.
[5] II, 1002. [6] II, 1898. [7] II, 2199. [8] II, 3347.
[9] *M.P.*, 665; E. P. Hammond, *English Verse . . .*, p. 149; also in *Anglia*, 38 (1914), p. 125; in eight ballad stanzas.

means whereby he can be rescued, as the refrain emphasizes, is 'with silver plate, enprinted with coynage'. The pert humour, for which the envoy apologizes, is decked out with witty playing upon words and sense: for gold and silver he uses the alchemist's terms Sol and Luna; instead of coin he writes Tower (where the Mint was situated), and the metaphorical ship is an allusion to the minting of gold nobles. This posing of riddles accorded with the taste of the time, and Duke Humphrey was so delighted that he granted the poet's request in a generous manner. Lydgate returned thanks for this gift in the prologue to Book III: poverty and old age are close at hand, and he was almost driven to despair at the task entrusted to him; but now his patron's generosity has given him courage once more, and he can set to work again feeling a new man.

In Book III we have in fact a fresh start. Almost unconsciously Lydgate had been obliged by his material to set himself a new objective: the compilation of a great historical work. Before this new purpose display of erudition and discussion of contemporary topics had to take second place; the introductory passages containing descriptions of nature, which were a feature of his earlier work, are here completely absent, and the stately solemnity of the envoy to Rome becomes ever more pronounced, as a tone deemed appropriate to such a major historical undertaking.

The theme of the whole of Book III is Roman history, of which elements were already present in Book II; but in addition to the Italian princes we have Greek and other heroes. His humanistic aspirations lead him to attempt an out-and-out historical treatment, for which he draws upon Justin's world history, Boccaccio's *De genealogiis*, and other historical works.[1] In this he shows an understanding for profane heroism that is astonishing in a medieval cleric. Thus, for example, he appreciates the heroic figure of Leonidas,[2] gives a complimentary portrait of Alcibiades,[3] and is full of admiration for Epaminondas,[4] whose contempt for death and eventual fall, in Lydgate's description, verge upon the sublime. The moralistic asides which in this connexion he casts at his own age lead to occasional deviations from his source. For instance, he turns Boccaccio's attack on judges into a tribute to the good old days, when nobles did

---

[1] Boccaccio supplied the examples for the chapter on covetousness (III, 4327); Justin was drawn upon for the chapter on Epaminondas (III, 4638), and a work not identified supplied copious additional material to the story of Amyntas (especially from III, 4579 onwards).

[2] III, 2297.          [3] III, 3284.          [4] III, 4635.

not abuse the law, clergy led model lives, merchants did not cheat, and women did not use cosmetics or wear horns on their heads or trailing dresses.[1] Such criticism is for the most part colourless and commonplace compared to that of Boccaccio. He is at his best in the warning he gives that 'he who takes revenge will reap vengeance'. To this he adds: 'princes, take pains to keep the fickle people from rebellion',[2] a remark in which his own personal apprehensions come clearly to the fore.

He continues in this grand manner appropriate to one writing a history of the world until Book VII. Admittedly, to the modern reader, less inspired by reverence for the material he is considering, this may savour of monotony. Humphrey drew Lydgate's attention to poetic models such as Virgil, Dante, and Petrarch;[3] and Lydgate, who stresses the patronage they enjoyed from their princes, takes this opportunity to send Humphrey another begging-letter.[4] To oblige Humphrey he interpolates literary digressions which do not have the standard his humanistic patron might have expected. These are continued in Book IV.

In the prologue he makes mention of a number of poets (Seneca, Vegetius, Persius, Virgil, Ovid, Petrarch, Dante, etc.), and also gives a list of works by Virgil and Petrarch. But from this one cannot infer that Lydgate was personally acquainted with these works or draw deductions as to his conception of poetry. Sometimes he endeavours to preach a gentle moral lesson in a witty or engaging style,[5] which was traditionally regarded, by the clergy in particular, as the function of poetry. But elsewhere he puts poetry on a par with historiography. His earlier reference to poets as those who handed down to posterity the glory of their princes is here amplified: it is from written records, he says, that we are familiar with the lives of the prophets, patriarchs, and martyrs; if 'writyng' did not exist, 'lawe' would be forgotten and 'our faith appalled':[6]

> *For all religioun and ordre of good lyuyng*
> *Takth ther exaumple be doctryn of lettrure.*[7]

---

[1] In the envoy to Appius, III, 3088.        [2] III, 4229.

[3] Cf. the reference to Dante (IV, 134–40) and the borrowing from manuscripts of works by Petrarch from Humphrey's library. E. P. Hammond, in *Mod. Phil.*, 25 (1927–8), pp. 49 ff.

[4] III, 3837–71.

[5] 'Ther cheeff labour is vicis to repreve / With a maner couert symylitude / And non estat with ther langage greve' (III, 3830).

[6] IV, 22.        [7] IV, 24.

# John Lydgate

The *Fall of Princes* complies absolutely with all these demands, and Book IV therefore diligently relates the fortunes of Manlius Marcus, Dionysius, Alexander and Callisthenes, Darius, Olympia, Agathocles, Arsinoë, Brennus, Pyrrhus, and others besides. The stories are told in a manner that will hardly arouse the interest of a reader today, but it must be said in Lydgate's favour that he often compresses Laurent's verbosity to advantage,[1] and occasionally surpasses him by making his version more dramatic.[2] Sometimes the horrors follow upon one another too closely for his own taste. In the tale of Olympia he exclaims: 'Off this processe write I will nomore / Cause the mateer is abhomynable'.[3] His guileless nature left him helpless when confronted with the all-too-human realities of life. He was the scholar who felt at home among his books; we can see him supplementing the story of Manlius Marcus by drawing upon Aulus Gellius[4] and compiling, from books we cannot identify, a grandiose description of Roman triumphs.[5] The moralistic asides in this book arise naturally out of the subject-matter, but are so emphatically keyed to one particular idea that we must assume that Lydgate had some contemporary issue in mind. Boccaccio and Laurent say that Fortune often elevates those of humble origin in order to overthrow them again later; Lydgate stresses the evil that results if a base-minded man comes to power. Even as king the base-minded man is no more than a crowned ass. No one is as arrogant and cruel as a beggar who rises to high station.[6]

This thesis, reiterated in the sentence 'Vertu is strenger than outher plate or maille',[7] is taken up again in Book V,[8] although we cannot identify whom he has in mind in drawing this picture of the crowned upstart; it may be intended metaphorically. The real interest of this and the subsequent book lies in the account given of Roman history. It is the figures of Marcus Regulus, Scipio, and Hannibal, and the conflict between Rome and Carthage that occupy the centre of the stage; in the following book it is Marius and Sulla and the wars between Pompey and Caesar. The subject is treated for the most part heroically. Regulus' voluntary self-sacrifice for the good of the State[9] is described with pathos, as though he were a Christian martyr.

---

[1] E.g., in the chapter on Alexius (IV, 1450) and in the story of Antipater (IV, 3109).
[2] Cf. the story of Belgius and Brennus (IV, 3570).
[3] IV, 2395.        [4] IV, 225.        [5] IV, 512.
[6] IV, 3151; cf. also IV, 3058.
[7] IV, 3741; cf. also the fine parallel with nature in IV, 2696.
[8] In the story of Andriscus (V, 2369-75 and 2467 ff.).        [9] V, 444 ff.

Lydgate would gladly tell his story in letters of gold. He is called the greatest of all Romans;[1] he is worthy to be crowned with a laurel wreath, and princes should take him as an ideal which they should seek to emulate. His treatment of the Punic Wars does not maintain this high level, but in his portrayal of the last Scipio,[2] whom he characterizes in a sense contrary to that of his source, he manifests the admiration for champions of liberty[3] which he already showed in his portrait of Cato.[4] The chapter on Caesar in Book VI is most original. Boccaccio had only mentioned the great Caesar in passing; Laurent had accorded him a special position on the grounds that he had not been overthrown on account of his vices. Lydgate refuses to grant him this special position; he finds him guilty of bringing about his own fall by his 'ambicious negligence',[5] and by seizing power when he was not allowed to have the triumph he wanted.[6] This had been the salient point in his prose work *The Serpent of Division*, in which the conflict between Caesar and Pompey had served as a warning of the evils of civil war. Since Lydgate rejects the deification of Caesar, but not his greatness, his account of his tragic fate is one of the most impressive tales in the whole work, and the envoy, with its sombre refrain 'Moordred at Roome of Brutus Cassius',[7] is also one of the best, on a par with the envoy to Rome in Book II. The impression of the hand of fate at work is heightened by the account, originating with Lucan and Laurent, given of the portentous marvels and omens which preceded the struggle between Caesar and Pompey.[8] Lydgate must have had a presentiment of the calamities which were later to befall England in the Wars of the Roses, and therefore combined his historical account with words of warning and exhortation. The story of Pompey and Caesar is given an ethical element in the refrain 'Pocessioun take no fors of wrong or riht: No cleym is worth withoute title of riht'. Lydgate's political outlook may be feudal and old-fashioned, but his conception of justice is based on personal conviction, and his rejection of violence is clear and unmistakable.

Lydgate's historical survey reaches its climax in Books V and VI; Book VII, on the other hand, gives evidence of fatigue and breaks off abruptly. This is apparent alone from its length: whereas all the other books run to an average of 3000–5000 verses, Book VII has

---

[1] V, 755.  [2] V, 1643.  [3] E.g., Juba (VI, 2727).
[4] III, 1226.  [5] VI, 2863.  [6] VI, 2815.
[7] VI, 2871.  [8] VI, 2283, and esp. 2388 ff.

# John Lydgate

only 1600 verses.[1] Another reason, apart from sheer exhaustion at the excessive volume of the work, lay in the content. The most important tales deal, on one hand, with Messalina, Caligula, and Nero, and on the other hand with the golden age, John the Baptist, and the destruction of Jerusalem; the path thus leads from Ancient Rome to Biblical history. The deeds of the Roman emperors arouse aversion and indignation in Lydgate; he makes abbreviations, or additions reflecting his own point of view, in which he contrasts the Roman world with the golden age. This necessitates a complete remodelling of Laurent's chapter. The latter's discussion of Saturn is reduced to a simple allusion. After this Lydgate[2] sets out to paint an ideal picture full of colour and containing echoes of Chaucer, which forms a separate poem in its own right, thanks to its slightly varying refrain:

> *For sobirnesse and attemperaunce*
> *Hadde in that world hooli the governaunce.*

This was the way in which Noah and Abraham had lived. Injustice and violence were unknown; youth was disciplined, and in middle age men devoted themselves to 'vertuous studie'; passions were curbed, and no one was guilty of slander. Knights respected chastity, heretics were punished, and the Church was held in high esteem. This theme brings out all Lydgate's didactic zeal. He embellishes his sermon with historical data: the golden age, he tells us, lasted until Jupiter overthrew his father, which turned the old order upside down; each class put aside moderation; reason ceased to rule, as it had done in the golden age; and the age of iron and cruelty began. To Lydgate the present day seems as changeable as the moon, unrestrained in the pursuit of pleasure.[3] He holds up the moderation of John the Baptist and Diogenes as an ideal for princes to follow.

Book VII comes to a worthy conclusion with the account of the destruction of Jerusalem.[4] Citing Josephus, he describes Vespasian's campaign and the annihilation of the city by Titus. Its fall is justified on the grounds that the Jews were to blame for treating Christ with such hostility; so great were the sins of the city that, if it had not been destroyed by the Romans, the earth would have opened and swallowed it up.[5] History is thus presented as a manifestation of

---

[1] Book I: 7070 verses; Book II, 4592; Book III, 5152; Book IV, 4066; Book V, 3145; Book VI, 3638; Book VII, 1663; Book VIII, 3381; Book IX, 3628.

[2] VII, 1157–1243.     [3] VII, 1251.     [4] VII, 1335 ff.

[5] This is not referred to by Laurent; Lydgate took it from John of Salisbury's *Polycraticus* (II, 5).

divine justice; it serves as a great *exemplum* to illustrate the meaning of virtue as taught and preached by the Church.

This moral lesson had at times been obscured in the course of Lydgate's long journey through pagan and heroic history. For the second time he has grown tired of these tales. The first occasion when this had happened was after Book II; but then, encouraged by Humphrey's support, he had begun afresh, after a pause, in a new style – the style appropriate to a great historical work. Now commences a new stage in the work, the third and last. He reveals his fatigue in an attractive addendum to the prologue, in which he makes Boccaccio his mouthpiece:

> *My lymys feeble, crokid and feynt for age,*
> *Cast in a dreed, for dulnesse of corage*
> *For to presume vpon me to take*
> *Of the eihte book an eende for to make.*[1]

He is not desirous of glory, but only to be well thought of by his fellow-men, which counts for much in a world where wealth and learning are soon forgotten and friendships fade. This original and personal note is again struck in the scene in which Petrarch appears to Boccaccio. Lydgate's words of welcome are directed less to the Italian poet laureate than to Chaucer:

> *Wolkome maister, crownid with laureer,*
> *Which han Itaille [= England] lik a sunne cleer*
> *With poetrie, pleynli to descryue,*
> *Most soueraynli enlumyned bi your lyue,—*
> *I haue desired, as it is weel kouth, . . .*
> *To doon you worshep fro my tendre youth, . . .*
> *. . . for treuli in substaunce*
> *Ye have been lanterne, liht and direccioun . . .*
> *To refourme the rudnesse of my stile*
> *With aureat colours of your fressh langage.*
> *But now fordullid be impotence of age, . . .*
> *My labour up of writyng I resigne.*[2]

Petrarch encourages the weary old man not to stop with Book VII, and after diverse examples of the diligence and perseverance shown by others adds as consolation that he will be recompensed for his

---

[1] VIII, 18.    [2] VIII, 67–84.

work by a certain highly-placed personage.[1] The humorous touch he shows when he makes another delightfully camouflaged request for Humphrey's support is also evident in the famous lines that follow, in which he tells of his origins in the village of Lidgate,[2] where Bacchus' potion, so essential to the well-being of his soul, flows but sparingly – a hint that Humphrey should also send him a small cask of wine. This prologue, originating from Lydgate himself, whose whole attitude is radically different from that of Boccaccio and Laurent, is, as it were, a pause for breath before launching into further work of translation.

The theme of Book VIII is in the main a continuation of the history of the Roman emperors (Diocletian, Maximian, Galerius, Valerian). It produces an effect different from that of Book III, when he launched into this material fresh in spirit; now he plods diligently and wearily through his endless subject, cutting it down as far as he can. But then he adds something new: a chapter on Constantine,[3] based on the *Legenda Aurea*, *Brut*, and other works. In view of these sources, Constantine's tragedy takes on the characteristics of a miraculous romantic legend which seems rather out of place amidst these historical accounts. Why did Lydgate introduce this tale? First and foremost, on patriotic grounds: according to legend, Constantine was born in Britain, and the poet calls upon Britons to rejoice in the fact that it was their country that gave the world its first emperor. This piece of hagiography with its marvels and omens thus served to rescue the poet from the immoralities of secular history and gave him the opportunity at last to devote himself entirely to a Christian theme. When we observe that the story of Constantine is effectively set off by the one that follows, on Julian the Apostate,[4] in which Lydgate illustrates the evil consequences of blasphemy, then it becomes patent that with Book VIII a new feature has entered into his treatment of history: it has now become pragmatic. The humanistic tinge of the earlier books has paled. He now abandons quite openly any claim to historical objectivity. When he reaches the story of Theodosius,[5] which he relates as a saint's life, with all the miraculous trappings (basing his account once again upon the *Legenda Aurea*, but making it more succinct and neat than that given by Laurent), his style departs from that appropriate to a great objective historical account. Now it is no longer Fortune but God who

[1] VIII, 145.     [2] VIII, 187 ff.     [3] VIII, 1170–1460.
[4] VIII, 1464–1708.     [5] VIII, 1891–2107.

punishes tyrants,[1] and it is by means of a miracle performed by God that Theodosius is rendered victorious.[2] Virtuous princes are urged to follow this example, which shows how the anger of the Lord may be assuaged: for Theodosius submitted himself to the Church without a murmur and is now enjoying his reward, seated with Christ in Heaven. If this may still be called a 'mirror for princes', then it is certainly a monkish one. From a general survey of Book VIII it may be said that among the great mass of characters mentioned four figures stand out: Constantine and Theodosius, both of whom are portrayed as saints rather than as tragic figures; then, as devil's advocate, Julian the Apostate; and lastly (after all manner of lesser tales[3] and passages of sermonizing)[4] King Arthur.[5] His story reads well. It is full of action, has a fervent patriotic tone, and is inspired by enthusiasm for the ideals of chivalry. It might be said that with Lydgate tradition flowed in his blood, whereas Laurent knew it only at second hand. Arthur is not a tragic figure, since he is free from guilt and is not responsible for his own fall. As the ideal of a Christian hero he is accepted into Heaven, a happy fate which Lydgate denies to his pagan heroes.[6] The envoys (of which there are actually two)[7] give the warning, then again topical, that conflict between members of high-ranking families endangers the unity of the realm, with an obvious reference to the breach that was now yawning in the Anglo-French empire[8] and a wistful glance back to the chivalrous days of the Round Table. The story of Rosamund, greatly abridged, with which the book concludes,[9] elicits from Lydgate the remark that he sees little profit ('litil frut') in this tale apart from recognition of the fact that murder brings divine retribution in its train. Lydgate

---

[1] VIII, 1996.　　　　　　　　[2] VIII, 2003.

[3] Boccaccio's *Dolentium descriptio breuis*, which Laurent expanded considerably, is very much shortened by Lydgate: e.g., he curtails the passages on Alaric, Radagaisus, etc. (VIII, 2108 ff.), and also on Odoacer, Boethius, etc. (VIII, 2626). The lines on Rome (Boccaccio's *In praesentem urbis Romae conditionem*) are translated in a listless and banal manner (VIII, 2528–69) that bears no comparison with that of his envoy to Rome.

[4] Cf. the chapter *On the conduct of things*, translated without abbreviation from Laurent (VIII, 2353 ff.), with some additional material of his own (VIII, 2451–7).

[5] VIII, 2661–3206.

[6] Cf. Romulus (II, 4201). Lydgate's remonstrance follows St Augustine (cf. Brie, op. cit.).

[7] The envoy proper (VIII, 3130–64) and the section headed: 'An exclamacion ageyn men þat been vnkynde to þeir kynrede' (VIII, 3165–206).

[8] 'The monarchie departid was on tweyne / That stood first oon' (VIII, 3195).

[9] VIII, 3256–381.

would not have made a remark such as this in the earlier books of *Fall of Princes*; then he had been content with the great historical drama of the transitoriness of worldly things. But now he has become a pragmatic historian, and evaluates the individual tales only according to their merits as *exempla*.

It is in this critical and sceptical mood that he sets about the translation of the last book, Book IX, in which he deals with the medieval tragedies of Brunhild, Guy de Lusignan, Charles of Anjou, the fortunes of the Knights Templar, Philippa Catanensi, and King John of France. He is in haste to bring the book to an end, and often makes such drastic cuts[1] that he would have been better advised to have followed Boccaccio in treating several figures together as a group.[2] In general this book is not dealt with fittingly,[3] although the near-contemporary characters who appear in it are of interest. The story of the Knights Templar[4] is informative and those of Charles of Anjou,[5] and John of France[6] excellent. The eventful career of Charles of Anjou, king of Jerusalem and Sicily, show Lydgate once more at the peak of his form. The sonorous envoy to Book IX, introduced by one of the very rare inaugural descriptions of nature, recalls some of the best poetry in the work. A still more memorable impression is left by the story of King John of France, taken prisoner by the English at Poitiers. Here Lydgate once again displays his great talents as a historian, since he has an opportunity to express his patriotic sentiments. The five stanzas in which he takes issue with Boccaccio for his biased attitude towards England are more forceful than one is accustomed to expect from Lydgate. With forthright conviction he advances the thesis that a historian ought to be impartial. He is enthusiastic in his praise of chivalrous valour, and his defence of Edward springs from his conviction that right is on his side. Thus the envoy comes to an end on the note that God has granted the victory to those whose cause was just, and that consequently the French empire is the lawful inheritance of the kings of England.

The great work was at an end. On the day when Lydgate laid down his pen he may well have thought back to that May morning eight

---

[1] E.g., Mohammed (IX, 50 ff.), Heraclius (IX, 533 ff., etc.), Duke Gaultier (IX, 2553).

[2] Cf. the series Aribertus, Desiderius, Pope Joan, the Byzantine emperors, etc.

[3] This is particularly true with regard to the visit of Dante (IX, 2511–52), but also the interesting material on Catanensi (IX, 2805–3056).

[4] IX, 2126–237.　　　　[5] IX, 1856–2048.　　　　[6] IX, 3134–238.

years earlier when he had accepted the commission to write this book. The *Fall of Princes* had become a child of sorrows for him, and more than once he had been on the verge of despair. The voice of the author makes itself heard through the traditional phrases in the final envoy addressed to his patron.[1] It was in any case the fashion to protest one's ignorance and lack of linguistic and metrical talent; but the phrase 'Ynglissh in ryme hath skarsete'[2] expresses truly the feelings of one who had wrestled with the task of keeping to a scheme of rhyme royal and French ballad stanzas. There is another personal touch in the customary reference to age or illness: already when he began the work Lydgate had been advanced in years and was no longer so enterprising as he had once been; many years spent toiling laboriously over his parchment had impaired his eyesight, so that he had to wear glasses.[3] One can imagine him poring over Laurent's text, deciphering the French – 'to which language my tounge was not affyled', as he says – and indeed, he often misunderstood what he was reading. His labours were compensated from time to time by the prospect of ample remuneration (for which he now again asks his patron), and of an occasional hour of leisure over a glass of wine.[4] The epilogue, which was beginning to run to excessive length, is brought to an end by a summary of the contents and a final re-capitulation of the moral. There follows the 'go litil book',[5] in which the author wishes his patron well and invokes God's blessing upon him, and then a second 'go litil book', in which he expresses the hope that his work will be spared the fate of being first raised up and then brought low by the wheel of Fortune – a long and repetitive finale appropriate to such a long and repetitive work.

The *Fall of Princes* had a large circulation and retained its sig-nificance for a long time as a model for others to follow. We have more than thirty manuscripts, some of them lavishly decorated,[6] and printed editions by Pynson (1494, 1527), Tottel (1554) and Wayland (1558). The fact that it was still reprinted in the mid-sixteenth cen-tury shows that it was valued as a historical epic, for the educated readers of the Elizabethan era were no longer interested in medieval

---

[1] IX, 3303–588 (34 + 6 stanzas).  [2] IX, 3312.
[3] 'Myn eyen mystyd, and dirked my spectacle' (IX, 3335).
[4] IX, 3338.  [5] IX, 3589.
[6] The most beautiful is the privately-owned MS. Phillips 4254, from the late fifteenth century, with seven fine miniatures and 260 large initial letters. The MSS. Ecton Hall-Huntington and Harley 1766 also have pictorial decoration. For further details, cf. the bibliographical introduction to Bergen's edition of the *F.o.P.* (Vol. IV).

# John Lydgate

compilations of tragedies such as that by Chaucer's monk.[1] The historical outlook of the Renaissance differed little from Lydgate's own: history was regarded as a mirror from which the present could derive knowledge and enlightenment from the past, by studying the fortunes and misfortunes that had befallen princes and peoples. Lydgate was outdated only in that he said little about more recent history, particularly English history. One can indeed see a kind of continuation or epilogue to his great work in a short poem he wrote entitled *Fates of Princes*, or *Of The Sodeine Fall of Princes in Oure Dayes*.[2] The personages whom he lamented in this poem are Edward II, Richard II, King Charles of France, the Duke of Orleans, Thomas, Duke of Gloucester, and Robert de Vere, Duke of Ireland. But since the poet here adopts a pro-Burgundian attitude and shows himself hostile to Armagnac, and since his approach here is comparatively immature, this seems more likely to have been written before the *Fall of Princes*, not after it.

The attempt was made to give Lydgate's work fresh validity by writing a continuation conceived on a grandiose scale. Thus originated the *Mirror for Magistrates*,[3] whose contributors oriented themselves on Lydgate, both in regard to material and to style.[4] The influence of Lydgate's mammoth work, which in modern times has often been played down, goes even farther: Shakespeare's histories are dramatic versions of the theme treated in the *Fall of Princes*.[5] This

[1] 'Sundry gentlemen very wel learned commended much the workes of Lydgate, chefely the Fall of Prynces' (Wayland's preface to the *Mirror for Magistrates* (1555), cited from L. B. Campbell's edition of this work (Cambridge, 1938)).

[2] *M.P.*, 660; *Englische Studien*, 43, 10 ff.; in seven Chaucerian stanzas.

[3] 'I have added [to Lydgate's work] a continuation of that Argument, concernynge the chefe Prynces of this Iland, penned by the best clearkes in such kinde of matters that be thys day lyuing, not vnworthy to be matched with maister Lydgate' (Wayland's preface, in Campbell, op. cit., p. 6). On the line leading from Lydgate's *F.o.P.* to the *Mirror for Magistrates*, and on to Shakespeare's historical tragedies, cf. W. F. Schirmer, 'The Importance of the 15th Century for the Study of the English Renaissance', in *English Studies Today: papers read at the International Conference of University Professors of English, Oxford, August 1950*, ed. by C. L. Wrenn and G. Bullough, O.U.P., 1951, pp. 104 ff.

[4] Cf., in addition to L. B. Campbell's edition of the *Mirror*, the introduction and notes to *The Complaint of Henry Duke of Buckingham, including the Induction, or, Thomas Sackville': Contribution to the Mirror for Magistrates*, ed. M. Hearsey, New Haven, 1936 (Yale Studies in English, 86).

[5] R. Chapman, 'The Wheel of Fortune in Shakespeare's Historical Plays', in *RES*, Jan. 1950. Cf. W. F. Schirmer, 'Glück und Ende der Könige in Shakespeares Historien', in *Arbeitsgemeinschaft für Forschung des Landes Nordrhein-Westfalen*, Heft 22, Cologne, 1953.

is not to place Lydgate and Shakespeare on the same level, but merely to point out the significance of the *Fall of Princes* for the literature of later ages. 'The morality that Lydgate preaches, though less poetical, is more of the Renaissance than Chaucer's.' [1]

[1] E. M. W. Tillyard, *Shakespeare's History Plays*, L., 1948, p. 72.

## Chapter 22

*Lydgate's Last Works*

*

Whilst Lydgate was writing his *magnum opus* for Humphrey many a summer had come and gone, and he felt the approach of autumn not only in his own life, but also in the world at large. Thus his adaptation of Boccaccio became a work in which his own life was reflected, and one seems to sense the rustling of withered leaves in the refrain of the transitoriness of earthly things, which one finds in several of the moralistic poems he wrote as parerga. The subject of his lament was not death but the process of dying, and this he treated magnificently in his variations on the elegiac *Ubi sunt* theme. He is too prone to adopt the tone of the schoolmaster or preacher, which to us seems to obscure the man and the poet, but this did not strike the reader of those days as in any way out of the ordinary. Nor is there anything surprising in the fact that Lydgate's religious verse to our minds seems more pompous than sincere, for this was an age in which the spiritual was overshadowed by the temporal and bishops and abbots had first and foremost to be able jurists, diplomats, officials, or administrators. As we look back from our own vantage-point we frequently gain the impression that the men and women of those days did not understand very clearly the age in which they lived, and that poets went on mechanically playing the same old tunes. This is not entirely so, and Lydgate, for all his rigid adherence to the traditional values, is one of the few who expressed the notion that this was the close of an era: not in a spirit of monkish asceticism, which is possible in any age, but, one might say, in the spirit of a secular schoolmaster. This admittedly was not an approach that was conducive to good poetry, but it was one that helped to explain the age in which he lived.

On 18th November 1434 Thomas Chaucer died,[1] and it may be assumed that Lydgate was present at his friend's funeral in the village church of Ewelme, which he knew well. One year afterwards, on 15th September 1435, came the death of his friend and patron John of Lancaster, Duke of Bedford.[2] He was the only one of Henry VI's counsellors who enjoyed general esteem. He was a statesman who was as far-sighted as he was unselfish – although even he could not have prevented the inevitable from happening in France. Shortly before his death came the additional misfortune of the failure of the conference of Arras, which sealed the fate of Paris. The Duke of Burgundy, who had secured sweeping concessions from Charles VII, made no secret of the fact that he was ready to change sides. He issued invitations to a peace conference at Arras, a proposal which Papal nuncios and delegates from the Council of Basle urged the English to accept. In July Cardinal Beaufort, Archbishop Kemp, and the Earls of Suffolk and Huntingdon were sent to Arras. They were instructed not to renounce Henry VI's claim to the French Crown. Since agreement on this question proved impossible the French put forward an ultimatum: Henry VI was to keep Normandy and marry one of the daughters of Charles VII, but was to renounce his claim to the French throne and give up Paris and other towns in northern France. At this the English envoys broke off the negotiations and left Arras. In the light of the military situation the attitude taken by the English was fatal. Since Bedford, who was on his deathbed, could no longer exercise a restraining influence, there now occurred what he had striven to avert at all cost: Philip the Good pardoned the murderers of his father and effected a reconciliation with Charles VII. The defection of Burgundy, which inaugurated the last phase of the Hundred Years' War, made a great impression in England. Here the idea of peace had been gaining ground. Those in power sought merely to avoid losing prestige; the people had awakened from their dreams of military grandeur, but had not yet grasped the possibility of utter defeat. The change of front by Burgundy altered the whole situation; the jealous hatred of the 'Flemings', which had been suppressed with difficulty during the last two decades whilst England had been allied to Burgundy, now flared up anew. The Government worked towards war, and the City mob

---

[1] His wife Mathilda died on 27th April 1437.
[2] He was buried in the choir of Rouen Cathedral. His magnificent monument of black marble was mutilated by the Calvinists in 1562 and totally destroyed in 1734.

[ 229 ]

pillaged the homes and warehouses of Philip's Flemish and Dutch subjects.

The agitation penetrated even into the monasteries. When Philip of Burgundy attacked and besieged Calais (only to be repelled later), Lydgate, who had hitherto shown remarkable reserve and had entered into controversy solely with the Lollards and other opponents of the Church, wrote his only political polemics. One of these poems is the short *Ballade in Despyte of the Flemynges*,[1] an attack upon the Duke of Burgundy, whose party Lydgate had still supported as late as 1428,[2] for breaking his treaty with England. The invective usual in such 'poems with a purpose' is, however, kept within the bounds of moderation.

The second attack upon Burgundy is interpolated into his didactic fable *Debate between the Horse, Goose and Sheep*.[3] It yields somewhat more information about Lydgate's political views.[4] In this work he is not concerned with the animals and their characteristics but with what they have to say. And this the ageing poet expresses with great prolixity. His efforts to achieve sententious diction result in a superabundance of maxims. In addition to this there is much erudite playing upon words and repetition of words and ideas, which produces a somewhat confused narrative.[5] It is difficult to summarize the con-

---

[1] *M.P.*, 600, in five ballad stanzas; printed by Brie in *Brut* (pp. 600 ff.) as by an anonymous author. Cf. MacCracken's article in *Anglia*, 33 (April 1910). Another ballad, *So Duke Philip and the Flemings departed from Calais with great shame*, in *Brut*, p. 582, and a lengthier poem describing the whole siege are in Wright, *Political Poems . . .* II, 151–6. The date of Lydgate's poem is sometimes (also by MacCracken in *M.P.*, xvii) given as 1424, which is clearly incorrect: the section in *Brut* begins with this year, but this can have no relation to the ballad.

[2] Cf. *A Thoroughfare of Woe*, *M.P.*, 822.

[3] *M.P.*, 539; ed. by M. Degenhart, Leipzig, 1900 (Münchner Beiträge zur roman. und engl. Philologie, 19); ed. by Furnivall, *Political, Religious and Love Poems*, EETS, OS., 15, pp. 15–42; C. F. Bühler, 'Lydgate's "Horse, Sheep, and Goose", and Huntington MS. HM 144', in *MLN* 55 (1940), pp. 563–70. Schick considers it one of Lydgate's early works. Degenhart, going by the political allusions it contains, dates it not earlier than 1436 and not later than 1440; Förster dates it 1437–40 on the grounds that lines 409–19 relate to the siege of Calais by the Duke of Burgundy in 1436 and the troubles in Holland in 1437. The fable, which is based on the *Gesta Romanorum* or the fables by Marie de France, comprises seventy-seven Chaucerian stanzas, supplemented by an envoy of fifteen ballad stanzas which emphasizes its moral message.

[4] The Burgundy passage, strictly speaking, only covers stanza 60 (ll. 413–20), and is thus only an allusion, though it is spun out into an extensive reflection.

[5] As an example of passages that are not narrative, cf. the horse's enumeration of great horse-owners: Alexander, Hector, etc. Among them is included the prophet Zechariah, with four horses which are then immediately described, and the parallel drawn with the four cardinal virtues; and it is only after these two stanzas that the

tents, for the most varied ideas are lumped together.[1] The introduction, reaching far back into the past, recalls that it was the custom in antiquity to hold disputations and to appoint judges to decide between the parties. Lydgate had himself seen one such debate in a picture showing a lion and an eagle acting as judges between a horse, a goose, and a sheep, who were arguing which of them was of the greatest benefit to man. Then follows, without any further introduction, the speech by the horse. It begins by emphasizing its martial qualities: the war-horse is a necessity for emperor and king; without horses there could be no knights. The horse is also extolled in poetry and religious allegory. Its importance is no less in everyday life, before the plough, at harvest-time, and when it draws to church the newly-cast bell. The goose feels itself superior to the horse because it is at home in two elements: it serves as weather prophet and in medicine; its feathers are used as quills for writing, as stuffing for pillows, and on the arrows of the English bowmen, without which neither horse nor horseman could defend the country. Even when dead, a goose is still of benefit, for its meat makes a delicious meal. It had once saved the Capitol; it is akin to the swan, and plays a part in the legend of the Knight of the Swan; therefore it is the goose that deserves the prize. The sheep is so gentle that it makes the ram speak on its behalf. The latter proves with the aid of quotations from St Augustine that the lamb has a religious significance, as the symbol of Christ. It is also of practical significance: the wool trade has helped England to attain the important position she now holds. Its skin is used as parchment. Its importance in history is attested by the story of the Golden Fleece and of Jason and Gideon. But above all it is the animal of peace, and for this reason merits the prize. There now follows the disputation: the horse rebuts the sheep's argument about peace by saying that the wool trade caused the war between England and Burgundy over Calais. The goose seconds this: together with

---

story is resumed. For an example of confused narrative, cf. the ram's tale, which begins in line 330 to enumerate the material advantages enjoyed by the lamb, but then deviates to repeat the idea of the lamb as an ideal for Christ, and only returns to the logical sequence of events in lines 350 ff. This should not be interpreted as negligence in construction, for this is elaborately contrived: after the five introductory stanzas the content is divided into four sections of equal length (seventeen, seventeen, sixteen, and nineteen stanzas). The first group contains the speech by the horse, the second that by the goose, the third that by the sheep, and the fourth the disputation and the delivery of judgement. The verdict passed by the lion and the eagle extends to six stanzas and corresponds to the five stanzas of the introduction. The envoy has fifteen stanzas.

[1] Contents as given by Degenhart, op. cit.

# John Lydgate

the horse it makes the defence of the country possible, whereas the wealth brought by the manufacture of wool invites enemy attack. The lamb retorts that it cannot be blamed if its gifts are abused. In their verdict the judges pronounce all three animals equally useful. The envoy, which points the moral, argues that the animals' satisfaction with their lot is applicable to humans as well. Many topics are touched upon here: the distribution of earthly goods, the uncertainty of fate, and the equality of all in death. Finally, the poet warns against arrogance on the part of rulers, particularly usurpers. In the final stanza he returns to the animals with which he began.

The trite, if kindly, view of life put forward here by the peace-loving Lydgate seems difficult to reconcile with his earlier views on chivalry and his national pride. But this apparent disparity can be interpreted differently in the light of the striking parallel that exists between this work and the *Lybelle of Englyshe Polycye*:[1] Lydgate's cardinal idea is the brotherly coexistence of peoples on the basis of commercial treaties (such as were the object of English policy at the time in relation to Flanders and the Hanseatic League). In other words, he rejects war (such as had flared up over the wool trade at Calais), revolts (such as had broken out in Flemish towns after the Burgundian defeat at Calais), and piracy (such as had been practised by the English against Flemish ships). When Lydgate endorsed chivalry and monarchy he did so not because he approved of their military connotations but because they were for him part of the divine order of society. He was anticipating the future; for after the present 'lack of governance' had come to an end Henry VII was to pursue an enlightened commercial policy and to act in the sense which Lydgate advocated. His ideas, it is true, are not clearly formulated, but he was forward-looking and had already moved far away from feudalism – as is shown by the fact that he makes no mention of a crusade, such as had been envisaged by Henry IV and Henry V, and by Joan of Arc as well.

It is tempting to see in Lydgate's political observations an echo of the conversations at Chaucer's house at Ewelme. In 1431, three years after Thomas Montacute's death, Alice Chaucer, Lydgate's most

[1] There are also literal parallels (Degenhart, p. 23):

Libel, 1100:  *And thus shuld every lond oon with another*
              *Entercomon as brother with his brother*

Lydgate 536:  *T'entrecommone as brother doth with brother.*

Or cf. Libel, 1900 and Lydgate, 456 ff.

active and faithful patroness, had married William de la Pole, Count (later Duke) of Suffolk (1396–1450). Under her influence he, too, became an admirer and patron of Lydgate. William de la Pole was an uncommon man. Historians have varied in their judgement of him: some call him a far-sighted loyal statesman, misunderstood by his own time, whilst others consider him an unscrupulous tyrant without the slightest ability.[1] In politics, as in literature, he was a dilettante. But here we are concerned with his private, not his public life. He met Alice Chaucer, and perhaps Lydgate too, for the first time as a young man of nineteen, when he attended the funeral of his brother Michael, who had been killed at Agincourt, and stayed with the Chaucers at Ewelme. Two years later he accompanied the expeditionary army to France, where he remained, with intervals, until 1431. He was held in high repute as a courageous officer and was present at many events of political importance, such as the wedding of Bedford and Anne of Burgundy (at Troyes in Champagne in June 1423), Henry VI's coronation in Paris in 1431, and his subsequent entry into London in February 1432. By that time his military career had already come to an end. As commander-in-chief of the English army (from 1428 onwards) he had been taken prisoner before Orleans (8th May 1429), but was released in 1430 upon his word of honour by the Bastard of Orleans, Jean Dunois. After this he pursued a career as a man of peace and also used his influence politically to work against the prolongation of the war. This brought him into conflict with Gloucester. The gulf between them was widened in 1431 when he married Alice Chaucer,[2] since the Chaucer family were supporters of the Beaufort party. His years at Ewelme were the happiest of his life. In possession of wealth, rank, and favour at court, he led the leisurely life of a country squire, a benefactor of his village,[3] and known, as Alice's father had been, for his delight in the company of educated people. He fitted into the Chaucer household, where there were books and the writing of poetry was cultivated. During his captivity in France he had himself composed verses in French, and this link with French poetry became stronger between 1433 and 1436, when he was charged with the custody of Charles d'Orléans.

---

[1] H. A. Napier, *Historical Notices of Swyncombe and Ewelme*, op. cit., pp. 31 ff., 47 ff.; Wylie, *Henry V*, op. cit., II, 47 ff.; *DNB*, 46, pp. 50 f.

[2] On 11th November 1430 Alice had received from Humphrey, in his capacity as 'Protector of the Kingdom', permission to marry William, Earl of Suffolk.

[3] Cf. Napier, *Historical Notices . . .*, p. 57.

# John Lydgate

This high-born French poet had been taken prisoner by the English at Agincourt and brought in Henry V's suite to England, where he lived for twenty-five years (until his release in 1440) in an honourable captivity that was more nominal than real.[1] During this period he could lay claim to the role of mediator between French and English poetry. He knew English, owned a manuscript by Chaucer, frequented Alice Chaucer's house,[2] and carried on a correspondence in gallant courtly verse with the ladies who taught him English. William de la Pole was an active member of this poetic coterie, and is believed to have been the author of the English poems that are to be found among the works of Charles d'Orléans.[3] It is not impossible that Lydgate may have met Charles in the set to which Suffolk and Chaucer belonged. Suffolk, in any case, admired Lydgate's works as warmly as he did those of the aristocratic French prisoner. The best MS. in existence of the *Siege of Thebes* bears de la Pole's coat-of-arms,[4] and in one poetic effusion Suffolk sang Lydgate's praises as the fitting successor to Chaucer.[5] It was for Suffolk's household that Lydgate composed his *Virtues of the Mass*,[6] and from him that he

---

[1] P. Champion, *Vie de Charles d'Orléans*, Paris, 1911; A. L. Champollion-Figeac, *Louis et Charles d'Orléans*, Paris, 1844; C. Beaufils, *Étude sur la vie et les poésies de Ch. d'O.*, Coutances, 1861. Works edited by J. M. Guichard, Paris, 1842; A. L. Champollion-Figeac, Paris, 1842; C. d'Héricault, Paris, 1874.

[2] In *Romania* 49 (1923) P. Champion adduces King René's testimony (*Livre de Cuer d'Amours épris*) that Charles of Orleans fell in love with the lady who taught him English and suggests that this was the Countess of Suffolk (Alice Chaucer). It is more probable that it was a certain Anna Molins, who is mentioned in a rondeau. Cf. E. P. Hammond, 'Ch. d'O. and Anne Molyneux', in *Mod. Phil.*, 22 (1924), pp. 215 f.

[3] MacCracken, 'An English Friend of Charles d'Orléans', in *PMLA*, 26 (1910), pp. 142–80; E. P. Hammond, *English Verse . . .*, pp. 215 ff.; P. Sauerstein, *Ch. d'O. und die englische Übersetzung*, Halle, 1899.

[4] Arundel 119; cf. Hammond, in *Anglia*, 36, p. 363, and Erdmann's edition, *EETS*, ES., 108, p. viii.

[5]
> O noble Chaucer passyd ben thy dayse
> Off poetry ynamyd worthyest
> And of makyng in alle othir days the best
>
> Now thou art go thyn helpe I may not haue
> Wherefor to god I pray ryght specially
> Syth thou art dede and buryde in thy grave
> That on thy sowle hym lyst to haue mercy
> And to the monke of bury now speke I
> Ffor thy coming ys syche and eke thy grace
> After Chaucer to occupye his place

(Poem printed by Hammond in *MLN*, 26, pp. 74 ff.; MacCracken adds to the probability that Suffolk was the author (*PMLA*, 26, pp. 142 ff.).)

[6] Cf. p. 175.

obtained support when in 1441 he submitted a petition for his charter to be renewed.

At this time Suffolk was already playing a part in national politics which in or about 1437 obliged him to terminate his peaceful residence at Ewelme. This year can be regarded as the turning-point between two epochs. On 12th November the minority of the king formally came to an end, but Cardinal Beaufort succeeded in ensuring that his influence should remain paramount, as it had been in the Regency Council. Since the king, owing to his nervous complaint, took little part in the business of government, the Lord Privy Seal, Adam Moleyns, was *de facto*, if not in name, the king's first secretary; decisions were taken by him in conjunction with the Steward, Suffolk, in a spirit that accorded with Beaufort's policy. In 1437 several famous representatives of the older generation died: among them were the two dowager queens, Joan of Navarre (widow of Henry IV) and Catherine of Valois (widow of Henry V). The death also occurred of Emperor Sigismund. Although he had frequently leaned towards Charles VII, he had remained loyal to the treaty of friendship which he had contracted with Henry V. In December requiems were sung for his soul in every cathedral in the country. England was anxious to secure the election of a new emperor who would be well disposed towards her, but her relations with the Continent were now in a state of dissolution. The conflict with Scotland, which had broken out in 1436, ceased with the murder of James I, but the hopeless war in France continued. In 1436 Paris was lost, and only near Calais and at Rouen could the English still hold out. The young commander-in-chief, Richard, Duke of York, lacked Bedford's experience and had to be recalled (July 1437). Richard de Beauchamp, Earl of Warwick, who was appointed to succeed him, died on 31st May 1439, and Richard was therefore again entrusted with supreme command. In 1439 there was a distant possibility that peace would be concluded, for the English were now prepared to surrender what they had refused to give up at Arras, and during the year conferences were held at Calais and Gravelines. But the French had now stepped up their claims, and although the conference at Gravelines, where England, Burgundy, and France were represented by large delegations, was attended by much splendid ceremonial, no agreement was reached.

\*

Lydgate was now approaching seventy years of age and events in
the world at large no longer made such a great impact on him as they
had once done. But whilst he was writing his *Legend of St Albon* he
must often have heard of the troubles that beset his king and
country. Together with the Count of Suffolk and others his abbot,
William Curteys, who as head of the important monastery of Bury
ranked among the most eminent men of East Anglia, was asked on
several occasions between 1440 and 1442 to enter into negotiations
with various ecclesiastical and secular dignitaries in the hope of
securing loans. The abbot enjoyed the king's full confidence; in the
letters which they exchanged[1] Henry asked 'oure trusty and welbeloved abbot of Bury' for money and also for advice in a tone such
as a young man would use when writing to a dependable older
friend. Henry tells the abbot of his concern about the French victories, requests his assistance in making preparations for a fitting reception to be accorded to the French princess he is to marry, and
asks him to act as his ecclesiastical representative at the laying of the
foundation-stone of King's College Chapel, Cambridge.[2] Once again,
shortly before their dissolution, the monasteries played a great role;
the guest-house at Bury will have harboured many visitors, and the
abbey will have been the scene of many important negotiations. In
connexion with these events Abbot Curteys, who earnestly desired
to restore the monastery to its former splendour, may have commissioned Lydgate to write his *Cartae versificatae*.[3] This was a verse
rendering of the charters granted to the monastery by various English kings, which were entered in Curteys' register. We can derive
little pleasure from seeing the charters of Hardecnut, Edward the
Confessor, William the Conqueror, and others compressed or expanded into ballad stanzas; but charters in verse were nothing unusual in an age when even Latin grammar was written in rhyme,
and we may assume that Lydgate's work was an object of pride
among his fellow-monks. In this connexion mention may be made
of another work, written by Lydgate shortly after 1442,[4] which
is also a versified history: *The Kings of England Sithen William Con-*

[1] Correspondence printed in *Memorials of Bury St Edmunds*, op. cit., III,
241 ff.
[2] The letter, in English, is in *ibid.*, p. 246.
[3] Or *Rimed Charters of English Kings presented to the Abbey of Bury*. (Brown's *Index*, No.
1513: 'probably by Lydgate'); printed in *Memorials of Bury St Edmunds*, III, 215–37 (not
in *M.P.*); 693 lines.
[4] *RES*, IX (1933), p. 47.

*querour*.[1] This poem, circulated in many manuscript versions, lists the kings of England from Alfred the Great to Henry VI. It is admittedly of no significance as a work of literature, but for the historian it is worthy of note on account of the accuracy with which Lydgate recorded events, particularly those that occurred from the end of the fourteenth century onwards.[2]

Of other works that presumably belong to his later years mention may be made of a brief occasional poem entitled *Verses on Cambridge*;[3] written in fourteen Chaucerian stanzas embellished with all manner of miscellaneous etymological information, it purports to give something akin to a history of the university in its early years. But it is colourless and remote from contemporary issues, so that there is reason to doubt whether it was actually connected with Henry VI's foundation of King's College Chapel in 1446, to which Curteys and some bishops were invited.

Of greater interest than these occasional verses designed for official functions is his *Fabula duorum mercatorum*,[4] which was presumably composed at the request either of a patron or of some highly-placed friend. This is the story of two merchants, one living in Egypt and the other in Syria, who become acquainted through a third person, maintain contact by means of messengers, and grow to be close friends. The Syrian makes a journey to Egypt and is welcomed by his friend, but falls ill. In a monologue he discloses to the reader that he is in love with a young woman whom the Egyptian has already chosen as his bride-to-be. They compete honourably for her hand, and the Syrian wins; his friend voluntarily gives her up, and they marry and leave for Syria. It now transpires that, by a whim of Fortune, the Egyptian merchant becomes impoverished. He sets out to see his friend, but dares not knock at his door to beg for shelter, and instead spends the night in a temple outside the town. During the night a quarrel occurs between two citizens; one of them is

---

[1] *M.P.*, 710 (expanded version in thirty Chaucerian stanzas; Brown's *Index*, No. 882); an abridged version (containing stanzas 16–30 of the above, with variants) in Brown's *Index*, No. 3632; a later version in couplets (192 lines) in *M.P.*, 717, and Brown's *Index*, No. 3431. Cf. J. P. Oakden, 'Lydgate's Verses on the Kings of England', in *RES*, IX (1933), pp. 47–53.

[2] Cf. Hammond, in *Englische Studien*, 43, pp. 23 ff.

[3] *M.P.*, 652; *Retrospective Review*, 2nd series, I, 498.

[4] Lydgate's *Fabula Duorum Mercatorum*, from J. Zupitzas, Nachlass, ed. G. Schleich, Strasbourg, 1897 (Quellen u. Forschungen zur Sprach- und Kulturgeschichte der germanischen Völker, 83). In 130 Chaucerian stanzas.

# John Lydgate

killed, and his murderer flees. The noise draws the townspeople to the spot. Weary of life, the Egyptian confesses that it is he who has committed the crime. He is sentenced to death, but as he is on his way to the place of execution he is seen by his friend, who takes his place and pleads guilty in his stead. In this situation he is seen by the real murderer, who is brought to reason by the thought of divine retribution. The judges send all three of them before the king, who promises to pardon them if they speak the truth. He rejoices to hear of such unbreakable bonds of friendship, and the Egyptian returns home having been given half his friend's possessions. This edifying tale of true friendship that is able to withstand all trials closes with a panegyric to divine justice. It contains in addition a sufficient element of suspense and surprise to make it a favourite theme among novelists. It is to be found in Bandello and Boccaccio, is related by Thomas Elyot in his *Governour*, and is also extant in several English verse renderings, which culminate in Goldsmith's *Tale of Alcander and Septimius*. Lydgate bases his account on the original story in Petrus Alphonsus' *Disciplina clericalis*. His augmentations consist of rhetoric rather than narrative. He describes the merchants, who in the source are referred to by name only, but in general and abstract terms, so that they have none of the vividness of Chaucer's pilgrims. Revelling in sententious moralizing, he delivers a sermon on friendship and elaborates on the conception which each friend had of the other before they met, and on the manner in which the yearning for friendship can be satisfied.[1] In his later period his work is characterized by verbose dialogues and monologues that could almost be called humanistic,[2] mysterious flourishes and a delight in obscure language. Even where he introduces a simile drawn from nature he uses far-fetched phrases that are suggestive of the style of the sixteenth and seventeenth centuries. Thus, for instance, the meeting of the two friends is depicted as fine weather driving away the evil of separation:

> *Her ioiful somer is tapited al in greene,*
> *Of stable blew is her bothen hewe.*[3]

Lydgate's old delight in playing on mythological names is illustrated by his invocations of Megaira, Tisiphone, and Myrrha;[4]

---

[1] E.g., lines 64, 96, 108, 211, 255, 344, 484, 579, 603, 666, 689, 701, etc.
[2] E.g., lines 221 ff.; 395–434; 549 ff.; 743 ff.; 785 ff.
[3] Line 194.          [4] Line 505.

whilst the introduction of Fortune[1] and the interpolation of remarks by the author himself[2] are familiar to us from other works. If in spite of these interruptions suspense is still maintained this is due to the fictional nature of the theme.

[1] Lines 503, 519 et al.
[2] E.g., stanza 2 (line 8); stanza 27 (line 183); stanzas 71 ff. (line 491); stanzas 129 f. (line 897).

## Chapter 23

*Lydgate's Last Years*

\*

During the last decade of Lydgate's life English history was no poorer in significant events than it had been in earlier years, but the aged poet no longer took such a prominent part in them. The great scandal of the year 1441 was the Eleanor Cobham affair.[1] Eleanor was one of the ladies-in-waiting of Humphrey of Gloucester's first wife, Jacqueline de Hainault. The marriage, which had been contracted in 1422 and extolled by Lydgate,[2] was not of long duration. Eleanor became Humphrey's mistress and later his wife. Her ascent from humble circumstances to the position of first lady of the land, whose status was recognized by the Pope and who was accepted into the *confrérie* of St Albans, caused rumours to spread that this uncommonly beautiful and ambitious woman practised sorcery. In the course of the conflict between the war party and those who advocated the conclusion of peace the story was bruited about – how much truth there was in it we do not know – that she had melted down a wax image of Henry VI in order to make Humphrey king. Such an accusation of witchcraft was calculated to arouse feelings of horror, and in an effort to eliminate Humphrey or to humiliate him Eleanor was put on trial. The sensation which this created is attested by numerous ballads and the detailed accounts of it given in the chronicles. The Duchess of Gloucester was tried by Cardinals Beaufort and Kemp (Chichele pleaded illness) and was sentenced to walk through the streets of London for three days barefoot and clad in a hair shirt, after which she was condemned to life-long solitary con-

---

[1] Eleanor, daughter of Reynold Cobham, Suffolk's successor as custodian of Charles d'Orléans.

[2] See p. 114.

finement, in which she remained for five years. Humphrey was powerless and had to let events take their course. For Lydgate this was yet another example of the drama of *sic transit gloria mundi*, for Humphrey, who had given him the commission to translate *De casibus*, had been one of the most eminent and proudest men in the country.

The king kept aloof from these events. He found contentment in such matters as founding Eton College, which was designed to prepare entrants to King's College, Cambridge, just as Winchester, which was more secular in character, was the first step to New College, Oxford. In the long term Henry VI thus rendered considerable service to his country, but at the time he faced a more urgent task – that of bringing about a settlement of the war with France. To achieve this Suffolk, the successor to Beaufort (who had retired from politics in 1443),[1] took up the latter's plan for Henry VI to marry a French princess. Early in 1444 he left with a delegation[2] for France to ask on Henry's behalf for the hand of Margaret, the daughter of René of Anjou, in return for which England was prepared to make peace and abandon her claims to the French Crown. But apart from agreement to the match Suffolk achieved only a twenty-two-month armistice, which he accepted in the vain hope of being able to turn it into a permanent peace. The betrothal was arranged on 24th May, and the armistice signed at Tours four days later.

Suffolk's concessions, the relinquishing of the title of King of France and the restitution of Anjou and Maine, were demagogically exploited by Gloucester's adherents, as were also Beaufort's close ties with the unpopular Pope Eugenius IV. The pious king allowed himself to be influenced by the arguments of Beaufort and Suffolk. He also had the advice of the Church in the person of Archbishop Stafford, who was so convinced of the soundness of this policy that he advanced 1000 marks to enable the king to pay for the expenses incurred in his wedding and the coronation of his queen. Abbot Curteys of St Edmunds, too, was prepared to provide carriages and horses for the queen. Margaret's father, René, King of Sicily, Naples, and Jerusalem, was a sovereign without a country. He had no dowry to give his daughter; nor could he pay for her journey to England. This suited the protagonists of the marriage on the English

---

[1] *d.* 11th April 1447 at Wolvesey Castle.
[2] Cf. M. A. Hookham, *Life and Times of Margaret of Anjou*, 2 vols., L., 1872, I, 233.

side, for they hoped thereby to ensure Margaret's gratitude.[1] In February 1445 a marriage by proxy was formally contracted in Nancy. The ceremonial was exaggerated and somewhat old-fashioned: Margaret chose the marguerite as her flower, and there was a tournament in which King Charles appeared together with King René, and Charles' mistress Agnes Sorel wore the armour of an amazon. The next celebrations took place in Rouen. Margaret, escorted by the Duke of York, made a triumphant entry into the town, where she was welcomed by English dignitaries; on 10th April, with Suffolk in command of her suite, she landed at Porchester. She was suffering from the ill effects of her voyage and had to recover from an attack of smallpox as well[2] before she could be married to Henry on 22nd April. The ceremony, at which Archbishop John Kemp of York officiated, took place at the Premonstrants' Abbey at Tichfield (or, according to another chronicle, in Southwich near Porchester). One month later, after the customary period of residence at Eltham, the royal couple made their way to London. On 28th May the ceremonial reception took place at Blackheath, at which Duke Humphrey, despite his disapproval of the match, was also present, with 500 horsemen wearing marguerites in their caps.

Fifteenth-century poetry is largely incomprehensible if it is regarded in isolation, divorced from the ostentatious ceremonial which formed an integral part of the age. Once again the call went out for Lydgate, who in his younger years had described so well in verse the ceremonies at Henry VI's coronation, to provide a festive poem for this occasion too, and perhaps also to superintend the pageants, as he had done before. Lydgate was certainly in London together with Abbot Curteys, who received a personal invitation from Henry VI to attend the coronation of his queen.[3] His *Verses for pageants at the Entry of Queen Margaret* (generally referred to as *Margaret's Entry into London*)[4] have not been preserved in full, and the

---

[1] Op. cit., I, 235 f. Description of Margaret's journey to England in *Life and Times of Margaret of Anjou*, I, 245–63 and in J. Stevenson, *Papers . . .*, (Rolls Series), op. cit., II, xxxvii ff.

[2] But cf. the different account given in Christie, *Henry VI*, op. cit., pp. 104 f.

[3] *Memorials of Bury St Edmunds*, I, 470.

[4] Ed. by C. Brown in *MLR*, 7 (1912), pp. 225–34. Cf. R. Withington in *Mod. Phil.*, 13 (1915–6), pp. 53–7. One hundred and seventy verses in ballad stanzas. The work is listed by Pits and Tanner, following Stow's list of Lydgate's works, which is to be found in Speght's edition of Chaucer (1598) after the *Siege of Thebes* (cf. MacCracken in preface to *M.P.*). Stow describes it in his *Annals of England*, 1592, p. 624. For a long time it was thought to have been lost (cf. MacCracken, *M.P.*, xl); it was found by C. Brown

description of the ceremony contained here must be supplemented by the accounts of it given in the chronicles.[1] For the royal procession three pageants were erected on London Bridge, symbolic representations recalling Lydgate's mummings and pantomimic spectacles at which the meaning was made clear by the recitation of verses of which Lydgate was the author. At the southern end of the bridge a stage was constructed inscribed with a verse from Genesis, '*Ingredimini et replete terram*'; on it stood the figures of Peace and Plenty, who welcomed the queen as she passed. Afterwards the procession came to a second pageant erected in the middle of the bridge, representing Noah's ark. Lydgate's verses extol Margaret as the harbinger of peace and order, comparing her with Noah, who once had provided safety from the 'flood of vengeance' for his companions in the Ark. Margaret is the dove with the olive-branch, the 'Sonne of Comfort'. Lydgate hoped that through Margaret the peace with France which he fervently desired would at last be realized – a pious hope which was evidence rather of his confidence in the Almighty than of his grasp of political realities.

The other pageants which followed transplanted this panegyric to the moral, allegorical, and visionary plane. The chronicles record that the procession passed along Fish Street and Gracechurch Street to Leadenhall. Here a proper stage had been constructed, on which, it seems, was performed a version of the play dealing with the Four Daughters of God.[2] The text, which has been preserved only in fragments, begins with a speech by Madame Grace, who appears as 'Chauncelere de dieu', whereupon the allegorical figures of Truth, Justice, and Peace reply by expressing the wish that the queen may enjoy a long life and happy reign. May truth be united with mercy, and justice and peace form indissoluble bonds of love between the two kingdoms; the two patron saints, St George and St Denis, are called upon to intercede for their two peoples.

---

in MS. Harl. 3869 (before a manuscript of the *Confessio Amantis*). R. Withington brought to light a further MS. fragment in Stow's handwriting from MS. Harl. 542, entitled *The Speches in the pagiauntes at the cominge of Qwene Margaret . . . the 28th of Maye 1445*. Cf. also R. Withington, *English Pageantry*, op. cit., I, 148.

[1] *Historical Collections of a Citizen of London in the 15th Century*, ed. J. Gairdner, Camden Soc., 1876, p. 186 (the account by Will. Gregory, who was Mayor of London in 1451 and was probably an eye-witness); *English Chronicle (Brut)*, ed. F. Brie, op. cit., pp. 489, 510.

[2] Cf. H. Traver, *The Four Daughters of God* (Bryn Mawr Monograph), 1907. Cf. Lydgate's version of this story in his legendary *Life of Our Lady*.

After listening to this play the procession turned west along Cornhill and Cheapside. In Cornhill, at the prison known as 'The Tun', there was a pageant symbolizing the legend of St Margaret. In it a parallel was drawn between the martyred saint and the queen: God rules over us all, and therefore none of the powers of evil can cause us any harm; earth, sea, and trees are subject to man; peace reigns between England and France, and we put our trust in God that Margaret will enable us to live in tranquillity. This vision of the divine era, rendered by Lydgate in a somewhat wearied style and without the sonorous versification of his earlier years, is continued in the next pageant, situated at the well in The Cheap, which treats the theme of the five wise and the five foolish virgins. Now a purely religious note is struck: the Dove of God will take under its wing all who seek peace once their labours are over; milk and honey will flow in the land, and in the world beyond there will be everlasting bliss. The religious element becomes more marked the closer one approaches St Paul's Cathedral. The pageant at the cross in The Cheap represents the celestial Jerusalem; it is a hymn of praise sung on the way to the House of God. The queen's procession through the City represents the working of Divine Providence. Man will ascend from virtue to virtue until he beholds God on Mount Zion. 'We pray that, with God's guidance, we shall enter with thee into the heavenly Jerusalem.'

Finally, the last station, a pageant erected by St Michael's Church in Querne (opposite St Paul's Gate), represented the Resurrection and Last Judgement. The poet implores the Virgin Mary to intercede with Christ to send Margaret a long reign and thereafter to crown her with eternal bliss. Lydgate's ceremonial verses are more religious and symbolic than before; now weary of the world, his gaze is fixed upon the life hereafter, and the joy he expresses is more suited to some feast of the Church than to the waving and cheering crowds in the streets of London. This sacred tone will doubtless have struck the pious Henry VI as appropriate.

St Paul's can have presented no very impressive sight on this occasion, for its tower had been struck by lightning, and had not yet been rebuilt.[1] All the more festive was the effect produced by the

[1] *Brut*, p. 487: 1445, 1st February, 'grete wedryng of wynde, hayle, snowe, rayne, thunder and lightnyng, at the after None; and it endured iiij oures; and it did grete harme to þe Cite of London, for it brent Seint Paules grete steple, bothe on the west syde and on þe south syde . . . it was quenched with vyneger.' It was not repaired until 1462.

City. Along its decorated streets the queen rode in a white carriage, escorted to her coronation in Westminster by forty-six newly-created knights belonging to the Order of the Bath. The ceremony was performed by John Stafford, Archbishop of Canterbury, on the following day, Sunday, 30th May. The three days of pageants and tournaments that ensued caused even those who had previously lent a willing ear to Humphrey and the war party to cheer their queen. In Parliament Suffolk was praised, even by Humphrey, for his work of mediation.

This optimism was scarcely justified. When Margaret (1430–82) came to England she was little more than a child. Polydori Virgilio calls her, with some exaggeration, '*puellam tam ultra alias foeminas pulchram quam prudentem*'. Good-looking and kind-hearted, she had received a good education in Naples and had inherited something of her father's literary taste. In Henry VI she found a man capable of appreciating French literature, and she sought to make the English court a brilliant centre of poetry and music. She patronized foreign authors (thereby arousing the jealousy of English writers), and showed her respect for learning by founding Queen's College, Cambridge (1449). Proud and ambitious, she possessed the will and determination to take over the reins of government. Henry VI idolized her, and was completely under her domination. She felt herself superior to her husband, whose inclinations were rather those of a monk and scholar than a ruler. Henry was now twenty-three; at that age his father had led armies in the field, but he was happiest when he could converse with the pupils of Eton or stroll about in the garden of the monastery of Bury St Edmunds.[1] He could thus be no more than a puppet in the hands of his ministers. Margaret was not content: she hated Humphrey as a possible successor to the throne should her marriage remain childless, and therefore relied upon Suffolk's party; to the old aristocratic families she adopted a defiant and provocative attitude. By treating those who opposed Suffolk and herself as personal enemies she offended the opposition and gave them ample grounds on which to attack her. When Suffolk openly displayed his French leanings and Henry spoke French during negotiations with French envoys (something his father would have never done), accusing fingers were pointed at the foreigner Margaret as the culprit who had caused Henry V's acquisitions to be abandoned. When Margaret won over members of the Privy Council by flattery

[1] On Henry's character, cf. the biography by his chaplain Blackman, printed as appendix to Hearne's edition of Otterbourne's *Chronicle*, Oxford 1732 (R.S.).

and maintained a close political liaison with Suffolk, this provided an opportunity to cast a slur upon her moral integrity.

Those who had hoped that her marriage to Henry would bring England diplomatic advantage were doomed to be disappointed. The king's attitude towards the French was so accommodating as to be almost undignified. At an audience given to some French envoys[1] Archbishop Stafford replied in carefully measured terms, but the king waved his hat and several times called out: 'St Jehan grant mercies, St Jehan grant mercies'. Suffolk urged the king to confirm his promise to cede Anjou and Maine as a pledge for the armistice.[2] Such an unsatisfactory arrangement, made without Parliament's sanction, could be exploited recklessly by the influential Gloucester, and Suffolk found it necessary to have him arraigned. His trial was planned to take place in Bury St Edmunds, where Suffolk's own influence was strong.

It was here that Parliament was summoned on 10th February 1447. It met in the spacious refectory of the abbey, in Margaret's presence; the proceedings were opened with an address by the chancellor, the Archbishop of Canterbury, who spoke of the continuation of the peace negotiations and the king's proposed journey to France. But the real purpose of the meeting was to obtain from Parliament a warrant for Gloucester's arrest. Eight days after the assembly had begun its deliberations Humphrey arrived from his castle at Devizes with a numerous suite. In the presence of the Dukes of Somerset and Buckingham he was arrested; five days later (23rd February) he was dead. There was reason to suspect foul play, a plot by Margaret and Suffolk; but according to the testimony of his friend, Abbot Whethamstede, Gloucester died a natural death. He was buried in St Albans Abbey. Nevertheless 'the murder of good Humphrey' is a stock theme for all Yorkist pamphleteers.

\*

We have no record of Lydgate's reactions to these events. He continued to live undisturbed in his monastery, and from 1439 onwards was in receipt of a comfortable pension from the Crown.[3] Nor does

---

[1] In July 1445, led by the Archbishop of Rheims.

[2] This Henry did in a letter written, probably under the influence of his wife, on 22nd December 1445 to his father-in-law René of Anjou.

[3] The documents concerning Lydgate are (following Steele, *EETS*, ES., 66, p. xxiii):

    1. Lease to Lydgate a.o. by Sir R. Rochford of the lands of the alien Priory of Long-

the abbey's chronicle make any mention of the alarming course of events on the battlefields of France or in the world of high politics; instead it records a storm that damaged the windows and extinguished all the lights in the monastery except the sanctuary lamp, a flood when the water rose so high that it came into the church,[1] and the reconstruction of the West Tower, completed in 1446. In the same year the death occurred of William Curteys, the last great abbot. With his death the monastery's importance declines. His successor, William Babington, abbot from 1446 to 1453, is no more than a name to us. The custom of keeping a register, a practice which Curteys had revived and which he strictly supervised, gradually ceased to be observed, so that we know little about the last ninety years of the monastery's existence.

---

ville Gifford, or Newenton Longville, with the pension of Spalding, formerly appertaining to the Abbey of Angers . . . 21st February 1423.

2. A grant of 10 marks to Lydgate from the Customs at Ipswich . . . 22nd April 1439.

3. Allowance of payment of this Grant, £6. 4s. 5¼d. being the proportion due at Easter 1440 . . . Lyddegate cui Rex xxij die Aprilis, Anno decimo septimo, concessit decem marcas percipiendas annuatim pro termino vitae sue.

4. The King cancels the previous grant of A.D. 1439 of 10 marks, and grants to Lydg. £7 13sh. 4d. per annum from the proceeds of the farm of Waytefee, to date from the Easter preceding . . . 7th May 1440.

5. An allowance to the Sheriff of £3. 16s. 8d. paid to Lydg. (and Baret) on account of the grant No. 7 for the year 1439–40 – (the grant of 21st November 1441 is quoted) – the grant due from Easter 1440 of £3. 16. 8. was paid for Mich. 19 Hen. VI. 1440.

6. Petition of Lydg. touching the invalidity of letters patent granting him £7. 13. 4 yearly, and praying new letters patent to him and John Baret, squire, granted [Proc. of the Privy Council]. Rex apud Westmonasterium xiiij° die Novembris anno XX [1441] concessit praesentem billam . . . presentibus Domino Suffolcie qui billam prosecutus est ac me, Adam Moleyns . . . 14th November 1441.

7. The King's patent granting to Lydg. and Baret, and to the survivor, the sum of £7. 13. 4 per annum. Concesserimus Joh. Lidgate . . . septem libras, tresdecim solidos et quatuor denarios, precipiendos annuatim a festo Pasche tunc ultimo preterito, durante vita sua, de exitibus et proficuis prouenientibus de alba firma et feodo vulgariter nuncupato Waytefe, per manus Abbatis de Bury Sancti Edmundi . . . 21st November 1441.

8. Payment to Michaelmas 1441.

9. Payment to Michaelmas 1443.

10. Receipt of Baret 2 oct. 1446 . . . recepisse pro me et Johanne Lydgate Monacho . . . de W. Tyrell, vicecomite Norffolcie et Suffolcie, tres libras, sexdecim solidos et quatuor denarios de illis septem libris, tresdecim solidis et quatuor denariis quos Rex concessit percipiendos annuatim datum 2. oct. 1446.

11. Payment to Michaelmas 1448 Philip Wentworth, late Sheriff . . . renders a further account, showing the payment to John Lidegate . . .

12. Payment to Michaelmas 1449 Giles Seintlo, Esq., late Sheriff . . . renders a further account, showing the payment to John Lidegate . . .

[1] *Victoria County History, Suffolk*, II, 66.

# John Lydgate

About Lydgate, too, first-hand evidence is lacking. On occasions, although comparatively rarely, he will have been in London and Windsor, and also at Ewelme or some other of Suffolk's country estates. He was acquainted with men of letters such as Shirley and Benedict Burgh.[1] From the latter we have a *Letter to Lydgate*[2] which he evidently sent him in the early 1440s. In it he extols effusively the poets from Homer to Boccaccio, all of whom, he says, are surpassed by Lydgate: 'maister lidgate, what man be ye'. So long as Lydgate lives, the art of poetry will not die. He hopes to see and hear him: 'that were my paradyse, that wer my heuen!' The purpose of this letter was clearly to obtain an introduction to the famous poet. It may be assumed that Lydgate and Burgh were together frequently between 1444 and 1450 – either at Bury or at Windsor, for the letter[3] bears the note: 'written by Mas Burgh in þe Prays of John Lidgate . . . boothe dwelyng at Windsor'.

It was also Burgh who, at the request either of the king or of Viscount Bourchier, completed Lydgate's last work, *The Secrees of [Olde] Philisoffres*.[4] This is the translation of a book popular in medieval times, the *Secreta Secretorum*, supposedly written by Aristotle in reply to questions put by Alexander. Of the numerous imitations and translations in Latin and in vernacular languages,[5] Lydgate's verse rendering[6] is the one that is conceived on the largest scale,[7] although it in fact consists only of fragments of a translation. Out of a feeling of reverence Burgh made no alterations, and the outcome is a work woefully lacking in structural shape. The theme changes continually; it is repeatedly interrupted by prologues written by one or other of its translators; part of it is in the first person and part in

---

[1] *Circa* 1413–83; his edition of *Cato* has been edited by M. Förster in *Archiv*, 115–16 (1905–6); ed. by P. Wilson, L., 1924.

[2] In E. P. Hammond, *English Verse . . .*, op. cit., pp. 188 ff.

[3] Dated 11th December (144?), Bylegh Abbey, Little Maldon (near Hatfield). Marginal note by J. Stow. Beginning of letter cut off.

[4] Lydgate and Burgh's *Secrees of Philisoffres*, ed. R. Steele, *EETS*, ES., 66, L., 1894.

[5] E.g., Egidio Colonna, *De regimine principum* (translated by (H)occleve); Thomas Aquinas, *De regimine principum*; Simon Islip (in 1366, when Archbishop of Canterbury), *Speculum Edwardi*. In English: Gower's treatment of this material in the 7th book of his *Confessio*; the translation by (H)occleve mentioned above (1412); a translation by James Yonge (1420) (ed. R. Steele, *EETS*, ES., 74 (1898), pp. 119–248); Lydgate's paraphrase; a version partly in prose, written by John Shirley for Henry VI (1460) from a French version; and a later translation, like Lydgate's composed in Chaucerian stanzas, *The Poesye of Princely Practise*, by William Forrest (1548, for Edward VI).

[6] Based on a faulty Latin text, and probably also on a French version.

[7] Lines 1–1491 composed by Lydgate, the remainder (lines 1492–2730) by Burgh.

the third; the initial epistolary form is later lost; and we are left with an overall impression of muddle both in regard to content and to form. Had Lydgate not died before the work was completed, he would probably have brought some order into this poetic jumble; but his hand was now shaky and infirm with age. We may charitably overlook the fact that occasionally he misunderstands the sense of the original,[1] that he makes mistakes in translation,[2] and that he heads part of Philip's prologue 'Alexander's letter';[3] but the defects of his peculiarly languid style are all too evident. Where he expands one short sentence in the original to a passage of seventy lines[4] he descends to the level of garrulity. The paraphernalia of erudition seem to us abstruse, although at the time the themes he dealt with may have had a fascinating appeal. Men were irresistibly attracted by the magic of alchemy, for the study of which Henry VI appointed several commissions.[5] Astrology, pyromancy (a term given to divination by fire), geomancy (the divination of earthquakes), and other matters of scientific speculation were looked upon as precious occult knowledge. Lydgate would like to see it reserved to kings, scholars, and universities.[6] The appeal which the work had for contemporaries explains why the king extended his patronage to it. Another reason is that it had the popular form of a 'mirror for princes', regarded as suited to a distinguished patron;[7] this gave Lydgate his last chance to express his convictions and tender advice. That Henry VI must have been the patron, although his name is not mentioned, is evident from the prologue, which states that the work was composed at the king's command,[8] and also from various allusions in the text, of which the plainest is the one referring to the rightful heir to two crowns.[9] The tone and content of this 'mirror for princes' and its divergences from the original show that this is Lydgate's final im-

---

[1] E.g., line 164; in line 210 he read Patricii as 'Parisii', and made Philip of Tripolis (the author of a thirteenth-century version of the *Secreta*) a 'Philip of Paris'.

[2] E.g., l. 469: 'magnanymyte' for *magnitudinem*; in l. 318 he writes 'Metropolitan' for Tripolitanus.

[3] line 477; it is doubtful, incidentally, whether the titles in the margin are Lydgate's.

[4] From l. 372 onwards.

[5] R. Steele, in *The Antiquary*, September 1891.

[6] lines 519 ff. Cf. also ll. 491–602 and the demand that the king's personal physician should understand astronomy and the constellations (ll. 1184 ff.).

[7] Shirley's prose translation is also dedicated to Henry VI, and the French translation (a printed edition of 1489) in the King's Library to Charles VIII (according to Steele's edition of the *Secrees*, p. 87).

[8] ll. 27 f.          [9] ll. 44 f.

ploring exhortation to the king. Indeed, it is his testament. Never before had he laid such emphasis upon the importance of learned counsellors: a university, he says, radiates light in a kingdom like the sun amidst the stars, and for this reason deserves the king's protection.[1]

> *Wheer is Clergye | ther is philosophye,*
> *Marchaundyse | plente and Rychesse*
> *prudent Counsayl | diffence of Chevalrye.*[2]

In his role as counsellor Lydgate urges upon the king his own favourite ideas. They are neither fresh nor original, but they have the pathos of conviction and were most opportune on the eve of a civil war. He longs for a restoration of the old patriarchal relationship between a ruler and his subjects; a king must win over his people, not suppress them by force. Wherever there is an atmosphere of Oriental despotism in his source Lydgate tones it down and makes alterations. Alexander asks, not how he can subjugate the Persians, but how he can win them over;[3] and his adviser recommends leniency and justice, since a kingdom can endure only if it is founded on love.[4] Here Lydgate speaks more warmly of the people than he did in the *Fall of Princes*. The final remark, that Alexander listened to the advice he was given and so won possession of Persia, is akin to a supplication addressed to Henry VI.[5] The qualities that make a king fit to govern are above all moderation ('attemperaunce'), courtly tact ('discrecioun'),[6] prudent reflection, which restrains him from undertaking military campaigns,[7] and fairness in dispensing justice among his subjects.[8] Generosity is extolled as the virtue of monarchs. The king must heed God's commandments and lead a model life;[9] he must be serious-minded and God-fearing, and must punish heretics who oppose the teaching of the Church.[10] The fervent, and indeed imploring tone which Lydgate adopts in this work compensates for its artistic shortcomings. Since his royal patron apparently fell short of the monarchic ideal, the *Secrees of Philisoffres* contain a wearisome reiteration of rather trite recommendations and moral injunctions.

---

[1] ll. 1174 ff.    [2] 1177 ff.    [3] l. 155.    [4] l. 195.

[5] Other departures from the original: in l. 1125 the passage in which the king is advised to make his favourites drunk more often in order to hear their opinions on his rule is radically changed, becoming a simple injunction to make merry; in ll. 1156 ff. the advice to buy up corn for sale in time of famine is omitted entirely.

[6] line 759 and elsewhere.    [7] l. 174.    [8] ll. 1058 ff.

[9] l. 1086 ff.    [10] ll. 1065 ff.

Today the content is of less interest to us than the picture it reveals of the author. Our interest is firmly held by the descriptions of the seasons,[1] which are only loosely appended but are more pleasing as poetry. The old monk in the garden and in the vicinity of his monastery had the ability to give nature topics the quality of his own intense experience. We see the bees bearing honey from the flowers by the river Lark to the hives in the monastery garden, and the cattle seeking the cool of a shady copse; we follow in Lydgate's footsteps as he goes into the orchard and vegetable garden, to the berries and beans, to the chickweed and lettuce, and we find ourselves wishing that Lydgate had given a detailed description of the *hortulus* of his abbey, as did Walahfrid Strabo, the monk from Reichenau. But to do this he was no longer granted the time. As, full of foreboding, he wrote his last words, 'deth al consumyth',[2] the pen fell from his hand.[3]

Benedict Burgh, his pupil, friend, and literary executor, wrote a prolix continuation of his last work in which he rendered Lydgate a well-intentioned but unfortunate service. Carefully emulating his style, he completed it in an impersonal didactic manner: it is an exhaustive doctrine of hygiene and physiognomy and a practical guide to the arts of government. It was written for Henry, the son of Lady Isabel Bourchier, who had patronized Osbern Bokenham's legends and who probably also appreciated the work of Lydgate.

\*

Another of Lydgate's literary friends was John Shirley.[4] He lived to the age of ninety (1366–1456), and it is possible that he may once have known Chaucer.[5] He was patronized by the nobility and the court of Henry VI, and is of importance as a copyist and a collector of manuscripts. Shirley copied a great many works by Chaucer and Lydgate, and by other writers as well, and for a fee lent out these MS. volumes, many of which have been preserved.[6] This 'lending library'

[1] ll. 1079 ff.   [2] l. 1491.

[3] After l. 1491, and before stanza 214, stands: 'here dyed this translator, and nobil poete: and the yonge folowere gan his prologe on this wyse.'

[4] O. Gaertner, *John Shirley: sein Leben und Wirken*, Diss., Halle, 1904; A. Brusendorff, *The Chaucer Tradition*, L., 1925, passim (cf. index); E. P. Hammond, *English Verse . . .*, p. 191.

[5] Shirley's father was a court official (armiger) and consequently a colleague of Chaucer's. In the inscription on his tomb Shirley is called 'Esquire', so that he probably followed his father in this post, or held some other court appointment.

[6] Harl. 78, 2251, 7333; Add. 5467, 16,165; Ashmole 59; Trin. Coll., Cambridge, R 3.20; Sion MS. of Chaucer (mostly folio), and many others.

# John Lydgate

proved so popular that at his death its owner possessed a house and four shops rented from St Bartholomew's Hospital. It was in Shirley's manuscripts that Lydgate read Chaucer's *Anelida and Arcite* and *The Book of Thebes*. Lydgate was undoubtedly acquainted with Shirley; indeed, one may presume that he introduced Shirley to Thomas Chaucer and his family:[1] the poems to Thomas Chaucer are only to be found in Shirley's manuscripts, and it is from Shirley that we have the only MS. of the French poems by the Count of Suffolk (the husband of Alice Chaucer). Of Lydgate's works thirty have been preserved exclusively in Shirley's manuscripts. Into two of his books Shirley inserted a list of the contents in verse,[2] in which he extolled Lydgate in phrases which testify to their close acquaintanceship;[3] to these Lydgate replied with a kind of poetic *ex libris* dedicated to Shirley.[4] That they were on terms of intimate friendship can be seen from the titles and marginal notes which Shirley added to Lydgate's poems, e.g., 'Beholdeþe nowe . . . þe translacyoune of Gaude virgo mater Christi made by . . . Lydegate by night as he lay in his bedde at London'.[5]

[1] This is Brusendorff's opinion (op. cit., p. 42).
[2] Brusendorff, op. cit., pp. 453 ff.; Hammond, op. cit., pp. 191 f.
[3]
> . . . ye humayne pilgrymage
> Sayd all by proose in fayre langage
> and many a roundell and balade
> wch ye munke of bury hath made   i. dane John lidgate
> and sayd them with hys sugred mouthe
> in straunge metre so vnkouthe
> of morall mater and holynesse
> of salmes and of ympnes expresse
> of loue and lawe and of pleyinges
> of lordes of ladyes of qwenes of kynges
> his rymyng so moralysed
> that hym aught well be solempnysed
> of all oure engelishe nacion
> ffor his famus translacyon
> of this booke and of other mo . . .

(Brusendorff, pp. 457 f.).
[4] Brusendorff, p. 460:
> Yee þat desyre in herte and have pleasaunce
> Olde stories in bokis for to rede
> Gode matiers putt hem in remembrance
> And of þe oþer take yee neuer hede
> Byseching yowe of your godelyhede
> Whane ye þis boke haue over redde and seyne
> To Johan Shirley restore yee it ageine
> Lenvoye by Lidegate

[5] *M.P.*, 288; cf. also the comments on the titles to *M.P.*, 35, 127, 315, 209, 809, 709.

These additions tell us its place of composition, and occasionally also its date and the name of the patron. Sometimes these remarks are entirely personal in character, and are quite amusing: the envoy to *Servant of Cupyde forsaken*,[1] in which Lydgate deplores the inconstancy of women, has the marginal note: 'Be stille daun Johan. Suche is youre fortune.' Similar points are made in his running commentary to the *Fall of Princes*.[2] In the case of the *Mumming for the Mercers of London*[3] Shirley endeavoured to annotate the mythological names and allusions, and in the *Mumming at Windsor*, where Lydgate has a line in praise of women,[4] Shirley adds: 'Dear friend, when you wrote this you must have been tipsy [yvray].'[5] In helping us to form an impression of Lydgate as a man such marginal remarks are just as useful as the painstaking interpretation of biographical data. Owing to the scarcity of such material we have attempted to fill out the picture by considering Lydgate in his broader historical setting. And now we have only to put the finishing touches to this canvas.

\*

With Humphrey's death Suffolk's most dangerous rival had been removed from the scene, and he was now complete master of the situation. He wished to continue Beaufort's policy, but he had entered into greater obligations to the French than were justifiable in the eyes of the English people. Only peace between England and France could make his policy tolerable, but this did not materialize. At the king's request he put his case before Parliament (25th May 1447). We know nothing of the manner in which it was received, but a proclamation was issued forbidding anyone to make further slanderous allegations against him on pain of incurring the king's displeasure.[6] In 1448 he was made Duke and reached the zenith of his political career, which now became an exemplary case of the 'fall of a prince'. The people were in a revolutionary mood, and could not forgive him for his surrender of Anjou and Maine. Suffolk was imprudent enough to recall Richard, Duke of York, the commander-in-chief in France (replacing him by Edmund, Duke of Somerset, who was then the head of the Beaufort family), and thus incurred York's lasting enmity. A succession of defeats in France, which by

---

[1] *M.P.*, 427.   [2] MS. Harl. 2251, f. 82–150; cf. Brusendorff, p. 465.
[3] *M.P.*, 695; the annotations reproduced *in extenso* in Brusendorff, pp. 466 ff.
[4] *M.P.*, 691, supplement to line 49.
[5] 'A daun Iohan, est yvray?'; cf. Brusendorff, pp. 465 f.
[6] Rymer, *Foedera*, XI, 173.

the end of 1449 resulted in the loss of almost the whole of Normandy,
aroused widespread indignation in England which developed into a
general campaign directed against Suffolk. In 1449 Charles VII declared war and the country found itself in the grip of a catastrophic
financial crisis. Suffolk was arraigned by Parliament and charged
with self-enrichment (1450). In an effort to save his life, the king
ordered him to be exiled for five years; but his ship was forced to
stop, and he was beheaded without trial in a boat on the high seas –
probably at the instigation of Richard, Duke of York. In Ports-
mouth the troops showed their fury by murdering Adam Moleyns,
who had once been one of Suffolk's loyal supporters. This gave the
signal for disturbances throughout the country. Jack Cade made
himself the spokesman of the malcontents, but he and his men were
regarded purely as trouble-makers. Richard of York landed in
Beaumaris in order to avert the danger. Edmund Beaufort, Duke of
Somerset, was recalled from France and made 'Constable of England'.
The barons were divided between York and Somerset – i.e., between
Yorkists and Lancastrians. The king was powerless. The civil war
began.

Lydgate did not live to see the unhappy fate that befell his friends,
his king, and his country. He died in 1449 or 1450, and was buried in
his abbey at Bury St Edmunds. Over his grave was placed the
epitaph:[1]

> *Mortuus seclo superis superstes,*
> *Hac jacet Lidgat tumulatus urna,*
> *Qui fuit quondam celebris Brittaniae fama Poesis.*

---

[1] Cited by Steele, *Secrees*, op. cit., p. 109, with a correction to the erroneous spelling
or reading of '*celebra*'. In Tanner, op. cit., '*cui*' stands in stead of *qui*, which is scarcely
justifiable.

# Appendix I

*

## *Lydgate's Reputation*

*

During his own lifetime and for three generations after his death Lydgate enjoyed a reputation equal to that of Chaucer. He himself called Chaucer his master, praising him for his mildness, kindness, and generosity. But of his literary attainments he admires only his excellence in the use of language: 'of owre language he was the lodesterre', he says in his *Fall of Princes* (Prologue, 252), and this is the substance of all his laudatory remarks on this theme. This was an appreciation of Chaucer which was endorsed by his contemporaries and immediate successors: Lydgate was merely speaking for his own time, when the title of poet was awarded to those who showed ability to handle form and style in their treatment of traditional subjects. The fifteenth century thus generally tended to regard poetry as rhetoric, and was especially fond of florid language. It is therefore not surprising that the three English poets Gower, Chaucer, and Lydgate were seen as models worthy of emulation. In 1470 George Ashby called these 'maisters' Gower, Chaucer, and Lydgate the 'Primier Poetes of this nacion'. That Lydgate's work was particularly highly appreciated is shown by the lines devoted to him by John Metham of Norwich (1458–9):

> *Eke Ion Lydgate, sumtyme monke of Byry,*
> *His bokys endytyd with termys of retoryk*
> *And halff chongyd Latyne, with conseytys off poetry*
> *And craffty Imagynacionys off ymagys ffantastyk*
> *But eke his qwyht her schewyd, & hys late werk*
> *How that hys contynwaun3 made hym bot a poyet & a clerk*
>
> (*EETS*, 15, p. 307).

# John Lydgate

This trinity of Gower, Chaucer, and Lydgate is also referred to by Osbern Bokenham, Gavin Douglas, Stephen Hawes, and Thomas Feylde. By the end of the fifteenth century it had become a stable formula which was repeated throughout the sixteenth century by such writers as John Rastell (1520), Skelton (1523), Lindsay (1530), Forrest (1545), G. Harvey (1577), John Lawson (1581), F. Meres (1598), and Bodenham (1600), appearing for the last time with the early seventeenth-century writer Freeman (1614) (cf. C. Spurgeon, *500 Years of Chaucer Criticism*, I, passim). This was not simply the meaningless transmission of a ready-made formula, as is clear from the fact that many sixteenth-century editions of Chaucer's works (e.g., those of Pynson in 1526 and Stowe in 1561) included a number of pieces by Lydgate, either because these were believed to have been written by Chaucer or because it was desired to emphasize the view that the two poets were of equal merit. In his *Pastyme of Pleasure* (1506) Stephen Hawes wrote:

> O Mayster Lydgate! the most dulcet sprynge
> Of famous rethoryke, wyth balade ryall
> The chefe orygynal

In or about 1450 an anonymous author called Lydgate 'a great Ornament of ye English toung'. His words were repeated, almost literally, a century later by Robert Breham (1555). The more literature was valued for its didactic content, the more brightly Lydgate's fame shone. John Metham's reverent eulogy of the scholar poet is echoed in a more banal tone in the following lines by Thomas Feylde (1509), which may be regarded as a summary of this survey:

> Chaucer floure of rethoryke eloquence
> Compyled bokes pleasaunt and meruayllous
> After hym noble Gower, experte in scyence
> Wrote moralytyes herde and delycyous
> But Lydgate's workes are fruytefull and sentencyous
> Who of his bokes hathe redde the fyne
> He wyll hym call a famus rethorycyne.

Lydgate must be acknowledged as the most representative poet of his day, so varied was the material he handled and the poetic media at which he tried his hand. His high reputation in the fifteenth century also finds expression in the eulogy by Caxton (in his *Book of Cur-*

*tesye*, *EETS*, ES., 3, pp. 36–40), in Hawes' acknowledgement (in Chapter 14 of his *Pastyme*), and in Bale's retrospective judgement: '*Omnium sui temporis in Anglia poetarum, absit inuidia dicto, facile primus floruit*' (*Catalogus*, p. 586). In the age of the Renaissance, Lydgate's inflated style was still an object of admiration. This is shown by the preface to the *Mirror for Magistrates*, which followed the pattern set by the *Fall of Princes*. But subsequently his fame evaporated, and with the changes that occurred in the English language his work, and Middle English literature in general, gradually lapsed into oblivion. During the seventeenth and eighteenth centuries his name is scarcely mentioned (though one may note as a curiosity that two anonymous writers, in *The Muses Mercury*, 1707, and in the *Encyclopaedia Britannica*, 1780, regarded him as greater than Chaucer). The pre-Romanticists revived interest in medieval literature, but among them it was only Thomas Gray who referred appreciatively to Lydgate (*Some remarks on the poems of John Lydgate* [1760, printed 1814], *Works*, Aldine ed., 1858 ff., V, 292; ed. Gosse, 1884, I, 387 ff.).

Evaluation of Lydgate's merit as a writer is necessarily conditioned by the literary fashions prevailing in the critic's own time. Such an assessment was in effect only possible up to the Renaissance; afterwards his work could only be judged from a historical point of view. This approach was inaugurated by Gray, in so far as he introduced historical comment into his appreciation, in which he followed aesthetic criteria (excessively so, as we may think). Another early critic who approached his subject historically was Thomas Warton (*History of English Poetry*, 1774–81):

'His muse was of universal access; and he was not only the poet of his monastery, but of the world in general. If a disguising was intended for the company of goldsmiths, a mask before his majesty at Eltham, a may-game for the Sheriffs and Aldermen of London, etc., etc., Lydgate was consulted, and gave the poetry. . . . I am of opinion that Lydgate made considerable additions to those amplifications of our language, in which Chaucer, Gower and Occleve led the way: and that he is the first of our writers whose style is clothed with that perspicuity, in which the English phraseology appears at this day to an English reader.'

One would have expected this to have been followed up by a proper assessment of Lydgate from a historical standpoint. In general nineteenth-century critics did adopt a historical approach, but so

# John Lydgate

far as Lydgate was concerned the century opened inauspiciously. In his *Bibliographia poetica* (1802, pp. 87 f.) Joseph Ritson wrote:

'This voluminous, prosaick, and driveling monk . . . in truth and fact these stupid and fatiguing productions which by no means deserve the name of poetry, and their still more stupid and disgusting author, who disgraces the name and patronage of his master Chaucer, are neither worth collecting (unless it be as typographical curiositys, or on account of the beautiful illuminations in some of his presentation-copys), nor even worthy of preservation: being only suitably adapted "ad ficum & piperem", and other more base and servile uses.'

If one is determined to take such a negative view, then it would have been better not to attempt an evaluation of Lydgate at all. English scholars have been inclined rather to give an 'appreciation' of literary works than to describe them in their historical context. It has become customary for the same deprecatory remarks to be handed down from one history of literature to the next. W. J. Courthope (in his *History of English Poetry*, 1895, I, p. 325 ff.), speaks of a 'desert of dulness' and of his 'incapacity as a poet'. This negative view was taken over by the author of the otherwise broad-minded *Literary History of the English People*, the Frenchman J. J. Jusserand (1895, I, 496). R. Garnett (*English Literature: an Illustrated Record*, 1903, I, 187 ff.) comes closer to Warton, but sticks to 'literary appreciation'. In the authoritative *Cambridge History of English Literature* (1908, II, 199 ff.) G. Saintsbury takes refuge in witty phrases: 'Chaucer's gold dew-drops of speech' are contrasted with Lydgate's 'leaden splashes', and it is stated that 'the 15th century adored him because he combined all its own worst faults'. In the *Concise C.H.E.L.* (1942, p. 85) G. Sampson added a corrective, saying that: 'There may be more in Lydgate than we have yet discovered.' Legouis, too, contents himself with ironical remarks (Legouis–Cazamian, *Histoire de la littérature anglaise*, 1924, p. 154). Even Grierson (H. J. C. Grierson and J. C. Smith, *A Critical History of English Poetry*, 1944, pp. 40 ff.), who mentions the threads linking Lydgate with the *Mirror for Magistrates*, concludes with the sentence: 'If he pleases yet it is . . . for the personal touches.'

Outside the British Isles Lydgate's significance has been more justly assessed. One may mention in the first place Hortis' *Studi sulle Opere Latine di Gio Boccaccio*, 1879, pp. 640 ff.) and the endeavour of the American John Churton Collins to save Lydgate's reputation in his reviews of the histories of literature by Saintsbury, Gosse, and Jusserand (reprinted in *Ephemera Critica*, L., 1901, pp. 98, 115, 199). Collins made the point that it was hardly fair to dismiss with half a page of remarks, mostly in a tone of ridicule, a man who in the fifteenth century was universally hailed as England's premier poet. The compiler of a history of literature, he argued, was actually faced with the stimulating task of showing why Lydgate, who has little to offer us, possessed the appeal he had for his contemporaries. Unfortunately Collins' polemic did not lead him to attempt such a historical exposition; instead he adopted the same aesthetic approach as the critics he attacked, merely substituting pluses for minuses. In the meantime, however, it had become possible to study Lydgate on a higher level than that of personal value-judgements; for the German philological school, which in the course of the nineteenth century was more or less accepted in England, had begun to make a study of Lydgate independent of aesthetic judgement. Its aim was to produce critical editions of the texts of Lydgate's works, which was done first in Germany and then in England by the *Early English Text Society*. Today almost all his works (with the exception of *Life of Our Lady*[1]) are available in scholarly editions in this series.

[1] While this book was in the press, there appeared *A Critical Edition of John Lydgate's 'Life of Our Lady'* by J. A. Lauritis, R. A. Klines-elter and V. F. Gallagher. (Duquesne Studies, Philological Series 11), Duquesne University, Pittsburgh, Pa, 1961.

# Appendix II

## *Survey of Lydgate Studies*

\*

The first edition of Lydgate's poems in the nineteenth century (disregarding the editions of various texts in the Roxburghe Club series (1818, 1822), Nicolas' *Chronicle of London* (1827) and Wright's *Political poems* (1859)) was J. O. Halliwell's *Selection from the Minor Poems of Lydgate* (L., 1840) in the second volume published by the Percy Society. This contained many poems which are no longer thought to have been written by Lydgate. The edition of part of *Life of Our Lady* in C. E. Tame's *Early English Religious Literature*, II, L., n.d. [1871– ] is also unreliable.

Scholarly editions began to appear with the work of J. Zupitza, C. Horstmann, and J. Schick. Zupitza edited *Guy of Warwick* (in *Sitzungsberichte der Wiener Akademie*, 1873; another text was edited by F. N. Robinson in *Harvard Studies*, V, 1896) and also *Aesop* (*Archiv*, 85 [1890], following Sauerstein's edition in *Anglia*, 9 [1886]). Horstmann edited *Life of St Edmund and Fremund* (in *Altenglische Legenden*, 1881); *The Lyfe of Seint Albon and lyfe of Saint Amphabel* (in *Festschrift der Realschule zu Berlin*, 1882). Schick edited *The Temple of Glas* (*EETS*, ES., 60 (1891)). This edition, which lifted Lydgate studies to a scholarly level, contains the first description of Lydgate's life and work, still of some value today, and the first critical guide to the transmission of Lydgate's works. The stimulus which Schick gave to Lydgate studies led to a number of editions of his works being produced during the 1890s. R. Steele's edition of the *Secrees of Philisoffres* (*EETS*, ES., 66 (1894)) added some valuable information to that given by Schick in his introductory essay. The articles on Lydgate by H. Morley (*English Writers*, VI (1891)), and S. Lee

(*D.N.B.*, 1893) were evidence of an increased readiness to adopt historical criteria in approaching the subject.

Stimulated by these efforts, E. Krausser edited the *Complaint of the Black Knight* with an exhaustive introduction (Diss., Halle, 1896, reprinted from *Anglia*, 19). In the same year there appeared the book by E. Gattinger, *Die Lyrik Lydgates* (*Wiener Beiträge zur engl. Phil.*, 4), a courageous but premature attempt to regard Lydgate's lyrics comprehensively and to assess their place in English literature. In view of the fact that the canon had not yet been firmly established, this led to dubious conclusions; it would perhaps have been better at this stage if Gattinger had restricted himself to a study of sources, as E. Köppel did with regard to the *Siege of Thebes* and the *Fall of Princes* (Munich, 1884 and 1885).

Using Zupitza's papers G. Schleich edited the *Fabula duorum mercatorum* (in *Quellen und Forschungen zur Sprach- und Culturgeschichte*, 83, Strasbourg, 1897) with a detailed essay and a valuable glossary of words used by Lydgate.

All the editions that followed were published in the *EETS* series. F. J. Furnivall began in 1899 his edition of *The Pilgrimage of the Life of Man*, Part I, in ES., 77 (1899), Part II, in ES., 83 (1901); K. B. Locock then provided, as Part III, an introduction, notes, and glossary, in ES., 92 (1904). In 1900 O. Glauning edited *Two Nightingale Poems* with a good commentary (ES., 80 (1900)), and M. Degenhart published *Horse, Goose, and Sheep*, also with comprehensive introduction and notes (*Münchner Beiträge zur romanischen und englischen Philologie*, 19). E. Sieper's edition of *Resoun and Sensuallyte* comprises one volume of text (Part I, ES., 84 (1901)) and one volume of *Studies and Notes* (Part II, ES., 89 (1903)). In addition to this there are the preliminary studies by J. Schick, in *Anglia*, Beiblatt, 1898, and by Sieper, in *Les Échecs Amoureux* (1898). In 1906 H. Bergen began to edit the *Troy Book* (Part I, ES., 97 (1906), Part II, ES., 103 (1908), Part III, ES., 106 (1910), Part IV, ES., 126 (1935)). This is the best edited of Lydgate's works, with sufficient excerpts from the sources to enable comparisons to be made and an excellent glossary.

The accompanying essays in these editions, which were supplemented by a number of articles in periodicals and sections in general works (e.g., B. R. Brotanek, *Die englischen Maskenspiele*, Vienna, 1902), encouraged H. N. MacCracken to undertake his comprehensive *Studies in the Life and Writings of John Lydgate* (Thesis, 891 pp., Harvard Univ. Lib., 1907). I have been able to see only rotograph parts of excerpts of this unpublished thesis, but the most essential parts of it have been made available in other publications: the text of *The Serpent of Division*, in his subsequent edition (L., 1910), with an essay 'The Lydgate Canon', published as appendix to the *Transactions of the Philological Society*, L., 1907–8, and in MacCracken's edition of the *Minor Poems* (Part I: Religious Poems, ES., 107 (1911); Part II, Secular Poems, OS., 192 (1934); Part III, which was to have included essays on the canon, a commentary, and glossary, did not appear). MacCracken's edition is not free from error (cf. O. Mahir, *J. Lydgate: einige religiöse Gedichte*, Berlin, n.d., [1910–15]); but it is nevertheless fundamental, since it contains all the shorter poetic works of Lydgate (including the mummings and the shorter legends), and the introduction to the first volume contains the Lydgate canon mentioned above.

From this time onwards the editions of his works in the *EETS* series were supplemented by short essays and dissertations. In 1911 there appeared the first volume of *The Siege of Thebes* edited by A. Erdmann (ES., 108); Part II, edited with most valuable studies by E. Ekwall, did not appear until 1930 (ES., 125). Shortly afterwards, almost simultaneously, there appeared two works basic for an understanding of Lydgate's style: G. Reismüller, *Romanische Lehnwörter bei Lydgate*, Leipzig, 1911 (with exhaustive tables), and A. Courmont, *Studies on Lydgate's Syntax in the Temple of Glas*, Paris, 1912, in which the author showed that Lydgate deliberately adopted an archaic style. The scholarly interest in Lydgate continued during and after the First World War. On Lydgate's diction there appeared the dissertations by R. Hingst (Greifswald, 1908), E. Hüttmann (Kiel, 1914), H. Juhl (Kiel, 1921), and the articles by J. F. Royster (*Mod. Phil.*, 1915; *Stud. Phil.*, 1916). Contributions to textual criticism were supplied by Th. Prosiegel (Diss., Munich, 1903). A number of studies continued the investigations into Lydgate's metre begun in the early editions of his works, e.g., B. H. Reger (Bayreuth, 1910), A. H. Licklider (Baltimore, 1910), C. F. Babcock (*PMLA*, 1914) and C. S. Lewis (*Essays and Studies*, 1938). Finally, there have appeared a large number of historical and literary studies, such as E. P. Hammond (*MLN*, 1911–12, and *Anglia*, 1914), F. Brie (*Engl. Studien*, 1929), C. Brown (*MLN*, 1925, and *PMLA*, 1935), K. Brunner (*Archiv*, 1932), J. P. Oakden (*RES*, 1933), and the dissertations by H. Koch (*Troy Book*, Berlin, 1935), E. Tilgner (*Aureate Terms*, Berlin, 1936), Th. Wolpers (*Mariendichtung*, Bonn, 1949, printed in *Anglia*,

69), H. Quistorp (*Lydgates Heiligenlegenden*, [unpublished], Bonn, 1951).

The editions of texts were brought to a close with H. Bergen's great edition of the *Fall of Princes* (*EETS*, ES., 121–4 (1924–7)) and the *Dance of Death*, edited by F. Warren and B. White (*EETS*, OS., 181 (1931)). Good editorial technique is combined with a scholarly literary essay in E. P. Hammond's anthology *English Verse between Chaucer and Surrey*, Durham and C.U.P., 1927. There remains room for a concordance and dictionary to the vocabulary used by Lydgate.

## Appendix III

### *The Lydgate Canon*

\*

1. List of works deemed to have been written by Lydgate.
2. List of works attributed to Lydgate, apparently in error:

(*a*) customary criteria for establishing authenticity;
(*b*) attributions made in general biographical works;
(*c*) list of dubious works;
(*d*) discussion of works listed.

There are two reasons why it will never be possible to establish which works were written by Lydgate and which by members of his school. In the first place, Lydgate was not – like Chaucer, for example – a towering genius, about whose canon doubt can hardly exist. In the case of Chaucer we can be guided by the poetic quality of his work and his unmistakable personal touch, in addition to philological tests (language, style, metre, and rhyme tests). In the second place, this technique of philological analysis has only a relative value in regard to Lydgate, since his significance lies above all in his pronounced rhetorical style; his use of language and metre, and his general manner, lent itself comparatively easily to imitation. The more rhetorical his style, the harder it is to distinguish his work from that of his followers. We therefore have to rest content with a canon that has limited pretensions to accuracy, that established by Mac-Cracken (*M.P.*, v–lviii). The list of Lydgate's works recognized as authentic by MacCracken is not entirely without error, if only because certain criteria which he applied are open to challenge. But by and large MacCracken's canon has found acceptance among scholars, and therefore the list given here is based upon it. All Lydgate's works are included, arranged in the categories according to which they have been discussed in this book. Each poem is listed by its title, with its opening words given in brackets, as well as its number in the Mac-Cracken canon (*M.P.*, pp. xl ff.), since this gives further details about the grounds for its attribution to Lydgate, and also, for the sake of clarity, its number in the *Index of Middle English Verse* by C. Brown and R. H. Robbins (N.Y., 1943). Where, as a result of recent research, the authenticity of a work has been contested, this is indicated in the footnotes.

C = MacCracken's *Canon* (from which the titles and orthography are taken); I = Brown's *Index*.

I. FABLES AND DEBATES:

Isopes Fabules (Wisdom is more . . .) C 59; I 4178.
The Churl and the Bird (Problemes of olde . . .) C 17; I 2784.
Debate between the Horse, Goose, and Sheep (Controversies pleis and . . .) C 56; I 658.

2. COURTLY POETRY:

Complaint of the Black Knight (In May, when . . .) C 20; I 1507.
Flour of Curtesye (In Fevrier, when . . .) C 44; I 1487.
A Gentlewoman's Lament (Allas I wooful . . .) C 48; I 154.
Ballade of Her that hath all Virtues (Fresshe lusty beaute . . .) C 7; I 869.
A Complaint for Lack of Mercy (Grettere mater of . . .) C 18; I 1017.[1]
The Servant of Cupid Forsaken (Ful longe I . . .) C 136; I 886.
A Lover's New Year's Gift (In honnour of . . .) C 85; I 1496.
My Lady Dere (Every maner creature . . .) C 85; I 1496.

3. ALLEGORIES:

Temple of Glas (For þouʒt constreint . . .) C 144; I 851.
Resoun and Sensuallyte (To alle folkys . . .) C 106; I 3746.[2]

---

[1] Brusendorff contests Lydgate's authorship, but does not give the grounds for his opinion (*The Chaucer Tradition*, L., 1925).

[2] Brusendorff, p. 185: 'ascribed to Lydgate on no better evidence than that of Stowe and some indifferent literary parallels'; p. 388: 'the author of Res. and Sens. who certainly was not Lydgate'.

4. ROMANCES:

Troy Book (O myhty Mars . . .) C 152; I 2516.
Siege (Story) of Thebes (Whan bright Phebus . . .) C 142;
I 3928.

5. SATIRES:

So as the Crabbe Goth Forward (þis worlde is . . .) C 137; I 3655.
Ryght as a Rammes Horne (Alle ryhtwysnes now . . .) C 109;
I 199.
The Order of Fools (The ordre of . . .) C 89; I 3444.
Against Millers and Bakers (Put out his . . .) C 73; I 2786.
Jak Hare (A froward knave . . .) C 60; I 36.
Payne and sorow of Evil Maryage (Glory unto God . . .) C 93;
I 919.[1,2]
Ballade on an Ale-seller (Remembrying on the . . .) C 1; I 2809.[1]
Ballade per Antiphrasim (Vndir youre hood . . .) C 8; I 3823.[2]
[Beware of] Doublenesse (This world is ful . . .) C 32; I 3656.
Examples against Women (To Adam and . . .) C 35; I 3744.[3]
Horns away (Of god and . . .) C 55; I 2625.
Bycorne and Chichefache (O prudent folkes . . .) C 13; I 2541.

6. POLITICAL VERSE:

A Praise of Peace (Mercy and Truthe . . .) C 94; I 2156.
On Gloucester's Marriage (Thorugh gladde aspectis . . .)
C 50; I 3718.
Complaint for my Lady of Gloucester and Holand (A solitary
sore . . .) C 19; I 92.
The Title and Pedigree of Henry VI (Troubled hertes to . . .)
C 95; I 3808.
Roundel for Coronation of Henry VI (Rejoice ye reames . . .)
C 108; I 2804.
Ballade to King Henry VI, on his Coronation (Moost noble
Prynce . . .) C 9; I 2211.
The Soteltes at the Coronation Banquet of Henry VI (Loo here
twoo. . .) C 138; I 1929.

---

[1] Lydgate's name not mentioned in Brown's *Index*.
[2] Brusendorff contests Lydgate's authorship, but does not give the grounds for his opinion.
[3] I: 'probably by Lydgate'; *Speculum*, 20 (1946), p. 109: 'definitely by Lydgate'.

On a New Year's Gift of an Eagle (þis hardy foole . . .) C 86;
I 3604.

Prayer for King, Queen and People (Most souereyne lord . . .)
C 97; I 2218.

Ballade in Despyte of the Flemyngs (Off stryvys new . . .) C 43;
I 2657.[1]

7. MUMMINGS AND ENTRIES:

Mumming at Eltham (Bachus which is . . .) C 77; I 458.

Mumming at Bishopswood (Myghty Flourra goddes . . .) C 76;
I 2170.

A Pageant of Knowledge (This worlde is borne . . .) C 90;
I 3651.

Mumming at London (Loo her this . . .) C 79; I 1928.

Mumming at Hertford (Moost noble prynce . . .) C 78; I 2213.

Mumming at Windsor (Mooste noble prynce . . .) C 80; I 2212.

Mumming for the Mercers of London (Moost mighty lord . . .)
C 81; I 2210.

Mumming for the Goldsmiths of London (þat worþi david . . .)
C 82; I 3301.

Pur le Roy: King Henry VI's Entry into London (Toward
the ende . . .) C 34; I 3799.

Margaret's Entry into London (Moost cristen Princesse . . .)
I 2200; not mentioned in C.

8. SECULAR KNOWLEDGE AND RULES OF CONDUCT:

Stans puer ad mensam (My dere child . . .) C 139; I 2233.

Treatise for Lavenders (Yee maistresses myne . . .) C 63;
I 4254.

Duodecim abusiones (Go forthe, King . . .) C 33; I 920.[2]

Four Things that Make a Man a Fool (Worshyp, wommen,
wyne . . .) C 45; I 4230.

Nine Properties of Wine (Wyne of nature . . .) C 88; I 4175.

A Dietary (For helth of . . .) C 30; I 824.[3]

Secrees of [olde] Philisoffres (God almyghty save . . .) C 132;
I 935.

---

[1] I: 'perhaps by Lydgate'.

[2] Brusendorff contests Lydgate's authorship, but does not give the grounds for his
opinion.

[3] A *Doctrine for Pestilence* is listed separately in C, No. 31.

9. TRANSLATIONS OF DEGUILEVILLE AND THE DANCE OF
DEATH:

The Pilgrimage of the Life of Man (Ye worldly folk . . .) C 96;
I 4265.

Daunce of Machabree (O ye folkes . . .) C 24; I 2591.

10. LEGENDARY LIVES OF SAINTS AND PIOUS TALES:

The Life of our Lady (O thoughtful herte . . .) C 68; I 2574.

Legend of St Margaret (At the reuerence . . .) C 123; I 439.

Legend of St George (O yee folk . . .) C 119; I 2592.

Legend of St Petronilla (The parfite life . . .) C 126; I 3446.[1]

How the Plage was Sesyd in Rome (So noble medesyne . . .)
C 57; I 3168.

Legend of St Giles (Of Agamemnon vndir . . .) C 120; I 2606.

Legend of St Austin at Compton (Lyk as the . . .) C 113; I 1875.

Legend of Dan Joos (O welle of . . .) C 64; I 2579.[2]

Lives of SS. Edmund and Fremund (The noble story . . .)
C 116; I 3440.[3]

Miracles of St Edmund (Laude of our . . .) C 74; I 1843.

The Lyfe of Seint Albon and the Lyfe of Saint Amphabel (To
call Clio . . .) C 110; I 3748.

Fabula duorum mercatorum (In Egipt whilom . . .) C 36; I
1481.

11. HISTORICAL WORKS:

Guy of Warwick (From tyme of . . .) C 52; I 875.

Fall of Princes (He that whilom . . .) C 37; I 1168.

The Sodeine Fall of Princes in Oure Dayes (Beholde this
gret . . .) C 38; I 500.

Cartae versificatae (In name of hym . . .) C 15; I 1513.[4]

The Kings of England Sithen William Conquerour (This
myghty William . . .) C 62; I 3632.

12. OCCASIONAL POEMS:

On the Departyng of Chaucer (O thow Lucyna . . .) C 28; I
2571.

[1] I: 'probably by Lydgate'.

[2] Brusendorff contests Lydgate's authorship, but does not give the grounds for his
opinion.

[3] C gives the initial line of the *Prayer to St Edmund* (I 53); cf. p. 271.

[4] I: 'probably by Lydgate'.

Valentine to Her I Love Best of All (Seynt Valentyne of . . .)
C 155; I 3065.

Letter to Gloucester (Right mighty prince . . .) C 66; I 2825.

Verses on Cambridge (By trewe recorde . . .) C 14; I 582.

13. PROSE WORKS:

Serpent of Division (Whilom as olde . . .) C 135; not mentioned
in I.

Brut C 12; not mentioned in I.

14. RELIGIOUS LYRICS:
'APPLIED ART':

Merita Misse (God of hewine . . .) I 957;[1] not mentioned in C.

A Kalendare (Iesu Lord! for . . .) C 61; I 1721.

Procession of Corpus Christi (þis hye feste . . .) C 100; I 3606.

Virtues of the Mass (Ye that beth . . .) C 70; I 4246.

Exortacion to Prestys (Ye holy prestes . . .) C 70; I 4249.[2]

On Kissing at Verbum caro factum est (ȝee deuout people
. . .) C 70; I 4245.[2]

Pater noster qui es in celis (Oure glorious fadyr . . .) C 92;
I 2711.

Exposition of the Pater noster (Atwixe drede and . . .) C 91;
I 448.

Stella celi extirpauit (Thow hevenly quene . . .) C 141; I 3673.

De Sancta Maria contra pestilenciam (O hevenly sterre . . .)
I 2459;[3] not mentioned in C.

Fifftene Toknys aforn the Doom (As the doctour . . .) C 42;
I 408[1,4]

PARAPHRASES OF HYMNS:

Benedic anima mea (O thou my soule . . .) C 10; I 1572.

Misericordias domini in eternum cantabo (Alle goostly songes
. . .) C 75; I 178.

Deus in nomine tuo salvum me fac (God in thy . . .) C 29; I 951.

De profundis (Having a conseit . . .) C 25; I 1130.

---

[1] I: Lydgate's name not mentioned.
[2] Not listed separately in C, as belonging to the *Vertues of the Masse.*
[3] I: Lydgate's name not mentioned.
[4] Brusendorff contests Lydgate's authorship, but does not give the grounds for his opinion.

# John Lydgate

Te Deum laudamus (Te deum laudamus . . .) C 143; I 3261.[1]

Vexilla regis prodeunt (Royal Baneris Unrolled . . .) C 157; I 2833.[1, 4]

Letabundus (Grounde take in . . .) C 65; I 1019.

Christe qui lux es et dies ([O] Christe þat arte . . .) C 22; I 614.

LONGER POEMS:

A saying of the Nihtingale (In Juygne whan . . .) C 87; I 1498.

The Testament of Lydgate (O how holsom . . .) C 146; I 2464.

HYMNS TO JESUS ON THE PASSION:

O Dolorous pyte of Crystes Passioun (Erly on morwe . . .) C 101; I 702.[2]

A Prayer upon the Cross (Upon the cros . . .) C 154; I 3845.

Cristes Passioun (Man to refourme . . .) C 23; I 2081.

Fifteen Ooes (O blyssid lord . . .) C 41; I 2394.

Quis dabit meo capiti fontem lacrimarum (Who shall give . . .) C 104; I 4099.

PRAYERS:

The eight Verses of St Bernard (O sothfast sonne . . .) C 114; I 2553.

Prayer in Old Age (All the trespas . . .) C 98; I 222.

To St Robert of Bury (O Blyssid Robert . . .) C 127; I 2399.

Prayers to ten Saints (Blyssid Denys of . . .) C 145; I 529.

Prayer to St Thomas (Blissed Thomas rubyfyed . . .) C 128; I 538.[2]

A Prayer to St Thomas of Canterbury (Synguler shepperde gardeyn . . .) C 129; I 3115.[3, 4]

Prayer to Sts Katherine, Margaret and Magdalene (Katerine with glorious . . .) C 121; I 1814.

Prayer to St Michael (O myghell by . . .) C 124; I 2513.[5]

Prayer to St Gabriel (Blissed Gabriel wich . . .) C 118; I 531.[6]

To St Leonard (Reste and reffuge . . .) C 122; I 2812.

To St Ursula (Ye Britoun martirs . . .) C 130; I 4243.

---

[1] I: 'attributed to Lydgate'.  [2] I: Lydgate's name not mentioned.
[3] I: 'attributed to Lydgate'.
[4] Brusendorff contests Lydgate's authorship, but does not give the grounds for his opinion.
[5] I: 'perhaps by Lydgate'.  [6] I: 'by Lydgate?'.

To St Ositha (Heyl hooly Sitha . . .) C 125; I 1050.[1]

Devowte Invocacioun to St Denys (O þow chosen . . .) C 115; I 2566.

A Glorious Prayer to St Edmund (Glorious Edmund Kyng . . .) C 117; I 915.

Prayer to St Edmund (Blyssyd Edmund Kyng . . .) C 116; I 53.

Praise of St Anne (He that intendeth . . .) C 112; I 1152.[2]

Invocation to St Anne (Thow first moever . . .) C 111; I 3671.

MARIAN HYMNS:

On the Image of Our Lady (Beholde and se . . .) C 58; I 490.

The Child Jesus to Mary, the Rose (My father above . . .) C 16; I 2238.[2]

Gaude Virgo mater Christi (Be gladde mayde . . .) C 47; I 464.

Ave Maria [Salutacio angelica] (Hayle gloryous lady . . .) C 4; I 1045.

Verses to the Virgin (Fragment) C 158; I *34.[2, 3]

Ave regina celorum (Hayle luminary and . . .) C 5; I 1056.

Regina celi letare (O thow ioyfull . . .) C 105; I 2270.

To Mary, the Star of Jacob (O sterre of . . .) C 140; I 2556.

Prayer to Mary, in whose Help is Affiaunce (O swettest bawme . . . .) C 99; I 2565.

Fifteen Joys and Sorrows of Mary (Atween mydnyht and . . .) C 39; I 447.

Fifteen Joys of (Mary) oure Lady (Blessed lady, o . . .) C 40; I 533.

Gloriosa dicta sunt de te (On hooly hilles . . .) C 49; I 2688.

To Mary the Quene of Hevene (Quene of Hevene . . .) C 103; I 2791.

Ave Jesse virgula (Hayle blissid lady . . .) C 3; I 1037.

Ballade at the Reverence of Our Lady Qwene of Mercy (A thowsande stories . . .) C 6; I 99.

MISCELLANEOUS:

Defence of Holy Church (Right mighty prince . . .) C 27; I 2219.

A Holy Meditation (Affter the stormy . . .) C 54; I 131.[4]

---

[1] I: 'perhaps by Lydgate'.

[2] Brusendorff contests Lydgate's authorship, but does not give the grounds for his opinion.

[3] I: 'possibly by Lydgate or one of his school'.

[4] Lydgate's authorship contested by C. Brown in PMLA, 50, pp. 997 ff.

# John Lydgate

[1] Brusendorff contests Lydgate's authorship, but does not give the grounds for his
opinion.

[2] I: 'by John Lucas (?)'.

[3] I: 'Proverbs ascribed to R. Stokys (by MacCracken to Lydgate)'.

[4] Brusendorff contests Lydgate's authorship, but does not give the grounds for his
opinion.

[5] Lydgate's name not mentioned in I; the first five stanzas included as the introduction
to No. 4042 with the comment 'attributed to Lydgate'.

[6] I: 'perhaps by Lydgate'.

[7] I: 'possibly by Lydgate'.

[8] Lydgate's name not mentioned in I.

Timor mortis conturbat me (So long as . . .) C 151; I 3160.[1]
Benedictus Deus in donis suis (God departith his . . .) C 11;
  I 943.
God is myn Helpere (God is myn . . .) C 51; I 953.
Epistle to Sibille (The chief ginnyng . . .) C 67; I 3321.

The authenticity of a number of the works listed above is open to
question. In the case of many works traditionally regarded as written by Lydgate there are such strong doubts as to his authorship
that it is impossible to ascribe them to him. A list of these is given
below, together with a brief discussion of the plausibility of the
claim that he was the author. It would require too much space to
examine all the arguments for and against, and in most cases one can
only follow one's own personal opinion. For the sake of clarity, one
may first of all summarize the criteria that were adopted by Mac-
Cracken in the introduction to his *M. P.* to establish the authenticity
of Lydgate's works (cf. on this point the article by E. P. Hammond in
*Anglia*, Beiblatt, 24 (1913), pp. 140 ff.; *Anglia*, 28 (1905), pp. 1 ff.;
*Anglia*, 30 (1907), pp. 320 ff.).

The most important criteria are statements by Lydgate himself
about his work and attributions made by scribes of contemporary
MSS. (in particular by J. Shirley). But since we have reason to doubt
the authenticity of many works signed by scribes with Lydgate's
name, and since later bibliographies give a list of Lydgate's works
that is inordinately long, attempts have been made to attain a greater
degree of certainty by analysing his rhyme, metre, and style.

(a) *Rhyme.* Study of works of which Lydgate is known to have
been the author shows that he rhymes accurately, but does not distinguish between opened and closed 'e' and 'o' sounds, and that he
rhymes -er and -ere with -ir and -ire, words that end in -e with those
that do not, and (in his early works) -y with -ye or -ie. These departures from Chaucer's practice were quite common during the
fifteenth century. But in Lydgate's authentic works we do not find
the poetic licence taken by some of his contemporaries, who rhymed
-igne and -ighte with -ine or -ite, -orie and -arie with -ie, and -ees with
-esse. Likewise he avoids assonance and makes use of the popular
rhyme in -oun only when the rhyming words are actually stressed on
the last syllable, and not on the penultimate or the second from last
(but cf. C. Brown in *PMLA*, 50, pp. 997 ff.). These criteria do not

[1] Lydgate's name not mentioned in I.

provide convincing proof by themselves, but can serve as supporting evidence.

(b) *Metre.* This cannot be said of metrical criteria. MacCracken can only point to the fact that Lydgate sought to give his verse a smooth rhythm, and regards jerky metre as evidence against Lydgate's authorship. But unfortunately students of Lydgate are not in agreement as to what constitutes a smooth metre.

(c) *Style.* Stylistic criteria can also only lead to hypotheses, not to convincing proof. MacCracken is inclined not to regard the degree of Chaucer's influence as a valid measure, since this can be found in the work of all the poets of the time. But on the other hand he considers it reasonable to classify his religious poems into the *Pearl* and *Quia amore langueo* type. He takes as another criterion Lydgate's use of double expressions and rhyme-tags (cf. the list of these compiled by Sieper, *EETS*, ES., 84). Finally, one may mention the factor of Lydgate's own personality: his modesty and reluctance to thrust himself forward, which was more marked than literary convention required.

Looking at these criteria set out by MacCracken, it is difficult to avoid the impression that in the last instance the student must be guided by his own personal expertise. This MacCracken himself seems to admit when he singles out as characteristic of Lydgate's work 'a certain smoothness of verse, a certain dignity and elevation of sentiment, a certain polish as of the court'. Elsewhere (*Anglia*, 33, p. 286) he speaks in similar terms of the general impression produced by Lydgate's style: it is difficult to define, but unmistakably apparent to the expert.

Another criterion, far removed from this imprecise realm of emotional appreciation, is Lydgate's treatment of the final -e. Here Lydgate by and large agrees with Chaucer, whereas works by other authors are more advanced in this respect.

\*

The first list of Lydgate's works was made by John Bale in his *Scriptorum illustrium Maioris Britanniae Catalogus*, 1548 (reprinted as *Index Britanniae Scriptorum*, ed. by R. L. Poole and M. Bateson, Oxford, 1902). This contains forty-eight titles, of which 18 must be queried (following MacCracken, *M.P.*, pp. xxxvi ff.). Bale's list was adopted almost literally by John Pits in his *Relationum Historicarum de Rebus Anglicis*, Tom. I, Paris, 1619. John Stow gives in Speght's edition of Chaucer (1598) a much-expanded list of 114 works by Lydgate based on the MSS. in his possession. But Stow appears to ascribe indiscriminately all the secular works to Chaucer and all the religious ones to Lydgate. The next list to be compiled was that in Bishop Thomas Tanner's *Bibliotheca Britannico-Hibernica* (ed. by D. Wilkins, 1748), which was based upon Stow and Pits. Finally, there is the list of Joseph Ritson in his *Bibliotheca Anglo-Poetica* (1802); in this Lydgate's works are covered by no less than 251 entries, of which MacCracken queries over forty-five.

The works of which Lydgate was probably *not* the author are as follows (title, opening words, no. in Brown's *Index* and Ritson's list; enumeration taken from MacCracken):

1. *Courtly poetry and Chaucer*: Maunciples Tale; Prioresses Tale; St Cecilia; Gentilesse; Stedfastnesse; Fortune; ABC. – Complaint d'amours. – Assemble of damys; Craft of lovers; A praise of women; Ballade warning men; Complaint against hope; Remedie of love; A lover's plaint; To his mistress.

2. *Moralistic allegories*: Court of Sapience; Assembly of Gods.

3. *Romances and dramatic pieces*: Siege of Jerusalem. – High astrapotent auctor of all.

4. *Satires*: Satirical description of his lady; Prohemy of a marriage; Treatise of a Galaunt; Ragmanys rolle; London Lickpenny.

5. *Fabliaux*: Lady Prioress and her suitors; Smith and his dame; Childe of Bristow; Piers of Fulham.

6. *Historical and political works*: Petigree of Emperors; On the Reconciliation, 1457; Battle of Agincourt; Battle of Barnet; Expedition of Henry V into France; Epitaphium Ducis Gloucestriae.

7. *Secular knowledge and rules of conduct*: Praeceptiones Gall. Ling.; Proprietates nationum; Dantis opuscula; Petrarchae quaedam; Cato's distichs; De re militari; Summum sapientiae.

8. *Legends and pious tales*: Life of St Anne; St Barbara; St Denis; St Erasmus; Story of Job. – Three kings of Cologne; Monk of Paris; Legend of Wulfrike.

9. *Religious lyrics*: Conditor alme siderum; De coelorum gaudiis; The Nightingale. – Psalmi passionis; Hymn to the Creator; Appeal of Christ; Testamentum Christi; Prayer to Christ's name; Song of love to Jesus; Prayer to Jesu. – Lamentacyoun of Magdaleyne; Prayer to bedward and at rising; Lydgate's prayer to St

T

# John Lydgate

Edmund; Aureate prayer to B.V.; Quia amore langueo; Stabat mater; Lament of our lady; Maria virgo assumpta est; Veni coronaberis; Prayer to the B.V.; Salue regina; Hymn on the 5 joys; Prayer to the B.V. and several saints; Gaude flore virginali; Regina celi laetare; Lenvoy to Mary; Balade in praise of the B.V.; O flos pulcherrime. – Exhortation against the deadly sins; Magnificence of the church.

10. *Moralistic poems*: Chaunse of the dyse; Folly of heaping up riches; Make amendes; Thank God for all; For the better abyde; Poem against idleness; Hoc factum est.

Since Lydgate was a disciple of Chaucer, many of the latter's works were attributed to him: by Ritson *The Maunciples Tale* (46), *The Prioresses Tale* (239), St Cecilia [*Second Nun's Tale*] (235); as well as the ballads *Gentilesse* (31), *Lak of Stedfastnesse* (81) and *Fortune* (21, 86), and *ABC* (206), which Lydgate incorporated into his translation of Deguileville. The *Complaint d'amours* (85), which Skeat attributes to Chaucer (I, 411 f.), is perhaps by one of Chaucer's disciples, but not by Lydgate.

Among the other courtly poems wrongly attributed to Lydgate were: the charming *Boke called Assemble of Damis* (In Septembre at the fallyng of the leef) [Rits. 27; I 1528], printed by Skeat, *Chaucerian Pieces*, p. 380; 107 Chaucerian stanzas; the dialogue between Cupid and Diana, or *Craft of Lovers* (To moralise o similitude) [Rits., 30, 109; I 3761], a poem in twenty-six ballad stanzas that in early editions (e.g., Johnson – Chalmers, *English Poets*, I, 558 f.) was attributed to Chaucer; the poem *A praise of women* (Al tho the lyste of women) [Rits., 28; I 228], printed by Chalmers (I, 344), which is also generally printed with Chaucer's works; MacCracken calls it 'a cheap imitation of Chaucer'; it dates from approx. 1475.

Other poems of the courtly type are: *Balade warning men against deceitful women* (Lok wel aboute, ye that lovers be) [Rits., 24; I 1944], printed in *Chaucerian Pieces*, p. 295 (also in Chalmers, I, 564), six ballad stanzas; *Complaint against Hope* (As I strode in studyinge allone) [Rits., 87; I 370], unprinted; *Remedie of love* (Seeing the manifolde inconuenience) [Rits., 29; I 3084], printed by Chalmers, (I, 538). All the above are certainly not by Lydgate; but MacCracken attributed to Lydgate's immediate entourage two ballads (printed in *Archiv*, 127 (1911), pp. 323 ff.): *A Lovers Plaint* (As ofte as syghes ben in herte trewe) [I 402, Lydgate's name not mentioned], thirteen ballad

[ 276 ]

stanzas; and *To his Mistress* or *Complaint for Lac of Sight* (For lac of sighte grete cause haue I to pleyn) [I 828] (also in H. L. Cohen, *The Ballade*, pp. 287 ff.).

Among lengthy allegories the following have often wrongly been attributed to Lydgate (following St. Hawes' *Past. of Pleas.*, ll. 1282 ff.): *Court of Sapience* (The laborous and the most meruelous werkes) [I 3406; cf. also 168], listed more than once by Ritson (e.g., 12, 51); it has been edited by R. Spindler, Leipzig, 1927; cf. E. P. Hammond, *English Verse*, p. 258, and C. Bühler, *The Sources of the C. of S.*, Leipzig, 1932 (Beitr. z. engl. Phil., 33). – The poem differs radically from Lydgate's work in metre, rhyme, and style (cf. the arguments of Spindler, in his ed., pp. 46–72, 97 ff.). It may probably be dated to about 1475, and may have been written to order for Edward IV. In addition to this, W. de Worde printed in his edition of Chaucer (1498), with an attribution to Lydgate, *The Assembly of Gods* (Whan Phebus in the Crabbe had nere hys cours ronne) [Rits., 13; I 4005, 'perhaps by Lydgate'], ed. O. L. Triggs, *EETS*, ES., 69; cf. E. P. Hammond, *Chaucer Manual*, p. 407, and A. Rudolph, *Lydgate und die A. of G.*, Berlin, 1909 (Diss., Würzburg, 1908). The work imitates Lydgate's style of diction but is very different in its metre, in the careless handling of rhyme and the forceful expressions incorporated from everyday speech; like *London Lickpenny*, it has a totally different air about it which distinguishes it from Lydgate's work.

Rits. (38) also ascribed to Lydgate a romance: *Siege of Jerusalem* (Listeneth alle þat ben in liue) [I 1881]. It is also known as *Destruction of Jerusalem* or *Titus and Vespasian*; (the best known version, in alliterative verses, is in I 1583). The version thought to be by Lydgate (in doggerel couplets) has been edited by J. Herbert (Roxburghe Club), 1905; cf. Fischer in *Archiv*, 111, p. 289.

The poem *The high astrapotent auctor of all* [I 3376] in seven Chaucerian stanzas (attributed to Lydgate by Ritson (173)) belongs to the category of drama ('Lines for a mumming spoken by Law'); it is unprinted.

Among satirical pieces Shirley attributed to Lydgate *A Satirical Description of his lady*, also known from its refrain as *Hood of Green* (My fayr lady so fresshe of hew) [Rits., 108, I 2237]. The words 'Explicit quod Lydgate' in the MS. Harl. 2255, dating from the time of Edward IV, have been explained by MacCracken as an error (for a contrary view, cf. Köppel, in *Engl. Studien*, 24, p. 290); it is printed in Halliwell's anthology (Percy Soc.), p. 199. A similar delight in obscenity occurs in *Prohemy of a Marriage betwix an olde Man and a yonge wife*, also entitled *Advice to an old Man* or *Decembre and July* (A philisophre a good clerk secular) [Rits., 50 ; I 86] in seventy-two Chaucerian stanzas with an envoy, printed in Halliwell, pp. 27 ff. It is far removed from Lydgate's work not only in its theme but also in its delight in narrative and its brevity and wit.

Bishop J. Alcock (*d.* 1500) ascribed to Lydgate a work listed by Stow (101) and Ritson (155), namely *Treatise of a Galaunt*, also known as *Ballade of a Galaunt* or *Gallande Ballade* (Galawnt pride thy father is dede) [I 892]; it is a short poem of ten quatrains with refrain, directed against French fashions but attacking all classes in a popular sharply satirical tone. The roughness of the metre and irregularities of rhyme are also evidence that it was not written by Lydgate. Printed in W. C. Hazlitt, *Remains of the Early Popular Poetry of England*, 4 vols., 1864, III, 147 ff., and by Furnivall in *Academy*, 29th August 1896. *Ragmanys rolle* (My ladyes and my maistresses), twenty-six ballad stanzas [I 2251], printed in W. C. Hazlitt, op. cit., I, 69 ff., is said by Mac-Cracken to have been written 'by a witty Chaucerian', like *Chaunse of the dyse* (see below). – The last and simultaneously the best of these satirical pieces that have been ascribed to Lydgate is *London Lickpenny* (To London once my stepps I bent) [Rits., 35; I 3759]. This lively poem in sixteen ballad stanzas, which gives a good picture of the age in which it was composed, has been preserved in a manuscript by John Stow (*d.* 1605), who makes use of it in his *Survey of London* (ed. by Kingsford, Oxford, 1928, I, 217). It has often been reprinted, most recently by Hammond in *Anglia*, 20 (1898), pp. 404 ff. (parallel edition of both extant versions) and in *English Verse . . .*, p. 237. 'Style and rhyme are utterly at variance with Lydgate's practice' (MacCracken).

In connexion with these satires one may mention two *fabliaux* ascribed to Lydgate by Ritson which are equally alien to his conception and style: *Lady Prioress and her suitors* (O gloryous God our governor) [Rits., 41; I 2441], in twenty-seven tail-rhyme stanzas each of nine lines, printed by Halliwell, pp. 107 ff., and *Smith and his Dame* (God that dyed on a tre) [Rits., 44; I 978], in tail-rhyme stanzas of sixteen lines, totalling 575 lines in all, a version of the familiar humorous tale, which comes close to being a legend; it is printed in Hazlitt, *Remains*, III, 201, and in Horstmann, *Altenglische Legenden*, 1881, p. 322. Another work that is part *fabliau* and part legend is *The Childe of Bristow* (He that made bothe Heuene and Helle) [Rits., 42;

I 1157], 'a poor piece of popular versification' in twelve-line tail-rhyme stanzas, 558 lines in all; it is printed in Horstmann, op. cit., pp. 315 ff. The tale of *Piers of Fulham* (A man that lovith ffisshing and fowlyng bothe) [Rits., 48; I 71], in 182 couplets, can be characterized as a sketch for a *fabliau*; it has become a pointless piece of moral instruction. It may be found in C. H. Hartshorne, *Ancient Metrical Tales*, L., 1829, pp. 117 ff.

Of historical or political poems, *Petigree of Emperors* [Rits., 130] is unidentifiable, and *On the Reconciliation 1457*, printed by Sir Harris Nicolas in *Chronicle of London* (1827) was written after Lydgate's time. Among the other pieces printed by Nicolas, *The Battle of Agincourt* (Stedes ther stumbelyd in that stownde) [I 3213], in eight ballad stanzas, refers, as MacCracken makes clear, to a minstrel. It is couched in a tone that is quite impossible for Lydgate, as a court poet, to have adopted, particularly towards his patron Henry V. It is printed in Wright, *Political Poems*, II, 125, and in Kingsford, *Chronicles of London*, 1915, p. 120. Much the same may be said of *Song on the Battle of Barnet*, mentioned by Stow and Ritson [174], or *Gaudete iusti in domino* (the opening line), [I 899], in four ballad stanzas. According to MacCracken this poem gives expression to an opinion held by people in London about Edward IV. MacCracken prints it in *Archiv*, 130, pp. 309 f. Also minstrel-like is *The Expedition of Henry V into France* (God that all this worlde gan make) [I 969], in sixty-nine ballad stanzas with short lines. This poem is to be found already in Elmham's *Vita Henrici Vi.* (Hearne's ed., p. 359) and is reprinted by Nicolas in his *Chronicle of London*, pp. 216–33; the ascription the latter gives is unfounded. The position is rather different with regard to *Epitaphium Ducis Glowcestrie* (1446) (Souerayne immortal euerlasting god) [I 3206], in thirteen ballad stanzas, discussed by Schick in *Temple of Glas*, pp. xcvi f., and by MacCracken in *M.P.*, p. xl.: the latter considers that it was not written by Lydgate but admits that it is in his style. Brown (*Index*) states: 'perhaps by Lydgate'.

The poems of which Lydgate may have been the author that fall into the category of 'secular knowledge and rules of conduct' are not all identifiable. This applies to *Praeceptiones Gall. ling.* [Rits., 145], *Proprietates nationum* [Rits., 143], and also *Dantis opuscula* and *Petrarchae quaedam* [Rits., 159 and 160], already listed by Bale, which one may mention here. – Other poems in this category which can be proved not to have been written by Lydgate are *Cato's Distichs*, listed twice by Rits. [11, 54], composed by Lydgate's disciple Benedict Burgh. Nor did Lydgate write the translation of Vegetius' *De re militari*, or *Of Knyghthode and Bataile* (Sum tyme it was the gise among the wise) [Rits., 53; I 3185], 3023 lines in Chaucerian stanzas; it is printed in *EETS*, 221; cf. MacCracken in *Kittredge Anniversary Papers*, p. 389. On the other hand, Förster and Hammond support (but MacCracken contests) the possibility that Lydgate was the author of the poem variously entitled *Summum Sapientiae*, *Liber Proverbiorum*, or *Sayings of old Philosophers* (þe tyme approcheþe of necessite . . .) [Rits., 76; I 3487]. This translation, in 116 Chaucerian stanzas, is devoid of literary merit, and is unprinted.

Since Lydgate was such a successful compiler of legends it is not surprising that he should have been credited with many more of which he was not the author. Ritson [248] ascribes to him a version of the life of St Alexes, but it is not clear which of the numerous versions he has in mind [cf. I, under 'Alexis']. The attribution to Lydgate of a *Life of St Anne* (O blessed Jesu that art fulle of myght) [Rits., 231; I 2392], in ninety-four Chaucerian stanzas, printed in *EETS*, 174, pp. 90 f., and by MacCracken in *Archiv*, 130 (1913), pp. 286 ff., is probably due to the fact that Lydgate wrote a lyrical piece called *Praise of St Anne* and that his friend and admirer Bokenham composed a *vita* of this saint (in Chaucerian stanzas, the form which Lydgate had introduced in this genre). This is also probably the case with *Life of St Barbara* (Whan Maximian for alle his tyrandyse) [Rits., 237; I 3994], unprinted, and *Life of St Denis*; in the latter instance it is not clear which version is implied to have been written by Lydgate (possibly I 2882: Seint Denis was in þe olde lawe). The attribution to Lydgate of the legend of *St Erasmus* entitled *Passio Sancti Erasmi* (Alle cristen peple listeneth ye & here) [Rits., 240; I 173], in 172 lines, is understandable, since the author attempted to emulate Lydgate's style. It is printed by Horstmann, in *Archiv*, 62, pp. 414 ff. and in *Altenglische Legenden*, 1878, pp. 198 ff. – MacCracken prints in *Archiv*, 126, pp. 365 ff., *The Story of Job* (Most mercifull lorde by thyne habundant goodnesse) [I 2208], in twenty-six Chaucerian stanzas, which shows evidence of Lydgate's school both in the use of metre and in the fact that it was composed as the accompanying text to some pictures. On the border between legend and pious tale stands *The Three Kings of Cologne* (For wynde or Rayne, ffor water or colde or hete), 859 lines in Chaucerian stanzas [I *31]. The text, preserved only in fragments (about 100 lines at the beginning appear to be missing), is thought by MacCracken (*Archiv*, 129 (1912), pp. 50 ff.) to have been composed by a northern writer in Lydgate's style shortly after he had completed his *Legend of St Edmund* (1433). The *Legend of a Monk of Paris* (Remembryd by scriptures we fynde) is a short (four Chaucerian stanzas) version of the story of the dead man's gratitude [I 2810], printed in Halliwell, pp. 73 f. Another short piece which is also printed in Halliwell (pp. 72 f.) is the *Legend of Wulfrike, a priest of Wiltshire* (In Wiltshire of England two pristis ther were) [I 1590; Rits., 43, under the title *Two priests of Wiltshire*].

Most of the anonymous poems that have been ascribed to Lydgate are naturally religious ones. Thus Stow [22] gave Lydgate as the author of the paraphrase of the hymn *Conditor alme siderum*; none of the extant versions (which include those of Ryman [I 1231] and Herebert [I 2433]) can be identified as by Lydgate, and we may therefore perhaps consider that a part of his *Laetabundus* poem is implied here. Ritson [180] lists a paraphrase of *De coelorum gaudiis*, which is likewise an unproven supposition. Someone who was almost Lydgate's contemporary, the scribe Humphrey Newton (born *ca.* 1466), ascribed to him the poem *The Nightingale* (Go lityll quayere And swyft thy prynses dresse) [I 931], which reaches almost to epic proportions. This claim is repeated by Tanner and others, but it is possible that these writers are confusing this poem with Lydgate's *A sayenge of the Nyghtingale* (In June whan Titan was in Crabbes hede) [I 1498]. Both poems are printed by O. Glauning in *Two Nightingale Poems*, EETS, ES., 80 (1900). Glauning supports the view that both these poems are by Lydgate, but this opinion is challenged by Mac-Cracken. Another group of poems which have been ascribed to Lydgate are the 'Psalmi passionis'. These include the works listed by Stow [13] and Ritson [221]; Stow also attributes to Lydgate a poem entitled *Of Christ's Passion* [14], and Ritson [220] follows him in this. Possibly in this case, as in others, we are dealing with a double reference to the same work, and the work indicated is *Psalms of the Passion* (O lord omnipotent fadyr of oure creacyoun) [I 2493]. The poem, which runs to twenty-four Chaucerian stanzas, is wholly in Lydgate's style, but is assigned to a later date by MacCracken on the basis of an analysis of the rhyme; he suggests that it may be the work of the author of *Magnificentia Ecclesiae*. It is printed in *Archiv*, 130, pp. 299 f. Another of these paraphrases is *A Hymn to the Creator*, or *Haue Mercy on me!* (Almyhti God, maker of Heuene), in five ballad stanzas [I 253], printed in *Archiv*, 131, p. 43, C. Brown, *Religious*

# John Lydgate

*Lyrics of the XVth Century*, pp. 214 f., *EETS*, 155, pp. 67 ff. – Of the numerous poems to Jesus composed under Lydgate's influence which were formerly ascribed to him personally the *Appeal of Christ* (Bannatyne MS., 1568, Hunterian Club, pp. 112 f., O creaturis creat of me your creator) has been shown by MacCracken, on the basis of rhyme-tests, not to be his work. The *Testamentum Christi* listed by Ritson [208] is in the absence of further details not identifiable. Other hymns to Jesus composed by members of Lydgate's school are: *A Prayer to Christ's Name*, or *A Prayer to Christ against perils* (O cryste Jesu mekely I pray to the), which is close to the first part of Lydgate's *Testament* [Rits., 217; I 2401]; it is in three Chaucerian stanzas and is printed in *Archiv*, 131, 43, and in *Religious Lyrics of the XVth Century*, p. 191; further, *A Song of love to Jesus* (Ihesu þi swetnes whoso myȝte it se) [I 1781], fifteen ballad stanzas, printed by Horstmann, *Yorkshire Writers*, vol. I, p. 368, and in *EETS*, 98, p. 45; *A Prayer to Jesu* (Jesu Crist kepe our lyppes from pollucioun) [I 1682], six ballad stanzas, unprinted. – The hymn addressed to Mary Magdalene [Rits., 26] entitled *The Lamentatyoun of M. Magdaleyne* (Plonged in the wawe of mortal distresse) [I 2759], a lengthy (102 Chaucerian stanzas) poem wrongly attributed to Lydgate, is printed in Miss B. M. Skeat's diss., Zurich, 1897. – Of prayers, *Praier to bedward and at rising*, listed by Stow [46] and Ritson [92], is not identifiable, unless the two authors are referring to the following two poems, neither of which has any connexion with Lydgate: *A deuout prayere toward thy bedde at nyht* (Now Jesu lord . . .) [I 2345], in six quatrains, printed in *Archiv*, 130, p. 304, and in *Religious Lyrics of the XVth Century*, pp. 194 f., and *A deuout prayere at thy vprysyng* (In nomine patris . . .) [I 1720], in eight quatrains, printed in *Archiv*, 130, p. 305, and in *Religious Lyrics of the XVth Century*, p. 195. *Lydgates Prayer to St Edmund on behalf of Henry VI* (O gloryous Martyr wiche of deuout humbles // ffor Crystys . . .), in eight ballad stanzas [I 2445], is genuine; it is an insertion into the *Legend of St Edmund*. It is printed by Horstmann in *Altenglische Legenden*, 1881, pp. 438 f.

Particularly numerous are the Marian hymns that have been attributed to Lydgate. Lydgate's contemporary Shirley gives him as the author of *An aureate prayer to the Blessed Virgin*, or *Dilectus meus*, or alternatively *Rex Salamon* (Rex Salamon summus of sapience) [I 2816; Rits., 98]. MacCracken hesitates to accept it as genuine because the metre and rhyme tests do not support the theory that it was written by Lydgate. A prominent place in English medieval Marian

[ 282 ]

poetry is occupied by the prayer *Quia amore langueo*,[1] a lament of the Blessed Virgin (In a tabernacle of a Toure / As I stode . . .) [I 1460], in twelve ballad stanzas. Not only Ritson, but also the authors of contemporary MSS. (Shirley) attribute it to Lydgate, and this view has been endorsed in recent times.[2] The question is an important one, because this is one of the finest Middle English religious poems, which has often been printed (most recently in *Religious Lyrics of the XIVth Century*, pp. 234–7 and Weston, p. 347), and because one essential criterion in evaluating its authenticity has hitherto been left out of account. MacCracken considers that this work, 'generally admitted to be the highest poem of the type in English, the finest expression of the Virgin's sorrow' (*M.P.*, xxxii), lies beyond Lydgate's powers. It has the depth of feeling of the Marian hymns of the thirteenth century, still to be found (or again to be found) in fifteenth-century carols, as well as the declamatory persuasive note struck in fourteenth-century religious poetry. Maria is made touchingly human instead of being portrayed enthroned in majesty. This criterion seems to me decisive: the poem is completely untypical of Lydgate and has nothing of the invocatory style that characterizes his Marian hymns. Nowhere else in Lydgate's works do we find such a simple human conception of the Virgin; this would have seemed to him profane. MacCracken is far from the truth when he says that Lydgate's religious poetry can be classified in the *Quia amore langueo* school, and even takes this as a criterion of authenticity. In my opinion Marian hymns of which the author is unknown can only be attributed to Lydgate where the Virgin is portrayed as a divine figure far removed from the mundane and earthly world and where the style is correspondingly rich in sonorous and elevated invocations. – It is from this point of view that one must approach the other Marian hymns attributed to Lydgate, all the more so since this generally confirms MacCracken's conclusions. The Marian hymns, poems, and prayers are as follows: first, two laments: *Stabat mater*

---

[1] Three poems with this title are extant. In addition to the Marian hymn mentioned above, there is a lament of Christ, based on the Song of Songs: *In a valey of this restles mynde* (I soughte . . .) [I 1463], in sixteen ballad stanzas, printed in E. K. Chambers, *Early English Lyrics*, pp. 151 f., and a stanza incorporated in Rolle's prose, *Qwen wil þu come & comforte me* [I 4056], printed in Horstmann, *Yorkshire Writers*, II, 34. Both the first-mentioned versions are printed by Furnivall, *EETS*, 15, 148 ff., 151 ff.

[2] Brusendorff (*The Chaucer Tradition*) asks why Shirley's authority should be contested in this instance when it is accepted in nine pieces of the same MS. (Ashmole 59); but cf. MacCracken, p. xxxii.

*dolorosa* (Heyle goddes moder dolorous) [Rits., 196; I 1048], printed
by Brunner in *Anglia*, 61, 142 f. and in Brown's *Religious Lyrics of the
XVth Century*, pp. 22 f., and *A Lament of our Lady at the Passion* (There
stood besyde the crosse) [Rits., 6; I 3543], in fifteen ballad stanzas,
which is probably not by Lydgate despite the note to this effect on
the MS. by Stow. MacCracken, who prints it in *Archiv*, 130 (1913),
pp. 305 ff., describes it as 'a late attempt to rival the beautiful earlier
lyrics in this manner'. – Nor is there sufficient evidence to ascribe
to Lydgate the following poems: *Maria virgo assumpta est* (this is the
title given by Ritson, [192]), or *Mystical invitation of the Blessed Virgin
to man* (Regina celi, qwene of thy sowth) [I 2803], in ten ballad stanzas
with the refrain 'Maria virgo assumpta est'; it is printed in *Archiv*,
131, pp. 50 f. by MacCracken, who sees similarities with the style
of the Vernon poems. *Veni coronaberis, a song of Christ to the Blessed
Virgin* (Surge mea sponsa so swete in sight) [Rits., 188; I 3225], in
nine ballad stanzas, is a poem which in Lydgate's manner draws
greatly upon the Song of Songs; it is printed by Furnivall in *EETS*,
24, 1–3 and in *Religious Lyrics of the XVth Century*, pp. 65 f. One of
the invocatory poems and hymns that follow will be the *Ave Maria*
listed by Ritson as No. 198, unless by this he means Lydgate's *Ave
regina celorum* (*M.P.*, 291). (An attempt to identify this as one of the
*Aves* listed by Brown (*Index*, p. 743) can have no positive result since
none of these shows any marked evidence of having been written by
Lydgate.) These are *A Prayer to the Blessed Virgin* (All hayle, Mary,
ful of grace) [I 183], in six ballad stanzas, printed in *Religious Lyrics
of the XVth Century*, p. 28, and in *Archiv*, 131, p. 45, and *Salue regina, a
hymn to the Blessed Virgin* (Salue wyth all obaysans to God in humble-
nesse) [I 3074], in four or five ballad stanzas, printed in *Archiv*, 131,
pp. 44 f., by Flügel in *Anglia*, 26, p. 172, and in *EETS*, *ES.*, 101,
pp. 60 f. The hymns in the following list are similar to those by
Lydgate, which does not prove his authorship, but indicates that
they were written by his disciples, who often imitated his rhetorical
manner so well that it is difficult to distinguish their works from his.
An example of this is *A hymn on the five joys of the Virgin* (Heyl, glorius
virgyne, ground of all our grace) [I 1046], in five ballad stanzas,
printed in *Archiv*, 131, p. 49, and in *Religious Lyrics of the XVth
Century*, pp. 53 f., which is attributed by Shirley in his MS. Ashmole
59 to a 'holy ankaresse of Mansfeld'. Close to Lydgate's litany in
style and rhythm is *A prayer to the Blessed Virgin and several saints*
(Mercyful Quene, as ye best kan and may) [I 2154], in four ballad

and five Chaucerian stanzas, printed in *Archiv*, 131, p. 46, and in *Religious Lyrics of the XVth Century*, pp. 200 ff. The poem *Gaude flore virginali* (Ioy blissid lady with pure virgynal flowre) [I 1804], in eight Chaucerian stanzas, which was included in the canon already by Ritson [202], is regarded by Hammerle (*Anglia*, 55, p. 429) as Lydgate's version of this popular theme (cf. I 897 and 1807), but according to MacCracken the metre and rhyme tests point the other way. In many cases, however, it is impossible to come to definite conclusions. In the 'macaronic hymn to the Blessed Virgin' *Regina celi letare* (Regina celi letare // In whome fyrste þis worlde began) [I 2802], in four ballad stanzas, printed in *Archiv*, 131, pp. 48 f. and in *Religious Lyrics of the XVth Century*, pp. 52 f., the metre, stanza, and refrain are identical with those in Lydgate's poem of the same name. – *Lenvoy to Mary* (Goe lytyll byll, and doe me recommende) [I 927], in six ballad stanzas, printed in *Archiv*, 131, p. 47, and *Religious Lyrics of the XVth Century*, pp. 75 f., recalls Lydgate's *Valentine*. The acrostic on the name Mary in Lydgate's poem *Ave Jesse Virgula* is imitated in *A balade in praise of the Blessed Virgin with acrostic* (Awey, ffeint lufe, full of varyance) [I 456], in fifteen Chaucerian stanzas, printed in *Archiv*, 131, pp. 51 ff. – We may conclude this survey, which testifies to the influence of Lydgate's style upon the members of his school, with the *Hymn to the Virgin O flos pulcherrime!* (With humble hert I preye iche creature – or rather, since the first line is missing in Mac-Cracken's edition, Myght wisdom goodnesse of the Trinite) [I 2168], in twenty-three ballad stanzas with the refrain 'O florum flos, O flos pulcherrime'; it is printed in *Archiv*, 131, pp. 60 ff. Of religious poems with a mixed content the pieces mentioned by Stow (No. 45) and Ritson (No. 114) may be identical, i.e. *An exhortation against the Deadly Sins* (Syth in thys world þer can no þyng be sewre) [I 3129], a poem in ten Chaucerian stanzas, printed by MacCracken in *Archiv* 130 (1913), pp. 308 f., and which he admits 'approaches most closely in its imitation to the genuine work of Lydgate'. – The work, already mentioned, *Magnificence of the Church*, or *Parvus tractatus de magnificentia ecclesiae* (Emperour of all emperours omnipotent) [Stow 16; Rits., 127; I 723] is characterized by MacCracken as most remarkable but rough in metre; he is inclined to attribute it to the author of the *Psalms of the Passion* (q.v.). It is in thirty-nine ballad stanzas and is printed by MacCracken in *PMLA*, 24, pp. 688–98.

As the author of so many moralistic and didactic poems, Lydgate was credited with others which he did not actually write. Among

# John Lydgate

these are two pieces listed by Ritson [60, 88], *On the Chaunse of the dyse* (First myn vnkunnynge) [I 803], in fifty-nine Chaucerian stanzas. printed by Hammond in *Engl. Stud.*, 59, pp. 5 ff., and in part in H. L. Cohen, *The Ballade*, N.Y., 1915. Ritson also mentions [No. 18; I 1936] *On the folly of heeping up riches* (Long wil be water in a welle), a short poem with a faulty metre, printed in *Religious Lyrics of the XVth Century*, p. 288. – Halliwell (p. 228) prints *Make Amendes* (Bi a wode as I gone ride) [I 563], in twelve ballad stanzas with refrain, with a beginning similar to that of a verse epic, which drives home the moral contained in the title. He also prints (on p. 225) *Thank God for all* (By a wey wandryng as y wente) [I 562], in seventeen ballad stanzas with a refrain, also printed in *Religious Lyrics of the XIVth Century*, pp. 157 ff. (cf. *Englische Studien*, 41, pp. 374 ff.). Further he prints (on p. 222) *For the better abyde*, or *A ditty upon improvement* (I see a rybaun ryche and newe) [I 1355], a poem in seven ballad stanzas, also printed in *Religious Lyrics of the XVth Century*, p. 283. *A Poem against idleness* (Two maner of folkes to put in remembraunce), in forty-one Chaucerian stanzas, printed by Halliwell on pp. 84 ff., cannot be identified under this title or opening line in MacCracken's Canon or Brown's *Index*. Finally, to this group belongs *On the mysteries of Creation* (O man thow marrest in thy mynd) [I 2503], also known as *Hoc factum est a domino* after the refrain, in twelve ballad stanzas, printed in *Archiv*, 131, pp. 41 ff.

Index

# Index

(N.B.—*19th- and 20th-century critics and editors are not listed
in this index. Cf. footnotes and appendices.*)

# Index

# Index

U                    [ 291 ]

# Index

# Index

Eltham Palace, 30, 56, 66, 101, 105, 115, 242

Ely, Bishop of: *see* Fordham, John

Elyot, Thomas, 238

*Epitaphium Ducis Glowcestrie*, 275, 279

Estfeld, William, 107 f.

Ethelred, King, 56, 165

Eton, 13, 144, 241, 245

Eugenius IV, Pope, 144 n., 241

Eusebius, 86

Ewelme (manor and village), 60 ff., 229, 232 f., 235, 248

Exeter, Duke of: *see* Beaufort, Thomas

Exeter, William de, Abbot of Bury St Edmunds, 18 n., 21 n., 51, 91, 118, 138

Exeter's Registrum, 51

*Exhortation against the Deadly Sins, An*, 276, 285

*Expedition of Henry V into France*, 275, 279

Eynsham, monastery of, 9

Fabyan, Robert, chronicler, 67 n., 93, 132 n., 140 n.

Faure, Pierre, 209 n.

Feylde, Thomas, 256

Fordham, John, Bishop of Ely, 21, 51

Forrest, William, 248 n., 256

Fortescue, Sir John, 214

*For the better abyde*, 276, 286

Fortune, 48, 49, 50, 84, 87, 105, 108, 125, 126, 129, 194, 200, 202, 203, 204, 206, 207, 210, 213, 218, 222, 225, 237, 239

Fouquet, Jean, 209

*Four Daughters of God, The*, 121 n., 152 n., 243

Freeman, Sir Ralph, 256

Fremund, King of Mercia, 162 ff.

Froissart, Jean, 3, 4, 26, 32, 101, 137

Gallopes, Jean de, 122

*Gaude flore virginali*, 276, 285

*Gawain and the Green Knight*, 4, 36

Gelebronde, Ralph, 128 n., 191 n.

Gerardus (Girardus) Cornubiensis, Cornish monk, 93, 94 n.

Glastonbury, monastery of, 22 n.

Glendower, Owen, 29, 57

Gloucester, monastery of, 9

Gloucester Hall, Oxford, 22

Gloucester, Humphrey, Duke of, 13, 19 n., 28, 60, 61, 69, 77, 81, 82, 97, 110, 113 ff., 121, 135 n., 139, 146, 171 n., 208, 209 n., 211 f., 215 ff., 221 f., 226, 233, 240 f., 245, 246, 253

Gloucester, Duke of (Thomas of Woodstock), 25, 226

Golden Age, 201, 220

Goldsmith, Oliver, 238

Gosford, John, Prior of Bury St Edmunds, 13

Gower, John, 33, 36, 44, 71, 151, 169, 211, 248 n., 255, 256, 257

Grafton, Richard, chronicler, 93

Granson, Oton, 32

Gray, Thomas, 202 n., 257

Gray, Sir Thomas, 55 n.

Gregory XI, Pope, 7

Gregory, William, chronicler, 130 n., 243 n.

Grosseteste, Robert, 110 n.

Guido delle Colonne, 42 n., 43, 45, 46, 248 n.

Guillaume de Berneville: *see* Berneville

Guillaume de Lorris: *see* Lorris

Gulle, William, Prior of Hatfield, 91

Hall, Edward, chronicler, 27

Hardecnut, King of Denmark and England, 236

Harvey, Gabriel, 256

Hatfield Regis, 90 ff., 116, 118, 138, 248 n.

Hawes, Stephen, 256, 257, 277

Hengham, Richard de, Abbot of Bury St Edmunds, 21 n.

Henri II of France: *see* Henry VI

Henry II of Anjou, King of England, 62

Henry III, King, 15

Henry IV, King, 24–30, 35, 40, 51, 52 f., 55, 101, 214, 232, 235

# Index

Henry V, King, 24, 25 n., 28 ff., 40, 41, 42 f., 48 f., 50, 52 f., 60, 62, 66 ff., 81, 82, 89, 101, 105, 113, 114, 116 f., 119, 122 n., 132, 133, 137, 140, 144, 151, 155 n., 187, 200 n., 202 f., 232, 234, 235, 245, 279

Henry VI, King, 10, 13, 18, 19 n., 51, 53 n., 56 n., 60, 62, 68, 81 ff., 92, 93, 101, 103 n., 106 f., 111, 113, 115, 117 f., 130–8, 140 ff., 144 ff., 163, 170, 171 n., 189, 190, 209, 229, 233, 235 ff., 241 ff., 249 ff., 254

Henry VII, King, 25 n., 232

Henry, Abbot of Bury St Edmunds, 21 n.

Henryson, Robert, 23

Herebert, William, 281

Hertford Palace, 100, 106, 133

Hervé, 12th-century architect, 11

*High astrapotent auctor, The*, 275, 277

(H)occleve, Thomas, 34, 54, 59, 248 n., 257

*Hoc factum est*, 276, 286

Holland, John: *see* Huntingdon, Earl of

Homer, 43, 167, 248

*Hood of Green*, 96, 275, 277

*How the good wife taught her daughter*, 110

*How the wise man taught his son*, 110

Hugo, sacristan of Bury St Edmunds, 12

Hugo I, Abbot of Bury St Edmunds, 21 n.

Hugo II, Abbot of Bury St Edmunds, 21 n.

Humphrey, Duke of Gloucester: *see* Gloucester

Hunstanton, Henry (de), Abbot of Bury St Edmunds, 20 n.

Huntingdon, Anne: *see* Mortimer, Anne

Huntingdon, Earl of (John Holland), 155 n., 229

*Hymn on the five joys, A*, 276, 284

*Hymn to the Creator, A*, 275, 281

*Hymn to the Virgin: O flos pulcherrime*, 276, 285

Idley, Peter, 110

Insula, Richard de, Abbot of Bury St Edmunds, 21 n.

Interludes, 103, 105

*Ipomydon*, 33

Isabeau of Bavaria, wife of Charles VI of France, 58, 62, 68, 137

Isabeau of France, wife of King Edward II, 137

Isabel, wife of the 5th Earl of Warwick, 19 n.

Isabella of France, 2nd wife of King Richard II, 25, 30 n., 56

Islip, Simon, 248 n.

Ixworth, Robert de, Abbot of Bury St Edmunds, 21 n.

Jacqueline of Hainault or Holland (Jacobea of Bavaria), wife of Humphrey, Duke of Gloucester, 68, 114 f., 240

Jacqueline of Luxembourg, 2nd wife of the Duke of Bedford, 144

James I, King of Scotland, 28, 69, 115, 235

Jean de Meung: *see* Meung

Joan of Arc, 107, 135, 232

Joan of Navarre, wife of King Henry IV, 27, 55, 235

Jocelin de Brakelond, 10 n., 15

John, King of England, 15

John II, King of France (Jean le Bon), 3, 5 n., 207, 224

John of Gaunt, Duke of Lancaster, 5, 20, 30, 35 f.

John of Lancaster, Duke of Bedford: *see* Bedford

John of Salisbury, 83, 151 n., 214, 220 n.

John the Fearless, Duke of Burgundy, 27, 30, 58, 64, 119, 137

Josephus Flavius, 215, 220

*Journal d'un Bourgeois de Paris*: see *Bourgeois*

Justin (Justinus, Marcus Junianus), 216

# Index

# Index

# Index

# Index

# Index

# Index

# Index

## DATE DUE

| | | | |
|---|---|---|---|
| | | | |
| | | | |
| | | | |
| | | | |
| | | | |
| | | | |
| | | | |
| | | | |
| | | | |
| | | | |
| | | | |
| | | | |
| | | | |
| | | | |
| | | | |
| | | | |
| | | | |
| | | | |
| | | | |